# THE BILL JAMES
# GOLD MINE

2010

# THE BILL JAMES GOLD MINE 2010

## by Bill James

ACTA SPORTS

**The Bill James Gold Mine 2010**

by Bill James

Edited by John Dewan and Gregory F. Augustine Pierce
Cover Design by Tom A. Wright
Book Design and Typesetting by Michael Babin
Cover Photo by Samara Pearlstein

Published by:     ACTA Sports, a division of ACTA Publications
                  5959 W. Howard Street, Skokie, IL 60077
                  800-397-2282, www.actasports.com, info@actasports.com

Printed in the United States of America by WorldColor

ISBN: 978-0-87946-411-0
ISSN: 1940-7998
Year: 13 12 11 10
Printing: 5 4 3 2 First Printing

# Contents

# 'Knowledgements

by Bill James

AS I HAVE SAID BEFORE, THE TERM "ACKNOWLEDGEMENTS", while it is the conventional usage, is not exactly what we're trying to say. What we're trying to convey here is more along the lines of "thanks", "appreciation", or "gratitude", rather than "acknowledgement".

The first two people who should be thanked are John Dewan and Greg Pierce. This is Bill James speaking, and my name is on the book, but I didn't pull the book together. I write articles, during the course of the year, for Bill James Online. Greg Pierce reviews all of those articles, suggests articles that would be appropriate for use in this book, and in some cases suggests revisions to those articles to make them more appropriate to book form. Greg also commands the publishing company, ACTA publishing, which brings this book to you.

*Writing books is stressful, and this is hard as well on wives and children, dogs and goldfish.*

John Dewan is in charge of the assembly of the "nuggets", the small pieces of information which are found with each team. As each nugget is intended to be something which is a) interesting, and which b) virtually no one knows until he reads the book, this is a very difficult and time-consuming task, in which many people participate.

And, as many people participate, that becomes a task in itself: assigning the research to individuals, routing it through me, keeping track of who has done what and what has been done, getting it assembled in book form and getting it fact-checked. It's a lot of work.

The three of us — Greg, John and myself — are essentially co-authors of the book, and, while I want to express my gratitude to John and Greg, I am also speaking on behalf of them in offering our appreciation to the many others who have worked on the book.

Mike Webber has been responsible for many of the nuggets. Well, no…I am responsible for them, in the sense that if there is something amiss, that would be my responsibility. Mike Webber is responsible for many of them, in the sense that he did the work of finding most of the nuggets for the Royals, Indians, Twins, Tigers, Pirates, Rockies, Mariners, Nationals, Cubs, Giants, and the new National League expansion team, the Ottawa Physicians. Thank you, Michael.

Mat Olkin is also responsible for many of the nuggets; thank you, Mat. Mat did the Angels, Cardinals, Dodgers, Phillies, Blue Jays, Rangers, Marlins, Brewers, and the new American League expansion team, the Maryland Horse Farmers.

Dave Studenmund works with us on Bill James Online, and also did some nuggets; thank you Dave. Charles Fiore did nuggets and proof-reading; we are grateful for your help, Charles. Ben Jedlovec does research with John Dewan, and did work which is reflected in this book; thanks, Ben.

We contract with Baseball Info Solutions, run by the inestimable Steve Moyer, with help from the estimable Damon Lichtenwalner, to provide the stats and double-check the facts in the book. This year that latter task fell into the capable hands of Jon Vresics; thank you, Jon. On occasion I ignore his suggestions, so that errors in the book remain my responsibility. Rob Burckhard of BIS also works with John on nuggets and research; thank you, Rob.

This book was designed by Michael Babin, for which we wish to express our appreciation. The cover was designed by Tom Wright, and we appreciate this as well. Also, in this connection, Andrew Yankech of ACTA runs interference on the production of the book, and Donna Ryding, Mary Eggert, Brendan Gaughan and Richard Struben make sure the books get to you, once you order them. Thank you, ladies and gentlemen.

Writing books is stressful, even when there are three people primarily involved, and this is hard as well on wives and children, dogs and goldfish. We appreciate the patience and support of those who love us, and we appreciate each of you who reads the book.

Bill James
Lawrence, Kansas
February 8, 2010

# Comparing Starting Pitchers Across History

by Bill James

THIS STARTED OUT AS SOMETHING ENTIRELY DIFFERENT, and I'm not going to tell you what it was because it didn't work and it wasn't important. For something else I was trying to do I needed a list of the best starting pitchers each year. I used the Season Score system to generate that list, and then I got interested in that list and what one could do with it. I wound up with a new way to rate starting pitchers across history. There are ten million ways to rate starting pitchers and this is just another one, but…I learned some things I didn't know, I thought it was interesting, and I decided to share it with you.

Suppose that we look at the top ten pitchers in each league each season, and then we compare pitchers based on how they rank among their peers. Our first problem is, how do we rank the pitchers?

*There are ten million ways to rate starting pitchers and this is just another one.*

I ranked them based on Season Scores. Season Scores is a simple system that I introduced a couple of years ago and revised last August; it scores a pitcher by his wins, losses, innings pitched, ERA, strikeouts and walks, and also Saves, but Saves are not too important for a starting pitcher. I've explained the Season Scores system before and this isn't the place to re-visit that, but the point of the system is to evaluate a pitcher's record without context. In sabermetrics we are usually meticulous about evaluating statistics in context. About 2007 it occurred to me that we were missing something. Suppose that we compare Mike McCormick in 1967 (22-10, 2.85 ERA) to Mark Buehrle in 2004 (16-10, 3.89 ERA.) McCormick was a lot like Buehrle — a cagey lefty who was sneaky fast and would make you beat him. He won the Cy Young Award in '67.

In context, Buehrle's numbers are actually much better than McCormick's. McCormick had a 2.85 ERA, but the league ERA in '67 was 3.38. In 2004 the league ERA was 4.64. Buehrle's ERA was 75 points (or 16+%) better than league — and he was working in a hitter's park. McCormick's ERA was 53 points (or 16-%) better than league — and he was working in a pitcher's park. In context and adjusting for run support, Buehrle was no doubt better than McCormick, but still, 16-10 is not better than 22-10, and a 3.89 ERA is not better than a 2.85 ERA. This was a way of trying to say "How good are the numbers themselves?", rather than "How good was the pitcher who compiled these numbers?"

This turned out to be useful for a lot of different reasons, in part because it tracks the way that people think in a normal context. The highest-scoring pitcher in the league is usually the Cy Young winner; not always, usually. When there is a difference between the two — when the award goes one way and the Season Score the other — it is probably true that the Season Score is "right" as often as the voters. Since 2000 there have been 20 Cy Young Awards. Seventeen of those have gone to the highest-scoring pitcher in the league. The only awards in the last ten years that did *not* go to the highest-scoring pitcher in the league were the 2005 American League Award, which went to Bartolo Colon although Johan Santana had a higher Season Score, and both awards in 2009. In 2009 Felix Hernandez had a higher score than Greinke, and Adam Wainwright a higher score than Lincecum.

Maybe our system was right about those judgments; maybe it was wrong. I'm not arguing that the Season Score system is better than the judgment of the Cy Young voters. I am arguing that it is usually about the same as the judgment of the Cy Young voters, and it has certain advantages. The advantages are that it can be easily figured for any pitcher, rather than just the Cy Young candidates, and that it can be looked at for all of baseball history on a constant scale, rather than just the years 1956-2008 and on a scale that has changed

numerous times.

We use the Season Score method, then, to look at the issue of "Who are the best pitchers in each league each year?" Our next problem is, how do we give credit to those pitchers?

My first thought was to give credit to the top ten pitchers in each league each year, ten points to the #1 pitcher, 9 to the #2 pitcher, etc. The problem with this is that it treats unequally the pitchers from different eras. The NL now has 16 teams. From 1900 to 1962 it had only eight teams. For a couple of years in the 19th century, it had only six. With that system, in 1950 there would be 55 points for the pitchers on eight teams, or 6.9 points per team. In 2000 there would be 55 points for 16 teams, or 3.4 points per team.

How do we fix that? Let's try this: let's fix the points at 5.5 points per team. We can do that by this method:

*The advantages are that it can be easily figured for any pitcher, and that it can be looked at for all of baseball history on a constant scale.*

- In a six-team league we give points to the league's six best starting pitchers, on an 8-7-6-5-4-3 scale. Six teams, 33 points, 5.50 points per team.

- In an eight-team league, we give points to the league's eight best starting pitchers, on a scale of 9-8-7-6-5-4-3-2. Eight teams, 44 points, 5.50 points per team.

- In a ten-team league, we give points to the league's ten best starting pitchers, on a scale of 10-9-8-7-6-5-4-3-2-1. Ten teams, 55 points, 5.50 points per team.

- In a twelve-team league, we give points to the league's eleven best starting pitchers, on a scale of 11-10-9-8-7-6-5-4-3-2-1. Twelve teams, 66 points, 5.50 points per team.

- In a fourteen-team league, we give points to the league's eleven best starting pitchers, on a scale of 12-11-10-9-8-7-6-5-4-3-2. Fourteen teams, 77 points, 5.50 points per team.

- In a sixteen-team league, we give points to the league's eleven best starting pitchers, on a scale of 13-12-11-10-9-8-7-6-5-4-3. Sixteen teams, 88 points, 5.50 points per team.

It's basically a ten-best-pitchers list, but we give the pitcher more credit for being the best pitcher in a sixteen-team league than in an eight-team league.

I figured the best pitchers in baseball by that system and totaled up the points, but there was a problem. I had Roy Oswalt ahead of Sandy Koufax. Doesn't sound right.

I am willing to argue for any outcome that is rational, even if it is surprising, but is this a rational outcome? Studying the data, I decided that the biggest problem came from the lack of adequate recognition for truly outstanding seasons. In 1978 Ron Guidry was the best pitcher in the American League, with a won-lost record of 25-3 and an ERA of 1.74. Gaylord Perry was the best pitcher in the National League, but he was 21-6 with an ERA of 2.73.

These seasons are not the same, nor even in the same group. Guidry's season was historic. Dwight Gooden's season in 1985 was historic, as was Pedro's season in 1999, the Big Unit in 2002, and Steve Carlton in 1972. These seasons are something *more* than the best season in that league that year; they are historic.

I added to the counts three kinds of "historic season bonus points". I gave the pitcher an additional 3 points for

1) Any season in which he led the league in Season Score by 50 points or more,

2) Any season in which he had a Season Score of 400 or higher, post-1900, or

3) Any season which was among the top four seasons of the decade (thus, the top 20% of the first-in-league seasons).

In the years before the Cy Young Award, a pitcher who led the league in Season Score by 50 points or more would very often be the Most Valuable player. Pitchers don't win the MVP Award anymore, but a pitcher who has the highest season score by 50 points or more is virtually always the Cy Young Award winner. There are only a few cases in which this was not true.

A 400-point season is an even more difficult achievement than leading the league by 50 points. A 20-game winner typically has a Season Score between 250 and 300. A 400-point season is *big* numbers. The last two pitchers to get to 400 points were Guidry in '78 and Doc Gooden in '85.

Those seasons are special, so we treat them as special. These three bonuses are not mutually exclusive; one can get the 3 points for leading the league in Season Score by 50 points or more, the 3 points for having one of the top four seasons of the decade, *and* the 3 points for having a Season Score of 400. Since 1930 twelve pitchers have gotten all nine points:

- Lefty Grove in 1930 and 1931
- Carl Hubbell in 1933
- Dizzy Dean in 1934
- Robin Roberts in 1952
- Sandy Koufax in 1963, 1965 and 1966
- Denny McLain in 1968
- Steve Carlton in 1972
- Ron Guidry in 1978
- Doc Gooden in 1985

*A pitcher who has the highest season score by 50 points or more is virtually always the Cy Young Award winner.*

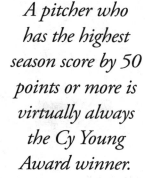

Those were all incredible seasons, and I don't think anyone would question that they all deserve to be distinguished from the "ordinary" Cy Young seasons.

OK, two more little wrinkles I have to explain. First, no points are awarded to any season with a Season Score less than 100. This is a rule which only applies to a handful of seasons in 19th century baseball, and has no impact on the historic standing of any significant pitcher. Second, I created a "damaged goods list", which includes twenty leagues—the Union Association in 1884, all three major leagues in the "strike season" of 1890, the Federal League in 1914 and 1915, both leagues in the war-shortened 1918 seasons, both leagues in 1942, 1943, 1944 and 1945, both leagues in 1981, and both leagues in 1994. In 1994 and 1981 a strike wiped out a third of the season, so the best pitchers in the league had records like 13-4 in 190 innings. That's not *exactly* the same as a Cy Young season in a normal season, is it? It isn't, so I reduced the points awarded in a "damaged season" from 5.50 points per team to 4.50 points per team, and also, pitchers from "damaged seasons" were not eligible for historic season bonus points, no matter how good their numbers were. Logically, I probably should have done *more* than that to discount performances in the damaged seasons, but...at least it is something.

## What I Learned

What I learned from doing this is that our modern pitchers stack up extremely well by historical standards. The "recently retired pitchers" list, of course, is a bestiary; Clemens, Maddux, Randy Johnson and others yield to no one in terms of the number of top-rank seasons that they produced—and there are others beyond them, others who perhaps we don't think of as historic pitchers because they don't stack up impressively next to Clemens and Maddux and the Big Unit, but who *do* stack up surprisingly well when compared to other great pitchers from history.

There were eight pitchers active in the 2009 season who have already done enough, by historic standards, to go into the Hall of Fame, based on the number of high-impact seasons they have already recorded. Two of those — Tim Hudson and Andy Pettitte — are marginal, close calls. They're over the Hall of Fame line, but still close enough that you can argue about it. The other six, based on the big seasons that they have *already* had, are Randy Johnson, Pedro Martinez, Roy Halladay, John Smoltz, Johan Santana and Roy Oswalt. I know the inclusion of Oswalt on this list may be surprising, but...I'll talk about it later.

Before 1890 there were two semi-established quasi-major leagues, the National League and the American

*What I learned from doing this is that our modern pitchers stack up extremely well by historical standards.*

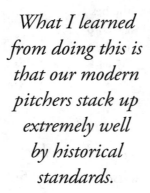

Association. In 1890, due to a labor/management dispute, most of the best players in the National League and some of the best players in the American Association started a new league, the Player's League. This a) weakened the competition in all three leagues, and b) opened the door to many new players. Two of the new pitchers were Kid Nichols and Cy Young.

Although Amos Rusie was the dominant pitcher of the early 1890s in terms of public recognition as a superstar, by the late 1890s Kid Nichols and Cy Young had become the two greatest pitchers in baseball's short history up to that point—Nichols number one, and Cy Young number two. In 1900-1901 there was another period of labor strife, with new rival leagues starting up. Cy Young signed in a league — the American League — which *did* become a major league, while Kid Nichols signed in a league which didn't. Young thus moved ahead of Nichols, becoming — in 1901 — the greatest pitcher in baseball history up to that point, as measured by the number of outstanding seasons in his career.

Cy Young got to 500 career wins in part because he pitched in an era when a good pitcher could win 30 games in a season. Thirty wins, for most of Cy Young's career, meant less than twenty wins does today. We routinely and appropriately discount Young's career record because of this.

But discounted or not, Cy Young had one hell of a career. Cy Young pitched in the major leagues from 1890 to 1911—22 years. In five of those years (1890, 1906, 1909, 1910 and 1911) he was *not* one of the top pitchers in the league. The other 17 seasons, he was:

| Year | G | W | L | WPct | IP | SO | BB | ERA | Score | League Rank | SS Points | Bonus | Total |
|------|-----|-----|-----|------|-------|-----|-----|------|-------|-------------|-----------|-------|-------|
| 1891 | 55 | 27 | 22 | .551 | 423.2 | 147 | 140 | 2.85 | 264 | 7 | 3 | 0 | 3 |
| 1892 | 53 | 36 | 12 | .750 | 453.0 | 168 | 118 | 1.93 | 549 | 1 | 11 | 6 | 17 |
| 1893 | 53 | 34 | 16 | .680 | 422.2 | 102 | 103 | 3.36 | 338 | 2 | 10 | 0 | 10 |
| 1894 | 52 | 26 | 21 | .553 | 408.2 | 108 | 106 | 3.94 | 175 | 4 | 7 | 0 | 7 |
| 1895 | 47 | 35 | 10 | .778 | 369.2 | 121 | 75 | 3.24 | 392 | 1 | 11 | 0 | 11 |
| 1896 | 51 | 28 | 15 | .651 | 414.1 | 140 | 62 | 3.24 | 327 | 1 | 11 | 0 | 11 |
| 1897 | 46 | 21 | 19 | .525 | 335.0 | 88 | 49 | 3.79 | 172 | 9 | 3 | 0 | 3 |
| 1898 | 46 | 25 | 13 | .658 | 377.2 | 101 | 41 | 2.53 | 349 | 4 | 8 | 0 | 8 |
| 1899 | 44 | 26 | 16 | .619 | 369.1 | 111 | 44 | 2.58 | 328 | 4 | 8 | 0 | 8 |
| 1900 | 41 | 19 | 19 | .500 | 321.1 | 115 | 36 | 3.00 | 224 | 2 | 6 | 0 | 6 |
| 1901 | 43 | 33 | 10 | .767 | 371.1 | 158 | 37 | 1.62 | 522 | 1 | 9 | 6 | 15 |
| 1902 | 45 | 32 | 11 | .744 | 384.2 | 160 | 53 | 2.15 | 474 | 1 | 9 | 6 | 15 |
| 1903 | 40 | 28 | 9 | .757 | 341.2 | 176 | 37 | 2.08 | 443 | 1 | 9 | 6 | 15 |
| 1904 | 43 | 26 | 16 | .619 | 380.0 | 200 | 29 | 1.97 | 450 | 2 | 8 | 3 | 11 |
| 1905 | 38 | 18 | 19 | .486 | 320.2 | 210 | 30 | 1.82 | 316 | 7 | 3 | 0 | 3 |
| 1907 | 43 | 21 | 15 | .583 | 343.1 | 147 | 51 | 1.99 | 370 | 4 | 6 | 0 | 6 |
| 1908 | 36 | 21 | 11 | .656 | 299.0 | 150 | 37 | 1.26 | 404 | 3 | 7 | 3 | 10 |

In 1892, 1895, 1896, 1901, 1902 and 1903 Young scores as the best pitcher in his league. In four others seasons he was the second-best or the third-best. In six seasons beyond that, he was one of the seven best. Four times he was the best pitcher in his league by a margin of 50 points or more. By 1901 Cy Young was the greatest pitcher in the history of baseball, by this method — and he held that position into the 21st century.

## The Hall of Fame Line

I was trying to level the playing field. I was trying to say "the league ERA may be 3.00 one year and 5.00 another year, but let's level the playing field by comparing each pitcher to those pitchers that he actually competed with. Pitchers may pitch 300 innings in one season and lead the league with 200 in another because of the use of bullpens and a five-man starting rotation, but let's compare everyone on a fair basis versus his contemporaries."

Our system has its limitations and its flaws, certainly, but it also has this additional benefit: it gives the pitcher no credit whatsoever for hanging around as a .500 pitcher. Sandy Koufax had 165 career wins and Dizzy Dean 150, but they easily outpoint Jim Kaat and Tommy John, who hung around a long time and won 280+ games.

The essential reason that this system works as well as it does, and the reason I decided to write about it, is that it draws a relatively bright line between Hall of Fame and non-Hall of Fame pitchers. There are, as I said, millions of ways to rank starting pitchers, and this is just one more. In any of those ways that one can rank starting pitchers, there is a "Hall of Fame line"; there is some point above which most players are in the Hall of Fame, and below which most players are out.

Ordinarily, however, there is a substantial gray area. Usually, when you rank pitchers, you have four things:

- An "in" line,
- An "out" line,
- A gray area between the lines, and
- Outliers.

Outliers on both ends; players who shouldn't be in but are; players who should be in but aren't.

What makes this methodology interesting is that the gray area goes from black to white very, very quickly. The line is: 43 points. At 43, you're in; below 43, you're not in. Setting aside active and recently retired pitchers, there are 17 players who score between 43 and 50. Thirteen of those 17 — 76% — are in the Hall of Fame. There are 21 players who score between 35 and 42. Only six of those 21 — 29% — are in the Hall of Fame. 43 you're in; 42, you're out. One rarely sees that. This is a summary of the Hall of Famers by ten-point ranges, excluding active and recently-retired pitchers:

| Range | Population | Hall of Famers | HOF Pct |
|---|---|---|---|
| 100+ points | 7 | 7 | 100% |
| 90-99 points | 3 | 3 | 100% |
| 80-89 points | 2 | 2 | 100% |
| 70-79 points | 6 | 5 | 83% |
| 60-69 points | 8 | 7 | 88% |
| 50-59 points | 10 | 9 | 90% |
| 40-49 points | 18 | 12 | 67% |
| 30-39 points | 42 | 8 | 19% |
| 20-29 points | 76 | 4 | 5% |
| 10-19 points | 166 | 3 | 2% |
| 1-9 points | 337 | 2 | 1% |

So this enables us to say, with a fair degree of confidence, what a Hall of Fame career is in terms of having a necessary number of seasons as one of the best pitchers in the league. I decided to refer to each eleven points, on occasion, as a "strong season". There are 5.5 points per team; 11 points is as many points as there would be on two teams. It's just more convenient sometimes to say that a pitcher had eight strong seasons than that he had a score of 43 points in our strong seasons evaluative system. Comments on individual pitchers are summarized below in alphabetical order.

### Chief Bender

Bender is among the weakest Hall of Fame starting pitchers by this method, checking in with only 23 points. Bender was never the best pitcher in his league in any season, and ranks among the top pitchers in his league in only five seasons.

### Vida Blue

By this method as by so many others, Vida Blue's career appears to be of Hall of Fame stature. With a career won-lost log of 209-161, Blue certainly has a record comparable to some Hall of Fame pitchers like Don Drysdale (209-166) and Hal Newhouser (207-150)—but also Milt Pappas (209-164) and Lew Burdette (203-144). Pitchers in this group generally go into the Hall of Fame if they have dominant seasons — like Drysdale and Newhouser — and are left out if they do not.

Vida Blue had one of the most dominant seasons of the modern era, winning the American League MVP award in 1971, and won 18 to 22 games four other times. By our system he scores at 50, and almost everybody in that range has been elected to the Hall of Fame. Not counting active and recently retired pitchers, he is the third best-qualified pitcher who has not been elected to the Hall of Fame, behind...well, I'd better save the names.

### Bert Blyleven

With 71 points — six strong seasons — Blyleven ranks as ridiculously over-qualified for the Hall of Fame. He is one of three pitchers in history who has not been elected to the Hall of Fame despite several years on the ballot and more than four strong seasons. Our study in this regard is thus consistent with numerous other methods tending to show Blyleven as a Hall of Fame quality pitcher.

By this method Blyleven ranks as the #1 starting pitcher in his league in 1984, and among the best starting pitchers in his league in 13 different seasons.

*What makes this methodology interesting is that the gray area goes from black to white very, very quickly.*

These are the only pitchers in baseball history who were among the best pitchers in their league in ten or more different seasons:

| Player | Yr Count | Player | Yr Count |
|---|---|---|---|
| Warren Spahn | 17 | Steve Carlton | 11 |
| Cy Young | 17 | Whitey Ford | 11 |
| Roger Clemens | 15 | Tom Glavine | 11 |
| Greg Maddux | 14 | Randy Johnson | 11 |
| Tom Seaver | 14 | Kid Nichols | 11 |
| Walter Johnson | 13 | Eddie Plank | 11 |
| Pete Alexander | 13 | Carl Hubbell | 10 |
| Lefty Grove | 13 | Pedro Martinez | 10 |
| Bert Blyleven | 13 | Jim Palmer | 10 |
| Christy Mathewson | 12 | Red Ruffing | 10 |
| Mike Mussina | 12 | Don Sutton | 10 |

### Tommy Bond

Tommy Bond was the number one pitcher in the National League in 1877 and 1878. I figured the all-time top-ten list as it stood after every season beginning in 1876, and Bond, of course, was at the top of the list in the early years, with a total accumulating to 40 points. Bond held the top spot on the chart from 1877 through 1883, being pushed out of the #1 all-time spot by Old Hoss Radbourn in 1884. He remained on the top-ten list into the early 20th century.

### Tommy Bridges

Bridges, a famous curveball pitcher of the 1930s, had a nice run, being listed among the top pitchers in the American League in seven different seasons from 1934 to 1943, and ranking first in 1936. His career total was 28 points.

### Kevin Brown

Kevin Brown does extremely well in our survey, being listed among the best pitchers in his league in 1992,

'96, '97, '98, '99, 2000, and 2003. His career total of 72 points is well above the level that has historically indicated a Hall of Fame career.

Although Tom Glavine won the NL Cy Young Award in 1998, our method lists Brown as the league's best pitcher, Glavine as the third-best. Comparing Glavine to Brown in that season, Brown pitched 28 more innings, had a better ERA, had 100 more strikeouts (257-157) and 25 fewer walks. Glavine was supported by 5.15 runs per nine innings; Brown, by 4.37.

Again, I'm not saying that our system is right; merely that it is reasonable. Glavine won the Cy Young Award, and he will always have that — but it doesn't mean that he gets *all* recognition from everybody as the league's best pitcher. Brown has an argument, too.

### Mark Buehrle

After ranking among the best pitchers in the American League in 2001, 2002, 2004 and 2005, Buehrle has not been able to crack the top-pitchers list since 2005. He has 29 points and is holding.

### Jim Bunning

In his first season as a rotation starter (1957), retiring Senator Jim Bunning ranks as the #1 pitcher in the American League, finishing 20-8 with a 2.70 ERA; in fact, by the season score there is only one other pitcher (Billy Pierce) within 60 points of him.

In the two seasons after that Bunning finished 14-12 and 17-13, in both cases just missing the league's best-pitchers list. In 1960 Bunning — despite a won-lost record of 11 and 14 — ranks as the fourth-best starting pitcher in the American League. There was a shortage of good pitchers in the American League that year. Two young pitchers, Jim Perry and Chuck Estrada, won 18 games each, but both had ERAs about 3.60, and the league ERA was well under 4.00. Whitey Ford and Camilo Pascual, two of the league's best pitchers in that era, had ERAs around 3.00, but missed time with injuries and finished 12-9 and 12-8. Frank Baumann led

*Blyleven ranks as ridiculously over-qualified for the Hall of Fame.*

the league in ERA (2.67), but made only 20 starts and had a strikeout-to-walk ratio of 71-53. Bunning, leading the league in strikeouts and second in ERA, nearly ranks as the league's best pitcher despite his 11-14 record.

In 1961, of course, Whitey Ford had a historic season, while Bunning's teammate Frank Lary also had a Cy Young-quality campaign, but Bunning, at 17-11 with a better ERA than either Ford or Lary, ranks as the league's number three pitcher. In 1962, at 19-10, he once more ranked among the league's best.

In 1963 Bunning had a poor year, finishing 12-13 with a worse-than-league ERA, failing to place on or near the league's best-pitchers list for the first time in his career. That winter the Tigers traded him to the National League for Don Demeter, an outfielder. It was a poor trade; indeed, it was a stupid trade.

Early in 1964 Bunning pitched a perfect game, baseball's first regular-season perfect game in more than 40 years. In mid-September, 1964, Jim Bunning seemed poised to win his first Cy Young Award. Entering September he was 14-4 with a 2.17 ERA. Koufax was at 19-5 but done for the season with an injury. Starting (always on three days' rest) Bunning pitched complete games on September 1, 5 and 13, and took a no-decision on September 9. On September 13 he pitched 10 innings, ultimately winning the game 4-1, making him 17-4 with a 2.23 ERA.

Now let me pause for a moment to defend the reputation of the late Gene Mauch. In popular history, what happened next was that as soon as the Phillies' lead began to slip, Mauch panicked and started Bunning on two days rest to try to arrest the slide. Bunning was shelled, didn't pitch well the rest of the year, and the Phillies had a monumental collapse.

Elements of that are certainly true, but it's not exactly right. Gene Mauch did in fact make an utterly inexplicable decision to start Jim Bunning on two days' rest on September 16, 1964. Bunning did get hit hard, was highly ineffective late in the year, and the Phillies did do an absolutely amazing pennant race pratfall. No one can understand why Bunning made that September 16 start. The Phillies were playing Houston, a team which

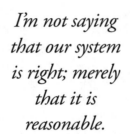

*I'm not saying that our system is right; merely that it is reasonable.*

had a team batting average for the season of .229 and a team OPS for the season of — I am not making this up — .599. They were one of the worst-hitting teams in the history of baseball. Bunning had pitched a ten-inning complete game just two days earlier. The Phillies had the pennant virtually wrapped up, six games ahead with a little over two weeks to play. The decision to start Bunning in that game is simply flabbergasting. Bunning was hit hard, and the Phillies lost.

The Gene Mauch blew it story, however, is not exactly right. First, the Phillies lead was not slipping at that time. The Phillies had a 6 ½ game lead on September 20 — four days *after* Bunning's loss to Houston.

Second, Bunning started against Los Angeles on September 20, on his normal rest, and was highly effective, giving up five hits, no walks and no earned runs (two un-earned) in a 9-inning complete-game victory. That made him 18-5 with a 2.33 ERA.

Third, Bunning's next start after that, on September 24, was on normal rotation, and Bunning did not pitch badly, although he lost.

The Phillies' collapse started on September 21. They lost on the 21st, 22nd and 23rd, lost on the 24th with Bunning, and lost again on the 25th and 26th. Bunning started again on two days' rest on the 27th and the 30th — but by then, it was high time to panic. By September 27 the Phillies had lost 6 games of a 6 ½ game lead in six days. You know the old joke: If you can keep your head while those around you are panicking, you may not understand the situation. By September 27 the Phillies' house was engulfed in flames; it was time to panic.

There is no defense for the decision to start Bunning on the 16th — but there is also no clear connection between that game and the collapse of the Phillies, which started five days later, after Bunning had pitched an outstanding game on September 20. The Phillies lost six straight games of which Bunning pitched only one, on normal rest, and gave up only three runs. *Then* he started again on three days' rest, lost, started again on three days' rest, lost again, and pitched a shutout on the last day of the season to finish 19-8, 2.63 ERA.

But also, it wasn't *that* unusual for a pitcher to start on two days' rest in that era; not common, but not as bizarre as it seems now. Koufax pitched a complete game on September 10, 1963, in the pennant race, came back and started against the Phillies on September 13; nobody says Walt Alston was an idiot for doing that. Warren Spahn in July, 1961, pitched ten-innings, and then came in to pitch relief two days later. He was 40 years old. Nobody said anything about that.

In any event Bunning scores, in 1964, as the number four starting pitcher in the National League, behind fellow Hall of Famers Koufax, Marichal and Drysdale — another really solid season. In 1965 he had almost the same numbers as 1964 (19-9, 2.60 ERA) and scores again as the number four pitcher in the National League, behind the same three pitchers. In 1966 he won 19 games for the third straight season, and this time scores as the #3 pitcher in the league, behind Koufax and Marichal.

So that is seven times in ten years that Bunning has been listed among the best pitchers in his league. In 1967 Koufax was retired and Marichal was hurt, and Bunning finished only 17-15 — but ranks as the best pitcher in the league. Bunning's 17-15 record in 1966 is the worst won-lost record ever for a league-best pitcher, other than Dazzy Vance in 1930, who also finished 17-15. The Cy Young Award went to Mike McCormick because of his 22-10 won-lost record, but look at the facts: McCormick pitched 262 innings with a 2.85 ERA. Bunning pitched 40 more innings — 302 — with an ERA more than half a run lower, 2.29. McCormick struck out 150 hitters; Bunning struck out 253. McCormick walked 81 hitters; Bunning walked 73. The park factor in San Francisco, where McCormick pitched, was 98; the park factor in Philadelphia was 108.

Obviously Bunning was better in 1967 than McCormick; he just didn't get the won-lost record he deserved, and thus lost the first Cy Young contest in years in which he would not have had to beat Koufax, Marichal and Drysdale, not to mention Bob Gibson. That was his last good year, but not a lot of pitchers can

match that record. Bunning ranks, by this method, as the #31 starting pitcher of all time.

### Steve Carlton

Carlton ranks among the best pitchers in the National League eleven years, and ranks first or second five times (1972, 1977, 1980, 1981 and 1982). With 98 points he ranks as the 14th greatest starting pitcher of all time by this method.

### Chris Carpenter

Chris Carpenter piled up 29 points before his injury, based on being among the best pitchers in the league in 2004, 2005 and 2006. Adding 12 points in 2009 — he ranks as the league's #2 starting pitcher — he now has 41 career points — just short of a Hall of Fame career, in terms of having seasons ranking him among the best pitchers in the league.

*By this method, Roger Clemens now ranks as the #1 starting pitcher of all time.*

### Bob Caruthers

Caruthers, seen by some people as a Hall of Fame candidate, was the best pitcher in the American Association in 1885, but is credited with only three strong seasons (32 points). He does, of course, have some other credentials, in that he was also a good-hitting outfielder when he didn't pitch.

### Jack Chesbro

Chesbro is in the Hall of Fame despite earning only 37 points in our survey — a number that leaves him behind Lew Burdette, Dennis Martinez and Frank Viola. He had a historic season in 1904, of course, and he was also the best pitcher in the National League in 1902. Otherwise his credentials are very modest, and I have long felt that his Hall of Fame selection was a mistake.

### Roger Clemens

By this method, Roger Clemens now ranks as the #1 starting pitcher of all time. You can agree with that, you can disagree, you can talk about steroids; that's up to you. In terms of having a large number of dominant seasons, Roger Clemens is the greatest starting pitcher of all time.

By our method, Clemens ranks as the number one starting pitcher in his league in eight different seasons — 1986, 1987, 1990, 1991, 1997, 1998, 2001 and 2004. No one in history can match that:

| Player | Seasons as League's #1 Starting Pitcher |
|---|---|
| Roger Clemens | 8 |
| Walter Johnson | 7 |
| Christy Mathewson | 7 |
| Lefty Grove | 6 |
| Jim Palmer | 6 |
| Cy Young | 6 |
| Grover Cleveland Alexander | 5 |
| Randy Johnson | 5 |
| Greg Maddux | 5 |
| Christy Mathewson | 5 |
| Tom Seaver | 5 |
| Warren Spahn | 5 |

Clemens ranks *among* the best pitchers in the league in 15 seasons, a figure exceeded only by Spahn and Cy Young, with 17 each.

In the eight seasons in which Clemens ranks as his league's #1 starting pitcher, his career won-lost record was 162-49 — an average of 20-6. But even if you set all eight of those seasons aside, Clemens might still be a Hall of Famer. His record in the rest of his career was 192-135—about the same as the career record of Hall of Fame pitchers Jack Chesbro, Rube Waddell, Ed Walsh and Dazzy Vance.

### David Cone

In our analysis David Cone is a "recently retired" pitcher, meaning that he has earned points in our method since 1990. There are many "recently retired" pitchers who show by our method as qualified Hall of Famers, and David is easily among them. With the Mets in 1988 (when Cone was 20-3) he ranks as the number two pitcher in the National League, behind Orel Hershiser. In 1990 and 1992 he ranks among the best pitchers in his league, and picks up a few points each year. In 1994, when he won the Cy Young Award for Kansas City, he ranks as the number one pitcher in the league, although we discounted this because it was a strike-shortened season (Cone went 16-5 in a 115-game schedule.) In 1995, splitting the year between the Blue Jays and the Yankees, he went 18-8 and ranks as the number three pitcher in the league. In 1997 he picked up a few points at the bottom of the list; in 1998 he won 20 games, and ranks as the fourth-best pitcher in the American League. In 1999, although his won-lost record was just 12-9, he was still the ninth-best pitcher in the league. Adding it all up, he has eight seasons ranking among the best seasons in his league, which is more than most Hall of Fame pitchers, and he has 60 points — about 40% above the Hall of Fame threshold.

Cone had a career won-lost log of 194-126, which, again, is similar to Hall of Famers Chesbro, Vance, Waddell and Walsh. In the last fifty years pitchers with those kind of won-lost records generally have *not* been selected for eternal fame, as the emphasis has been on career totals, rather than dominating seasons.

### Mort Cooper

Mort Cooper ranked as the #1 or #2 pitcher in the National League three straight years (1941-42-43), but pulled up with just 23 strong-season points.

### Stan Coveleski

Stan Coveleski had seven seasons ranking among the best pitchers in his league and was the top dog in 1925. He had a career total of 43 points, which puts him right on the line between "in" and "out".

*There are many "recently retired" pitchers who show by our method as qualified Hall of Famers, and David Cone is easily among them.*

### Mike Cuellar

Mike Cuellar had major league opportunities as early as 1959, but struggled for many years to establish himself as a major league pitcher, with a career won-lost record of 6-9 through 1965. He was always regarded as a very talented pitcher.

Finally getting his feet on the ground in 1966, Cuellar ranks among the best pitchers in the National League in two seasons (1966-1967), and among the best in the American League in five (1969-1970-1971-1972-1974). In 1969 he split the Cy Young Award with Denny McLain, a tie vote. Our system sees him as the #2 pitcher in the American League in that season, behind McLain, and #3 in 1970. He had a career total of 34 points, and would be in the Hall of Fame if he had gotten traction about three years earlier.

### Paul Derringer

Paul Derringer was 18-8 in 1931, 22-13 in 1935, 21-14 in 1938, 25-7 in 1939, and 20-12 in 1940. He ranks among the best pitchers in the league in all of those seasons, and was the #2 pitcher in the league in 1938 and 1939. However, Derringer's career total of 29 points is well short of the Hall of Fame standard.

### Don Drysdale

Drysdale ranks among the best starting pitchers in the National League in 1957 and in every season between 1959 and 1965. In 1962, when he won the Cy Young Award with a 25-9 record, we do have him ranked as the #1 starting pitcher in either league.

Interestingly, Drysdale does *not* rank among the best starting pitchers in the National League in 1968, when he had the famous consecutive-scoreless-inning streak — and does not deserve to. His won-lost record was just 14-12. His ERA was good, 2.15, but that was only sixth in the league in 1968, and he was nowhere near the top ten in the league in innings pitched or strikeouts.

He does, however, clear the Hall of Fame standard by this method, with a career total of 50 points.

### Dennis Eckersley

Dennis Eckersley ranked among the best starting pitchers in the American League in 1978 and 1979, and earned 18 points by this method as a starting pitcher. His biggest credentials, of course, are in his relief career.

### Bob Feller

Bob Feller ranks as the number one starting pitcher in the American League in 1939, 1940, 1946 and 1947, and ranks second in 1941 (behind Thornton Lee). He also made the list in 1938, 1948, 1950 and 1951.

Despite missing four prime seasons due to World War II, Feller still ranks as the #17 starting pitcher of all time by this method, actually tied for 17th with Carl Hubbell. His career total was 83 points. If one assumes that he would have been healthy and productive through the War years, he would probably have ranked about 5th or 6th all-time.

### Wes Ferrell

Wes Ferrell, although seen by some people as deserving of Hall of Fame status, was never the best pitcher in his league, and had only two seasons ranking among the top three in his league. His career total is only 35 points. Few pitchers in that range of accomplishment have been named to the Hall of Fame.

### Fat Freddie Fitzsimmons

Fat Freddie Fitzsimmons was not exactly fat, until the end of his career; he was kind of built like a hobbit. He was quite short with extremely short legs but a large, powerful torso and long arms. He had a big neck and a big head. He was odd-looking, like an oversized dwarf. He is listed now at 5-11; I don't know where that comes from. He was probably 5-8, but a big man from the waist up.

He threw some knuckleballs and/or knuckle curves, but he made his living off a sinker. He wasn't someone you would look at and say "Wow; there's a Hall of Famer" — yet he won 217 games in his career, and

*If one assumes that Feller would have been healthy and productive through the War years, he would probably have ranked about 5th or 6th all-time.*

lost only 146. His won-lost record is better than many Hall of Famers, yet in our system he has only 17 points, nowhere near a Hall of Fame number.

He never got above 6% in the Hall of Fame voting, and this is sort of what I am getting at. The Hall of Fame voters look for certain things, like dominant seasons and dominant performances. Don Drysdale things. Freddie Fitzsimmons had more wins than Don Drysdale and fewer losses, but he had hardly any of the things that made Drysdale a Hall of Famer. I didn't design this system to track the way that Hall of Fame voters think, but it just accidentally does. This is useful, and instructive.

### Whitey Ford

Ford had a historic season in 1961, leading the American League in Season Score by more than 50 points, and a career total of 72 points (six strong seasons). He ranks as the #22 starting pitcher of all time by this method.

### Bob Gibson

I know that many people have come to think of Bob Gibson as the paragon of pitching virtues, but in all candor, he doesn't do great by this method. He has 61 points in his career, a Hall of Fame number, but not a front-rank Hall of Fame number. He ranks as the number one pitcher in the National League in 1968 and 1970, his two Cy Young seasons, and also ranks second in 1969, fourth in 1972. 1968 was a historic season, obviously.

Gibson is held back a little, of course, because he was going head-to-head in his best seasons with Koufax and Marichal and Don Drysdale, and they couldn't *all* be the best pitcher in the league—but then, so was Jim Bunning, and Bunning got 63 points. He was slow getting started. Everybody remembers that Koufax struggled for years before he found himself, but Gibson was the same age as Koufax (a few weeks older, actually), and he was two or three years later than

Koufax in harnessing his ability. He had seven years as one of the best pitchers in the National League. He can accurately be described as a great pitcher, but somehow he has become the archetype of a great pitcher. I'm not sure that's justified by the record.

Within the last year, we have begun to hear the argument that Gibson was held back because he started on a five-man rotation while others in his league were working on a four-man rotation. This is not entirely untrue, but show me the season in which Gibson would rank better with more starts. Gibson ranked 1-4 in the National League in innings pitched in 1964, 1965, 1966, 1968, 1969, 1970 and 1972. He was ninth in 1963, and had in-season injuries in 1967 and 1971. He ranks below Koufax, Marichal, Bunning and Drysdale in the early part of that era not because he didn't pitch as much, but because he didn't pitch as well. He did out-last them all, and this gave him a couple of years as the league's best pitcher.

### Tom Glavine

Tom Glavine, Warren Spahn Lite, had eleven seasons among the best pitchers in the National League, and ranked first in 1991, when he did win the Cy Young Award. His career total was 90 points.

### Lefty Gomez

With 48 points, Gomez is over the Hall of Fame line with a half-season to spare. He was the best pitcher in the American League in 1934 and 1937 — posting a 2.33 ERA both years — and was among the best pitchers in four other seasons. See comments on Ron Guidry.

### Dwight Gooden

Gooden compiled 59 strong season points in his relatively short career. He is listed in my study as a "recently retired" pitcher.

### Lefty Grove

With 13 seasons among the best pitchers in the American League and six seasons as the best pitcher

*Bob Gibson doesn't do great by this method.*

in the American League, Grove ranks as the sixth-best starting pitcher in baseball history by this analysis. Had we done this study a decade ago, Grove would have ranked third, behind Cy Young and Walter Johnson.

### Ron Guidry

There are four pitchers in this study who are "true outliers" — that is, real and dramatic exceptions to the general patterns of the data. Those four are Bert Blyleven, Ron Guidry, Jesse Haines and Rube Marquard. There are several "marginal exceptions" to the rules, marginal outliers. Billy Pierce is a few points over the Hall of Fame line but never got a nibble from the Hall of Fame voters; Eppa Rixey and Herb Pennock are a few points below the Hall of Fame line but did go in, as did a dozen or so other pitchers. These are marginal calls.

Jesse Haines and Rube Marquard are "negative outliers" — pitchers who made the Hall of Fame despite a serious shortage of meaningful credentials — and then there are Bert Blyleven, at 71 points, and Ron Guidry at 60.

Blyleven and Guidry are so far above the Hall of Fame line that one would think that their Hall of Fame selection would not be an issue. Blyleven, of course, has become a popular candidate. Guidry has not.

Guidry's career in several respects parallels that of Lefty Gomez. Gomez' career record was 189-102; Guidry's was 170-91. Gomez' ERA was 3.34; Guidry's was 3.29. Both were Yankees, both left-handers, both hard throwers, both thin. Guidry had three 20-win seasons; Gomez had four.

In the past, I have analyzed this comparison in this way:

1) Gomez was fortunate to make the Hall of Fame, being very marginally qualified,

2) Guidry was similar but a little bit *behind* Gomez, thus not in a range where his Hall of Fame selection was likely,

3) Gomez had three outstanding seasons; Guidry only one, 1978, and

4) Gomez made the Hall of Fame, in part, based on his post-career reputation as an entertainer and ambassador for the game.

But the implications of this new method are totally incompatible with that analysis. As this method sees it, putting Gomez in the Hall of Fame was *not* a reach. Gomez is well qualified based on the number of high-quality seasons that he produced. And Guidry, rather than ranking behind Gomez, in fact ranks far ahead of him.

How does that happen? These are Ron Guidry's six point-producing seasons, in the form I used earlier for Cy Young:

| Year | G | W | L | W Pct | IP | SO | BB | ERA | Score | Rank | SS Points | Bonus | Total |
|------|----|----|----|-------|-------|-----|----|------|-------|------|-----------|-------|-------|
| 1977 | 31 | 16 | 7 | .696 | 210.2 | 176 | 65 | 2.82 | 237 | 6 | 7 | | 7 |
| 1978 | 35 | 25 | 3 | .893 | 273.2 | 248 | 72 | 1.74 | 439 | 1 | 12 | 9 | 21 |
| 1979 | 33 | 18 | 8 | .692 | 236.1 | 201 | 71 | 2.78 | 268 | 3 | 10 | | 10 |
| 1982 | 34 | 14 | 8 | .636 | 222.0 | 162 | 69 | 3.81 | 165 | 11 | 2 | | 2 |
| 1983 | 31 | 21 | 9 | .700 | 250.1 | 156 | 60 | 3.42 | 257 | 4 | 9 | | 9 |
| 1985 | 34 | 22 | 6 | .786 | 259.0 | 143 | 42 | 3.27 | 289 | 2 | 11 | | 11 |

*I am not suggesting that my new method here should substitute for all other judgment about Hall of Fame selections, not at all.*

A total of 60 points. It takes 43, historically, to be a Hall of Famer. Although Bret Saberhagen won the Cy Young Award in 1985, Guidry's record is just as good; I have Saberhagen with a Season Score of 290, Guidry 289. That gives Guidry four seasons among the league's four best pitchers, and he was competing in a 14-team league. Gomez had four such seasons, competing in an eight-team league.

What happened to Guidry, in a sense, was that Guidry's 1978 season was *so* good that it made the rest of his career look bad by comparison. Also, Guidry competed in the middle of a historic outbreak of 300-game winners and near-300-game winners. He was competing on the ballot with Steve Carlton, Phil Niekro, Don Sutton, Nolan Ryan, Jim Kaat, Tommy John, Bert Blyleven and others. He was 100+ wins behind them.

By Guidry's era, career win totals had come to dominate the Hall of Fame discussion. Perhaps this is right; perhaps it is wrong. I am not suggesting that my new method here should substitute for all other judgment about Hall of Fame selections, not at all. There are many other ways to look at the issue. Perhaps those other ways are better.

But while those other pitchers have 100+ wins more than Guidry, Guidry's winning percentage was far better than Carlton's, or Sutton's, or Niekro's, or Kaat's, or Tommy John's, or Ryan's, or Blyleven's or Gaylord Perry's; it was even far better than Tom Seaver's. Guidry was further over .500 — wins minus losses — than most of those pitchers.

Steve Carlton's ERA was 41 points better than the league norm for his career. Don Sutton's ERA was 45 points better-than-league, Tommy John's was 42 points better, Blyleven's 50 points better. Jim Kaat was 15 points better than league. Ron Guidry's ERA was 76 points better than the league average.

I am merely pointing this out: in general, through baseball history, pitchers who have this many seasons as one of the best pitchers in their league have been almost automatic Hall of Fame selections. Historically, the Hall of Fame has made room for all pitchers with 250+ wins—but also for pitchers who were more dominant in shorter careers.

*Through baseball history, pitchers who have this many seasons as one of the best pitchers in their league have been almost automatic Hall of Fame selections.*

### Jesse Haines

The only starting pitchers who have been selected with less than 23 points are Dennis Eckersley, Rube Marquard, Jesse Haines, Babe Ruth, Albert Spalding and Hoyt Wilhelm. All of those except Haines and Marquard, of course, have other credentials. Eckersley and Wilhelm were relief pitchers. Babe Ruth, I believe, was an outfielder. Albert Spalding was a millionaire businessman who was one of baseball's most powerful behind-the-scenes executives from 1877 into the 20th century.

And then there is Jesse Haines, whose "other accomplishment" was that he was a friend of Frankie Frisch, the central figure on the Hall of Fame Veteran's Committee at the time Haines was elected. Haines' playing credentials consist of only three seasons among the league's best pitchers, totaling 19 points. He misses by 16 points the *bottom* of the gray area. He is perhaps the worst-qualified pitcher in the Hall of Fame.

### Roy Halladay

Roy Halladay through 2009 has 60 points worth of strong seasons, putting him already over the Hall of Fame line.

### Mel Harder

Mel Harder's career won-lost record (223-186) is similar to but better than that of his close contemporary Paul Derringer (223-212). Derringer, whose career was a mixture of good and awful seasons, scores at 29 points in our system, Harder at 28.

### Orel Hershiser

While Hershiser has not become a popular Hall of Fame candidate and may never do so, with only 204 career wins, he scores at 45 points in our system, which would put him just *over* the Hall of Fame line. In that he pitched until 2000, we considered him a "recently retired" pitcher.

### Carl Hubbell

Tied with Bob Feller for the 17th spot all-time.

### Catfish Hunter

Catfish Hunter, as you probably know, was elected to the Hall of Fame in his third year of eligibility despite a won-lost record — and an overall record — no better than other pitchers who were not selected. Catfish's won-lost record was 224-166. Luis Tiant, whose career ran almost exactly the same years in the same league, was 229-172. Their ERAs were almost the same (3.30 vs. 3.26, edge to Catfish), although Tiant pitched in much more difficult parks. Catfish in his career was only 56 runs better than league average, park-adjusted — an extremely low number, for a Hall of Famer — whereas Tiant was 172 runs better than an average pitcher.

However, while I am not arguing that the selection of Hunter/dismissal of Tiant was *right*, it is *consistent* with the voting history of the institution, when looked at from this standpoint. Both Hunter and Tiant had six seasons among the best pitchers in the American League, but Hunter had three seasons ranking #1 or #2. Tiant had only one (1968). Hunter had 44 points in our system — over the Hall of Fame line — Tiant had 28, which is well under the line.

In all candor, this argument represents the weakness or failure of this line of analysis, rather than its strength. Catfish was *not* better than Tiant; he merely looked a little bit better because he pitched in a pitcher's park for a team that won three consecutive World Series. Our system makes no adjustment for that, and thus signs on to the wrongheaded supposition that Hunter was greater than he was. That is the strength and weakness of our system — that it tracks conventional wisdom about pitchers, right or wrong, and this enables us to spot cases where the conventional analysis for some reason misfired.

### Larry Jackson

One of the favorites of my childhood — as was Catfish — Jackson won 194 games in his career, but

*Our system tracks conventional wisdom about pitchers, right or wrong, and this enables us to spot cases where the conventional analysis for some reason misfired.*

earned only 10 points as one of the better pitchers in his league.

### Ferguson Jenkins

An obvious Hall of Famer, ranks among the best pitchers in his league in all seven of his 20-win seasons, plus 1978 (when he was 18-8 with Texas). He does, however, rank well below Bert Blyleven, a contemporary pitcher with a similar won-lost record.

### Tommy John

John has a similar career won-lost record (288-231) to Ferguson Jenkins (284-226) and Blyleven (287-250). His ERA is also the same as Jenkins' (3.34), which is only three points different from Blyleven (3.31). However, while Blyleven comes in at 71 points in this system and Jenkins at 59, John comes in at 36. He had a lot of seasons in a very long career in which he pitched well, but just not enough innings to be considered one of the best pitchers in the league. He was 10-5 in 1968, 11-5 in 1972, 13-3 in 1974, 5-3 in 1986 and 13-6 in 1987. He also had a lot of 10-10, 9-8 type of seasons. These seasons add up to essentially the same totals as Blyleven and Jenkins, but they don't have the same impact on Hall of Fame voters. What puts you in the Hall of Fame is if voters look at you and decide "That guy is one of the best pitchers in the league", and then you stay there for several years.

I do believe that Tommy John will eventually be in the Hall of Fame. Historically, the Hall of Fame has eventually selected everybody with 250+ wins. The very large number of pitchers from the 1970s and 1980s with 250+ wins made it impossible to select them all in the BBWAA vote, but I do believe that, in time, they will all or almost all get in. And Tommy John, whose name has entered the American Language, is not likely to be forgotten.

### The Johnson Twins

Walter Johnson, as noted earlier, had as many seasons as his league's best starting pitcher — 7 — as anyone in history B.C. (Before Clemens). By this method, Cy Young at the end of his career was the number one pitcher of all time by the margin of 159 to 99. Christy Mathewson got to 121 points, and he then ranked as the #2 starting pitcher in MLB's brief history. Walter Johnson passed Mathewson in 1924, added a few more points in 1925, and retired with a career total of 135. Lefty Grove got to 122 points, one up on Matty, in 1939.

And there the leaders sat, for several generations: Cy Young, 159, Walter Johnson, 135, Grove 122, Mathewson, 121. That was the leader board in 1940, in 1950, in 1960, in 1970. Spahn in 1963 tied Christy Mathewson for the #4/#5 spot on the list, but through the 1970s, 1980s and 1990s there was no change to the all-time historical starting rotation: Cy Young, Walter Johnson, Lefty Grove, Mathewson or Spahn. By 1990 this was the all-time top ten list:

| Rank | Player | Career |
|---|---|---|
| 1. | Cy Young | 159 |
| 2. | Walter Johnson | 135 |
| 3. | Lefty Grove | 122 |
| t-4. | Christy Mathewson | 121 |
| t-4. | Warren Spahn | 121 |
| 6. | Pete Alexander | 116 |
| 7. | Tom Seaver | 113 |
| t-8. | Kid Nichols | 99 |
| t-8. | Jim Palmer | 99 |
| 9. | Steve Carlton | 98 |
| t-10. | Carl Hubbell | 83 |
| t-10. | Bob Feller | 83 |

But for that word "tie", the top four had not changed in 51 years. Roger Clemens claimed the #10 spot in 1992. He added a few points in 1994, and then was his league's top pitcher again in 1997 and 1998. By the close of the millennium the top four had not changed for 60 years, but a challenge was on the horizon:

| Rank | Player | Career |
|---|---|---|
| 1. | Cy Young | 159 |
| 2. | Walter Johnson | 135 |
| 3. | Lefty Grove | 122 |
| t-4. | Christy Mathewson | 121 |
| t-4. | Warren Spahn | 121 |
| 6. | Roger Clemens | 119 |
| 7. | Pete Alexander | 116 |
| 8. | Tom Seaver | 113 |
| 9. | Greg Maddux | 107 |
| t-10. | Kid Nichols | 99 |
| t-10. | Jim Palmer | 99 |

Finally, as we skated by the millennium bug, a new order arrived:

| Rank | Player | Career |
|---|---|---|
| 1. | Cy Young | 159 |
| 2. | Walter Johnson | 135 |
| 3. | Roger Clemens | 125 |
| 4. | Lefty Grove | 122 |
| t-5. | Christy Mathewson | 121 |
| t-5. | Warren Spahn | 121 |
| 7. | Greg Maddux | 119 |
| 8. | Pete Alexander | 116 |
| 9. | Tom Seaver | 113 |
| t-10. | Kid Nichols | 99 |
| t-10. | Jim Palmer | 99 |

Randy Johnson at that moment was at 80 points, in 15th place all-time — but Clemens, Maddux and Randy Johnson were not old pitchers ready to retire; they were still among the best in baseball. The list began to move every year. In 2001 Greg Maddux joined Clemens in the all-time starting rotation:

| Rank | Player | Career |
|---|---|---|
| 1. | Cy Young | 159 |
| 2. | Roger Clemens | 137 |
| 3. | Walter Johnson | 135 |
| 4. | Greg Maddux | 128 |
| 5. | Lefty Grove | 122 |
| t-6. | Christy Mathewson | 121 |
| t-6. | Warren Spahn | 121 |
| 8. | Pete Alexander | 116 |
| 9. | Tom Seaver | 113 |
| t-10. | Kid Nichols | 99 |
| t-10. | Jim Palmer | 99 |

Roger Clemens had pushed Walter Johnson from his post as the #2 starting pitcher of all time — a position he had held for more than a lifetime (76 years). Meanwhile Randy Johnson — almost as old as Clemens — was having a string of incredible seasons, and charging up the all-time list, and when Clemens had a so-so season in 2002, Greg Maddux actually moved ahead of him.

| Rank | Player | Career |
|---|---|---|
| 1. | Cy Young | 159 |
| 2. | Greg Maddux | 138 |
| 3. | Roger Clemens | 137 |
| 4. | Walter Johnson | 135 |
| 5. | Lefty Grove | 122 |
| t-6. | Christy Mathewson | 121 |
| t-6. | Warren Spahn | 121 |
| 8. | Pete Alexander | 116 |
| 9. | Randy Johnson | 115 |
| 10. | Tom Seaver | 113 |

The Unit had broken into the top ten. Clemens edged back ahead of Maddux in 2003, and in 2004 came back with yet another Cy Young season, going 18-4 for Houston. Randy Johnson, though stuck with a 16-14 won-lost log due to poor offensive support, actually pitched just about as well. Maddux wasn't bad, either; he was 16-11 for the Cubs. This was the leaderboard after the 2004 season:

| Rank | Player | Career |
|---|---|---|
| 1. | Cy Young | 159 |
| 2. | Roger Clemens | 153 |
| 3. | Greg Maddux | 138 |
| 4. | Walter Johnson | 135 |
| 5. | Randy Johnson | 125 |
| 6. | Lefty Grove | 122 |
| t-7. | Christy Mathewson | 121 |
| t-7. | Warren Spahn | 121 |
| 9. | Pete Alexander | 116 |
| 10. | Tom Seaver | 113 |

Maddux began to run out of gas in 2005, finishing 13-15 with a 4.24 ERA, but Clemens and Randy Johnson — both of them several years older than Maddux — remained among the best pitchers in the game. Clemens posted a 1.87 ERA for Houston — and became, by this method, the greatest starting pitcher of all time:

| Rank | Player | Career |
|---|---|---|
| 1. | Roger Clemens | 162 |
| 2. | Cy Young | 159 |
| 3. | Greg Maddux | 138 |
| 4. | Walter Johnson | 135 |
| 5. | Randy Johnson | 133 |
| 6. | Lefty Grove | 122 |
| t-7. | Christy Mathewson | 121 |
| t-7. | Warren Spahn | 121 |
| 9. | Pete Alexander | 116 |
| 10. | Tom Seaver | 113 |

What was the world coming to? For more than 60 years the all-time starting rotation was Cy Young, Walter Johnson, Lefty Grove and Christy Mathewson. Only Spahn had climbed into the discussion — and he had to share a berth with Matty. It disturbed the natural order of the universe to see new pitchers doing things the all-time greatest never could. This was disorienting, and it created a sense, among a lot of fans, that "something is not right here." Something is not right here, when all of these modern players begin to do things that have never been done before. It's not natural and it's not right.

I see it a little differently. To me, for new players to challenge constantly for their position among the greatest ever *is* the natural order of the universe. What was un-natural was for the list not to change for 60 years. I'm entirely willing to accept Clemens and Randy and Greg Maddux all being among the five greatest starting pitchers of all time. I don't have any problem at all with their all being part of the same generation, and I don't see anything about that fact which is in any way suspicious or disturbing. After all, Cy Young, Christy Mathewson and Walter Johnson were all in the major leagues from 1907 through 1911, a five-year span. Does that mean they can't all be considered all-time greats?

I regard Randy Johnson as one of the greatest pitchers of all time. He's fifth on the list, just a hair behind The Big Train. Has he *really* been as great as Walter Johnson? En. . .I don't know. I'd put him on the same level. I'll worry about ranking them another time.

### Addie Joss

The Hall of Fame rules had always stated that a player had to play in the majors for ten years to qualify for the Hall of Fame. Addie Joss played only 9 years, but the Veteran's Committee elected him anyway. The Hall of Fame amended the rules to make this legal. My belief is that they actually amended the rules after the fact. The Veteran's Committee elected him; the Hall of Fame realized that this was not within the rules, so they amended the rules and pretended that it had all been done in legal order to avoid there being a stink about it.

Joss was elected essentially on the strength of the argument that he was comparable to Sandy Koufax. Koufax pitched twelve years and was 165-87; Joss pitched nine years and was 160-97. Koufax had won-lost records of 25-5, 26-8 and 27-9; Joss was 27-11, 24-11 and 21-9.

Of course, Joss in reality was not remotely comparable to Sandy Koufax, but the people who elected him were told that he was, and they believed it. Joss was a very fine pitcher, but he won 27 games in an era in which the best pitchers won 35 and 40. This is a list of the most wins in the American League in a season between 1901 and 1910:

| Rank | Player | Year | W |
|---|---|---|---|
| 1. | Jack Chesbro | 1904 | 41 |
| 2. | Ed Walsh | 1908 | 40 |
| 3. | Cy Young | 1901 | 33 |
| 4. | Cy Young | 1902 | 32 |
| 5. | Jack Coombs | 1910 | 31 |
| 6. | George Mullin | 1909 | 29 |
| 7. | Cy Young | 1903 | 28 |
| t-8. | Addie Joss | 1907 | 27 |
| t-8. | Doc White | 1907 | 27 |
| t-8. | Rube Waddell | 1905 | 27 |
| t-8. | Al Orth | 1906 | 27 |

Joss was a fine pitcher, but winning 27 games when the other best pitchers are winning 40 is not the same as winning 27 games when the other best pitchers are winning 20. This is what our system measures: how the player compares to his contemporaries. Sandy Koufax, 76, Addie Joss, 35.

*To me, for new players to challenge constantly for their position among the greatest ever is the natural order of the universe.*

### Jim Kaat

Similar to Tommy John, he won 280 games in an era in which a lot of pitchers did, thus earning him only 39 points in our evaluation. I still believe that he should and will eventually be in the Hall of Fame, but he ranks far behind Blyleven.

### Bob Lemon

Bob Lemon was one of the best pitchers in the American League for seven years between 1948 and 1956, and earned 45 points in our system, making him a qualified Hall of Famer despite a career total of "just" 207 wins.

### Mickey Lolich

Lolich was among the best pitchers in his league in 1964, 1965, 1969, 1972 and 1973, and earned a career total of 31 points. In terms of big seasons versus his contemporaries he ranks about even with Kevin Appier, Rick Sutcliffe and CC Sabathia.

### Ted Lyons

Made it into the Hall of Fame with 33 points, or three strong seasons. Credentials similar to Herb Pennock, Red Faber, Waite Hoyt; got into the Hall of Fame because he had 250+ wins and everybody with 250+ wins got in, even though his "good seasons" count is a little on the short side.

### Greg Maddux

See comments on the Johnson Twins.

### Juan Marichal

Ranked among the best pitchers in the National League eight times, and ranked second five times — behind Koufax in '63, ' 64, '65 and '66, Gibson in '68.

### Rube Marquard

A Hall of Fame anomaly with only 21 points in our survey and only 201 career wins. Elected in large part because of his appearance in *The Glory of Their Times*, which was an enormously popular book and helped to put several players in the Hall of Fame.

### Pedro Martinez

Attempting a comeback at this time, he has 104 points by our method — making him the #11 pitcher of all time — and is still young enough to add to that total if he can get back to being one of the best pitchers in the game. He is way, way beyond the line of being a Hall of Fame pitcher, whatever his career win total.

### Carl Mays

Probably a Hall of Famer, were it not for the fact that he was the most hated man in baseball in his era. He has 47 points by this system, putting him above the Hall of Fame line, and surrounded by Hall of Fame pitchers.

### Jack Morris

Jack Morris has for some reason become the counterweight to Bert Blyleven in the Hall of Fame debate; whenever somebody argues for Blyleven, somebody else always says they liked Jack Morris better. Morris does well in our analysis — not as well as Blyleven, but still very well. He has 64 points, which is 50% above the Hall of Fame line. As he did earn points after 1990, I counted him in my analysis as a "recently retired" pitcher.

### Jamie Moyer

Moyer had zero career points and only 72 career wins at the age of 33; he now has 41 points and 258 career wins. The Cubs came up with Moyer and Maddux in the same season, 1986. They were building for 2003.

### Mike Mussina

Mike Mussina did stunningly well in our study, ranking as the #15 starting pitcher of all time. Mussina had no seasons as the league's number one pitcher, but twelve seasons in which he ranked among the best starting pitchers in his league. In the last 50 years only Clemens, Maddux, Seaver and Blyleven have had as many.

 *Mike Mussina did stunningly well in our study.*

### Kid Nichols

Throughout the 1890s Nichols ran neck and neck with Cy Young. The number one pitcher on the all-time list, at the start of their careers, was Tim Keefe. Nichols and Young both made it on to the leaderboard in 1894, Nichols moving into fifth place, Young into tenth. After 1895 Nichols was in fourth place, Cy Young in fifth, and after the 1896 season they were tied for second. From 1897 to 1900, Nichols was the number one pitcher of all time, with Cy Young second. Both of them were having great years every year. Amos Rusie was the most famous pitcher of that era, but Nichols and Young were better; not as flashy, didn't throw as hard, didn't dominate the news coverage in the same way, but they were better pitchers.

After 1900 Nichols' career kind of stalled out, and Cy Young pulled gradually away from him. The interesting thing is that Nichols' career stalled out not from injury or ineffectiveness, but for a variety of other reasons. His team collapsed underneath him. In 1900 Nichols was 39 runs better than an average pitcher, park-adjusted, which is a huge number, but finished just 13-16 due to poor offensive support. After the turn of the century there was a period of economic turmoil, like that in 1890, in which new leagues formed and players who were unhappy with their National League contracts jumped to other leagues. But whereas Cy Young, Jack Chesbro and others jumped to the American League, Nichols jumped instead to the Kansas City franchise in the Western League. The Western League failed to establish itself as a rival major; Nichols went 26-7 there in 1902 and 21-12 in 1903, but this doesn't count because it's now regarded as a minor league. Cy Young, winning 30 games a year in the American League, pulled far ahead of him.

Nichols returned to the National League in 1904 as player/manager of the St. Louis Cardinals. The Cardinals were a sad sack operation, finishing in last-place at 43-94 in 1903. Nichols improved them to near .500 in 1904 (75-79), in part because he himself won 21 games (21-13) — but was fired early in the 1905 season in a dispute over watching the gate. Major league players in that era were supposed to stand at the gates before the game and take tickets; in fact, even *during* the game players who were

*Stats, of course, can be looked at through a limitless variety of lenses.*

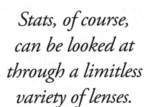

not actually in the contest were delegated to stand at the gate to prevent people from sneaking in without a ticket. Nichols said that he had plenty to do with managing the team and pitching, and refused to take a turn watching the gates, and he was fired as manager and then traded to Philadelphia as a result of this dispute. He went 10-6 for Philadelphia with a 2.27 ERA.

He started slowly in 1906, however, and was released early in the season. He wound up his career with 99 points in our system, making him the number two pitcher in baseball history up to that point. He remained in the top ten list until pushed off of the list by Greg Maddux in 1999.

### Roy Oswalt

One of the most surprising things about this study was the stunning performance of Roy Oswalt. Oswalt has already ranked among the best pitchers in the National League in six seasons—every season from 2001 through 2007 except 2003, when he pitched well but had some injuries. Because he has not had a Cy Young season he is, I think, not generally regarded as a Hall of Fame pitcher. But by our method, six seasons among the best pitchers in your league is a lot, and six seasons ranking among the best pitchers in a 16-team league is more impressive than six seasons among the best pitchers in an 8-team league. We credit Roy Oswalt with 54 points through 2008, which is well above the standard of a Hall of Fame career.

Stats, of course, can be looked at through a limitless variety of lenses, and I am in no way suggesting that this one will or should take precedence over the others. Oswalt has 137 career wins as of now; to be a serious Hall of Fame candidate he certainly needs to push that up past 200, and probably up somewhere around 250. But what he has already done is extremely impressive. Until I did this study, I really had no idea how impressive. He enters the 2010 season 67 games over .500 in his career. That is a Hall of Fame number. Maybe it's not a Hall of Fame number if, like Johnny Allen or Vic Raschi, you only win 140 games in your career; maybe it's not a Hall of Fame number if, like Dave McNally, you only win 184. But many of the pitchers who are in the Hall of Fame aren't 67 games over .500.

### Jim Palmer

99 points, an obvious Hall of Famer.

### Billy Pierce

Not counting active and recently retired pitchers like Jack Morris, Doc Gooden and David Cone, there are five pitchers in history who are not in the Hall of Fame although they had 44 or more strong season points: Blyleven, Guidry, Vida Blue, Carl Mays and Billy Pierce. Pierce drew 5 votes for the Hall of Fame in 1970 (2%), 7 in 1971 (still 2%), and never more than 4 after that. We might safely say that most people did not think of him as a Hall of Fame pitcher.

His record, however, has its points. We rank him among the best pitchers in the American League in 1952, when he pitched 255 innings with an ERA of 2.58. He was certainly among the best pitchers in the league in 1953, when he was 18-12, was second in the league in ERA at 2.72, and led the league in strikeouts with 186. He was certainly among the best pitchers in the American League in 1955, when he became the only major league ERA qualifier of the 1950s to have an ERA starting with "1" — 1.97. The best ERA of the decade.

He was certainly among the best pitchers in the American League in 1956, when he was 20-9, and he was certainly among the best pitchers in the American League in 1957, when he was 20-12. He was certainly among the best pitchers in the American League in 1958, when he was 17-11 and second in the league in ERA. We have him among the best pitchers in the American League in 1960, but granted, that was because the American League in 1960 had a serious shortage of quality pitchers; see comments on Jim Bunning. We gave him nothing for 1962; he was 16-6 for the Giants, helping to lift them to the National League pennant, but we do not rank him among the best pitchers in the league.

Pierce had a career record of 211 wins, 169 losses. There are quite a few pitchers with records like that, and some of them are in the Hall of Fame (Jesse Haines, 210-158, Don Drysdale, 209-166, Hal Newhouser, 207-150,

*I am not saying that Pierce should be in the Hall of Fame, but it does seem that he was just overlooked somehow.*

Rube Marquard, 201-177), and some of them are not (Milt Pappas, 209-164, Vida Blue, 209-161, Bob Welch, 211-146). One of the things that seems to distinguish the Hall of Famers from the non-Hall of Famers is good ERAs. Don Drysdale is in the Hall of Fame in part because he was 229 runs better than an average pitcher; Milt Pappas and Vida Blue had basically the same record, but they were 130 runs and 89 runs better than average, not 229. Bob Welch had basically the same won-lost record as Hal Newhouser, but Welch was 56 runs better than an average pitcher, park-adjusted; Newhouser was 309 runs better than league.

But Billy Pierce was 224 runs better than an average pitcher, park adjusted — about the same number as Drysdale. Among the pitchers with comparable records he ranks better than anyone except Newhouser, Drysdale and Kevin Brown. I am not saying that Pierce *should* be in the Hall of Fame, but it does seem that he was just overlooked somehow, and that he should have been taken more seriously as a candidate than he was.

### J. R. Richard

Got to 30 points quickly before his health condition stopped him. (His career was ended suddenly in 1980 by a stroke, or something very much like a stroke.) Actually a contemporary American League pitcher, Dennis Leonard, was piling up points just as quickly. Leonard got to 29 points in the same years, 1976-1980.

### Eppa Rixey

Only 39 points in this system; got to the Hall of Fame by hanging around long enough to win 266 games, although he lost 251. Rixey was the Jim Kaat of the 1920s — a big left-hander who was very graceful on the mound, fielded his position extremely well and had excellent control.

### Kenny Rogers

Another pitcher with a career won-lost record like Pierce and Drysdale. Had five seasons ranking among the best pitchers in his league, earning him 25 points in this analysis.

### Babe Ruth

Ranks as the second-best pitcher in the American League in 1916, behind Walter Johnson, third in 1917, behind Cicotte and Jim Bagby. 15 points.

### Nolan Ryan

Because of his walks and losses, we do not rank Ryan as the #1 pitcher in his league in any season; of course, some people do. He has eight seasons among his league's best pitchers and 45 points in our system, which is a Hall of Fame number.

### CC Sabathia

32 points so far. Needs two more seasons among the league's best pitchers to meet the "star" requirements of the Hall of Fame; needs to pile up about 125 more wins to meet the "bulk" requirements.

### Johan Santana

With 54 points through 2009, he has already done the heavy lifting for a Hall of Fame career. What he has to do from now on is basically to stay healthy for six or eight years and not embarrass himself.

### Curt Schilling

Somewhat like Juan Marichal in a Hall of Fame analysis, we credit him with no seasons as his league's best pitcher, but three seasons ranking second or third, and nine seasons ranking among his league's best pitchers. We see him as being beyond a Hall of Fame standard, with 74 points. He's actually close to twice the Hall of Fame cutoff — ignoring entirely his post-season exploits.

### Herb Score

12 points in two seasons before being stopped by injury.

### Curt Simmons

Like Larry Jackson. He won 193 games in an impressive career, but had only four seasons ranking among the best pitchers in his league, and never ranked higher than seventh. 9 points.

### John Smoltz

Comparable to Schilling. We have him with 58 points, which is well beyond a Hall of Fame standard, but this ignores his fine post-season record and his years as a reliever, which would push him up even higher.

### Warren Spahn

Had five seasons as his league's best pitcher and 17 seasons as one of the best pitchers in his league, which ties with Cy Young for the top spot.

### Luis Tiant

See comments on Catfish Hunter.

### Fernando Valenzuela

Earned 35 points in his first six years in the National League, appearing to be on a Hall of Fame path, but ran out of gas at that point.

### Dazzy Vance

One of the most striking things about this study is the dearth of dominant pitchers after Walter Johnson and Grover Cleveland Alexander. After Alex and Walter there really isn't another great pitcher who comes along until Lefty Grove.

Not quite getting to my point. There are really no great pitchers in the 1920s. There is Vance, who was a phenomenal pitcher but had only half of a career, although that half a career was certainly enough to put him in the Hall of Fame. In the past I have tended to look at this as a function of the norms of the era. The teens were a pitchers' era; pitchers won 30 games, struck out 300 batters, and had ERAs in the ones. The twenties were a hitter's era, so the norms were different.

But this system adjusts *those* differences out of existence by comparing each pitcher to the other pitchers in the

*The Hall of Fame doesn't much like those guys who bounce around like loose tennis balls, and I don't either.*

same league in the same year, and this enables us to see that the pitchers of that era are not merely weaker because the norms were down. They're also weaker because different pitchers were the best in the league every year. There's just nobody in that era who stands out consistently in the way that Mathewson and Cy Young and Kid Nichols and Walter and Alex stand out from the previous decades. The great pitchers of the 1920s are like Waite Hoyt and Pennock and Shocker and Shawkey and Burleigh Grimes and Remy Kremer. They're good, but they're not all that good. Walter and Alex continued to dominate until they were almost 40 because there just wasn't anybody coming up behind them who was on the same level except Vance.

The 1930s, now; the 1930s have truly great pitchers — Grove, of course, but also Carl Hubbell, Dizzy Dean, Bob Feller, Lefty Gomez and Red Ruffing. OK, Gomez and Ruffing weren't on the same level as Walter and Alex, but they were better than Waite Hoyt and Herb Pennock. Dazzy Vance is really the only great pitcher of the 1920s. 51 points — a Hall of Fame number.

### Rube Waddell

Slides over the Hall of Fame line with 46 points. A colorful character but, with 193 career wins, not overwhelmingly qualified for immortality.

### Ed Walsh

64 points. A lot of people now confuse Waddell and Walsh because they pitched in the same league in the same era and have similar names and similar career records (193-143 for Waddell, 195-126 for Walsh), but it's like confusing Albert Belle and Albert Pujols. As personalities, you can't get much more different than Rube Waddell and Ed Walsh.

### Bucky Walters

Does not do particularly well in this analysis, with only four seasons among the best in his league and a career total of 32 points.

### Lon Warneke

Warneke's records are a lot like Billy Pierce's — 22-6, 18-13, 22-10, 20-13, 16-10, 17-9. He had six seasons among the best pitchers in the National League, and in 1932-33 appeared to be poised to be the best. But he had some little injuries, and Hubbell and Dean zoomed past him like he was standing still. With 43 points in this analysis he stands right on the border of a Hall of Fame career, and could as well be in as out.

### David Wells

I got to see David Wells a lot in 2005, when he was 15-7 for the Red Sox, and he was amazing. He was 42 years old by then and fat, but he had phenomenal strength in his back and shoulders, and just amazing balance. His bread and butter pitch was a big 12-to-6 curveball, and he could spin that thing in there and nail the bottom of the strike zone with it like it was nothing. That wasn't all he had; his fastball was still pretty good, and he had A+ control of everything. If the hitter leaned in he would put the fastball high and tight; if the hitter leaned back he would pitch away.

He was one of those guys, like Vladimir and Bo Jackson and Ron Cey, that sometimes you felt like you should check his DNA and make sure he was all human. I certainly have never seen anyone else who had the same level of command of his curveball, and in terms of things like repeating his delivery and changing the hitter's eye level, I never saw anybody better.

But his career is chopped up into a million little pieces, in Toronto and Detroit and New York and Boston and San Diego, and mostly that was his own doing; he was always looking for the next opportunity. The Hall of Fame doesn't much like those guys who bounce around like loose tennis balls, and I don't either. When you're building a team, you need people you can count on to be there for a while. We credit him with 36 points for seasons among the best in his league — about 15% short of a Hall of Fame career.

# Arizona Diamondbacks

## Key Players

| Pos | Player | G | AB | R | H | 2B | 3B | HR | RBI | SB | CS | BB | SO | AVG | OBP | SLG | OPS | WS |
|---|---|---|---|---|---|---|---|---|---|---|---|---|---|---|---|---|---|---|
| C | Miguel Montero | 128 | 425 | 61 | 125 | 30 | 0 | 16 | 59 | 1 | 2 | 38 | 78 | .294 | .355 | .478 | .832 | 13 |
| 1B | Chad Tracy | 98 | 257 | 29 | 61 | 15 | 0 | 8 | 39 | 1 | 0 | 26 | 38 | .237 | .306 | .389 | .695 | 3 |
| 2B | Felipe Lopez | 85 | 345 | 44 | 104 | 18 | 1 | 6 | 25 | 6 | 3 | 34 | 59 | .301 | .364 | .412 | .775 | 10 |
| 3B | Mark Reynolds | 155 | 578 | 98 | 150 | 30 | 1 | 44 | 102 | 24 | 9 | 76 | 223 | .260 | .349 | .543 | .892 | 20 |
| SS | Stephen Drew | 135 | 533 | 71 | 139 | 29 | 12 | 12 | 65 | 5 | 1 | 49 | 87 | .261 | .320 | .428 | .748 | 16 |
| LF | Gerardo Parra | 120 | 455 | 59 | 132 | 21 | 8 | 5 | 60 | 5 | 7 | 25 | 89 | .290 | .324 | .404 | .729 | 9 |
| CF | Chris Young | 134 | 433 | 54 | 92 | 28 | 4 | 15 | 42 | 11 | 4 | 59 | 133 | .212 | .311 | .400 | .711 | 8 |
| RF | Justin Upton | 138 | 526 | 84 | 158 | 30 | 7 | 26 | 86 | 20 | 5 | 55 | 137 | .300 | .366 | .532 | .899 | 19 |

## Key Pitchers

| Pos | Player | G | GS | W | L | SV | IP | H | R | ER | SO | BB | BR/9 | ERA | WS |
|---|---|---|---|---|---|---|---|---|---|---|---|---|---|---|---|
| SP | Dan Haren | 33 | 33 | 14 | 10 | 0 | 229.1 | 192 | 83 | 80 | 223 | 38 | 9.18 | 3.14 | 20 |
| SP | Doug Davis | 34 | 34 | 9 | 14 | 0 | 203.1 | 203 | 101 | 93 | 146 | 103 | 13.72 | 4.12 | 10 |
| SP | Max Scherzer | 30 | 30 | 9 | 11 | 0 | 170.1 | 166 | 94 | 78 | 174 | 63 | 12.63 | 4.12 | 9 |
| SP | Jon Garland | 27 | 27 | 8 | 11 | 0 | 167.2 | 188 | 90 | 80 | 83 | 52 | 13.20 | 4.29 | 8 |
| SP | Yusmeiro Petit | 23 | 17 | 3 | 10 | 0 | 89.2 | 102 | 62 | 58 | 74 | 34 | 13.65 | 5.82 | 1 |
| CL | Chad Qualls | 51 | 0 | 2 | 2 | 24 | 52.0 | 53 | 23 | 21 | 45 | 7 | 10.73 | 3.63 | 8 |
| RP | Juan Gutierrez | 65 | 0 | 4 | 3 | 9 | 71.0 | 67 | 33 | 32 | 66 | 30 | 12.68 | 4.06 | 7 |
| RP | Jon Rauch | 58 | 0 | 2 | 2 | 2 | 54.1 | 57 | 27 | 25 | 35 | 17 | 12.42 | 4.14 | 4 |

## But When He Makes Contact. . .

Mark Reynolds struck out a major-league record 223 times (wiping out his old record by 19) while batting .260. That means that he batted .423 when he actually hit the ball in fair territory, the highest batting average on batted balls in the majors. The top five in this category were:

| Player | AB | H | 1B | 2B | 3B | HR | AVG |
|---|---|---|---|---|---|---|---|
| 1. Mark Reynolds, Ari | 355 | 150 | 75 | 30 | 1 | 44 | .423 |
| 2. Joey Votto, Cin | 363 | 151 | 87 | 38 | 1 | 25 | .416 |
| 3. Joe Mauer, Min | 460 | 191 | 132 | 30 | 1 | 28 | .415 |
| 4. David Wright, NYM | 395 | 164 | 112 | 39 | 3 | 10 | .415 |
| 5. Hanley Ramirez, Fla | 475 | 197 | 130 | 42 | 1 | 24 | .415 |

## Misleading Errors

This is why we need better fielding statistics: Justin Upton made more errors than any other major league outfielder (12), but still saved eleven runs more than the average right fielder with his range and arm.

**Justin Upton — Defensive Runs Saved**

| Year | Plus/Minus | OF Arm | Total |
|---|---|---|---|
| 2007 | 2 | 0 | 2 |
| 2008 | 2 | 3 | 5 |
| 2009 | 8 | 3 | 11 |

## Up in the Air

Chris Young in 2009 was the most extreme fly ball hitter in the majors. 56% of his balls in play were fly balls (the highest figure among major-league qualifiers) and only 26% were ground balls (the lowest). The rest were line drives.

A2
ks +
Reynold

## Haren's Opponent OPS

If you look at his stats from a certain viewpoint — the batter's viewpoint — Dan Haren had his best year yet. Batters hit only .224 with a .635 OPS against Haren last year, both career lows. The only chink in his armor was 27 home runs allowed.

**Dan Haren — Record of Opposing Batters**

| Year | AB | R | H | 2B | 3B | HR | RBI | BB | SO | SB | CS | GIDP | AVG | OBP | SLG | OPS |
|------|-----|-----|-----|----|----|----|-----|----|-----|----|----|------|------|------|------|------|
| 2005 | 830 | 101 | 212 | 40 | 4 | 26 | 90 | 53 | 163 | 19 | 5 | 26 | .255 | .303 | .407 | .710 |
| 2006 | 869 | 109 | 224 | 43 | 6 | 31 | 99 | 45 | 176 | 10 | 4 | 16 | .258 | .301 | .428 | .729 |
| 2007 | 867 | 91 | 214 | 43 | 7 | 24 | 83 | 55 | 192 | 20 | 6 | 9 | .247 | .292 | .396 | .687 |
| 2008 | 825 | 86 | 204 | 45 | 4 | 19 | 77 | 40 | 206 | 9 | 2 | 12 | .247 | .286 | .381 | .667 |
| 2009 | 856 | 83 | 192 | 38 | 5 | 27 | 78 | 38 | 223 | 18 | 6 | 12 | .224 | .260 | .375 | .635 |

## Mirror, Mirror, on the Wall

In 2008 Dan Haren struck out 206 hitters, and Mark Reynolds struck out 204 times. In 2009 Haren struck out 223 hitters, and Reynolds struck out 223 times.

## Bearing Down

With no one on base, batters facing Doug Davis hit .308 with a slugging percentage of .507. With men on base, those numbers dropped to .215 and .322.

## Setting the Table

Overall, Arizona's first batter in each game batted .338 with a .395 on-base percentage. Both figures were best in the National League.

## Baserunning Struggles

Gerardo Parra, the D'backs rookie left fielder, was expected to add some speed to the lineup, having stolen 29 bases in the minors in 2008. For some reason that didn't work out. He was 5-for-12 as a base stealer, and grounded into 18 double plays, which was almost twice as many as anybody else on the team (granted that most of the Arizona hitters are too busy striking out to ground into very many double plays.) With the exception of backup catcher Chris Snyder, Parra was the worst baserunner on the team.

## Offensive-Minded Catchers

The best-hitting catcher in the National League is Brian McCann. But, led by Miguel Montero, Diamondback catchers posted the second-best slugging percentage, home run total and OPS among all National League catchers.

### Batting Stats among National League Catchers (By Team)

| Team | PA | R | H | 2B | 3B | HR | RBI | AVG | OBP | SLG | OPS |
|------|-----|----|-----|----|----|----|-----|------|------|------|------|
| Braves | 693 | 83 | 169 | 40 | 1 | 28 | 110 | .278 | .353 | .484 | .837 |
| D'backs | 673 | 84 | 158 | 35 | 0 | 22 | 79 | .266 | .345 | .437 | .782 |
| Marlins | 669 | 84 | 164 | 35 | 1 | 16 | 75 | .276 | .350 | .419 | .769 |
| Rockies | 648 | 71 | 140 | 28 | 3 | 18 | 89 | .255 | .347 | .415 | .761 |
| Phillies | 617 | 54 | 134 | 39 | 1 | 14 | 57 | .252 | .348 | .409 | .757 |

## Win Share Age

Arizona was the youngest team in the majors last year, as measured by their "Win Shares Age" — the average age of the team weighted by the Win Shares contributed by each player.

| Team | Win Shares Age |
|---|---|
| 1. D'backs | 26.5 |
| 2. Pirates | 26.7 |
| 3. Marlins | 26.8 |
| 4. Royals | 27.1 |
| 5. Padres | 27.4 |

## Glory Days

The worst pitching mismatch of the last ten years occurred on April 16, 2002, at Bank One Ballpark in Arizona, when Randy Johnson opposed Cardinal left-hander Bud Smith. Johnson wound up the 2002 season 24-5 with a 2.32 ERA, 334 strikeouts. Smith wound up the year 1-5 with an ERA of 6.94. Arizona won the game, 5-3.

The best pitching matchup of the last ten years, in terms of having two great pitchers on the mound, occurred on June 8, 2002, at Fenway Park — Curt Schilling (then with Arizona) against Pedro Martinez. Schilling came into the game 11-1. He wound up the season 22-6 with 293 strikeouts, 39 walks and an ERA of 2.98.

Martinez came into the game 7-0. He wound up the season 20-4 with 239 strikeouts, 40 walks and a 2.26 ERA.

Schilling struck out 9 batters in the game; Martinez struck out 10 — but Schilling won the ballgame, 3-2.

Just thought you would want to know.

# Atlanta Braves

## Key Players

| Pos | Player | G | AB | R | H | 2B | 3B | HR | RBI | SB | CS | BB | SO | AVG | OBP | SLG | OPS | WS |
|---|---|---|---|---|---|---|---|---|---|---|---|---|---|---|---|---|---|---|
| C | Brian McCann | 138 | 488 | 63 | 137 | 35 | 1 | 21 | 94 | 4 | 1 | 49 | 83 | .281 | .349 | .486 | .834 | 20 |
| 1B | Casey Kotchman | 87 | 298 | 28 | 84 | 20 | 0 | 6 | 41 | 0 | 0 | 32 | 28 | .282 | .354 | .409 | .764 | 9 |
| 2B | Martin Prado | 128 | 450 | 64 | 138 | 38 | 0 | 11 | 49 | 1 | 3 | 36 | 59 | .307 | .358 | .464 | .822 | 12 |
| 3B | Chipper Jones | 143 | 488 | 80 | 129 | 23 | 2 | 18 | 71 | 4 | 1 | 101 | 89 | .264 | .388 | .430 | .818 | 20 |
| SS | Yunel Escobar | 141 | 528 | 89 | 158 | 26 | 2 | 14 | 76 | 5 | 4 | 57 | 62 | .299 | .377 | .436 | .812 | 24 |
| LF | Garret Anderson | 135 | 496 | 52 | 133 | 27 | 0 | 13 | 61 | 1 | 0 | 27 | 73 | .268 | .303 | .401 | .705 | 7 |
| CF | Nate McLouth | 84 | 339 | 59 | 87 | 20 | 1 | 11 | 36 | 12 | 6 | 47 | 70 | .257 | .354 | .419 | .773 | 11 |
| RF | Jeff Francoeur | 82 | 304 | 32 | 76 | 12 | 2 | 5 | 35 | 5 | 1 | 12 | 46 | .250 | .282 | .352 | .634 | 3 |

## Key Pitchers

| Pos | Player | G | GS | W | L | SV | IP | H | R | ER | SO | BB | BR/9 | ERA | WS |
|---|---|---|---|---|---|---|---|---|---|---|---|---|---|---|---|
| SP | Derek Lowe | 34 | 34 | 15 | 10 | 0 | 194.2 | 232 | 109 | 101 | 111 | 63 | 13.82 | 4.67 | 7 |
| SP | Jair Jurrjens | 34 | 34 | 14 | 10 | 0 | 215.0 | 186 | 71 | 62 | 152 | 75 | 11.05 | 2.60 | 17 |
| SP | Javier Vazquez | 32 | 32 | 15 | 10 | 0 | 219.1 | 181 | 75 | 70 | 238 | 44 | 9.40 | 2.87 | 16 |
| SP | Tommy Hanson | 21 | 21 | 11 | 4 | 0 | 127.2 | 105 | 42 | 41 | 116 | 46 | 11.00 | 2.89 | 10 |
| SP | Kenshin Kawakami | 32 | 25 | 7 | 12 | 1 | 156.1 | 153 | 73 | 67 | 105 | 57 | 12.43 | 3.86 | 7 |
| CL | Rafael Soriano | 77 | 0 | 1 | 6 | 27 | 75.2 | 53 | 25 | 25 | 102 | 27 | 9.63 | 2.97 | 12 |
| RP | Peter Moylan | 87 | 0 | 6 | 2 | 0 | 73.0 | 65 | 29 | 23 | 61 | 35 | 12.58 | 2.84 | 7 |
| RP | Mike Gonzalez | 80 | 0 | 5 | 4 | 10 | 74.1 | 56 | 28 | 20 | 90 | 33 | 11.62 | 2.42 | 9 |

## Starting Strong

If the games had ended after the third, the 2009 Braves would have had the best record in the major leagues. They were 80-42 — ahead 80 times after three innings, behind only 42. It was all downhill from there.

**Atlanta Braves — 2009 Innings Ahead/Behind/Tied**

| Inning | 1 | 2 | 3 | 4 | 5 | 6 | 7 | 8 | 9 | Extra | Final |
|--------|---|---|---|---|---|---|---|---|---|-------|-------|
| Ahead | 37 | 63 | 80 | 78 | 82 | 75 | 78 | 77 | 76 | 9 | 86 |
| Behind | 29 | 36 | 42 | 45 | 53 | 65 | 65 | 67 | 69 | 7 | 76 |
| Tied | 96 | 63 | 40 | 39 | 27 | 22 | 19 | 18 | 16 | 23 | -- |

## Challenge Trades

The Braves started the 2009 season 32-36, but played well over the last 15 weeks of the season. Key to this were two "challenge" trades — straight-up trades of a right fielder for a right fielder and a first baseman for a first baseman.

**Comparative Batting in Braves Uniform**

| Player | G | AB | R | H | 2B | 3B | HR | RBI | BA | OPS |
|--------|---|----|----|----|----|----|----|-----|------|------|
| Casey Kotchman | 87 | 298 | 28 | 84 | 20 | 0 | 6 | 41 | .282 | .764 |
| Adam LaRoche | 57 | 212 | 30 | 69 | 11 | 1 | 12 | 40 | .325 | .957 |
| | | | | | | | | | | |
| Jeff Francoeur | 82 | 304 | 32 | 76 | 12 | 2 | 5 | 35 | .250 | .634 |
| Ryan Church | 44 | 127 | 20 | 33 | 12 | 0 | 2 | 18 | .260 | .749 |

## Jurrjens and Kawakami

The Braves outscored their opposition in Jair Jurrjens' starts by 40 runs, but finished just 17-17. With Kenshin Kawakami starting they were outscored by 32 runs, but finished 12-13. They were 5.3 wins short of expectation with Jurrjens, second-most in the majors behind Zach Duke — but 3.2 wins ABOVE expectation with Kawakami, second-most in the majors behind Justin Verlander.

| Games Started | GS | Run Support | Runs Allowed | Won | Lost |
|---------------|----|-----|-----|-----|------|
| Jair Jurrjens | 34 | 146 | 106 | 17 | 17 |
| Kenshin Kawakami | 25 | 91 | 123 | 12 | 13 |
| **Team Totals** | **162** | **735** | **641** | **86** | **76** |

## Hitting Third (or Not)

With Chipper Jones having a poor year, Atlanta's number-three hitters were by far the worst in the National League, finishing last in the league in batting, slugging, RBI and OPS:

| G | AB | R | H | 2B | 3B | HR | RBI | BB | SO | AVG | BA | SLG | OPS |
|---|----|---|---|----|----|----|-----|----|----|-----|----|----|----|
| 162 | 608 | 90 | 150 | 28 | 2 | 18 | 71 | 111 | 106 | .247 | .361 | .388 | .749 |

### National League — 2009
### Number-Three Hitters Ranked by OPS

| Team | R | RBI | BA | OBP | SLG | OPS |
|------|---|-----|----|-----|-----|-----|
| 1. Cardinals | 124 | 135 | .320 | .436 | .636 | 1.072 |
| 2. Marlins | 115 | 121 | .335 | .413 | .535 | .948 |
| 3. Brewers | 115 | 115 | .313 | .379 | .541 | .919 |
| 4. Phillies | 123 | 103 | .282 | .392 | .515 | .908 |
| 5. Reds | 104 | 103 | .295 | .383 | .519 | .902 |
| 6. Rockies | 92 | 100 | .313 | .403 | .471 | .874 |
| 7. Padres | 92 | 99 | .262 | .371 | .495 | .866 |
| 8. Dodgers | 102 | 109 | .277 | .369 | .486 | .855 |
| 9. Cubs | 96 | 99 | .275 | .372 | .481 | .854 |
| 10. Nationals | 109 | 101 | .282 | .352 | .488 | .840 |
| 11. Astros | 95 | 98 | .264 | .366 | .463 | .829 |
| 12. D'backs | 92 | 92 | .275 | .340 | .458 | .798 |
| 13. Giants | 86 | 81 | .283 | .337 | .460 | .797 |
| 14. Mets | 99 | 82 | .285 | .362 | .434 | .796 |
| 15. Pirates | 78 | 90 | .260 | .338 | .448 | .785 |
| 16. Braves | 90 | 71 | .247 | .361 | .388 | .749 |

## I Ain't 'Fraid of No Ghost

Chipper may have contributed a bit more than his stats indicate. Jones had the second-most "Ghost RBI" in the majors last year (only Ryan Braun had more). A Ghost RBI is defined as a batter advancing a runner who later scores, and who would not or might not have scored had the batter not advanced him.

### Atlanta Braves — 2009  Top Five Ghost Run Producers

| Player | Ghost Runs Scored | Ghost RBI | Total Ghost Runs |
|--------|-------------------|-----------|------------------|
| Chipper Jones | 1 | 26 | 27 |
| Brian McCann | 2 | 19 | 21 |
| Yunel Escobar | 1 | 17 | 18 |
| Martin Prado | 1 | 14 | 15 |
| Garret Anderson | 1 | 9 | 10 |

## They Can Get On, but They Can't Score

Only 24% of batters who reached base against Jair Jurrjens in 2009 eventually scored. The major league average was 33%. The savings to Jurrjens was about 25 runs.

The key element: The batting average against Jurrjens with runners in scoring position was .192.

**Jair Jurrjens — 2009**
**Runs Allowed Analysis**

|  | Reached | Scored | Pct |
|---|---|---|---|
| Single | 127 | 26 | 20% |
| Double | 39 | 15 | 38% |
| Triple | 5 | 1 | 20% |
| Homer | 15 |  |  |
| Walk | 75 | 10 | 13% |
| HBP | 3 | 0 | 0% |
| Error | 9 | 3 | 33% |
| FC - Out | 25 | 1 | 4% |
| **Total** | **298** | **71** | **24%** |

## The Secret to Their Success

The Braves didn't strike out the most batters in the league (they were fifth) nor did they walk the least batters (fifth), but they allowed only 119 home runs, the best figure in the majors.

**Major League —**
**Least Home Runs Allowed**

| Team | HR |
|---|---|
| Braves | 119 |
| Cardinals | 123 |
| Dodgers | 127 |
| Giants | 140 |
| Rockies | 141 |

## Chipper V. History

Who is the greatest third baseman in the history of the Braves' franchise: Eddie Mathews or Chipper Jones?

In the interest of fool disclosure, the Braves have had really good third basemen through most of their history. At the end of the 19th century their third baseman, Jimmy Collins, was probably the best in baseball for a few years, and could be in the Hall of Fame, although he isn't. Two other Brave third baseman won MVP Awards, Bob Elliott in 1947 and Terry Pendleton in 1992, and Darrell Evans was pretty good. Bob Horner had a couple of good years.

Anyway, Mathews is a Hall of Famer and Chipper will be, but which was the greater of the two? Let us look at this by Win Shares and Loss Shares. Everything a player does — a double, a single, an error, turning a double play or grounding into one — everything can be stated as a small part of a win or a small part of a loss. We call these Win Shares and Loss Shares.

Eddie Mathews came to the majors in 1952, at the age of 20, and had a decent first season, hitting .242 with 25 homers. We credit him with a won-lost record for the season of 17-13:

| Year | Player | Age | HR | RBI | AVG | SLG | OBP | OPS | WS | LS | W PCT |
|------|--------|-----|-----|-----|------|------|------|------|-----|-----|-------|
| 1952 | Mathews | 20 | 25 | 58 | .242 | .447 | .320 | .767 | 17 | 13 | .558 |

Like a pitcher being 17-13; it means essentially the same thing, if you don't take that too literally. Chipper wasn't in the majors at age 20, but got three at-bats in September, 1993, aged 21. But at age 21, Eddie Mathews had perhaps the greatest season ever by a 21-year-old player, hitting .302 with 47 homers, 135 RBI. We credit him with 31 Win Shares, no losses — 31 and 0:

| Year | Player | Age | HR | RBI | AVG | SLG | OBP | OPS | WS | LS | W PCT |
|------|--------|-----|-----|-----|------|-------|------|-------|-----|-----|-------|
| 1993 | Jones | 21 | 0 | 0 | .667 | 1.000 | .750 | 1.750 | 0 | 0 | 1.000 |
| 1953 | Mathews | 21 | 47 | 135 | .302 | .627 | .406 | 1.033 | 31 | 0 | .994 |

Now I have to explain something. We assign Win Shares and Loss Shares in two processes. In one, we assign responsibility for "games" — actually thirds of games — to each player. In the other, we assign him credit for Wins, which are actually thirds of wins. Occasionally, a player of great quality will wind up with more credit for wins than the area of responsibility assigned to him, which leads to a winning percentage greater than 1.000. It's illogical, but it's less illogical than the alternatives, so we live with it.

Mathews at age 22 was over 1.000. Chipper was in the minors:

| Year | Player | Age | HR | RBI | AVG | SLG | OBP | OPS | WS | LS | W PCT |
|------|--------|-----|-----|-----|------|------|------|-------|-----|-----|-------|
| 1954 | Mathews | 22 | 40 | 103 | .290 | .603 | .423 | 1.026 | 28 | -1 | 1.029 |

Chipper, 40 years and a few months younger than Mathews, had his rookie season in 1995, and it was a good one. But Mathews in 1955 was an established player, and a great one:

| Year | Player | Age | HR | RBI | AVG | SLG | OBP | OPS | WS | LS | W PCT |
|------|--------|-----|-----|-----|------|------|------|-------|-----|-----|-------|
| 1995 | Jones | 23 | 23 | 86 | .265 | .450 | .353 | .803 | 17 | 12 | .594 |
| 1955 | Mathews | 23 | 41 | 101 | .289 | .601 | .413 | 1.014 | 26 | 2 | .939 |

Jones' rookie season was of essentially the same quality as Eddie Mathews' rookie season, and that's fairly near the top end of what rookies usually do. Chipper was named the Rookie of the Year.

But Mathews, by this time, was far, far ahead. Chipper Jones through age 23 had a career won-lost record of 18-12. Eddie Mathews was 102-15. If Mathews had gone forward after age 23 — as most players do — he would now be mentioned with Babe Ruth and Willie Mays, and there would be no way Chipper could catch up to him.

But Chipper became a superstar, too, beginning in 1996:

| Year | Player | Age | HR | RBI | AVG | SLG | OBP | OPS | WS | LS | W PCT |
|------|--------|-----|-----|-----|------|------|------|------|-----|-----|-------|
| 1996 | Jones | 24 | 30 | 110 | .309 | .530 | .393 | .923 | 22 | 9 | .703 |
| 1956 | Mathews | 24 | 37 | 95 | .272 | .518 | .373 | .892 | 24 | 7 | .785 |

Mathews was maybe a hair better, park and league adjusted, but the two were now competing on an even basis. Both players were similar at age 25:

| Year | Player | Age | HR | RBI | AVG | SLG | OBP | OPS | WS | LS | W PCT |
|------|--------|-----|-----|-----|------|------|------|------|-----|-----|-------|
| 1997 | Jones | 25 | 21 | 111 | .295 | .479 | .371 | .850 | 21 | 12 | .640 |
| 1957 | Mathews | 25 | 32 | 94 | .292 | .540 | .387 | .927 | 28 | 3 | .906 |

But at age 26, Chipper had his best year so far, and Mathews his worst since 1952:

| Year | Player | Age | HR | RBI | AVG | SLG | OBP | OPS | WS | LS | W PCT |
|------|--------|-----|-----|-----|------|------|------|------|-----|-----|-------|
| 1998 | Jones | 26 | 34 | 107 | .313 | .547 | .404 | .951 | 27 | 6 | .829 |
| 1958 | Mathews | 26 | 31 | 77 | .251 | .458 | .349 | .807 | 24 | 8 | .741 |

At age 27 both players had monster seasons. Chipper won the MVP Award. Mathews finished second in the MVP voting — but as we figure it, he was actually better:

| Year | Player | Age | HR | RBI | AVG | SLG | OBP | OPS | WS | LS | W PCT |
|------|--------|-----|-----|-----|------|------|------|-------|-----|-----|-------|
| 1999 | Jones | 27 | 45 | 110 | .319 | .633 | .441 | 1.074 | 27 | 3 | .907 |
| 1959 | Mathews | 27 | 46 | 114 | .306 | .593 | .390 | .983 | 30 | 1 | .958 |

Why does Eddie Mathews, with a .983 OPS, score as better than Chipper Jones, with similar numbers but an OPS 100 points higher?  Context.  The National League ERA in 1959 was 3.95, and Mathews was playing the league's worst hitter's park.  In 1999 the league ERA was 4.56.  When there are more runs scored it takes more runs to equal a win, so each run created is a smaller part of a win.

Jones was now moving parallel to Mathews, but he was still several laps behind.  Jones' career record through age 27 was 115-41, which is a Hall of Fame caliber record.  Mathews was 208-34 — and had another great year in 1960:

| Year | Player | Age | HR | RBI | AVG | SLG | OBP | OPS | WS | LS | W PCT |
|------|--------|-----|----|----|------|------|------|------|----|----|-------|
| 2000 | Jones | 28 | 36 | 111 | .311 | .566 | .404 | .970 | 23 | 8 | .755 |
| 1960 | Mathews | 28 | 39 | 124 | .277 | .551 | .397 | .948 | 28 | 3 | .895 |

Both players were tremendous at age 29:

| Year | Player | Age | HR | RBI | AVG | SLG | OBP | OPS | WS | LS | W PCT |
|------|--------|-----|----|----|------|------|------|-------|----|----|-------|
| 2001 | Jones | 29 | 38 | 102 | .330 | .605 | .427 | 1.032 | 25 | 4 | .848 |
| 1961 | Mathews | 29 | 32 | 91 | .306 | .535 | .402 | .937 | 26 | 4 | .854 |

At age 30 Mathews slipped just a little bit.  His slugging percentage slipped under .500.  His RBI dropped all the way to — gasp! — 90.  Chipper was distinctly better:

| Year | Player | Age | HR | RBI | AVG | SLG | OBP | OPS | WS | LS | W PCT |
|------|--------|-----|----|----|------|------|------|------|----|----|-------|
| 2002 | Jones | 30 | 26 | 100 | .327 | .536 | .435 | .972 | 25 | 3 | .890 |
| 1962 | Mathews | 30 | 29 | 90 | .265 | .496 | .381 | .877 | 23 | 8 | .737 |

Here again I have something I must explain.  In 1963 Major League Baseball expanded the strike zone, pitching the game into a historic six-year run shortage.  Mathews' numbers dropped even further on a superficial level in 1963, but this is an illusion: everybody's numbers were down from 1963 to 1968.  In reality, he was still a dominant player:

| Year | Player | Age | HR | RBI | AVG | SLG | OBP | OPS | WS | LS | W PCT |
|------|--------|-----|----|----|------|------|------|------|----|----|-------|
| 2003 | Jones | 31 | 27 | 106 | .305 | .517 | .402 | .920 | 22 | 8 | .738 |
| 1963 | Mathews | 31 | 23 | 84 | .263 | .453 | .399 | .852 | 26 | 5 | .844 |

Jones' career won-lost contribution was now 210 and 64, a wonderful record.  Mathews was 310 and 54 — but he had had his last great year.  Beginning in 1964, Eddie Mathews was an old player.  In 2004, Chipper also appeared to be entering his decline phase:

| Year | Player | Age | HR | RBI | AVG | SLG | OBP | OPS | WS | LS | W PCT |
|------|--------|-----|----|----|------|------|------|------|----|----|-------|
| 2004 | Jones | 32 | 30 | 96 | .248 | .485 | .362 | .847 | 16 | 10 | .612 |
| 1964 | Mathews | 32 | 23 | 74 | .233 | .412 | .344 | .756 | 17 | 12 | .579 |

At age 33 both players bounced back, to a degree:

| Year | Player | Age | HR | RBI | AVG | SLG | OBP | OPS | WS | LS | W PCT |
|------|--------|-----|-----|-----|------|------|------|------|-----|-----|-------|
| 2005 | Jones | 33 | 21 | 72 | .296 | .556 | .412 | .968 | 15 | 4 | .799 |
| 1965 | Mathews | 33 | 32 | 95 | .251 | .469 | .341 | .810 | 21 | 10 | .666 |

To this point Jones has not really gained on Mathews. He is still essentially where he was at age 31 — 100 Win Shares behind. But Mathews continued to decline from that point. Chipper, on the other hand, rallied to new heights:

| Year | Player | Age | HR | RBI | AVG | SLG | OBP | OPS | WS | LS | W PCT |
|------|--------|-----|-----|-----|------|------|------|-------|-----|-----|-------|
| 2006 | Jones | 34 | 26 | 86 | .324 | .596 | .409 | 1.005 | 21 | 0 | 1.009 |
| 1966 | Mathews | 34 | 16 | 53 | .250 | .420 | .341 | .761 | 15 | 10 | .591 |

And newer heights:

| Year | Player | Age | HR | RBI | AVG | SLG | OBP | OPS | WS | LS | W PCT |
|------|--------|-----|-----|-----|------|------|------|-------|-----|-----|-------|
| 2007 | Jones | 35 | 29 | 102 | .337 | .604 | .425 | 1.029 | 28 | -3 | 1.114 |
| 1967 | Mathews | 35 | 16 | 57 | .236 | .392 | .333 | .725 | 13 | 13 | .503 |

At the age of 35 Eddie Mathews was holding on. Jones, although his playing time was dropping off, was hitting better than ever — while numbers around the league were down. At age 36 Eddie Mathews played his last major league game, while Chipper Jones hit a career-high .364:

| Year | Player | Age | HR | RBI | AVG | SLG | OBP | OPS | WS | LS | W PCT |
|------|--------|-----|-----|-----|------|------|------|-------|-----|-----|-------|
| 2008 | Jones | 36 | 22 | 75 | .364 | .574 | .470 | 1.044 | 25 | -4 | 1.197 |
| 1968 | Mathews | 36 | 3 | 8 | .212 | .385 | .281 | .665 | 2 | 1 | .554 |

At age 37 Chipper struggled by his own standards — but was still a very good player if compared to league norms. Mathews was retired:

| Year | Player | Age | HR | RBI | AVG | SLG | OBP | OPS | WS | LS | W PCT |
|------|--------|-----|-----|-----|------|------|------|------|-----|-----|-------|
| 2009 | Jones  | 37  | 18  | 71  | .264 | .430 | .388 | .818 | 20  | 7   | .739  |

So Jones, since 2006, has been gaining on Mathews by leaps and bounds.

In the end, who has had the better career? We don't know. We haven't reached the end yet. They're essentially the same. We have Mathews with a career won-lost record of 377-101. Chipper, so far, is 336-78. Both players are far above the threshold of a Hall of Fame career, and we do not yet know whose totals will be better. They will be about the same.

This chart compares the two, strictly as hitters:

| Player | Wins | Losses | Pct |
|--------|------|--------|------|
| Mathews | 311 | 48 | .867 |
| Jones | 290 | 32 | .900 |

And this one compares them as fielders:

| Player | Wins | Losses | Pct |
|--------|------|--------|------|
| Mathews | 65 | 53 | .550 |
| Jones | 47 | 46 | .503 |

Chipper isn't a great defensive player — but neither was Mathews. Both of them were competent, coping-skills fielders who played a relatively difficult defensive position, the hot corner, but not terribly well. They're comparable hitters; they're comparable fielders. They have had a comparable number of outstanding seasons.

If I had to choose? If I had to choose an all-time, all-city Braves team or else go bungee jumping, I would choose Chipper. They're both great players.

## Hanging Fire

Hanging fire is a military term for a mortar shell that doesn't go off when it is supposed to, but doesn't go out, either; the fuse does a slow burn and may eventually ignite, usually about a quarter of a second after some moron puts his eyeball on the muzzle face to see what's happening. Melky Cabrera's career, so to speak, has been hanging fire. When he was 20 years old Melky hit .280 with 75 runs scored, and 56 walks. Those are still his career highs, and it's been a few years. Melky will be 25 this year, and the Braves have decided to peer down the barrel and see if there's something still burning in there.

Who is older, Melky Cabrera or Nate McLouth? McLouth is actually three years older; he just seems newer because he came to the majors very quietly, in some city where not many people are aware that there is a baseball team. My question is, is Cabrera's age an illusion? Having played 569 major league games, shouldn't he have gotten wherever he is going, whether he is 32 or 22?

I did a search to see if I could find any players who were like Melky in that they came to the majors very early, played at a level like Melky's for several years, but then did become the players they were supposed to be. This is what I came up with:

1) Dave Winfield. Winfield skipped the minors, went straight to the majors at 21 and competed immediately. After that, though, he wasn't really that good for several years. At age 24 he had the same year

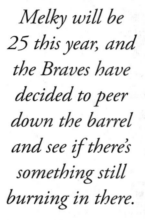

*Melky will be 25 this year, and the Braves have decided to peer down the barrel and see if there's something still burning in there.*

Melky did, basically, hit .283 with 13 homers, 69 RBI (Melky was .274 with 13 and 68). His career numbers at that time weren't a lot better than Melky's although they were a little better. He started to get good the next year, and he's in the Hall of Fame now.

2) Roberto Clemente. Clemente came to the majors at age 20, like Melky, and through age 24 he was no better than Melky at the bat, no better at all. His career highs after five years were 7 homers and 60 RBI, 69 runs scored. At the same age he had 627 major league games, with a .706 OPS—ten points lower than Melky's. But he got started at age 25, and is now part of the game's mythology.

3) Al Oliver. Al Oliver came to the majors in 1970, had a pretty good rookie year at age 21. For three years after that he really didn't do much. At age 24 he hit .282 with 14 homers, 64 RBI. . .about the same as Melky. His career numbers were a little better, not much. He retired with 2700 hits and a career average of .300.

4) Dwight Evans. Evans was in the majors at the age of 21, didn't really do anything for years. At the age of 24 he hit .242 with 17 homers, 62 RBI. Through the age of 24 he had played 548 games with a .254 average and 51 homers—and he was still several years away from getting really good. But he eventually did.

There are others we could mention here. Rusty Staub. Bernie Williams. B. J. Surhoff. You never know. I wouldn't give up on Melky, and I wouldn't discount the fact that he is still very young.

# Explaining Defensive Win Shares to a Deceased Sportswriter

by Bill James

LET ME TRY TO EXPLAIN DEFENSIVE WIN SHARES AS IF I WERE explaining them to Arthur Daley. Daley was a *New York Times* sportswriter of the 1950s, famous for his antagonism toward statistics — like Dan Shaughnessy, except that, being dead, Daley is much easier to communicate with than Shaughnessy.

**Daley:** I don't understand what making outs has to do with playing defense.

**James:** Defensive responsibility is both created and assigned. It is assigned from the team to the player by the team's action in sending the player out to the field. But before those defensive innings are assigned to the individual they must be created on the team level. It is making outs that creates the need to play defense on the team level.

**Daley:** How's that?

**James:** For every three outs that a team makes at bat, they have to play one inning of defense. This is the law of the game.

**Daley:** So if a player makes more outs at bat or on the bases, that makes him a worse defensive player?

*It is making outs that creates the need to play defense on the team level.*

**James:** If a player makes more outs, that gives him a larger responsibility to play defense, because it means that more defense must be played.

**Daley:** Suppose that Gary Sheffield and Ruben Sierra are teammates.

**James:** They must have been, somewhere.

**Daley:** And suppose that they alternate between playing left field and right field.

**James:** They could.

**Daley:** And suppose that their defensive statistics are just the same.

**James:** Which they could be.

**Daley:** Sheffield, because he has a .400 on-base percentage, is going to make fewer outs than Sierra, whose on-base percentage is close to the Neifi Perez line.

**James:** That's right.

**Daley:** But in your system, you're going to conclude that Sheffield is a better defensive player than Sierra.

**James:** He is a better defensive player.

**Daley:** Let's assume he's not.

**James:** Not better in the field?

**Daley:** Let's assume they are just the same in the field. You're going to conclude that Sheffield is better, because he makes fewer outs.

**James:** He *is* better because he makes fewer outs.

**Daley:** He is better at bat because he makes fewer outs. But he's not better in the field because he makes fewer outs.

**James:** Yes, in fact, he is. He is better in the field because he makes fewer outs at bat.

**Daley:** Why?

**James:** Because making outs increases the team's responsibility to play defense. When you make more outs, that increases the team's responsibility to play defense.

Therefore, if two players are the same in the field but one of them makes more outs, the one who makes fewer outs has to come out ahead when you compare the player's defensive contribution to his defensive responsibility.

**Daley:** I don't want to think about it in those terms.

**James:** How you want to think about it, how I want to think about it, has nothing to do with it. That's the way it is. Unless you can explain to me logically why it isn't.

**Daley:** Suppose that somebody else has a different fielding system.

**James:** Like John Dewan, or Tom Tippett, or Tom Tango, or Dave Pinto.

**Daley:** Or many others.

**James:** Or many others.

**Daley:** Are those systems wrong, to ignore the batter's outs in assessing fielding performance?

**James:** Well, I'm not here to say that anybody else is wrong. I'm trying to explain why I did it the way I did it; I'm not saying other people are wrong.

**Daley:** But you are, aren't you? If you argue that this is a necessary logical inference, aren't you saying that anybody who fails to take this into account is doing it wrong?

**James:** It's a necessary logical step, given the way that I am approaching the subject. I am assigning the responsibility for playing defense from the team to the individual. In doing that, it is a necessary logical step to take into account the outs the player has made. But other defensive systems approach the issue from different angles, and they may have it right, given their assumptions.

**Daley:** But then the way they look at it *may* be wrong?

*I am assigning the responsibility for playing defense from the team to the individual.*

**James:** Of course, the way that anyone looks at any issue could be wrong.

**Daley:** Do you think it's wrong?

**James:** I think it could be incomplete. One difference between what I am doing and what other people may be doing is that mine is a global system. It is attempting to make an accounting of how everything in the game fits together.

I think that, if you are attempting to make an accounting of how everything in the game fits together, you need to take into account the effect of outs in increasing defensive responsibility. But many, most or all of those other defensive systems that we talked about earlier are *not* attempting to make an accounting of how everything in the game fits together.

**Daley:** Let me try again.
**James:** Go ahead.

**Daley:** Suppose that you have two teams which are identical in every respect, except that the right fielder on one team is Gary Sheffield, and on the other team it is Ruben Sierra.
**James:** OK.

**Daley:** Suppose that Sierra and Sheffield are the same in the outfield.
**James:** OK.

**Daley:** Will the team with Sierra in the outfield allow more runs?
**James:** No. They will win fewer games, but they will not allow more runs.

**Daley:** They will win fewer games because they score fewer runs, but they will not allow more runs?
**James:** I suppose not.

**Daley:** Then why are the players not even, as defensive players?
**James:** Because the teams you have postulated cannot exist. You've created an imbalanced statistical universe.

**Daley:** How so?
**James:** If one player makes more outs than the other, then one team must make more outs than the other. If one team makes more outs than the other, then they must play more innings of defense. You're creating a situation in which one team makes 4400 outs at bat and the other makes 4300 outs at bat, everything else is the same, but they play the same number of innings on defense. That can't happen. Your theoretical universe cannot exist.

**Daley:** But we account for that difference on offense.
**James:** You can account for that difference on offense if you want to. But it isn't on offense. It's on defense.

What I am saying is that, while we are in the habit of thinking of offense and defense in baseball as un-connected, they are in fact *not* un-connected. There is a very important connection between them, which is the rule that for every out you make on offense, you must record an out on defense. Ninth innings for home teams excepted, of course.

**Daley:** I think we should make a rule requiring the home team to bat in the ninth inning if they are ahead, just so the stats balance.
**James:** Right. It's like those games they play in September after both teams are eliminated. If they don't matter, why do they play those games? And if it's for the integrity of the schedule, why don't they make the home team hit in the bottom of the ninth?

**Daley:** Anyway.
**James:** Seriously.

*The teams you have postulated cannot exist.*
*You've created an imbalanced statistical universe.*

**Daley:** If you look at this as a practical issue rather than a theoretical one, does this policy help or hinder?

**James:** It both helps and hinders, but it helps a great deal more than it hinders.

**Daley:** Where does it hinder?

**James:** Ted Williams vs. Vic Power. Ted Williams rates as a better defensive player than he was commonly perceived to be through much of his career, and no doubt this is because of his very good on-base percentages, which reduce his responsibility to play defense. Vic Power, on the other hand…while my system does a very good job of getting higher defensive values for the Gold Glove first basemen than for the Jason Giambis of the world, it doesn't do well by Vic Power. His low on-base percentages don't cause this, but they don't help, either.

**Daley:** And where does it help?

**James:** Over the course of a career, this practice is a tremendous help in pushing players toward the defensive winning percentages that they deserve. Over the course of a career a good defensive player who is a weak hitter will virtually always have a high ratio of defensive innings to outs made, because he will virtually always be deployed by a manager so as to maximize his defensive innings and minimize his at-bats, whereas a good hitter who is not a good fielder will virtually always be deployed by his manager, at some points in his career, so as to maximize his at-bats and minimize his innings in the field. The result of this is that defense-first players, in our system, will virtually always wind up with high defensive winning percentages, while poor defensive players will virtually always wind up with low defensive winning percentages, for their careers. A highly desirable outcome.

**Daley:** I'm not sure I am following you. Why exactly does this element of the system create a bias toward the better fielders?

**James:** A player is given defensive accountability both for his innings played, and for his outs made, but he only has the opportunity to earn defensive credits — defensive win shares — while he is in the field. He has to offset the outs he makes at bat while he is in the field. If a player is used as a defensive sub, or if he is pinch hit for, he tends to have a high ratio of innings in the field to plate appearances, and thus a high ratio of defensive innings to outs made. This gives him a larger opportunity to earn defensive credits, compared to his defensive responsibility, so he tends to do well. Conversely, if the player is used as a pinch hitter, or if he is taken out of the game for defense, then he tends to have a low ratio of defensive innings to plate appearances, and thus a low ratio of defensive innings to outs made. Thus, he has less opportunity to contribute in the field, relative to the defensive responsibility he is assigned.

**Daley:** So it is biased against that player.

**James:** If assigning high defensive winning percentages to good defensive players and low defensive winning percentages to poor defensive players is a bias, then yes, it's biased. But I don't think you can go to hell for that.

**Daley:** But there must be some problems with the system, right?

**James:** Sure.

**Daley:** We'll get to those in a minute. First, I wanted to ask about a couple of other features of your stupid system.

**James:** Go ahead.

**Daley:** You assign the same responsibility to play defense to a shortstop that you do to a left fielder.

**James:** Right.

**Daley:** Do you really believe that a left fielder has the same responsibility to play defense that a shortstop does?

**James:** From a certain perspective, no, but from a certain perspective, yes.

*While we are in the habit of thinking of offense and defense in baseball as un-connected, they are in fact not un-connected.*

**Daley:** A weasel answer if I've ever heard one.

**James:** It depends on exactly what you mean by the word "responsibility". We're trying to represent the impact of the player on the team. From the perspective of the team, everybody has to take responsibility for getting the other team out of the dugout and back into the field. I don't know that Phil Rizzuto has more *responsibility* for that than Johnny Mize, just because Rizzuto is playing shortstop and Mize is playing first. Rizzuto has more *skill* at playing defense than Mize, and he is more "responsible" for getting the other side out, in a certain sense, because he accomplishes more toward that goal. But he is not more "responsible" in the sense that it's one player's job more than the others'.

**Daley:** But the average shortstop is contributing more to the defense than the average left fielder, surely?

**James:** Certainly. And our system reflects that.

**Daley:** But if the average shortstop is contributing more to the defense than the average left fielder, wouldn't it be easier to just assign him a larger responsibility for playing defense, and thus compare the player to the average at his position? The average left fielder is 1x; the average shortstop is 2x.

**James:** If you can figure out how to make it work that way, more power to you. I can't. That is what most global analytical systems do, but I think it creates both logical and practical problems. Logically, if you have a first baseman who creates 70 runs and makes 300 outs and a teammate shortstop who creates 70 runs and makes 300 outs, they are the same as offensive players. If we say that they are even as hitters but that the shortstop is more valuable because of his defense, that, to me, is more accurate than saying that the shortstop is a better hitter because he plays shortstop. He's not a better hitter because he plays shortstop. He plays shortstop because he is a better fielder.

That said, I am far from convinced that I have exactly the right structure in place to address those issues. I tried it every different way that I could think of, and this seemed to create fewer analytical absurdities than anything else. I experimented with assigning a larger defensive responsibility to the players at the right end of the defensive spectrum (shortstop and center field) than to those on the left end (first base and left field). It just doesn't really work, for me. If you assign the shortstop 10 game shares and the first baseman 3, then the average shortstop is a .500 fielder and the average first baseman is a .500 fielder, which means that, when you consider hitting as well, the average first baseman has a higher winning percentage than the average shortstop, which is irrational, so then you have to go back to pretending that the shortstop who creates 70 runs is somehow a better hitter than the first baseman who creates 70 runs. But if a shortstop who creates 70 runs is equal, as a hitter, to the first baseman who creates 90 runs, then why does the first baseman hit third and the shortstop hit seventh?

My system says instead that "first basemen are better hitters than shortstops; shortstops are better fielders than first basemen." I think that statement more accurately describes the real universe than does the other alternative.

**Daley:** Let's talk about parts of your system that don't work.

**James:** OK.

**Daley:** What parts of your system don't work?

**James:** Well, one thing that doesn't work as well as it should is the team performance bias in the individual fielding records.

**Daley:** Team performance bias…?

**James:** Take a 90-win team that allows 700 opposition runs and a 60-win team that allows 850 opposition runs. It is overwhelmingly likely that the 90-win team is a better defensive team than the 60-win team. In fact, the

*It causes players who play on good teams to rank as better defensive players than players who play on bad teams.*

Royals…the reason they have been getting blown out the last week is their fielding. Their defense over the past week has just been horrific.

The problem is, when you look at 60-win teams and 90-win teams in the fielding stats, there isn't much difference. There's a small difference in fielding percentages, but that's just a few plays. No matter how good you are or how bad you are, as a team, you're going to record 27 outs a game. If you're a bad team, you'll have just as many double plays, on average, and if you're a bad team you'll actually have more outfield assists, and more assists at the positions where assists tend to carry more weight on defense.

To correct for this, we start with the assumption that a 90-win team allowing 700 opposition runs is better in the field than a 60-win team allowing 850 runs, as they almost always would be. Then, starting with the assumption that there is more defense being played on the Dodgers than on the Royals, we assign credit for that defensive accomplishment from the team to the individual players.

This has the effect, over a career, of biasing the system in the direction of the truth. It causes players who play on good teams to rank, over the course of a career, as better defensive players than players who play on bad teams. It causes them to rank that way because they are that way.

The problem is, the bias works well over the course of a career, but it causes off-the-wall variations year to year. If you take a team that has an off season, you will very often find that the second baseman has defensive records over a period of years that read 5-2, 4-1, 1-6, 4-2, 4-3. Everybody on the team gets hammered for their defense in the off season, and there clearly is some problem with the system, because the player shouldn't be punished for the failures of his team, beyond the extent to which his personal failures have contributed to the failure of the team. I know there is some problem related to this element of the system, but I don't know what it is and I don't know how to fix it.

**Daley:** Thank you for your time. This is the first interview I have done since I died in the mid-1950s.

**James:** I hope it was worth waiting for.

# Baltimore Orioles

| 2009 TEAM OVERVIEW | ML RANK | 16th | 13th | 7th | 24th | 15th | 21st |
|---|---|---|---|---|---|---|---|
| **64-98** | **Team** | **741** | **160** | **.268** | **517** | **.747** | **76** |
| | | RUNS | HOME RUNS | BATTING AVG. | WALKS | OPS | STOLEN BASES |
| **5**th place AL East | **Opp.** | **876** | **218** | **.288** | **546** | **.828** | **119** |
| | ML RANK | 28th | 26th | 30th | 12th | 29th | 20th |

## Key Players

| Pos | Player | G | AB | R | H | 2B | 3B | HR | RBI | SB | CS | BB | SO | AVG | OBP | SLG | OPS | WS |
|---|---|---|---|---|---|---|---|---|---|---|---|---|---|---|---|---|---|---|
| C | Matt Wieters | 96 | 354 | 35 | 102 | 15 | 1 | 9 | 43 | 0 | 0 | 28 | 86 | .288 | .340 | .412 | .753 | 9 |
| 1B | Aubrey Huff | 110 | 430 | 51 | 109 | 24 | 1 | 13 | 72 | 0 | 6 | 41 | 74 | .253 | .321 | .405 | .725 | 8 |
| 2B | Brian Roberts | 159 | 632 | 110 | 179 | 56 | 1 | 16 | 79 | 30 | 7 | 74 | 112 | .283 | .356 | .451 | .807 | 20 |
| 3B | Melvin Mora | 125 | 450 | 44 | 117 | 20 | 0 | 8 | 48 | 3 | 3 | 34 | 60 | .260 | .321 | .358 | .679 | 7 |
| SS | Cesar Izturis | 114 | 387 | 34 | 99 | 14 | 4 | 2 | 30 | 12 | 4 | 18 | 38 | .256 | .294 | .328 | .622 | 8 |
| LF | Nolan Reimold | 104 | 358 | 49 | 100 | 18 | 2 | 15 | 45 | 8 | 2 | 47 | 77 | .279 | .365 | .466 | .831 | 10 |
| CF | Adam Jones | 119 | 473 | 83 | 131 | 22 | 3 | 19 | 70 | 10 | 4 | 36 | 93 | .277 | .335 | .457 | .792 | 13 |
| RF | Nick Markakis | 161 | 642 | 94 | 188 | 45 | 2 | 18 | 101 | 6 | 2 | 56 | 98 | .293 | .347 | .453 | .801 | 16 |
| DH | Luke Scott | 128 | 449 | 61 | 116 | 26 | 1 | 25 | 77 | 0 | 0 | 55 | 104 | .258 | .340 | .488 | .828 | 11 |

## Key Pitchers

| Pos | Player | G | GS | W | L | SV | IP | H | R | ER | SO | BB | BR/9 | ERA | WS |
|---|---|---|---|---|---|---|---|---|---|---|---|---|---|---|---|
| SP | Jeremy Guthrie | 33 | 33 | 10 | 17 | 0 | 200.0 | 224 | 120 | 112 | 110 | 60 | 13.19 | 5.04 | 7 |
| SP | Brad Bergesen | 19 | 19 | 7 | 5 | 0 | 123.1 | 126 | 52 | 47 | 65 | 32 | 11.89 | 3.43 | 9 |
| SP | Jason Berken | 24 | 24 | 6 | 12 | 0 | 119.2 | 164 | 92 | 87 | 66 | 44 | 16.09 | 6.54 | 1 |
| SP | David Hernandez | 20 | 19 | 4 | 10 | 0 | 101.1 | 118 | 62 | 61 | 68 | 46 | 14.65 | 5.42 | 3 |
| SP | Rich Hill | 14 | 13 | 3 | 3 | 0 | 57.2 | 68 | 53 | 50 | 46 | 40 | 17.01 | 7.80 | 0 |
| CL | George Sherrill | 42 | 0 | 0 | 1 | 20 | 41.1 | 34 | 11 | 11 | 39 | 13 | 10.67 | 2.40 | 8 |
| RP | Danys Baez | 59 | 0 | 4 | 6 | 0 | 71.2 | 59 | 36 | 32 | 40 | 22 | 10.80 | 4.02 | 5 |
| RP | Jim Johnson | 64 | 0 | 4 | 6 | 10 | 70.0 | 73 | 32 | 32 | 49 | 23 | 12.73 | 4.11 | 7 |

## The Long Man

Brian Bass has come to be the definition of middle relief for the Orioles. In 2009, he led all major league pitchers in both "Early Entries" and "Long Outings".

| Player | Games | Early Entries | | Player | Games | Long Outings |
|---|---|---|---|---|---|---|
| 1. Brian Bass, Bal | 48 | 29 | | 1. Brian Bass, Bal | 48 | 30 |
| 2. D.J. Carrasco, CWS | 48 | 27 | | 2. D.J. Carrasco, CWS | 48 | 25 |
| 3. Brandon Medders, SF | 61 | 26 | | 3. Alfredo Aceves, NYY | 42 | 25 |
| 4. Zach Miner, Det | 46 | 26 | | 4. Burke Badenhop, Fla | 33 | 22 |
| 5. Justin Miller, SF | 44 | 26 | | 5. Luis Perdomo, SD | 35 | 21 |

## Stop That

There were 82 games in 2009 in which the Baltimore Oriole pitchers issued more walks than their batters received. The Orioles' record in those games was 21-61.

## Rotational Gyrations

The Orioles' original 2009 starting rotation — Jeremy Guthrie, Koji Uehara, Alfredo Simon, Mark Hendrickson and Adam Eaton — wound up starting only 66 Oriole games. This was the lowest such figure in the major leagues.

## You've Got to Know Your Strengths and Weaknesses

Adam Jones in 2009 hit only 107 fly balls — one of the lowest fly ball totals among major league regulars. When he did get the ball in the air he hit .365, with a slugging percentage of 1.029.

When he hit the ball on the ground, he hit .227 with a slugging percentage of .261. Unfortunately, he hit almost twice as many ground balls (211) as flies (107).

## At Home in the Two

Adam Jones split his 2009 season between the second and third spots in the batting order. His OPS was almost 300 points higher when he batted second.

| Lineup | PA | BA | OBP | SLG | OPS |
|---|---|---|---|---|---|
| Batting 2nd | 359 | .305 | .362 | .520 | .882 |
| Batting 3rd | 132 | .198 | .265 | .322 | .587 |

## Sparkling in September

Promoted to the majors in late May, hotshot rookie Matt Wieters hit under .250 through the end of June. But his performance in September speaks for itself.

| Month | AB | R | HR | RBI | BA | OBP | SLG | OPS |
|---|---|---|---|---|---|---|---|---|
| May | 11 | 1 | 0 | 0 | .182 | .182 | .455 | .636 |
| June | 74 | 7 | 2 | 7 | .257 | .313 | .378 | .691 |
| July | 62 | 4 | 1 | 6 | .323 | .364 | .403 | .767 |
| August | 96 | 8 | 2 | 13 | .250 | .298 | .354 | .652 |
| Sept./Oct. | 111 | 15 | 4 | 17 | .333 | .395 | .486 | .882 |

## Positions Available, Starting Pitcher

The Orioles were the only team in the majors that did not get at least one start with a Game Score of 80 or more from its starting pitchers. The Cardinals and Giants had ten games each with Game Scores of 80 or above.

**Baltimore Orioles 2009**

| Game Score | Times | ERA | W-L |
|---|---|---|---|
| 70 to 79 | 7 | 1.80 | 6-1 |
| 60 to 69 | 16 | 2.15 | 11-5 |
| 50 to 59 | 40 | 3.36 | 22-18 |
| 40 to 49 | 39 | 5.52 | 13-26 |
| 30 to 39 | 34 | 5.90 | 7-27 |
| 20 to 29 | 20 | 9.10 | 4-16 |
| Below 20 | 6 | 10.59 | 1-5 |

## Losing a Little Each Year

Brian Roberts' range has fallen from the sixth-best in the majors in 2005 to the 29th-best last year.

**Brian Roberts**

**Plus/Minus**

| Year | Inn | Outs Made | To His Right | Straight On | To His Left | GB | Air | Total | Runs Saved | Rank |
|---|---|---|---|---|---|---|---|---|---|---|
| 2005 | 1208.0 | 453 | +8 | +2 | +6 | +16 | +2 | +18 | 14 | 6 |
| 2006 | 1167.2 | 397 | -4 | +8 | +4 | +8 | -1 | +7 | 5 | 12 |
| 2007 | 1329.2 | 488 | +1 | +3 | -2 | +1 | -1 | 0 | 0 | 15 |
| 2008 | 1320.0 | 474 | +13 | +2 | -15 | -1 | -3 | -4 | -3 | 20 |
| 2009 | 1340.2 | 435 | -5 | -4 | +2 | -7 | -3 | -10 | -8 | 29 |

## Markakis' Strike Zone Judgement

On the surface, Nick Markakis had another fine year, but his on-base percentage plummeted from .406 in 2008 to .347 in 2009. His plate discipline fundamentally turned upside-down: He took more pitches in the strike zone and swung at more pitches outside the strike zone.

**Nick Markakis**

| Pitches Taken | 2008 | 2009 |
|---|---|---|
| Taken for a Strike | 30% | 36% |
| Called a ball | 70% | 64% |
| | | |
| In Strike Zone | 31% | 37% |
| High | 14% | 10% |
| Low | 21% | 21% |
| Inside | 9% | 10% |
| Outside | 25% | 23% |

| Swung At | 2008 | 2009 |
|---|---|---|
| Missed | 15% | 13% |
| Fouled Off | 40% | 38% |
| Put in Play | 44% | 48% |
| | | |
| In Strike Zone | 78% | 71% |
| High | 4% | 5% |
| Low | 7% | 7% |
| Inside | 5% | 7% |
| Outside | 6% | 9% |

### Mora No More?

Is Melvin Mora finally done? I always liked Melvin Mora. He was a good egg.

When Mora was seven years old his father took him to a candy store in Venezuela to buy some candy. Somebody mistook his father for somebody else, and murdered him in the candy store. In spite of this, Mora always seemed like a decent person. He himself, of course, became the father of quintuplets.

What is this, Oprah? Mora was late getting started in the major leagues, 27 years old when he played his first major league game, 29 when he became a regular. He's kind of a modern Al "Fuzzy" Smith. Al Smith was late starting his career, too, a Negro League star who joined the Indians in 1953. Like Mora, he bounced between positions for a good part of his career. . .this is a scan of their games played by position:

| Player | C | 1B | 2B | 3B | SS | LF | CF | RF | PH | PR | DH |
|--------|---|----|----|----|----|----|----|----|----|----|----|
| Al Smith | 0 | 0 | 2 | 379 | 9 | 402 | 86 | 676 | 82 | 19 | 0 |
| Melvin Mora | 0 | 1 | 29 | 815 | 195 | 170 | 158 | 29 | 43 | 18 | 14 |

And their career batting stats are almost the same:

| Player | Years | G | AB | R | H | HR | RBI | SB | AVG | OBP | SLG | OPS |
|--------|-------|---|----|----|----|----|-----|----|-----|-----|-----|-----|
| Al Smith | 12 | 1,517 | 5,357 | 843 | 1,458 | 164 | 676 | 67 | .272 | .358 | .429 | .787 |
| Melvin Mora | 11 | 1,401 | 4,979 | 750 | 1,384 | 164 | 693 | 91 | .278 | .352 | .436 | .788 |

Fuzzy Smith is now so obscure that I think he doesn't even have a Wikipedia entry. I don't know; I think somehow that Baltimore will remember Melvin Mora, and remember him fondly.

# Boston Red Sox

**2009 TEAM OVERVIEW**

**95-67**

**2** nd place **AL East**

## Key Players

| Pos | Player | G | AB | R | H | 2B | 3B | HR | RBI | SB | CS | BB | SO | AVG | OBP | SLG | OPS | WS |
|---|---|---|---|---|---|---|---|---|---|---|---|---|---|---|---|---|---|---|
| C | Jason Varitek | 109 | 364 | 41 | 76 | 24 | 0 | 14 | 51 | 0 | 0 | 54 | 90 | .209 | .313 | .390 | .703 | 7 |
| 1B | Kevin Youkilis | 136 | 491 | 99 | 150 | 36 | 1 | 27 | 94 | 7 | 2 | 77 | 125 | .305 | .413 | .548 | .961 | 28 |
| 2B | Dustin Pedroia | 154 | 626 | 115 | 185 | 48 | 1 | 15 | 72 | 20 | 8 | 74 | 45 | .296 | .371 | .447 | .819 | 24 |
| 3B | Mike Lowell | 119 | 445 | 54 | 129 | 29 | 1 | 17 | 75 | 2 | 1 | 33 | 61 | .290 | .337 | .474 | .811 | 13 |
| SS | Nick Green | 104 | 276 | 35 | 65 | 18 | 0 | 6 | 35 | 1 | 4 | 20 | 69 | .236 | .303 | .366 | .669 | 6 |
| LF | Jason Bay | 151 | 531 | 103 | 142 | 29 | 3 | 36 | 119 | 13 | 3 | 94 | 162 | .267 | .384 | .537 | .921 | 30 |
| CF | Jacoby Ellsbury | 153 | 624 | 94 | 188 | 27 | 10 | 8 | 60 | 70 | 12 | 49 | 74 | .301 | .355 | .415 | .770 | 21 |
| RF | J.D. Drew | 137 | 452 | 84 | 126 | 30 | 4 | 24 | 68 | 2 | 6 | 82 | 109 | .279 | .392 | .522 | .914 | 17 |
| DH | David Ortiz | 150 | 541 | 77 | 129 | 35 | 1 | 28 | 99 | 0 | 2 | 74 | 134 | .238 | .332 | .462 | .794 | 11 |

## Key Pitchers

| Pos | Player | G | GS | W | L | SV | IP | H | R | ER | SO | BB | BR/9 | ERA | WS |
|---|---|---|---|---|---|---|---|---|---|---|---|---|---|---|---|
| SP | Josh Beckett | 32 | 32 | 17 | 6 | 0 | 212.1 | 198 | 99 | 91 | 199 | 55 | 11.02 | 3.86 | 16 |
| SP | Jon Lester | 32 | 32 | 15 | 8 | 0 | 203.1 | 186 | 80 | 77 | 225 | 64 | 11.20 | 3.41 | 17 |
| SP | Tim Wakefield | 21 | 21 | 11 | 5 | 0 | 129.2 | 137 | 67 | 66 | 72 | 50 | 13.67 | 4.58 | 8 |
| SP | Brad Penny | 24 | 24 | 7 | 8 | 0 | 131.2 | 160 | 89 | 82 | 89 | 42 | 14.15 | 5.61 | 3 |
| SP | Clay Buchholz | 16 | 16 | 7 | 4 | 0 | 92.0 | 91 | 44 | 43 | 68 | 36 | 12.62 | 4.21 | 6 |
| CL | Jonathan Papelbon | 66 | 0 | 1 | 1 | 38 | 68.0 | 54 | 15 | 14 | 76 | 24 | 10.85 | 1.85 | 15 |
| RP | Hideki Okajima | 68 | 0 | 6 | 0 | 0 | 61.0 | 56 | 23 | 23 | 53 | 21 | 11.66 | 3.39 | 7 |
| RP | Ramon Ramirez | 70 | 0 | 7 | 4 | 0 | 69.2 | 61 | 26 | 22 | 52 | 32 | 12.53 | 2.84 | 8 |

## Man Versus Mirror

Tim Wakefield in 2009 had a won-lost record of 11-5. The starting pitchers who opposed him, you will not be shocked to learn, had a won-lost record in those games of 5-11. Josh Beckett was 17-6; the pitchers who took the mound against him were 5-17. Jon Lester was 15-8; the pitchers who opposed him were 8-14.

You could pretty much figure out that much, but what about the rest of their records? What was the full record of the pitchers who took the mound against Josh Beckett? On the theory that interesting things sometimes happen when you stand records on their heads and look at them upside-down, I thought I would take a look. These are the records of the Red Sox' starting pitchers in 2009 (as starting pitchers, not including relief appearances) — and the records of those who took the mound against them.

| Player | GS | W | L | WPct | IP | H | R | ER | K | BB | ERA |
|--------|----|----|----|------|-----|-----|-----|-----|-----|-----|------|
| John Beckett | 32 | 17 | 6 | .739 | 212.1 | 198 | 99 | 91 | 199 | 55 | 3.86 |
| Opp. Pitchers | 32 | 5 | 17 | .227 | 176.0 | 202 | 127 | 120 | 136 | 81 | 6.14 |
| Jon Lester | 32 | 15 | 8 | .652 | 203.1 | 186 | 80 | 77 | 225 | 64 | 3.41 |
| Opp. Pitchers | 32 | 8 | 14 | .364 | 184.2 | 191 | 94 | 85 | 137 | 76 | 4.14 |
| Brad Penny | 24 | 7 | 8 | .467 | 131.2 | 160 | 89 | 82 | 89 | 42 | 5.61 |
| Opp. Pitchers | 24 | 10 | 8 | .556 | 135.1 | 166 | 93 | 87 | 112 | 60 | 5.79 |
| Tim Wakefield | 21 | 11 | 5 | .688 | 129.2 | 137 | 67 | 66 | 72 | 50 | 4.58 |
| Opp. Pitchers | 21 | 5 | 11 | .313 | 124.0 | 126 | 78 | 72 | 95 | 49 | 5.23 |
| Clay Buchholz | 16 | 7 | 4 | .636 | 92.0 | 91 | 44 | 43 | 68 | 36 | 4.21 |
| Opp. Pitchers | 16 | 4 | 11 | .267 | 81.2 | 99 | 61 | 52 | 69 | 36 | 5.73 |
| Daisuke Matsuzaka | 12 | 4 | 6 | .400 | 59.1 | 81 | 38 | 38 | 54 | 30 | 5.76 |
| Opp. Pitchers | 12 | 6 | 5 | .545 | 63.2 | 65 | 37 | 33 | 50 | 28 | 4.66 |
| John Smoltz | 8 | 2 | 5 | .286 | 40.0 | 59 | 37 | 37 | 33 | 9 | 8.33 |
| Opp. Pitchers | 8 | 5 | 2 | .714 | 47.2 | 48 | 31 | 27 | 38 | 19 | 5.10 |
| Justin Masterson | 6 | 2 | 2 | .500 | 35.1 | 38 | 18 | 18 | 28 | 13 | 4.58 |
| Opp. Pitchers | 6 | 2 | 2 | .500 | 35.0 | 36 | 14 | 12 | 22 | 18 | 3.09 |
| Paul Byrd | 6 | 1 | 3 | .250 | 31.0 | 44 | 20 | 20 | 10 | 11 | 5.81 |
| Opp. Pitchers | 6 | 3 | 1 | .750 | 35.0 | 39 | 16 | 12 | 28 | 15 | 3.09 |
| Junichi Tazawa | 4 | 2 | 2 | .500 | 20.0 | 32 | 16 | 14 | 8 | 3 | 6.30 |
| Opp. Pitchers | 4 | 2 | 1 | .667 | 18.0 | 22 | 14 | 14 | 16 | 6 | 7.00 |
| Michael Bowden | 1 | 0 | 1 | .000 | 3.0 | 7 | 7 | 7 | 3 | 1 | 21.00 |
| Opp. Pitchers | 1 | 1 | 0 | 1.000 | 6.0 | 6 | 4 | 4 | 3 | 2 | 6.00 |

## I've Heard of That Second Guy

Through the 2009 season, Jon Papelbon has pitched 298 career innings with a career ERA of 1.84.

The last pitcher to get as much as 298 innings into his career with an ERA that low was Bob Lee, a 1960s reliever. Through June, 1966, Lee had pitched 322 career innings with an ERA of 1.81. He was hit hard in July, 1966, and never got his ERA that low again.

The last pitcher before Lee to get 298 innings into his career with an ERA that low was Walter Johnson in 1921.

## But Remember, Those Records Only Go Back About 50 Years

The Red Sox in 2009 allowed 151 stolen bases, while throwing out only 23 would-be base stealers. This was the worst stolen base percentage allowed (86.8%) in the history of the American League. The only major league team ever to do worse was the 2007 San Diego Padres.

## Clean Sweep

There are only three players in major league history whose names begin with the letters "Kot" — Casey Kotchman, Mark Kotsay, and George Kottaras. The 2009 Red Sox had them all.

This understates the fact. Those three players are not merely the only players whose names begin "Kot"; they are actually the only three players whose names — first name or last — contain the letters "Kot" in that order.

## Doubles

David Ortiz has 1,458 career hits, of which 380 are doubles.  As noted elsewhere in this book, this is the highest doubles percentage of all time for a player with 5,000 or more plate appearances.  The list of the all-time top seven includes three current Red Sox:

| | Player | H | 2B | Pct |
|---|---|---|---|---|
| Bos | David Ortiz | 1458 | 380 | 26.1% |
| | Scott Rolen | 1810 | 446 | 24.6% |
| Bos | Mike Lowell | 1567 | 381 | 24.3% |
| | Todd Helton | 2134 | 509 | 23.9% |
| | Carlos Delgado | 2038 | 483 | 23.7% |
| | Ronnie Belliard | 1342 | 318 | 23.7% |
| Bos | Jason Varitek | 1232 | 290 | 23.5% |

However, *many* active players have higher percentages than this with less than 5,000 plate appearances, and most of these players will be pushed far down the list within the next ten years.  Mid-winter acquisition Bill Hall, for example, is at 26.4%, Kevin Youkilis is at 24.7%, and Dustin Pedroia has 145 doubles among 580 hits, which is 25.0%.

## Noted in Passing

Jon Lester, with a career won-lost record of 42-16, has the highest career winning percentage since 1900 for a pitcher with 50 or more decisions.  The only pitcher in baseball history with a higher winning percentage was Albert Spalding (1876-1877), who was 48-12.

But, not to mislead you, this is a record that you definitely should not take too seriously at this time.  Many young pitchers *have had* very high career winning percentages early in their careers.  Whitey Ford, for example, was 105-40 through 1958, the same percentage as Lester's, and Ron Guidry was 76-29 through 1980, also the same percentage.  Sooner or later, everybody has a bad year, and his percentage goes down.

## It Has To Sometime

After six years in the majors, Kevin Youkilis' OPS has never gone down. His OPS line reads .780, .805, .810, .843, .958, .961.

That's five years of improvement. The major league record for most consecutive years improving your OPS from the previous season is six, held by 13 players, most recently David Ortiz (2002-2007).

## Red Sox First Basemen

In the last two seasons, Red Sox first baseman Kevin Youkilis has finished third and sixth in the MVP voting. This is an accomplishment of some historic stature. Only very, very good players are able to make multiple runs at an MVP Award.

Still, this does not make Kevin Youkilis the greatest first baseman in Red Sox history. The Red Sox have been playing for 109 years, they have had many first basemen having tremendous seasons, and two of them (Jimmie Foxx in 1938 and Mo Vaughn in 1995) have actually won the Award. The position has been manned for a total of 13 years by players now in the Hall of Fame (Foxx — 6, Yastrzemski — 5, Tony Perez — 2). Where does Youkilis rank, among Red Sox all-time first basemen, and, more to the point, what exactly would he have to do to become the greatest Red Sox first baseman of all time?

I decided to do one of my long-winded and stupid studies about this issue. First, I made a list of all Red Sox regular first basemen, 1901 to 2009, one first baseman a year. Second, I ranked them, 1 through 109. Third, I awarded points — 109 points for the best season ever, 108 points for the second-best, etc. The worst Red Sox first baseman of all time — George Scott in 1968, hitting .171 with 3 homers in 350 at-bats — received 1 point for that accomplishment. I then totaled up the points.

In a moment I'll show you what I have, but first let me share the list with you. These are the top ten seasons ever by Red Sox first basemen, as I rate them:

| Rank | Player | Year | AB | H | HR | RBI | AVG | OPS |
|---|---|---|---|---|---|---|---|---|
| 1. | Jimmie Foxx | 1938 | 565 | 197 | 50 | 175 | .349 | 1.166 |
| 2. | Jimmie Foxx | 1936 | 585 | 198 | 41 | 143 | .338 | 1.071 |
| 3. | Jimmie Foxx | 1939 | 467 | 168 | 35 | 105 | .360 | 1.158 |
| 4. | Mo Vaughn | 1996 | 635 | 207 | 44 | 143 | .326 | 1.003 |
| 5. | Carl Yastrzemski | 1970 | 566 | 186 | 40 | 102 | .329 | 1.044 |
| 6. | Mo Vaughn | 1998 | 609 | 205 | 40 | 115 | .337 | .993 |
| 7. | Walt Dropo | 1950 | 559 | 180 | 34 | 144 | .322 | .961 |
| 8. | Dwight Evans | 1987 | 541 | 165 | 34 | 123 | .305 | .986 |
| 9. | Mo Vaughn | 1995 | 550 | 165 | 39 | 126 | .300 | .963 |
| 10. | Jimmie Foxx | 1940 | 515 | 153 | 36 | 119 | .297 | .993 |

And this is how the rest of them rate, without the stats:

| Rank | Player | Year | Rank | Player | Year | Rank | Player | Year |
|---|---|---|---|---|---|---|---|---|
| 11. | J. Foxx | 1937 | 44. | B. Daubach | 2001 | 77. | D. Hoblitzell | 1915 |
| 12. | K. Youkilis | 2008 | 45. | J. Stahl | 1909 | 78. | C. Metkovich | 1945 |
| 13. | M. Vaughn | 1997 | 46. | J. Stahl | 1910 | 79. | M. Grimshaw | 1906 |
| 14. | K. Youkilis | 2009 | 47. | B. Daubach | 2002 | 80. | D. Gernert | 1959 |
| 15. | B. Freeman | 1901 | 48. | B. Buckner | 1986 | 81. | P. Todt | 1929 |
| 16. | M. Vaughn | 1993 | 49. | V. Wertz | 1960 | 82. | H. Agganis | 1954 |
| 17. | D. Evans | 1988 | 50. | C. Yastrzemski | 1975 | 83. | S. McInnis | 1919 |
| 18. | J. Foxx | 1941 | 51. | P. Todt | 1925 | 84. | M. Vaughn | 1992 |
| 19. | G. Burns | 1923 | 52. | B. Goodman | 1948 | 85. | B. Unglaub | 1908 |
| 20. | M. Vaughn | 1994 | 53. | C. Quintana | 1991 | 86. | C. Engle | 1911 |
| 21. | N. Esasky | 1989 | 54. | E. Morgan | 1934 | 87. | C. LaChance | 1902 |
| 22. | G. Scott | 1977 | 55. | G. Scott | 1966 | 88. | B. Sweeney | 1931 |
| 23. | D. Stuart | 1963 | 56. | B. Goodman | 1951 | 89. | D. Hoblitzell | 1914 |
| 24. | C. Yastrzemski | 1973 | 57. | C. Engle | 1913 | 90. | D. Hoblitzell | 1917 |
| 25. | B. Buckner | 1985 | 58. | N. Zauchin | 1955 | 91. | P. Todt | 1926 |
| 26. | C. Yastrzemski | 1974 | 59. | S. McInnis | 1921 | 92. | D. Alexander | 1933 |
| 27. | M. Vernon | 1956 | 60. | G. Scott | 1971 | 93. | M. Vernon | 1957 |
| 28. | R. York | 1946 | 61. | B. Daubach | 2000 | 94. | D. Stapleton | 1983 |
| 29. | K. Youkilis | 2007 | 62. | J. Stahl | 1912 | 95. | S. McInnis | 1920 |
| 30. | D. Stuart | 1964 | 63. | D. Gernert | 1953 | 96. | B. Freeman | 1905 |
| 31. | D. Alexander | 1932 | 64. | D. Gernert | 1952 | 97. | G. Scott | 1978 |
| 32. | P. Runnels | 1962 | 65. | B. Dahlgren | 1935 | 98. | C. LaChance | 1903 |
| 33. | J. Harris | 1924 | 66. | D. Gernert | 1958 | 99. | T. Perez | 1981 |
| 34. | K. Millar | 2003 | 67. | P. Runnels | 1961 | 100. | L. Finney | 1944 |
| 35. | K. Youkilis | 2006 | 68. | P. Todt | 1930 | 101. | B. Unglaub | 1907 |
| 36. | K. Millar | 2004 | 69. | C. Quintana | 1990 | 102. | D. Hoblitzell | 1916 |
| 37. | G. Scott | 1967 | 70. | T. Lupien | 1942 | 103. | T. Lupien | 1943 |
| 38. | T. Perez | 1980 | 71. | B. Goodman | 1949 | 104. | S. McInnis | 1918 |
| 39. | L. Thomas | 1965 | 72. | J. Jones | 1947 | 105. | P. Todt | 1927 |
| 40. | G. Burns | 1922 | 73. | K. Millar | 2005 | 106. | D. Cater | 1972 |
| 41. | C. Yastrzemski | 1976 | 74. | P. Todt | 1928 | 107. | D. Jones | 1969 |
| 42. | B. Watson | 1979 | 75. | B. Buckner | 1984 | 108. | C. LaChance | 1904 |
| 43. | M. Stanley | 1999 | 76. | D. Stapleton | 1982 | 109. | G. Scott | 1968 |

Following through on the methodology I outlined at the top, we give Jimmie Foxx 109 points for his 1938 season, 108 for 1935, 107 for 1939. You might think that this would make Foxx the #1 Red Sox first baseman of all time, but it doesn't. These are the top 20:

| Rank | Player | Seasons | Points | Rank | Player | Seasons | Points |
|---|---|---|---|---|---|---|---|
| 1. | Mo Vaughn | 7 | 618 | 11. | Jake Stahl | 3 | 177 |
| 2. | Jimmie Foxx | 6 | 615 | 12. | Dick Stuart | 2 | 167 |
| 3. | Carl Yastrzemski | 5 | 404 | 13. | Dick Gernert | 4 | 167 |
| 4. | Kevin Youkilis | 4 | 350 | 14. | George H. Burns | 2 | 161 |
| 5. | George Scott | 6 | 280 | 15. | Billy Goodman | 3 | 151 |
| 6. | Dwight Evans | 2 | 195 | 16. | Pete Runnels | 2 | 121 |
| 7. | Phil Todt | 6 | 190 | 17. | Buck Freeman | 2 | 109 |
| 8. | Kevin Millar | 3 | 187 | 18. | Walt Dropo | 1 | 103 |
| 9. | Bill Buckner | 3 | 182 | 19. | Mickey Vernon | 2 | 100 |
| 10. | Brian Daubach | 3 | 178 | 20. | Stuffy McInnis | 4 | 99 |

So Youkilis ranks, at this time, as the fourth-greatest first baseman in Red Sox history. What he would have to do, to rank as the greatest first baseman in Red Sox history, is to hold the job another four years and play about as well as he has played so far.

See, part of the deal is, *the Red Sox have never had a career first baseman.* Ever. The most seasons that anyone has played there, as a regular, is seven, by Mo Vaughn (1992-1998). The position has been played, for almost all of Red Sox history, by people who came in and were there for a couple of years and then were gone, like Kevin Millar and Dick Stuart and Mickey Vernon and Bill Buckner. Jimmie Foxx hit 222 homers with the Red Sox, 312 with other teams. Phil Todt and Brian Daubach spent basically their whole careers as Red Sox first basemen, but they were very modest careers. Scott was the Red Sox' first baseman, spent a couple of years at third base, came back for a year, got traded to Milwaukee, and came back again toward the end of his career. Dick Gernert played the position throughout the 1950s whenever nobody else wanted to. If Youkilis puts in his whole career as the Red Sox' first baseman, he will be the best they've ever had.

## Playing Possum

The Red Sox in 2009 scored 136 runs after there were two out and nobody on — the most of any major league team. Think about it. It's almost one run a game after there were two out and nobody on.

The Mets scored 56.

| Red Sox | | | | Mets | | | |
|---|---|---|---|---|---|---|---|
| Situation | Occurred | Runs | Pct | Situation | Occurred | Runs | Pct |
| None on, none out | 1513 | 931 | .615 | None on, none out | 1476 | 682 | .462 |
| None on, one out | 1056 | 375 | .355 | None on, one out | 1022 | 205 | .201 |
| None on, two out | 818 | 136 | .166 | None on, two out | 813 | 56 | .069 |

## When He Was Good

A "gem" is any game in which the starting pitcher pitches 6 or more innings of shutout ball, or any game in which the starting pitcher has a game score of at least 65.

Between August 29 and the end of the season, Clay Buchholz pitched four gems. Combining the four games he pitched 29 innings, giving up 16 hits and 2 runs, with a strikeout-to-walk ratio of 27 to 6.

**Boston Red Sox — 2009**

| Pitcher | Date | Game Score | IP | H | R | ER | BB | SO |
|---|---|---|---|---|---|---|---|---|
| Clay Buchholz | 8/29/2009 | 80 | 8.1 | 3 | 1 | 1 | 2 | 9 |
| Paul Byrd | 8/30/2009 | 64 | 6.0 | 3 | 0 | 0 | 3 | 1 |
| Jon Lester | 9/6/2009 | 75 | 7.0 | 4 | 0 | 0 | 2 | 8 |
| Clay Buchholz | 9/8/2009 | 75 | 7.0 | 3 | 0 | 0 | 1 | 5 |
| Clay Buchholz | 9/13/2009 | 65 | 7.0 | 5 | 1 | 1 | 3 | 5 |
| Jon Lester | 9/13/2009 | 82 | 8.0 | 2 | 0 | 0 | 3 | 7 |
| Daisuke Matsuzaka | 9/15/2009 | 68 | 6.0 | 3 | 0 | 0 | 3 | 5 |
| Clay Buchholz | 9/24/2009 | 72 | 6.2 | 5 | 0 | 0 | 0 | 8 |
| Jon Lester | 10/1/2009 | 75 | 6.1 | 2 | 0 | 0 | 1 | 7 |

## Frittered

On August 6, 2009, at Yankee Stadium, the Red Sox got their leadoff man on in eight consecutive innings — and were never in the game. They left 15 runners on base, and lost by seven runs.

There was only one other major league game in which a team got the leadoff man on eight times. That was done by Kansas City.

| Leadoff Hitter Reached | W-L |
|---|---|
| 8 times | 0-1 |
| 7 times | 0-1 |
| 6 times | 6-0 |
| 5 times | 15-7 |
| 4 times | 24-10 |
| 3 times | 23-12 |
| 2 times | 16-23 |
| 1 times | 9-7 |
| 0 times | 2-6 |
| Total, 4 or more LO men on | 45-19 |
| Total, 3 or less LO men on | 50-48 |

# The Doubles Record

by Bill James

I WANTED TO GO ON RECORD, MORE FORCEFULLY THAN I have before, in stating that the career record for doubles will be broken within twenty years.

Why?

Because everybody tells me that I'm wrong.

I remember in the 1970s, trying to argue that there would be a flood of pitchers from that generation who won 300 games. People gave me every reason under the sun why this couldn't possibly happen — but Carlton, Sutton, Seaver, Gaylord Perry, Nolan Ryan and Phil Niekro all won 300 games, after we had had only two 300-game winners in the previous 50 years.

I remember in the 1980s, when Cal Ripken had played in about 350 consecutive games, I wrote a Cal Ripken comment in one year's *Abstract* arguing that Lou Gehrig's "invincible" consecutive-game streak was in fact a vulnerable record that could well be broken. People gave me 500 reasons why I was wrong.

*Much of sabermetrics is about recognizing sustainable and unsustainable ratios. That's an unsustainable ratio.*

I remember when I first went to the Red Sox, Derek Lowe won 21 games with 127 strikeouts my first year there, and I made a chance remark that of course he couldn't do that again. Much of sabermetrics is about recognizing sustainable and unsustainable ratios. That's an unsustainable ratio. You can't win one game for every six strikeouts, consistently; it just can't be done — but Red Sox fans gave me 40 or 400 reasons why this didn't apply to Derek Lowe. It did.

And, since I observed last year that Tris Speaker's career record of 792 doubles has perhaps become vulnerable, y'all have given me about 40 reasons why I'm wrong about this. It's stuff like, "right-handed hitters don't hit many doubles after they're 30" and "doubles are different than homers and stolen bases because the same people don't lead the league in doubles every year."

Well, OK. You can believe that if you want to. I'm telling you, this record is going to be broken.

In modern baseball, the league leader in doubles normally hits about 54 doubles. That's less than a 15-1 ratio between the league leader and the all-time record. History shows that a 15-1 ratio between the league leader and the all-time record is an unsustainable ratio. You can give me 360 more reasons why that doesn't apply here, but it won't stop the record from being broken.

## Doubles as a Percentage of Hits

It occurred to me that perhaps we could gain some insight into this subject by looking at the percentage of a player's hits that were doubles, let's call it their "doubles percentage". In other words, Speaker hit 792 doubles in his career, which is the record. Is it reasonable to think that his record could be broken by a player getting 2,800 hits, let's say? Or 2,900 hits, or 3,000, or 3,100? At what doubles percentage does it become conceivable that a player could break the doubles record? And how many players are there today who could break the doubles record if they sustained their doubles percentage for 3,000 hits? For 3,100 hits? Etc. Once we know that, then we're in a better position to estimate what the chances are that the doubles record will be broken.

This was an eye-opening question, and I will now state that, beyond any question, the doubles record will be broken in the next generation, unless the game goes backward in this respect...goes backward in a way that it has been moving forward since the late 1970s. The percentage of doubles hit (doubles as a percentage of hits) in this generation is totally out of line with all previous generations, in a way that makes it apparent that this is just a different problem than it was ten years ago.

OK, let's start here. I figured the doubles percentage after every season for every player who had played at least 1,000 games in his career. In other words, after the 1922 season there were 155 active major league players who had played at least 1,000 games. Among those players, the highest doubles percentage was by Tris Speaker, who had at that time collected 545 doubles among 2,576 career hits, or 21.2%. The only other player over 20% was Steve O'Neill, who was Speaker's protégé, sort of, who was at 20.3%, and they were followed by Del Pratt (19.3%), Bobby Veach (18.8%) and Jack Graney (18.6%).

Speaker's doubles percentage went up in his declining years. In his last year, 1928, he had only 51 hits, but 22 of them were doubles. His final doubles percentage was 22.5%, which was the high-water mark of his career. At that time, this was the highest figure on record. The highest ever, through 1930, were:

| Player | Through | Pct |
|---|---|---|
| Tris Speaker | 1928 | 22.5% |
| Tris Speaker | 1927 | 22.2% |
| Ira Flagstead | 1928 | 22.1% |
| Tris Speaker | 1926 | 22.1% |
| Bob Meusel | 1928 | 22.1% |
| George H. Burns | 1929 | 22.0% |

And then more years of the same players. It is apparent that the numbers for that generation of players were higher than for any previous generation. When I run charts like this in the future I will list only players at their *highest* level, the highest doubles percentage that they ever had at the end of a season, past 1,000 career games played.

OK, let me focus your attention on that number: .225. Speaker had a hell of a lot of hits in his career — 3,514. Lot of hits. He had a huge number of hits, and he had the highest doubles percentage (among his hits) of any player in history. That combination put him in a position that would prove unassailable through the next 80 years.

*I'm telling you, this record is going to be broken.*

This, however, was not apparent for the first few years. Speaker's doubles percentages were an all-time record through 1930, but several players sailed past him in the 1930s. Through 1940, the all-time leaders were:

| Player | Through | Pct |
| --- | --- | --- |
| Hank Greenberg | 1940 | 24.4% |
| Chick Hafey | 1933 | 24.1% |
| Joe Medwick | 1939 | 23.7% |
| Joe Cronin | 1938 | 23.1% |
| Gabby Hartnett | 1932 | 22.7% |
| Tris Speaker | 1928 | 22.5% |
| Odell Hale | 1940 | 22.5% |
| Val Picinich | 1933 | 22.3% |
| Pepper Martin | 1939 | 22.2% |
| Bob Meusel | 1929 | 22.1% |

And, of course, many other years of the same players, but I'm leaving those out. Through 1940, it appeared that Speaker was being pushed down this list so rapidly that he would soon disappear from it, and thus that someone could break his doubles record without even getting real close to 3,514 career hits.

During World War II, however, doubles totals dropped off — and never really recovered. In 1950 this list was essentially the same as it had been in 1940:

| Player | Through | Pct |
| --- | --- | --- |
| Hank Greenberg | 1941 | 24.4% |
| Chick Hafey | 1933 | 24.1% |
| Joe Medwick | 1939 | 23.7% |
| Joe Cronin | 1938 | 23.1% |
| Lou Boudreau | 1947 | 23.0% |
| Gabby Hartnett | 1932 | 22.7% |
| Tris Speaker | 1928 | 22.5% |
| Odell Hale | 1940 | 22.5% |
| Val Picinich | 1933 | 22.3% |
| Pepper Martin | 1939 | 22.2% |

Lou Boudreau broke onto the list in 1947, but then in 1948, when he had his MVP year, hit "only" 34 doubles, so that his percentage went down. His percentage went down for the rest of his career, so that

the post-1947 figure was his high-water mark.

And there the list sat, for thirty years. No one broke onto the list in the 1950s or the 1960s. The list in 1977 was exactly the same as it had been in 1947. The player who finally ended that was Hal McRae, who hit 54 doubles in 1977. He hadn't played 1,000 career games at that time, but he appeared on the list when he went over 1,000 games in 1978, and then his number went up in 1979 and up again in 1980. By 1980 this was the list:

| Player | Through | Pct |
| --- | --- | --- |
| Hank Greenberg | 1941 | 24.4% |
| Chick Hafey | 1933 | 24.1% |
| Hal McRae | 1980 | 24.0% |
| Joe Medwick | 1939 | 23.7% |
| Joe Cronin | 1938 | 23.1% |
| Lou Boudreau | 1947 | 23.0% |
| Gabby Hartnett | 1932 | 22.7% |
| Tris Speaker | 1928 | 22.5% |
| Odell Hale | 1940 | 22.5% |
| Val Picinich | 1933 | 22.3% |

McRae was an outstanding hitter who, had he not had a very serious leg injury at the start of his career, very probably might have hit 750+ doubles. Pete Rose had a huge number of hits, but his doubles percentage was just 17.5. If McRae had had as many hits as Pete Rose, his doubles total would have been 985. In 1988 McRae was bumped out of the third spot by, improbably enough, Rance Mulliniks:

| Player | Through | Pct |
| --- | --- | --- |
| Hank Greenberg | 1941 | 24.4% |
| Rance Mulliniks | 1988 | 24.3% |
| Chick Hafey | 1933 | 24.1% |
| Hal McRae | 1980 | 24.0% |
| Joe Medwick | 1939 | 23.7% |
| Joe Cronin | 1938 | 23.1% |
| Fred Lynn | 1982 | 23.0% |
| Lou Boudreau | 1947 | 23.0% |
| Gabby Hartnett | 1932 | 22.7% |
| Tris Speaker | 1928 | 22.5% |

And also Fred Lynn made the list for a minute. Mulliniks was a left-handed hitter, originally a shortstop but not really quick enough to play shortstop, who settled into a role as a platoon third baseman. He never played against lefties, and he pulled the ball right down the first base line a lot, almost like a left-handed Kevin Millar or Gary Sheffield; Millar and Sheffield rip the ball right down the third-base line all the time.

Anyway, the list was beginning to move; Tris Speaker was now down to the 10th position in doubles percentage, although some of those ahead of him dropped below him before their careers ended. In the 1990s, Speaker was pushed farther down the line by an improbable array of players, most of whom you probably never thought of as hitting a lot of doubles:

| Player | Through | Pct |
|---|---|---|
| Hank Greenberg | 1941 | 24.4% |
| Mike Macfarlane | 1999 | 24.4% |
| Rance Mulliniks | 1988 | 24.3% |
| Chick Hafey | 1933 | 24.1% |
| Edgar Martinez | 1997 | 24.0% |
| Hal McRae | 1980 | 24.0% |
| Joe Medwick | 1939 | 23.7% |
| Tim Teufel | 1993 | 23.4% |
| Sid Bream | 1994 | 23.3% |
| John Olerud | 1997 | 23.2% |
| Joe Cronin | 1938 | 23.1% |
| Fred Lynn | 1982 | 23.0% |
| Lou Boudreau | 1947 | 23.0% |
| Ray Lankford | 1999 | 23.0% |
| Luis Gonzalez | 2000 | 22.9% |
| Larry Walker | 1998 | 22.8% |
| Albert Belle | 1998 | 22.8% |
| Gabby Hartnett | 1932 | 22.7% |
| Jeff Kent | 1999 | 22.6% |
| Tris Speaker | 1928 | 22.5% |

Greenberg held on to the number one spot, where he had been since he passed 1,000 career games in 1940, but Speaker dropped from tenth to twentieth on this list in ten years, due to the unexpected incursions of players like Tim Teufel and Sid Bream. Many of these men were not great hitters and were no threat to any record, but Albert Belle, Edgar Martinez and Larry Walker were formidable hitters. Had any of these men stayed healthy long enough, he could have made a run at 800 doubles. All of them, however, had injury-plagued careers.

Greenberg was finally knocked out of the top spot by an unlikely hero: John Valentin. Valentin crossed 1,000 games played in his last season, 2002, and with a higher doubles percentage than Greenberg. Since 2000, the incursion has become a full-fledged invasion. The current list is:

| Player | Through | Pct |
|---|---|---|
| David Ortiz | 2009 | 26.1% |
| John Valentin | 2002 | 25.7% |
| Mike Lowell | 2006 | 25.4% |
| Cliff Floyd | 2004 | 25.1% |
| Brian Roberts | 2009 | 25.0% |
| Doug Mientkiewicz | 2008 | 24.6% |
| Scott Rolen | 2009 | 24.6% |
| Carlos Delgado | 2003 | 24.6% |
| Hank Greenberg | 1941 | 24.4% |
| Orlando Cabrera | 2006 | 24.4% |

Not only is Speaker being rapidly pushed away from the top of the list, but Hank Greenberg, who ten years ago was the record-holder, may be pushed out of the top ten within the next year or two. Speaker has been surpassed in recent seasons not only by these eight players, but also by many, many more — Todd Helton, Jason Varitek, Jose Vidro, Michael Barrett, Ron Belliard, John Vander Wal, Geoff Jenkins, Kevin Millar, Bobby Abreu, Gerald Williams, Kevin Young, Jorge Posada, Frank Catalanotto, Lance Berkman, Deivi Cruz, and others. You know the two Alex Gonzalezes, the two shortstops who are so hard to keep straight unless one of them is local? Speaker's doubles percentage has been surpassed not only by one of them, but by both of them.

Simply stated, Tris Speaker's doubles percentage is no longer a high figure. I don't know if he's in the top 50 anymore. If he is, he won't be for long.

Doubles totals go up; they can go down. Nothing is inevitable before it is imminent, and Speaker's doubles total being broken is not imminent.

## Doubles and Career Length

At the start of this study, I posed the question, "could this record be broken by someone getting 2,800 hits in his career?" The answer to that is still "No". In order to get 792 doubles with 2,800 career hits, you would need a doubles percentage of 28.3. That's still well ahead of the record, currently 26.1. This is the chart:

| With Hits | Pct Needed |
|---|---|
| 2,800 | 28.3% |
| 2,900 | 27.3% |
| 3,000 | 26.4% |
| 3,100 | 25.5% |
| 3,200 | 24.8% |
| 3,300 | 24.0% |
| 3,400 | 23.3% |
| 3,500 | 22.6% |

Albert Pujols' doubles percentage is 22.5, the same as Speaker's. At that rate he would need 3,518 career hits, which is a lot of hits, but not necessarily an impossible number for somebody like Albert.

What is more likely, though, is that somebody will break the doubles record with 3,200 to 3,300 hits. There aren't a lot of players who get 3,200 or 3,300 hits. It will require a great player to break the record, and at this point we can't foresee who that will be. David Ortiz, for example, didn't get started soon enough.

Still, there are so many players now who hit doubles on 23 or 24% of their hits that the record is simply not what it was a few years ago. 792 doubles now is like 720 fifteen years ago. If doubles totals stay where they are, Speaker's record has to be broken.

There is an argument made that this is less likely because more players now go to college before entering pro baseball, which shortens their careers. That may be true on one level: there may be more players now who go to college, and it may be that college players are less likely to have very long careers.

But the number of players having very long careers isn't going down; it's going up, and going up very rapidly. To break the doubles record, you would need to play at least 2,500 career games. (Paul Waner, who played 2,549 games, had 3,152 hits, and Sam Crawford, who holds the career triples record, played 2,517 games.)

In all of baseball history up to 1970, there were only ten retired players who had played in 2,500 games (plus two active in 1970 who were past that mark). Since 1970 there have been 37 players who played 2,500 or more games — 8 who retired in the 1970s, 9 in the 1980s, 9 in the 1990s, and 14 who have played since 2000. More players active since 2000 have played 2,500 career games than in all of baseball history up to 1970.

The number of players having very long careers responds to many external variables — college, perhaps, but also the length of the schedule, the DH rule, expansion, financial incentives to keep playing, and better health care. The balance of these factors is not reducing the number of players who play long enough to hit 800 doubles; it is, in fact, dramatically increasing it.

As I said, the record for career doubles will be broken in the next twenty years.

(The lowest doubles percentage of all time, incidentally, was Roy Thomas through 1906. Through 1906 Thomas had played 1,115 games and had 1,240 major league hits, of which only 63 were doubles, or 5.1%. Other than Thomas, the champion "non-doubles" hitter of all time was Maury Wills, followed by Willie Keeler, Patsy Donovan, Al Bridwell and John McGraw.)

# Chicago Cubs

| | | | | | | |
|---|---|---|---|---|---|---|
| ML RANK | 22nd | 12th | 25th | 9th | 20th | 27th |

**2009 TEAM OVERVIEW**

**83-78**

**2**nd place **NL Central**

| | RUNS | HOME RUNS | BATTING AVG. | WALKS | OPS | STOLEN BASES |
|---|---|---|---|---|---|---|
| **Team** | **707** | **161** | **.255** | **592** | **.739** | **56** |
| **Opp.** | **672** | **160** | **.246** | **586** | **.715** | **89** |
| ML RANK | 4th | 9th | 3rd | 18th | 6th | 8th |

## Key Players

| Pos | Player | G | AB | R | H | 2B | 3B | HR | RBI | SB | CS | BB | SO | AVG | OBP | SLG | OPS | WS |
|---|---|---|---|---|---|---|---|---|---|---|---|---|---|---|---|---|---|---|
| C | Geovany Soto | 102 | 331 | 27 | 72 | 19 | 1 | 11 | 47 | 1 | 0 | 50 | 77 | .218 | .321 | .381 | .702 | 8 |
| 1B | Derrek Lee | 141 | 532 | 91 | 163 | 36 | 2 | 35 | 111 | 1 | 0 | 76 | 109 | .306 | .393 | .579 | .972 | 24 |
| 2B | Mike Fontenot | 135 | 377 | 38 | 89 | 22 | 2 | 9 | 43 | 4 | 1 | 35 | 83 | .236 | .301 | .377 | .677 | 7 |
| 3B | Aramis Ramirez | 82 | 306 | 46 | 97 | 14 | 1 | 15 | 65 | 2 | 1 | 28 | 43 | .317 | .389 | .516 | .905 | 15 |
| SS | Ryan Theriot | 154 | 602 | 81 | 171 | 20 | 5 | 7 | 54 | 21 | 10 | 51 | 93 | .284 | .343 | .369 | .712 | 17 |
| LF | Alfonso Soriano | 117 | 477 | 64 | 115 | 25 | 1 | 20 | 55 | 9 | 2 | 40 | 118 | .241 | .303 | .423 | .726 | 10 |
| CF | Kosuke Fukudome | 146 | 499 | 79 | 129 | 38 | 5 | 11 | 54 | 6 | 10 | 93 | 112 | .259 | .375 | .421 | .796 | 17 |
| RF | Milton Bradley | 124 | 393 | 61 | 101 | 17 | 1 | 12 | 40 | 2 | 3 | 66 | 95 | .257 | .378 | .397 | .775 | 11 |

## Key Pitchers

| Pos | Player | G | GS | W | L | SV | IP | H | R | ER | SO | BB | BR/9 | ERA | WS |
|---|---|---|---|---|---|---|---|---|---|---|---|---|---|---|---|
| SP | Ryan Dempster | 31 | 31 | 11 | 9 | 0 | 200.0 | 196 | 94 | 81 | 172 | 65 | 12.02 | 3.65 | 12 |
| SP | Ted Lilly | 27 | 27 | 12 | 9 | 0 | 177.0 | 151 | 66 | 61 | 151 | 36 | 9.61 | 3.10 | 14 |
| SP | Carlos Zambrano | 28 | 28 | 9 | 7 | 0 | 169.1 | 155 | 78 | 71 | 152 | 78 | 12.86 | 3.77 | 10 |
| SP | Randy Wells | 27 | 27 | 12 | 10 | 0 | 165.1 | 165 | 67 | 56 | 104 | 46 | 11.81 | 3.05 | 13 |
| SP | Rich Harden | 26 | 26 | 9 | 9 | 0 | 141.0 | 122 | 74 | 64 | 171 | 67 | 12.45 | 4.09 | 7 |
| CL | Kevin Gregg | 72 | 0 | 5 | 6 | 23 | 68.2 | 60 | 38 | 36 | 71 | 30 | 12.19 | 4.72 | 7 |
| RP | Aaron Heilman | 70 | 0 | 4 | 4 | 1 | 72.1 | 68 | 34 | 33 | 65 | 34 | 12.82 | 4.11 | 5 |
| RP | Carlos Marmol | 79 | 0 | 2 | 4 | 15 | 74.0 | 43 | 29 | 28 | 93 | 65 | 14.59 | 3.41 | 10 |

## League-Leading Lilly

Ted Lilly threw strikes 56.2% of the time, the highest percentage of strikes of any starting pitcher in the majors. He walked 1.8 batters per 9 innings pitched, a new career low. That is less than half the rate he walked batters from 2004 to 2006 when he was with Toronto.

Lilly also had the lowest ground ball to fly ball ratio in the league. Six of the ten pitchers in the two top tens overlapped.

| Lowest Ground Ball to Fly Ball Ratio | | | Percent of Pitches in the Strike Zone | |
|---|---|---|---|---|
| Player | Ratio | | Player | Pct |
| 1. Ted Lilly, ChC | .63 | | 1. Ted Lilly, ChC | 56.2% |
| 2. Johan Santana, NYM | .75 | | 2. Johan Santana, NYM | 53.8% |
| 3. Aaron Harang, Cin | .84 | | 3. Roy Oswalt, Hou | 52.7% |
| 4. J.A. Happ, Phi | .90 | | 4. Chris Carpenter, StL | 51.5% |
| 5. Matt Cain, SF | .92 | | 5. Cole Hamels, Phi | 51.4% |
| 6. Barry Zito, SF | .94 | | 6. J.A. Happ, Phi | 51.3% |
| 7. Randy Wolf, LAD | .94 | | 7. Joel Pineiro, StL | 51.2% |
| 8. Jonathan Sanchez, SF | .95 | | 8. Randy Wolf, LAD | 50.9% |
| 9. Clayton Kershaw, LAD | .95 | | 9. Matt Cain, SF | 50.6% |
| 10. Ricky Nolasco, FLA | .96 | | 10. Barry Zito, SF | 50.6% |
| Minimum 162 Innings Pitched | | | Minimum 162 Innings Pitched | |

## North Side Sliders

Ryan Dempster threw 1,067 sliders last season, 130 more than any other pitcher. Only seven starting pitchers in the National League used their slider more than 25%, and three of them were Cubs.

**Highest Percentage of Sliders**

| Player | Pct |
|---|---|
| 1. Ryan Dempster, ChC | 34.3% |
| 2. Kevin Correia, SD | 30.3% |
| 3. Johnny Cueto, Cin | 29.7% |
| 4. Chris Carpenter, StL | 27.6% |
| 5. Randy Wells, ChC | 27.4% |
| 6. Derek Lowe, Atl | 26.6% |
| 7. Ted Lilly, ChC | 25.9% |

Minimum 162 Innings Pitched

## Big Z Batting

Carlos Zambrano now has 563 major league at-bats — a normal full-season total for a position player — and has hit 20 home runs and 24 doubles, driving in 58 runs with a respectable .236 batting average. His strikeout-to-walk ratio is a little ragged. It's 203 to 6. Still, he is the second-best hitting pitcher in baseball. The best is Micah Owings.

## Excellence Unrewarded

Randy Wells finished 10th in the league in ERA at 3.05. He did his best work without being rewarded. His ERA of 1.27 in five starts where he received No-Decision was the lowest in No-Decisions of any pitcher who qualified for the ERA title.

**Randy Wells 2009**

| Group | G | IP | W | L | Pct | H | R | SO | BB | ERA |
|---|---|---|---|---|---|---|---|---|---|---|
| Wins | 12 | 78.2 | 12 | 0 | 1.000 | 73 | 19 | 51 | 15 | 2.06 |
| Losses | 10 | 58.1 | 0 | 10 | .000 | 69 | 39 | 36 | 22 | 5.25 |
| No-Decisions | 5 | 28.1 | 0 | 0 | ---- | 23 | 9 | 17 | 9 | 1.27 |

Quality Starts: 11 in Wins, 4 in Losses, 3 in No-Decisions

## Crowd the Plate at Your Own Risk

Carlos Marmol hit 12 batters in 74 innings pitched, one for every 6.17 innings he pitched.

Among pitchers since 1901 who have hit 10 batters or more in a season, Marmol's ratio of hit batters to innings pitched is the fifth-highest.

In 2000 Bulldog Hershiser hit 11 batters in just 24 innings pitched.

**Highest Ratio of Hit Batsmen per Inning Pitched**

| Player | Year | HBP | IP | IP/HB |
|---|---|---|---|---|
| 1. Orel Hershiser , LAD | 2000 | 11 | 24.2 | 2.24 |
| 2. Jack Warhop, NYY | 1913 | 12 | 62.1 | 5.19 |
| 3. Jerry Spradlin, Cle-SF | 1999 | 10 | 61.0 | 6.10 |
| 4. Jack Killilay, Bos | 1911 | 10 | 61.0 | 6.10 |
| 5. Carlos Marmol , ChC | 2009 | 12 | 74.0 | 6.17 |

Since 1901 – Minimum 10 HBP

## Oh, For the Long One

The Cubs in 2009 were 11-43 in games in which they did not hit a home run — the second-worst winning percentage in the majors in those games. The Cubs were 72-35 when they did hit a homer, sixth-best in the majors.

The difference in their winning percentages when they homered and they didn't was .469. The major league average difference was .267.

| Chicago Cubs 2009 | |
| --- | --- |
| **Home Runs** | **W-L** |
| 0 homers | 11-43 |
| 1 homer | 40-26 |
| 2 homers | 23-8 |
| 3+ homers | 9-1 |

## Lee's Other Half

Derrek Lee hit .336 in the second half of the season and his 1.092 on-base plus slugging percentage was the best in the majors.

| Best OPS — 2nd Half | |
| --- | --- |
| **Player** | **OPS** |
| 1. Derrek Lee, ChC | 1.092 |
| 2. Matt Holliday, Oak-StL | 1.048 |
| 3. Troy Tulowitzki, Col | 1.042 |
| 4. Adrian Gonzalez, SD | 1.018 |
| 5. Albert Pujols, StL | 1.009 |

Minimum 201 Plate Appearances

## Stolen Base Deficiency

The Cubs' 56 stolen bases were the fewest in the majors. They were thrown out 34 times and their 62% stolen base percentage was the worst in the majors.

### RBI the Easy Way

Geovany Soto had 18 plate appearances with the bases loaded and he drew a walk five times. That accounted for more than 10% of his total RBI.

### C'mon Guys — Bring Me In

Geovany Soto hit 41 singles in 2009 — but scored only 3 runs after reaching base on a single.

### Get 'em On, Get 'em Over, What Was Step Three Again?

Ryan Theriot led the National League with 139 singles, but his 38 runs scored after singles was not among the league's top ten.

**Ryan Theriot 2009**

| Reached on | | Runs Scored After | |
|---|---|---|---|
| Home Runs | 7 | | 7 |
| Triples | 5 | Scored after Triple | 1 |
| Doubles | 20 | Scored after Double | 9 |
| Singles | 139 | Scored after Single | 38 |
| Walk/HBP | 57 | Scored after Walk/HBP | 23 |
| Reached on Error | 3 | Scored after ROE | 1 |
| Reached on Forceout | 16 | Vultured Runs | 2 |
| | | **Total Runs Scored** | **81** |

### Not So Tough Competition

The Cubs had high hopes for 2009 after their playoff appearance in 2008. Not only were they disappointing, but according to Bill's new Season Score method (see p. 273), they faced the easiest opposition pitching in the entire National League.

# Four Chicagos for Cooperstown

## by Bill James

PLEASE REST ASSURED THAT I AM NOT ABOUT TO MAKE AN argument that Andre Dawson's selection to the Hall of Fame was a mistake. I don't think that, first of all, and, if I did, there is a time to say those things and a time to keep your thoughts to yourself. If that was what I thought, this would be a really good example of the latter. It is disrespectful to the Hall of Fame and to the player, in my view, to use the occasion of a player's Hall of Fame selection and induction to speak poorly of his accomplishments. If I didn't think Andre Dawson was a deserving Hall of Famer, I wouldn't be talking about it right now — next year, or last year, but not right now.

*I wouldn't be talking about it right now — next year, or last year, but not right now.*

I got interested in the question, however, of Minnie Minoso vs. Andre Dawson. Which player had the better career? Both players were outfielders. Both players have strong ties to Chicago, having played at least some of their best years there, and both players were very popular players, for different reasons. Dawson was popular because he was a class act, dignified and respectful of the game; Minoso was popular because he was colorful and exciting.

In other respects they are opposites. Andre Dawson came to the majors at the age of 21, had some fine years early in his career, and appeared, through much of his career, to be on a Hall of Fame glide path. He had a Hall of Fame career that could have been a lot better. At ages 22 and 23, 1977-1978, he was probably regarded as the best young outfielder in baseball:

| Year | Age | G | AB | HR | RBI | AVG | SLG | OBA | OPS | W | L | PCT |
|------|-----|-----|-----|----|-----|------|------|------|------|----|----|------|
| 1976 | 21 | 24 | 85 | 0 | 7 | .235 | .306 | .278 | .584 | 1 | 4 | .284 |
| 1977 | 22 | 139 | 525 | 19 | 65 | .282 | .474 | .326 | .800 | 17 | 11 | .617 |
| 1978 | 23 | 157 | 609 | 25 | 72 | .253 | .442 | .299 | .740 | 20 | 15 | .573 |

I'll have to explain a word about Win Shares and Loss Shares here, because you never know who might be reading. You might be a cop — or, worse yet, an architect. The theory of Win Shares and Loss Shares is that everything a player does on a baseball field can be described as a small part of a Win or a small part of a Loss. If a player strikes out, that's a piece of a loss. If he hits a home run, that's a piece of a Win.

The bits and pieces of wins and losses may be added up into "Shares" of Wins and "Shares" of Losses. Each Win and each Loss has three shares. Win Shares and Loss Shares are a way of adding together all of the things a player does to look at them in the terms that count — Wins and Losses. Andre Dawson in 1976, when he played only 24 games in September and hit just .237, earned only one Win Share, while taking four Loss Shares — one and four (1-4). In 1977, when he was NL Rookie of the Year, he earned 17 Win Shares, and was charged with 11 Loss Shares — 17 and 11. Like a pitcher's won-lost record, but for a position player as well. We try to state everything the player does — hitting, fielding, pitching and baserunning — as a Win Share or a Loss Share.

Minnie Minoso has different reported ages, and I don't claim to know when he was born. I think the most commonly listed birth date for him is November, 1922, but there may be better evidence for November, 1924. I'm going to treat his birth date as November, 1924, which means that he debuted at age 24 in late 1949, but did not play in the majors in 1950, when he was 25. Dawson, on the other hand, hit .308 with 34 stolen bases in 1980, when he was 25:

| Year | Player | Age | G | AB | HR | RBI | AVG | SLG | OBA | OPS | W | L | PCT |
|------|--------|-----|---|----|----|----|------|------|------|------|---|---|------|
| 1979 | Andre Dawson | 24 | 155 | 639 | 25 | 92 | .275 | .468 | .309 | .777 | 21 | 15 | .581 |
| 1949 | Minnie Minoso | 24 | 9 | 16 | 1 | 1 | .188 | .375 | .350 | .725 | 0 | 1 | .279 |
| 1980 | Andre Dawson | 25 | 151 | 577 | 17 | 87 | .308 | .492 | .358 | .850 | 24 | 8 | .756 |

Through the age of 25, Dawson had a career won-lost record of 84-52. Minoso at 25 — perhaps 27 — was 0 and 1. He was far, far behind.

Minoso was born in Cuba with very dark skin, and was clearly and absolutely covered by the color line. In the past, I have argued that he lost his best years due to segregation. There are people who argue that I am wrong about this, and I will give you their argument as best I understand it.

1) Minoso was not born in 1922, as listed, but 1924 (as assumed here). Thus, he was in the majors when he was 24 years old, not an unusual age to begin a career.

2) Minoso's late start, to the extent that he did start late, was caused not by the color line — which was broken in 1947 — but by Minoso's failure to hit in 1949.

I don't see it that way. First, even if we assume that Minoso was born in 1924, his career start is still very late. Duke Snider was born in 1926; he was in the majors in 1947, and a regular in 1949. Yogi Berra was born in 1925, and was a regular in 1948. Compared to guys like Snider and Berra, Minoso was either four years or six years late in getting his career started, depending on whether he was born in 1922 or 1924. In any case, he was hundreds of games behind schedule.

*The color line did not shatter suddenly and disappear in 1947.*

And second, of course his race had everything to do with that. The color line did not shatter suddenly and disappear in 1947. It eroded slowly over a period of many years. Minoso got a brief shot with the Indians in 1949, when Bill Veeck — an outspoken opponent of segregation — owned the team. When he reported to spring training in 1950, Bill Veeck no longer owned the team.

One of my favorite movies is *The Verdict,* which stars Paul Newman as a down-and-out, alcoholic lawyer doing battle on behalf of a woman put into a coma by a doctor's mistake. At one point Newman hires an expert to testify on his behalf, a doctor, not knowing that the doctor is an elderly black man. The expert is patronized by the court, and appears to have little impact on the jury.

When I watched the movie many years after it was made with my daughter, the movie held up extremely well, but my daughter couldn't relate to the stuff about the black doctor. "So he's black, so what?" she asked. "This was *after* the Civil Rights Act, wasn't it? What difference does it make that he's black?" I had to try to explain — racism didn't dissipate like the morning mist as soon as the Civil Rights Act was passed.

The same here; there wasn't a hard and fast color line after Jackie Robinson, but there was still a color line. If Minnie Minoso was *as good as* a white player, the white player was going to play. Minoso only got to play when he had clearly established that he was *better* than the white guys. Minoso's career started four years or six years late because he was black.

Anyway, he finally got started in 1951, when he was (let's say) 26, went 6-for-14 for Cleveland early in the season, and was traded to the White Sox. Minoso hit .326 in what was really his rookie season, scored 112 runs and stole 31 bases:

| Year | Player | Age | G | AB | HR | RBI | AVG | SLG | OBA | OPS | W | L | PCT |
|------|--------|-----|---|----|----|-----|-----|-----|-----|-----|---|---|-----|
| 1981 | Andre Dawson | 26 | 103 | 394 | 24 | 64 | .302 | .553 | .365 | .918 | 20 | 2 | .922 |
| 1951 | Minnie Minoso (Indians) | 26 | 8 | 14 | 0 | 2 | .429 | .571 | .529 | 1.101 | 1 | 0 | 1.000 |
| 1951 | Minnie Minoso (White Sox) | 26 | 138 | 516 | 10 | 74 | .324 | .498 | .419 | .917 | 24 | 4 | .846 |

Dawson, on the other hand, lost probably his best major league season to the 1981 strike. Dawson hit .302 that year, with 24 homers and 26 stolen bases, a career-high .918 OPS. We have his record at 20-2. It probably should have been 30-3 — his best year — but a third of the season was cancelled due to squabbling.

Minoso got to play in 1951 because the White Sox needed a third baseman, and Minoso could play a little bit of third base. He wasn't really a third baseman, though. He hit .320-something with walks, speed and power, so obviously he could play, but he went to the outfield in 1952. For two years after that, ages 27 and 28, Minoso and Dawson were past the things that had held them back, and both had fine seasons:

| Year | Player | Age | G | AB | HR | RBI | AVG | SLG | OBA | OPS | W | L | PCT |
|------|--------|-----|---|----|----|-----|-----|-----|-----|-----|---|---|-----|
| 1982 | Andre Dawson | 27 | 148 | 608 | 23 | 83 | .301 | .498 | .343 | .841 | 23 | 10 | .693 |
| 1952 | Minnie Minoso | 27 | 147 | 569 | 13 | 61 | .281 | .424 | .375 | .798 | 21 | 12 | .643 |
| 1983 | Andre Dawson | 28 | 159 | 633 | 32 | 113 | .299 | .539 | .338 | .877 | 24 | 11 | .687 |
| 1953 | Minnie Minoso | 28 | 151 | 556 | 15 | 104 | .313 | .466 | .410 | .875 | 22 | 10 | .691 |

Dawson at this point in his career was 151-75, apparently en route to the Hall of Fame. Minoso was 68-26 — a better percentage, but far behind in bulk.

In 1984, however, Dawson began to have trouble with his knees. He was playing in Montreal, a turf park, and the surface at Olympic Stadium was like concrete. Dawson's knees betrayed him, and his performance suffered:

| Year | Player | Age | G | AB | HR | RBI | AVG | SLG | OBA | OPS | W | L | PCT |
|------|--------|-----|---|----|----|----|-----|-----|-----|-----|---|---|-----|
| 1984 | Andre Dawson | 29 | 138 | 533 | 17 | 86 | .248 | .409 | .301 | .710 | 17 | 14 | .553 |
| 1954 | Minnie Minoso | 29 | 153 | 568 | 19 | 116 | .320 | .535 | .411 | .946 | 27 | 5 | .836 |
| 1985 | Andre Dawson | 30 | 139 | 529 | 23 | 91 | .255 | .444 | .295 | .739 | 16 | 14 | .536 |
| 1955 | Minnie Minoso | 30 | 139 | 517 | 10 | 70 | .288 | .424 | .387 | .811 | 19 | 11 | .635 |
| 1986 | Andre Dawson | 31 | 130 | 496 | 20 | 78 | .284 | .478 | .338 | .815 | 16 | 11 | .598 |
| 1956 | Minnie Minoso | 31 | 151 | 545 | 21 | 88 | .316 | .525 | .425 | .950 | 23 | 6 | .782 |

Minoso, outplaying Dawson every year, was catching up.

Minoso was a magnificent player. In 1954, when he hit .320 with 116 RBI, he also hit 18 triples, stole 18 bases, and scored 119 runs. He drew 77 walks, and struck out only 46 times. He was a Gold Glove outfielder. The Gold Gloves weren't introduced until 1957, when Minoso was well past 30, but Minoso won three Gold Gloves (1957-1959-1960). What he did well was "everything". He hit for high averages, walked, didn't strike out, hit for power, ran extremely well, was the most aggressive baserunner of his era, and played outstanding defense in the outfield. He was good every year. Beginning in 1951 he rang up ten straight outstanding seasons, 1955 being the weakest of them, and we have him at 19-11 in 1955.

He also did it with style. He was flashy, and he played hard. He was a great player. Dawson had more power and equal speed, as a young player, but Dawson didn't command the strike zone the way Minoso did.

In the winter of 1986-1987 baseball went through another difficult labor situation, as a part of which major league teams agreed not to sign one another's free agents. It was called "collusion". Collusion is prohibited by labor law. Businesses competing for employees cannot co-operate with one another to hold down wages. Eventually a court ruled against them, and Major League Baseball was ordered to pay some very large amount of money to the players in compensation for their illegal actions.

In the middle of this collusion, the only free agent who got signed was Andre Dawson, and the way he got signed was this. Dawson went to the Cubs and said (I am paraphrasing) "I want to play for the Cubs. I want to play for the Cubs because I like Wrigley Field, I like day baseball, and I really need to get off the artificial turf, which is killing my knees. Just pay me whatever you want to pay me; I'll play for you." He actually took a standard player contract, with no numbers in it, signed it, and handed it to the Cubs. You fill in the dollar amount; I'll play for whatever you choose to pay me.

*In the middle of this collusion, the only free agent who got signed was Andre Dawson.*

It was a dramatic gesture, and the teams were trying to pretend that there was no collusion going on, so they couldn't exactly refuse to sign Andre Dawson, since they could not pretend that his contract demands were unreasonable. Dawson signed with the Cubs, where, in 1987, he won the MVP Award:

| Year | Player | Age | G | AB | HR | RBI | AVG | SLG | OBA | OPS | W | L | PCT |
|------|--------|-----|---|----|----|----|-----|-----|-----|-----|---|---|-----|
| 1987 | Andre Dawson | 32 | 153 | 621 | 49 | 137 | .287 | .568 | .328 | .896 | 20 | 13 | .610 |
| 1957 | Minnie Minoso | 32 | 153 | 568 | 12 | 103 | .310 | .454 | .408 | .862 | 24 | 8 | .743 |

Dawson won the MVP Award because, following his dramatic gesture of the previous winter, he led the league in Home Runs and RBI. But he walked 32 times on the season, giving him a .328 on-base percentage. His on-base percentage was the league average, playing for a last-place team in a hitter's park, and he couldn't really run anymore. I saw him as a pretty good player, no more than that. Given a 20-person MVP ballot, I would not have listed Andre Dawson on the ballot. In my mind, it was one of the worst MVP selections of all time.

I didn't mean this to be disrespectful of Dawson; Dawson was a fine man and a fine player. But I still remember Harry Caray, Cubs broadcaster; I thought the world of Harry Caray, and he was always nice to me. I still remember watching the Cubs one afternoon early in 1988, and hearing Harry say "I still can't figure out why Bill James doesn't think that Andre Dawson was deserving of the NL MVP Award. I mean, look at this man…" and he ran though Dawson's virtues: his league-leading 49 homers, his grace on and off the field, his resolute action in coming to the Cubs at a price to be determined by the team. I don't deny any of that. You score runs by getting people on base, and the Cubs finished last.

At age 33 Dawson and Minoso had nearly identical seasons, apart from the fact that, of course, Minoso walked and Dawson didn't:

| Year | Player | Age | G | AB | HR | RBI | AVG | SLG | OBA | OPS | W | L | PCT |
|------|--------|-----|---|----|----|----|-----|-----|-----|-----|---|---|-----|
| 1988 | Andre Dawson | 33 | 157 | 591 | 24 | 79 | .303 | .504 | .344 | .849 | 20 | 11 | .648 |
| 1958 | Minnie Minoso | 33 | 149 | 556 | 24 | 80 | .302 | .484 | .383 | .867 | 21 | 10 | .684 |

*In my mind, it was one of the worst MVP selections of all time.*

Dawson was now 241-138 in his career, a .636 percentage; Minoso was 183-67, .731. Both players had two very good years left, ages 34 and 35:

| Year | Player | Age | G | AB | HR | RBI | AVG | SLG | OBA | OPS | W | L | PCT |
|------|--------|-----|---|----|----|----|----|----|----|----|---|---|-----|
| 1989 | Andre Dawson | 34 | 118 | 416 | 21 | 77 | .252 | .476 | .307 | .783 | 13 | 12 | .515 |
| 1959 | Minnie Minoso | 34 | 148 | 570 | 21 | 92 | .302 | .468 | .377 | .846 | 21 | 9 | .700 |
| 1990 | Andre Dawson | 35 | 147 | 529 | 27 | 100 | .310 | .535 | .358 | .893 | 18 | 10 | .645 |
| 1960 | MinnieMinoso | 35 | 154 | 591 | 20 | 105 | .311 | .481 | .374 | .855 | 21 | 12 | .635 |

At age 36 Dawson and Minoso both went into decline, but both stayed healthy and stayed in the lineup. Dawson's OPS was .790, Minoso's was .789, and I have them both with won-lost records of 16-14:

| Year | Player | Age | G | AB | HR | RBI | AVG | SLG | OBA | OPS | W | L | PCT |
|------|--------|-----|---|----|----|----|----|----|----|----|---|---|-----|
| 1991 | Andre Dawson | 36 | 149 | 563 | 31 | 104 | .272 | .488 | .302 | .790 | 16 | 14 | .528 |
| 1961 | Minnie Minoso | 36 | 152 | 540 | 14 | 82 | .280 | .420 | .369 | .789 | 16 | 14 | .539 |

At age 37 Dawson had one more good year. Minoso, traded to the Cardinals, got off to a slow start, and then got hurt in May, 1962:

| Year | Player | Age | G | AB | HR | RBI | AVG | SLG | OBA | OPS | W | L | PCT |
|------|--------|-----|---|----|----|----|----|----|----|----|---|---|-----|
| 1992 | Andre Dawson | 37 | 143 | 542 | 22 | 90 | .277 | .456 | .316 | .772 | 18 | 11 | .617 |
| 1962 | Minnie Minoso | 37 | 39 | 97 | 1 | 10 | .196 | .278 | .271 | .549 | 1 | 4 | .242 |

After that they were both just playing out the string, including a couple of famous late-in-life publicity stunt re-appearances by Minnie Minoso, then coaching for the White Sox:

| Year | Player | Age | G | AB | HR | RBI | AVG | SLG | OBA | OPS | W | L | PCT |
|------|--------|-----|---|----|----|----|-----|-----|-----|-----|---|---|-----|
| 1993 | Andre Dawson | 38 | 121 | 461 | 13 | 67 | .273 | .425 | .313 | .738 | 8 | 15 | .359 |
| 1963 | Minnie Minoso | 38 | 109 | 315 | 4 | 30 | .229 | .317 | .315 | .632 | 5 | 14 | .251 |
| 1994 | Andre Dawson | 39 | 75 | 292 | 16 | 48 | .240 | .466 | .271 | .737 | 4 | 11 | .235 |
| 1964 | Minnie Minoso | 39 | 30 | 31 | 1 | 5 | .226 | .323 | .351 | .674 | 1 | 1 | .587 |
| 1995 | Andre Dawson | 40 | 79 | 226 | 8 | 37 | .257 | .434 | .305 | .739 | 5 | 7 | .398 |
| 1996 | Andre Dawson | 41 | 42 | 58 | 2 | 14 | .276 | .414 | .311 | .725 | 1 | 2 | .416 |
| 1976 | Minnie Minoso | 51 | 3 | 8 | 0 | 0 | .125 | .125 | .125 | .250 | 0 | 1 | .000 |
| 1980 | Minnie Minoso | 55 | 2 | 2 | 0 | 0 | .000 | .000 | .000 | .000 | 0 | 0 | .000 |

On the bottom line, I have Dawson at 324-221, a .594 percentage, and Minoso at 248-122, or .670. Both players, by my account, are at least minimally qualified to be considered Hall of Fame candidates.

I use these standards, always with the caveat that I am not married to them, but I have yet to see the case where they didn't seem right. To be minimally qualified for the Hall of Fame, a player should have either 300 Career Win Shares, or 100 more Win Shares than Loss Shares. If a player meets *both* of those standards, he's a Hall of Famer. Andre Dawson meets both of those standards — thus, in my book, he's a Hall of Famer.

And Minoso, 126 Win Shares over .500 — he, too, is a Hall of Famer in my opinion. Breaking down Minoso and Dawson into offense and defense:

| Player | W-L | PCT |
|--------|-----|-----|
| Dawson at bat | 259-162 | .615 |
| Dawson in the field | 65-59 | .524 |
| Minoso at bat | 204-76 | .729 |
| Minoso in the field | 44-46 | .489 |

Dawson in the field was 38-26 through 1983, when his knees were good, but 27-33 the rest of his career, after his knees went. That's fairly typical. Minoso in the field was 32-23 through 1957, the year of the first Gold Glove Awards, but 12-23 after that year. Everybody's defense goes to hell in their thirties. Dawson was a very good player for a long time, and Minoso was a significantly better player than Dawson once he got a chance to play. I stay out of Hall of Fame debates when I can, but I advocate for Minoso because he was a childhood favorite, and because I believe that, given a chance to play at age 22 like Dawson or most other players of that caliber, he would have cleared the Hall of Fame bar with ease.

## Another Chicago Comparison

In a similar vein, I was interested in comparing the accomplishments of Bruce Sutter — a Hall of Famer — with those of Lee Smith. Bruce Sutter was the All-Star reliever of the Cubs in the late 1970s, the Cy Young Award winner in 1979, and elected to the Hall of Fame in 2006. Lee Smith was the All-Star reliever for the Cubs in the early 1980s, held the record for career Saves for a good many years, never won a Cy Young Award, and hasn't been elected to the Hall of Fame, although he has his advocates.

Sutter and Smith both really began their major league careers at age 23, although Smith pitched a few innings at age 22 — the year he and Sutter were teammates for a while:

| Year | Player | Team | Age | W | L | SV | G | IP | SO | BB | ERA | W | L | PCT |
|------|--------|------|-----|---|---|----|----|------|-----|----|------|----|---|------|
| 1980 | Lee Smith | Cubs | 22 | 2 | 0 | 0 | 18 | 21.2 | 17 | 14 | 2.91 | 2 | 1 | .583 |
| 1976 | Bruce Sutter | Cubs | 23 | 6 | 3 | 10 | 52 | 83.1 | 73 | 26 | 2.70 | 10 | 3 | .786 |
| 1981 | Lee Smith | Cubs | 23 | 3 | 6 | 1 | 40 | 66.2 | 50 | 31 | 3.51 | 4 | 4 | .513 |
| 1977 | Bruce Sutter | Cubs | 24 | 7 | 3 | 31 | 62 | 107.1 | 129 | 23 | 1.34 | 21 | 0 | 1.017 |
| 1982 | Lee Smith | Cubs | 24 | 2 | 5 | 17 | 72 | 117.0 | 99 | 37 | 2.69 | 12 | 5 | .693 |

Sutter had a much better year than Smith at age 23, and a much better year at age 24. Sutter at age 24 was one of the greatest relievers of all time, posting a 1.34 ERA and striking out 129 batters in 107 innings, in an era when pitchers just didn't do things like that. Signed as a non-drafted free agent in 1971, Sutter had been taught to throw a forkball in the minor leagues. The forkball was basically a dead pitch at that time; nobody had thrown it with notable success in the majors for several years, and Sutter's forkball was something special. The thing would get about 12-15 feet in front of home plate, belt high, and then just dive. Sometimes it would hit the ground. The batter couldn't take it, because if it was the fastball it was a strike, and he couldn't hit it because when he swung at it it wasn't there. By the end of his age-24 season Lee Smith was the Cubs' closer and a good one, but he was not — and would never be — at the level where Sutter was in 1977.

At age 25 Smith had the better year:

| Year | Player | Team | Age | W | L | SV | G | IP | SO | BB | ERA | W | L | PCT |
|------|--------|------|-----|---|----|----|----|-------|-----|----|------|----|---|------|
| 1978 | Bruce Sutter | Cubs | 25 | 8 | 10 | 27 | 64 | 99.0 | 106 | 34 | 3.18 | 13 | 7 | .636 |
| 1983 | Lee Smith | Cubs | 25 | 4 | 10 | 29 | 66 | 103.1 | 91 | 41 | 1.65 | 16 | 4 | .801 |

*Sutter at age 24 was one of the greatest relievers of all time.*

But at age 26 Sutter won the Cy Young Award:

| Year | Player | Team | Age | W | L | SV | G | IP | SO | BB | ERA | W | L | PCT |
|------|--------|------|-----|---|---|----|----|------|-----|----|------|----|---|------|
| 1979 | Bruce Sutter | Cubs | 26 | 6 | 6 | 37 | 62 | 101.1 | 110 | 32 | 2.22 | 18 | 3 | .870 |
| 1984 | Lee Smith | Cubs | 26 | 9 | 7 | 33 | 69 | 101.0 | 86 | 35 | 3.65 | 12 | 7 | .636 |

Sutter by age 26 had a career won-lost contribution of 62-12; Lee Smith, of 46-22. Smith's record was very, very good — but Bruce Sutter was 13 games ahead of him.

Sutter by 1979 was calling his pitch the "split-fingered fastball", which sounded cooler than a forkball although it amounted to about the same thing. The "forkball" in the 1960s, early 1970s, was an old man's pitch, almost a changeup. The split-fingered *fastball* had charisma. It wasn't exactly the same pitch; the splitter is jammed down into the fingers more, thrown harder, spins more, dives more. The Splitter — now one of the most common pitches in baseball — came into baseball almost directly from the Bruce Sutter experience, although the wheel has come full circle; the term "splitter" has replaced the term "split-fingered fastball", and there are now many pitchers who use the splitter as a change.

And also…I have told this story several times already, but it is integral to understanding Bruce Sutter. In both 1977 and 1978, Bruce Sutter was fantastic the first half of the season, and in the All-Star game. In both seasons, however, he was worked very hard in the first half of the season. In those days there was no such thing as a "Closer" role; there was a "Relief Ace". The Relief Ace pitched in the late innings of a close game — tied, up a run, down a run, didn't matter. The Relief Ace often pitched two and even three innings at a time, and a good Relief Ace might pitch 80 games and 140 innings in a season.

Sutter was a fantastic Relief Ace, but the job description was undisciplined, and Sutter was over-worked in both seasons, 1977 and 1978. He broke down the second half of the season both years. His manager, Herman Franks, announced before the 1979 season that, in the future, he would only use Sutter in "Save" situations. Herman Franks was fired before the season was over, but Bruce Sutter won the Cy Young Award, and this idea, to hold back your Relief Ace for Save situations, caught on like a house afire. Within three or four years after that, that was just the way it was done. Relief Aces became Closers. They only pitched in Save Situations, and, of course, in emergencies and to get some work, but basically, only in Save Situations. By the early 1980s, the way that Bruce Sutter was used had become the way that Relief Aces were used.

So Sutter had a huge impact on baseball history — first, by popularizing the "Splitter", and second, by playing a critical role in the evolution of the modern bullpen. Lee Smith is lacking this cachet. From ages 27 to 29, however, both Smith and Sutter were highly effective closers, not quite at a Mariano Rivera level:

| Year | Player | Team | Age | W | L | SV | G | IP | SO | BB | ERA | W | L | PCT |
|------|--------|------|-----|---|----|----|----|-------|-----|----|------|----|---|------|
| 1980 | Bruce Sutter | Cubs | 27 | 5 | 8 | 28 | 60 | 102.1 | 76 | 34 | 2.64 | 13 | 5 | .729 |
| 1985 | Lee Smith | Cubs | 27 | 7 | 4 | 33 | 65 | 97.2 | 112 | 32 | 3.04 | 17 | 4 | .805 |
| 1981 | Bruce Sutter | Cardinals | 28 | 3 | 5 | 25 | 48 | 82.1 | 57 | 24 | 2.62 | 10 | 5 | .674 |
| 1986 | Lee Smith | Cubs | 28 | 9 | 9 | 31 | 66 | 90.1 | 93 | 42 | 3.09 | 14 | 5 | .722 |
| 1982 | Bruce Sutter | Cardinals | 29 | 9 | 8 | 36 | 70 | 102.1 | 61 | 34 | 2.90 | 13 | 6 | .681 |
| 1987 | Lee Smith | Cubs | 29 | 4 | 10 | 36 | 62 | 83.2 | 96 | 32 | 3.12 | 13 | 6 | .672 |

After the 1980 season Bruce Sutter was traded to the Cardinals as a part of one of the most dramatic Winter Meetings ever. Whitey Herzog — the manager of the Cardinals and the *de facto* General Manager — went to the Winter Meetings needing a closer. He was able to trade for two Hall of Fame closers — Sutter and Rollie Fingers. Sutter was the guy he really wanted, so he traded Fingers to Milwaukee, where Fingers won the 1981 Cy Young Award.

I read somewhere recently that the Cubs were able to trade Sutter in the winter of 1980-1981 because they had Smith on hand. I don't think that's strictly true. In 1980 the Cubs still thought Lee Smith was going to be a starting pitcher. The Cubs traded Sutter in the winter of 1980-1981 because that's what they did with star players, in those years; they cashed them in while their value was high. They traded Sutter for Ken Reitz and Leon Durham in the same way, a few years earlier, they had traded Ferguson Jenkins for Bill Madlock and Vic Harris.

Lee Smith, I think it is fair to say, was not exceptionally well liked. He was a great big dude — 6-foot-5 and powerfully built — and he did not wear an inviting smile. He wasn't reporter-friendly. He lived off of high heat, and later, off a combination of high heat and pinpoint control. He was much more like Goose Gossage than he was like Sutter. He was a great pitcher and well respected, but not universally beloved.

By age 29, however, Smith was catching up to Sutter. Sutter's career record was now 98-28, still a fabulous .777 winning percentage, but Smith was now 90-38, a .706 percentage, and only nine games behind him. These, of course, are their records of Win Shares and Loss Shares, not their records of officially credited Wins and Losses, which are a sham for relievers anyway. Smith was traded to the Red Sox in 1988, and gained ground in the competition at age 30, as Sutter had his first poor season:

| Year | Player | Team | Age | W | L | SV | G | IP | SO | BB | ERA | W | L | PCT |
|------|--------|------|-----|---|---|----|----|------|----|----|------|----|----|------|
| 1983 | Bruce Sutter | Cardinals | 30 | 9 | 10 | 21 | 60 | 89.1 | 64 | 30 | 4.23 | 7 | 9 | .425 |
| 1988 | Lee Smith | Red Sox | 30 | 4 | 5 | 29 | 64 | 83.2 | 96 | 37 | 2.80 | 14 | 5 | .719 |

*The Cubs traded Sutter in the winter of 1980-1981 because that's what they did with star players, in those years; they cashed them in while their value was high.*

But Sutter stormed back in 1984 with 45 Saves and a 1.54 ERA in 123 innings:

| Year | Player | Team | Age | W | L | SV | G | IP | SO | BB | ERA | W | L | PCT |
|------|--------|------|-----|---|---|----|----|------|----|----|------|----|---|------|
| 1984 | Bruce Sutter | Cardinals | 31 | 5 | 7 | 45 | 71 | 122.2 | 77 | 23 | 1.54 | 19 | 3 | .862 |
| 1989 | Lee Smith | Red Sox | 31 | 6 | 1 | 25 | 64 | 70.2 | 96 | 33 | 3.57 | 12 | 5 | .705 |

Sutter was sixth in the National League MVP voting in 1984, third in the Cy Young voting. This made Sutter's career record 124-40, still eight and a half games ahead of Smith at 115-48.

But that was Bruce Sutter's last good year. He was a free agent that winter, signed with the Braves, and in all candor he never earned his money with the Braves.

| Year | Player | Team | Age | W | L | SV | G | IP | SO | BB | ERA | W | L | PCT |
|------|--------|------|-----|---|---|----|----|------|----|----|------|----|---|------|
| 1985 | Bruce Sutter | Braves | 32 | 7 | 7 | 23 | 58 | 88.1 | 52 | 29 | 4.48 | 8 | 8 | .504 |
| 1990 | Lee Smith | Red Sox | 32 | 2 | 1 | 4 | 11 | 14.1 | 17 | 9 | 1.88 | 2 | 0 | .883 |
| 1990 | Lee Smith | Cardinals | 32 | 3 | 4 | 27 | 53 | 68.2 | 70 | 20 | 2.10 | 12 | 2 | .844 |
| 1986 | Bruce Sutter | Braves | 33 | 2 | 0 | 3 | 16 | 18.2 | 16 | 9 | 4.34 | 2 | 1 | .567 |
| 1991 | Lee Smith | Cardinals | 33 | 6 | 3 | 47 | 67 | 73.0 | 67 | 13 | 2.34 | 16 | 3 | .823 |

Smith, on the other hand, had a couple of good years with the Red Sox, went to the Cardinals and was outstanding with the Cardinals in 1990-1991. By the end of his age 33 season, Smith's career Win Shares and Loss Shares were 146-54 (.731); Sutter's were 134-50 (.729).

Sutter was done. He didn't pitch at all in 1987:

| Year | Player | Team | Age | W | L | SV | G | IP | SO | BB | ERA | W | L | PCT |
|------|--------|------|-----|---|---|----|----|------|----|----|------|----|---|------|
| 1987 | Bruce Sutter | DNP | | | | | | | | | | | | |
| 1992 | Lee Smith | Cardinals | 34 | 4 | 9 | 43 | 70 | 75.0 | 60 | 26 | 3.12 | 11 | 7 | .597 |

Lee Smith was the first man to get 400 career Saves, and held the career Saves record, with 478, until Trevor Hoffman passed him in 2006. He had held the Saves record for about 15 years.

Sutter was done at age 35, but Smith was beginning to fade, too. Being a closer is different than any other job in baseball, in that the margin for error is thinner. You can stay in the league as a .450 second baseman, a .450 center fielder. A closer — if you're not good, you're not the closer. Smith after age 34 was sporadically but not consistently good, although he continued to rack up Saves until age 37:

| Year | Player | Team | Age | W | L | SV | G | IP | SO | BB | ERA | W | L | PCT |
|------|--------|------|-----|---|---|----|----|-----|----|----|-----|---|----|-----|
| 1988 | Bruce Sutter | Braves | 35 | 1 | 4 | 14 | 38 | 45.1 | 40 | 11 | 4.76 | 3 | 6 | .366 |
| 1993 | Lee Smith | Cardinals | 35 | 2 | 4 | 43 | 55 | 50.0 | 49 | 9 | 4.50 | 8 | 10 | .442 |
| 1993 | Lee Smith | Yankees | 35 | 0 | 0 | 3 | 8 | 8.0 | 11 | 5 | 0.00 | 2 | 0 | 1.157 |
| 1994 | Lee Smith | Orioles | 36 | 1 | 4 | 33 | 41 | 38.1 | 42 | 11 | 3.29 | 10 | 4 | .739 |
| 1995 | Lee Smith | Angels | 37 | 0 | 5 | 37 | 52 | 49.1 | 43 | 25 | 3.47 | 9 | 6 | .622 |
| 1996 | Lee Smith | Angels | 38 | 0 | 0 | 0 | 11 | 11.0 | 6 | 3 | 2.45 | 1 | 0 | .821 |
| 1996 | Lee Smith | Reds | 38 | 3 | 4 | 2 | 43 | 44.1 | 35 | 23 | 4.06 | 3 | 3 | .568 |
| 1997 | Lee Smith | Expos | 39 | 0 | 1 | 5 | 25 | 21.2 | 15 | 8 | 5.82 | 1 | 3 | .267 |

Lee Smith aged much better than did Bruce Sutter; of that there is no doubt. Smith made it to 1,000 games pitched in his career; Sutter petered out at 661. Lee Smith's final career Win Shares and Loss Shares are 192-85, a .692 percentage. Bruce Sutter's are 137-55, a .713 percentage. These records include the men's performance as hitters. Sutter had nine hits in his career; Smith had only 3, but one of them was a tater.

There may be three legitimate reasons why Bruce Sutter is in the Hall of Fame, and Lee Smith is not:

1) Sutter's peak period was more dominant,

2) Sutter introduced baseball to the power of the Splitter, and

3) Sutter played a critical role in defining the usage patterns of the modern bullpen.

Still, if it was up to me, I guess I would have voted for Lee Smith to go into the Hall of Fame before Bruce Sutter. I think, in the final analysis, that Smith had the better career.

# Chicago White Sox

## Key Players

| Pos | Player | G | AB | R | H | 2B | 3B | HR | RBI | SB | CS | BB | SO | AVG | OBP | SLG | OPS | WS |
|---|---|---|---|---|---|---|---|---|---|---|---|---|---|---|---|---|---|---|
| C | A.J. Pierzynski | 138 | 504 | 57 | 151 | 22 | 1 | 13 | 49 | 1 | 1 | 24 | 52 | .300 | .331 | .425 | .755 | 10 |
| 1B | Paul Konerko | 152 | 546 | 75 | 151 | 30 | 1 | 28 | 88 | 1 | 0 | 58 | 89 | .277 | .353 | .489 | .842 | 18 |
| 2B | Chris Getz | 107 | 375 | 49 | 98 | 18 | 4 | 2 | 31 | 25 | 2 | 30 | 54 | .261 | .324 | .347 | .670 | 10 |
| 3B | Gordon Beckham | 103 | 378 | 58 | 102 | 28 | 1 | 14 | 63 | 7 | 4 | 41 | 65 | .270 | .347 | .460 | .808 | 12 |
| SS | Alexei Ramirez | 148 | 542 | 71 | 150 | 14 | 1 | 15 | 68 | 14 | 5 | 49 | 66 | .277 | .333 | .389 | .723 | 15 |
| LF | Carlos Quentin | 99 | 351 | 47 | 83 | 14 | 0 | 21 | 56 | 3 | 0 | 31 | 52 | .236 | .323 | .456 | .779 | 8 |
| CF | Scott Podsednik | 132 | 537 | 75 | 163 | 25 | 6 | 7 | 48 | 30 | 13 | 39 | 74 | .304 | .353 | .412 | .764 | 15 |
| RF | Jermaine Dye | 141 | 503 | 78 | 126 | 19 | 1 | 27 | 81 | 0 | 2 | 64 | 108 | .250 | .340 | .453 | .793 | 14 |
| DH | Jim Thome | 107 | 345 | 55 | 86 | 15 | 0 | 23 | 74 | 0 | 0 | 69 | 116 | .249 | .372 | .493 | .864 | 11 |

## Key Pitchers

| Pos | Player | G | GS | W | L | SV | IP | H | R | ER | SO | BB | BR/9 | ERA | WS |
|---|---|---|---|---|---|---|---|---|---|---|---|---|---|---|---|
| SP | Mark Buehrle | 33 | 33 | 13 | 10 | 0 | 213.1 | 222 | 97 | 91 | 105 | 45 | 11.48 | 3.84 | 16 |
| SP | John Danks | 32 | 32 | 13 | 11 | 0 | 200.1 | 184 | 89 | 84 | 149 | 73 | 11.77 | 3.77 | 16 |
| SP | Gavin Floyd | 30 | 30 | 11 | 11 | 0 | 193.0 | 178 | 93 | 87 | 163 | 59 | 11.15 | 4.06 | 13 |
| SP | Clayton Richard | 26 | 14 | 4 | 3 | 0 | 89.0 | 94 | 50 | 46 | 66 | 37 | 13.55 | 4.65 | 5 |
| SP | Jose Contreras | 21 | 21 | 5 | 13 | 0 | 114.2 | 121 | 83 | 69 | 89 | 45 | 13.50 | 5.42 | 2 |
| CL | Bobby Jenks | 52 | 0 | 3 | 4 | 29 | 53.1 | 52 | 24 | 22 | 49 | 16 | 11.81 | 3.71 | 8 |
| RP | Matt Thornton | 70 | 0 | 6 | 3 | 4 | 72.1 | 58 | 22 | 22 | 87 | 20 | 9.83 | 2.74 | 12 |
| RP | Octavio Dotel | 62 | 0 | 3 | 3 | 0 | 62.1 | 54 | 26 | 23 | 75 | 36 | 12.99 | 3.32 | 6 |

## White Sox Starting Pitching

Since Ozzie Guillen took over the White Sox in 2004, the strength of the team has been the exceptional stability of their starting rotation. The White Sox play in a home run park. It would be easy for them to get gun shy, to start pitching away from the home run, overreact to a few bombs, and to see their pitching staff degenerate. They never have — to a quite remarkable extent. You can look at their pitching rotation in April and their pitching rotation in September, and it's the same guys. Nobody else in baseball has been able to do that.

In 2009 the White Sox did have to fix the rotation. Bartolo Colon got hurt or lost his marbles or something; anyway he was dropped from the rotation in July and released in September. Jose Contreras went out, Jake Peavy went in, Gavin Floyd skipped a few starts, and Ozzie spent September looking over the candidates for his 2010 rotation.

Still, the White Sox got 116 starts from their top four starting pitchers, 130 out of their top five. Those numbers are still far above average.

| Starter | Apr | May | Jun | Jul | Aug | Sep | Oct | Tot |
|---|---|---|---|---|---|---|---|---|
| Mark Buehrle | 4 | 6 | 5 | 6 | 6 | 6 | | 33 |
| John Danks | 4 | 6 | 5 | 4 | 6 | 6 | 1 | 32 |
| Gavin Floyd | 5 | 5 | 6 | 5 | 6 | 3 | | 30 |
| Jose Contreras | 4 | 2 | 4 | 5 | 6 | | | 21 |
| Bartolo Colon | 4 | 5 | 2 | 1 | | | | 12 |
| Clayton Richard | | 4 | 6 | 4 | | | | 14 |
| Carlos Torres | | | | 1 | 1 | 3 | | 5 |
| D.J. Carrasco | | | | 1 | | | | 1 |
| Freddy Garcia | | | | | 3 | 5 | 1 | 9 |
| Jake Peavy | | | | | | 2 | 1 | 3 |
| Daniel Hudson | | | | | | 2 | | 2 |
| Total | 21 | 28 | 28 | 27 | 28 | 27 | 3 | 162 |

## Pitchers Play Defense, Too

Led by Fielding Bible Award winner Mark Buehrle, the White Sox were the best defensive pitching staff in baseball last year, at 16 runs saved.

| Team | Pitcher Runs Saved |
|---|---|
| Chicago White Sox | 16 |
| New York Mets | 13 |
| Seattle Mariners | 12 |
| Cincinatti Reds | 11 |
| St. Louis Cardinals | 11 |

## Mark Buehrle — Gold Glover

After Mike Mussina and Kenny Rogers retired, the American League was left with no incumbent Gold Glove winner, and Mark Buehrle finally got the recognition he deserves. Additionally, he won the Fielding Bible Award as the best defensive pitcher in all of baseball. From *The Fielding Bible–Volume II*, Defensive Runs Saved combines pitchers' fielding with their ability to control the running game. It is no surprise that Buehrle posted the best mark in baseball last year with 11 runs saved. Here are his annual totals of estimated defensive runs saved based on his range around the mound (Plus/Minus) and his ability to hold runners (Stolen Bases):

| Year | Plus/Minus | Stolen Bases | Total |
|------|------------|--------------|-------|
| 2004 | 5 | 5 | 10 |
| 2005 | 2 | 2 | 4 |
| 2006 | 4 | 5 | 9 |
| 2007 | 2 | 3 | 5 |
| 2008 | 0 | 4 | 4 |
| 2009 | 7 | 4 | 11 |

## Mark Buehrle — Iron Man

Mark Buehrle has now pitched 200 innings for 9 straight seasons. He is the first pitcher to have a streak of 200-inning seasons that long since Mike Mussina (1995-2003), and the 25th to do so since World War II. Of the other 24 pitchers who have done this, 14 are now in the Hall of Fame, and at least two more are certain to join them.

| Years | Player | Streak | Years | Player | Streak | Years | Player | Streak |
|-------|--------|--------|-------|--------|--------|-------|--------|--------|
| 1947-1956 | Murry Dickson | 10 | 1962-1971 | Juan Marichal | 10 | 1967-1980 | Phil Niekro | 14 |
| 1948-1956 | Bob Lemon | 9 | 1963-1973 | Claude Osteen | 11 | 1968-1980 | Steve Carlton | 13 |
| 1949-1960 | Robin Roberts | 12 | 1965-1973 | Mel Stottlemyre | 9 | 1971-1980 | Bert Blyleven | 10 |
| 1950-1960 | Early Wynn | 11 | 1964-1975 | Mickey Lolich | 12 | 1983-1992 | Frank Viola | 10 |
| 1947-1963 | Warren Spahn | 17 | 1967-1976 | Ferguson Jenkins | 10 | 1988-2001 | Greg Maddux | 14 |
| 1955-1965 | Bob Friend | 11 | 1967-1976 | Catfish Hunter | 10 | 1995-2003 | Mike Mussina | 9 |
| 1957-1967 | Jim Bunning | 11 | 1967-1979 | Tom Seaver | 13 | 2001-2009 | Mark Buehrle | 9 |
| 1957-1968 | Don Drysdale | 12 | 1966-1980 | Don Sutton | 15 | | | |
| 1959-1968 | Larry Jackson | 10 | 1966-1980 | Gaylord Perry | 15 | | | |

## Don't Judge a Floyd by Its Cover

In 2008 Gavin Floyd went 17-8 with a 3.84 ERA. In 2009 his ERA went up to 4.06, and his won-lost mark went down to 11-11.

A closer look at his stats, however, shows that Floyd increased his strikeouts, reduced his walks, reduced the number of doubles, triples and homers he allowed, increased his double play support, and dramatically improved his stolen bases allowed, which were the worst in baseball in 2008.

What happened to Floyd in 2009, then, is something of a mystery. How can a pitcher give up fewer doubles, triples, homers, walks and stolen bases, get more strikeouts and more double plays, and yet lose effectiveness? It doesn't make any sense.

My first thought was that Floyd may have made a mistake by focusing on controlling the running game; he may have started using a slide step, which may have led to a higher batting average with runners on base and with runners in scoring position. A look at the data, however, shows that this isn't what happened, either. Floyd was more effective with the bases empty in both 2008 and 2009 — as many pitchers are — but the ratios did not meaningfully change. The batting average against Floyd with runners in scoring position was .233 in 2008, .231 in 2009.

To be honest, I do not know and do not understand what happened to Floyd. It is a puzzle. However, given that there is no apparent reason for his decline, I think one would have to bet heavy on Floyd's having a better year in 2010.

### Gavin Floyd — Record of Opposing Batters

| Year | AB | R | H | 2B | 3B | HR | RBI | BB | SO | SB | CS | GIDP | AVG | OBP | SLG | OPS |
|------|-----|-----|-----|----|----|----|-----|----|-----|----|----|------|------|------|------|------|
| 2008 | 787 | 107 | 190 | 48 | 5 | 30 | 96 | 70 | 145 | 37 | 5 | 17 | .241 | .309 | .429 | .738 |
| 2009 | 731 | 93 | 178 | 34 | 1 | 21 | 79 | 59 | 163 | 14 | 4 | 21 | .244 | .301 | .379 | .680 |

## Pinch, But No Punch

Ozzie Guillen sent to the plate 105 pinch hitters in 2009, third-most in the American League. His pinch hitters, unfortunately, were more like punch lines; they hit .106 as a group, with only 5 runs scored and 3 RBI.

One of the tasks of sabermetrics which as far as I know has not yet been accomplished is a survey of the leverage index of top pinch hitters. It seems to me possible that the great pinch hitters, like Jerry Lynch, John VanderWal, Wes Helms and David Dellucci, may have leverage indexes, as hitters, that would significantly increase our perception of their value.

## White Sox #3 Hitters

2009 was the first time in ten years that White Sox #3 hitters failed to hit at least 30 homers and drive in at least 100 runs. For years, the White Sox' #3 hitter was Frank Thomas. Even when The Big Hurt was Actually Hurt for half the season or more, he generally racked up such big numbers while he was in the lineup that whoever was there the rest of the year just had to chip in a few short putts to get the RBI count up to triple digits. In 2005, which was the White Sox' championship season, the third spot fell into the lap of Carl Everett and company. They were pretty awful, but the lineup around them was strong enough to keep the RBI count respectable, and then Jim Thome arrived; he was like Frank Thomas, except that he was left-handed and had funny ears.

In 2009, however, the third spot fell to an aging Jermaine Dye, an injured Carlos Quentin, and an out-of-position A. J. Pierzynski. It wasn't pretty. If Carlos Quentin's wrist and foot will allow him to play at full strength in 2010 this shouldn't be an issue.

| Year | AB | R | H | 2B | 3B | HR | RBI | BB | SO | AVG | OBP | SLG |
|------|-----|-----|-----|----|----|----|-----|-----|-----|------|------|------|
| 2000 | 615 | 120 | 199 | 48 | 1 | 42 | 145 | 115 | 101 | .324 | .429 | .610 |
| 2001 | 646 | 112 | 186 | 47 | 2 | 40 | 127 | 58 | 103 | .288 | .351 | .553 |
| 2002 | 610 | 106 | 160 | 29 | 2 | 30 | 103 | 99 | 120 | .262 | .365 | .464 |
| 2003 | 600 | 98 | 159 | 41 | 1 | 43 | 114 | 106 | 124 | .265 | .384 | .552 |
| 2004 | 648 | 119 | 189 | 30 | 2 | 40 | 121 | 62 | 100 | .292 | .360 | .529 |
| 2005 | 642 | 82 | 150 | 27 | 1 | 30 | 103 | 54 | 140 | .234 | .296 | .419 |
| 2006 | 616 | 136 | 185 | 32 | 2 | 44 | 123 | 102 | 159 | .300 | .403 | .573 |
| 2007 | 591 | 94 | 150 | 28 | 0 | 39 | 110 | 109 | 161 | .254 | .374 | .499 |
| 2008 | 623 | 109 | 165 | 34 | 0 | 40 | 114 | 86 | 120 | .265 | .366 | .512 |
| 2009 | 626 | 86 | 151 | 23 | 1 | 27 | 89 | 61 | 114 | .241 | .319 | .411 |

## Alas, Home Runs Only Count So Much

The White Sox lost 22 games in 2009 in which they hit more than one home run. Those 22 losses are more than the Braves, Dodgers and Giants combined.

## Alex Rios Hitting Analysis

What happened to Alex Rios in 2009? Simply stated, he did not hit line drives. He hit 110 line drives in 2007, 110 in 2008. Last year he hit 79. You hit .750 on your line drives. If you lose 30 of them, your average suffers.

Rios has never been a power hitter; he's been a line drive hitter. In 2009 he was a line drive hitter who wasn't hitting line drives.

| Year | Balls In Play | Line Drives | Pct |
|------|------|------|------|
| 2004 | 342 | 75 | 21.9% |
| 2005 | 385 | 76 | 19.7% |
| 2006 | 370 | 80 | 21.6% |
| 2007 | 547 | 110 | 20.1% |
| 2008 | 528 | 110 | 20.8% |
| 2009 | 482 | 79 | 16.4% |

## Jermaine Dye Hitting Analysis

Does this look familiar?

Jermaine Dye had the exact same problem as Alex Rios — he posted his worst line drive rate in recent memory. At age 36, Dye is a riskier bet to return to form.

| Year | Balls In Play | Line Drives | Pct |
|------|------|------|------|
| 2004 | 408 | 83 | 20.3% |
| 2005 | 431 | 89 | 20.6% |
| 2006 | 428 | 87 | 20.3% |
| 2007 | 405 | 77 | 19.0% |
| 2008 | 491 | 109 | 22.2% |
| 2009 | 397 | 67 | 16.9% |

# The 1959 Go-Go White Sox

by Bill James

WE HAVE JUST HAD THE HALF-CENTURY ANNIVERSARY OF THE Go-Go White Sox, further proof that the world is aging and gray and wears its pants above its navel. Baseball in the 1950s was a home run hitter's game. The difference between the good teams and the bad teams in the 1950s was that the bad teams had two big, slow power hitters and the good teams had four. The 1959 White Sox shook up the league, winning 94 games and making it to the World Series with speed, defense, pitching and bunts. Mike Scioscia would have loved them, but he was only a few months old at the time.

The White Sox in the late 1930s had a string of competitive seasons, finishing over .500 in 1936, '37, '39 and '40, and at .500 in 1941. They never won the American League, but they finished in the first division.

*Mike Scioscia would have loved them, but he was only a few months old at the time.*

In the late 1940s the sixteen major league teams were being sorted out as to how good a job they did of developing minor league operations. The teams that got ahead of the game in terms of developing farm systems — the Yankees, Dodgers, Giants, Red Sox, Cardinals, Tigers, Indians, Braves — those teams were doing well. The teams that didn't get interested in developing a farm system in the 1930s, by the late 1940s, were in deep trouble — and there was no reverse-order draft then to help them dig out.

They were in deep trouble, and most of them didn't get over it until the 1960s or 1970s. A couple of them did, however. The Phillies put a lot of money into a farm system in the mid-1940s, and pulled out of it as a competitive team in the early 1950s. And the White Sox hired Frank Lane.

Frank Lane was in his early fifties when he was hired to be the White Sox General Manager in 1948. Over a period of years he pulled off a series of spectacularly good trades, which overcame their weaknesses and put the White Sox back on the map. For Aaron Robinson, a catcher who would soon be out of the major leagues, he got Billy Pierce, who would win over 200 games. For Joe Tipton, another catcher of very modest talent, he got a Hall of Fame second baseman, Nellie Fox. For a package of players, none of them good, he got a catcher who was quite good, Sherm Lollar. For Gus Zernial — who was a very good slugging outfielder—he got Minnie Minoso, who probably should be in the Hall of Fame. For $75,000 and two players who couldn't play at all, he got a veteran pitcher named Virgil Trucks, who still had some mileage left on him. For cold cash, he picked up Chico Carrasquel, who would be an outstanding shortstop for several years. Also for cash he picked up a minor league slugging first baseman, Jack Harshman, who had recently converted to pitching, and who would be a rotation anchor for the White Sox for several years.

It was one of the best series of trades in the history of baseball — nor did he neglect the farm system. Lane, a minor league executive for years, also built up the White Sox scouting and development operation. To make all of this work, he hired a very fine manager, Paul Richards. Paul Richards is the subject of a new biography, *The Wizard of Waxahachie,* which I am told is outstanding.

In fact, the genius who made this work may well have been not Lane, but Richards. Frank Lane left the White Sox in 1955, had several other GM jobs, and performed very badly in all of them. He bounced from job to job, made a gigantic ass of himself everywhere, and got fired about five times in a period of just a few years. Paul Richards, on the other hand, left the White Sox in 1954, took over the Orioles, and built up the Orioles in the same meticulous way he had built up the

*Veeck knew how to sell tickets, and he knew how to generate excitement around a baseball team.*

White Sox. In any case, regardless of who gets the credit for it, the White Sox moved from 60 wins in 1950 to 81 in 1951, 81 again in 1952, 89 in 1953, and 94 in 1954.

The White Sox had winning records every year from 1951 through 1958, but the Yankees dominated the league. After Richards and Lane left the White Sox shifted into neutral, but they continued to hang around and do some things right. They signed Luis Aparicio, a Hall of Fame shortstop. They hired Al Lopez, a Hall of Fame manager; they stole both of them away from Cleveland, where General Manager Hank Greenberg had pissed them both off.

Charlie Comiskey, a 19th-century player, founded the White Sox, and owned the White Sox through and after the 1919 Black Sox scandal. After Comiskey died in 1931 the team passed to his relatives, from one to another; Lou Comiskey was listed as the owner for a while, Grace Comiskey, Dorothy Comiskey. These people would either die or lose interest, and the team lacked strong ownership.

After Frank Lane left the ownership didn't hire a new General Manager; rather, the GM duties were split between a couple of Comiskeys. One of the Comiskeys, however, was Johnny Rigney, a 1930s/1940s White Sox pitcher who had married Dorothy Comiskey. He wasn't a bad General Manager, but the team still had not won the pennant since 1919, when the team sold out the World Series, and several key members of the team were kicked out of baseball.

In 1959 the White Sox were purchased by a group of investors "led" by Bill Veeck. Bill Veeck became the public face of the White Sox ownership, although, in truth, not that much of the money was his. Veeck knew how to sell tickets, and he knew how to generate excitement around a baseball team. He was always up to something. In Chicago he put in an exploding scoreboard that sent off fireworks when the White Sox hit a home run, which was a new idea at the time. He put the player's names on the back of their uniforms, which was another new idea. He created a buzz about the White Sox.

The team started out 11-11, and they were four and a half games out of first by early May. A 10-1 stretch put them in first place by May 18, but then they were under .500 for the next month, and by June 20 were just 33-30.

33-30, however, was just one and a half games out of first; nobody in the league was playing all that well or all that badly. Everybody knew how these things ended: the Yankees took over. By the fourth of July the White Sox were 42-35, two games out of first place, but still two games ahead of the Yankees. Then they got hot. They won two, lost one, won five, lost one, won two, lost two, won five, lost one, won six, lost one. Let's add that up:

2-1
5-1
2-2
5-1
6-1

Totals up to 20-6. By August 5 the White Sox were in first place — only two ahead of Cleveland, but the Yankees had fallen eleven and a half back.

At this point the nation kind of adopted the White Sox, the can-do kids of the 1950s. They had little power on the team, no real cleanup hitter, but they had speed and defense and pitching and they could manufacture runs, and they were *fun*. For most of the year they had no first baseman, no right fielder, and no third basemen. Their infield was a mixture of Hall of Famers and Whoosez, two of each. They continued to win. By the end of August they were 80-49, sixteen and a half games ahead of the Yankees, and five and a half ahead of everybody.

*I have come to question, as a result of my studies upon the baseball operation, that Luis Aparicio actually deserved the credit that he has received for this team's success.*

They won it in a walk, five games ahead of Cleveland, 15 ahead of everybody else.

The media heroes were:

1) Nellie Fox, a diminutive second baseman who bunted and slapped the ball through the infield, sort of a combination of Dustin Pedroia and Ichiro Suzuki,

2) Luis Aparicio, who led the major leagues in stolen bases with the highest totals in fifteen years, and was acclaimed the greatest defensive shortstop since Marty Marion, and

3) Early Wynn, a crusty 39-year-old pitcher, fat and sometimes surly, who mixed in knuckleballs and fastballs directed at your head.

Somebody suggested to Early Wynn that he would knock down his own mother if she dug in on him. "Why wouldn't I?" he answered. "My mother was a damn good hitter." But while Wynn did not look like an athlete, he was. In addition to winning 22 games he hit .244 with 7 doubles and 2 homers.

Wynn won the Cy Young Award, and Fox, Aparicio and Wynn finished 1, 2 and 3 in the MVP voting. All three would eventually be in the Hall of Fame. But...and coming finally to my point...I have come to question, as a result of my studies upon the baseball operation, that Luis Aparicio actually deserved the credit that he has received for this team's success. Aparicio was a brilliant fielder and a brilliant base runner, but his on-base percentage for the Go-Go White Sox was .316. He scored 98 runs, but he made 497 outs — not a great ratio, and then, he drove in only 51.

But it raises a question: if Aparicio doesn't deserve the credit he has been given for the success of the 1959 White Sox, who does? These are the basic hitting statistics for the members of the 1959 White Sox, including pitchers:

## All 1959 CWS Hitting Stats

| Pos | Player | G | AB | R | H | 2B | 3B | HR | RBI | BB | SB | AVG | SLG | OBA | OPS |
|---|---|---|---|---|---|---|---|---|---|---|---|---|---|---|---|
| | Sherm Lollar | 140 | 505 | 63 | 134 | 22 | 3 | 22 | 84 | 55 | 4 | .265 | .451 | .345 | .796 |
| C | John Romano | 53 | 126 | 20 | 37 | 5 | 1 | 5 | 25 | 23 | 0 | .294 | .468 | .407 | .875 |
| | Earl Battey | 26 | 64 | 9 | 14 | 1 | 2 | 2 | 7 | 8 | 0 | .219 | .391 | .306 | .696 |
| | Cam Carreon | 1 | 1 | 0 | 0 | 0 | 0 | 0 | 0 | 0 | 0 | .000 | .000 | .000 | .000 |
| | Earl Torgeson | 127 | 277 | 40 | 61 | 5 | 3 | 9 | 45 | 62 | 7 | .220 | .357 | .359 | .716 |
| | Norm Cash | 58 | 104 | 16 | 25 | 0 | 1 | 4 | 16 | 18 | 1 | .240 | .375 | .372 | .747 |
| 1B | Ted Kluszewski | 31 | 101 | 11 | 30 | 2 | 1 | 2 | 10 | 9 | 0 | .297 | .396 | .351 | .747 |
| | Ray Boone | 9 | 21 | 3 | 5 | 0 | 0 | 1 | 5 | 7 | 1 | .238 | .381 | .400 | .781 |
| | Ron Jackson | 10 | 14 | 3 | 3 | 1 | 0 | 1 | 2 | 1 | 0 | .214 | .500 | .313 | .813 |
| 2B | Nellie Fox | 156 | 624 | 84 | 191 | 34 | 6 | 2 | 70 | 71 | 5 | .306 | .389 | .380 | .770 |
| | Bubba Phillips | 117 | 379 | 43 | 100 | 27 | 1 | 5 | 40 | 27 | 1 | .264 | .380 | .319 | .699 |
| 3B | Billy Goodman | 104 | 268 | 21 | 67 | 14 | 1 | 1 | 28 | 19 | 3 | .250 | .321 | .304 | .625 |
| | Sammy Esposito | 69 | 66 | 12 | 11 | 1 | 0 | 1 | 5 | 11 | 0 | .167 | .227 | .282 | .509 |
| | J.C. Martin | 3 | 4 | 0 | 1 | 0 | 0 | 0 | 1 | 0 | 0 | .250 | .250 | .250 | .500 |
| SS | Luis Aparicio | 152 | 612 | 98 | 157 | 18 | 5 | 6 | 51 | 53 | 56 | .257 | .332 | .316 | .647 |
| | Al Smith | 129 | 472 | 65 | 112 | 16 | 4 | 17 | 55 | 46 | 7 | .237 | .396 | .311 | .707 |
| LF | Johnny Callison | 49 | 104 | 12 | 18 | 3 | 0 | 3 | 12 | 13 | 0 | .173 | .288 | .271 | .560 |
| | Del Ennis | 26 | 96 | 10 | 21 | 6 | 0 | 2 | 7 | 4 | 0 | .219 | .344 | .250 | .594 |
| | Lou Skizas | 8 | 13 | 3 | 1 | 0 | 0 | 0 | 0 | 3 | 0 | .077 | .077 | .250 | .327 |
| CF | Jim Landis | 149 | 515 | 78 | 140 | 26 | 7 | 5 | 60 | 78 | 20 | .272 | .379 | .370 | .749 |
| | Joe Hicks | 6 | 7 | 0 | 3 | 0 | 0 | 0 | 0 | 1 | 0 | .429 | .429 | .500 | .929 |
| | Jim McAnany | 67 | 210 | 22 | 58 | 9 | 3 | 0 | 27 | 19 | 2 | .276 | .348 | .339 | .687 |
| RF | Jim Rivera | 80 | 177 | 18 | 39 | 9 | 4 | 4 | 19 | 11 | 5 | .220 | .384 | .266 | .650 |
| | Harry Simpson | 38 | 75 | 5 | 14 | 5 | 1 | 2 | 13 | 4 | 0 | .187 | .360 | .228 | .588 |
| | Larry Doby | 21 | 58 | 1 | 14 | 1 | 1 | 0 | 9 | 2 | 1 | .241 | .293 | .267 | .560 |
| PH | Don Mueller | 4 | 4 | 0 | 2 | 0 | 0 | 0 | 0 | 0 | 0 | .500 | .500 | .500 | 1.000 |
| | Early Wynn | 37 | 90 | 11 | 22 | 7 | 0 | 2 | 8 | 9 | 0 | .244 | .389 | .317 | .706 |
| | Bob Shaw | 47 | 73 | 7 | 9 | 1 | 0 | 0 | 2 | 5 | 0 | .123 | .137 | .179 | .316 |
| SP | Billy Pierce | 34 | 68 | 3 | 13 | 1 | 2 | 0 | 7 | 7 | 0 | .191 | .265 | .267 | .531 |
| | Dick Donovan | 31 | 61 | 4 | 8 | 4 | 0 | 1 | 5 | 5 | 0 | .131 | .246 | .197 | .443 |
| | Barry Latman | 37 | 47 | 3 | 6 | 1 | 0 | 0 | 6 | 4 | 0 | .128 | .149 | .189 | .338 |
| | Ray Moore | 29 | 23 | 0 | 2 | 1 | 0 | 0 | 0 | 1 | 0 | .087 | .130 | .125 | .255 |
| RP | Gerry Staley | 67 | 13 | 2 | 2 | 0 | 0 | 0 | 0 | 3 | 0 | .154 | .154 | .313 | .466 |
| | Turk Lown | 60 | 12 | 1 | 3 | 0 | 0 | 0 | 0 | 1 | 0 | .250 | .250 | .308 | .558 |
| | Ken McBride | 11 | 6 | 0 | 1 | 0 | 0 | 0 | 0 | 0 | 0 | .167 | .167 | .167 | .333 |
| XP | Rudy Arias | 34 | 4 | 0 | 0 | 0 | 0 | 0 | 0 | 0 | 0 | .000 | .000 | .000 | .000 |
| | Joe Stanka | 2 | 3 | 1 | 1 | 0 | 0 | 0 | 1 | 0 | 0 | .333 | .333 | .333 | .667 |

Aparicio and Fox became the stars of the team because they were virtually the only regulars having significant seasons — those two, and Sherm Lollar. These are the team's pitching stats:

### All 1959 CWS Pitching Stats

| Player | W | L | PCT | G | SV | IP | BB | SO | ERA |
|---|---|---|---|---|---|---|---|---|---|
| Early Wynn | 22 | 10 | .688 | 37 | 0 | 256 | 119 | 179 | 3.16 |
| Bob Shaw | 18 | 6 | .750 | 47 | 3 | 231 | 54 | 89 | 2.69 |
| Billy Pierce | 14 | 15 | .483 | 34 | 0 | 224 | 62 | 114 | 3.62 |
| Dick Donovan | 9 | 10 | .474 | 31 | 0 | 180 | 58 | 71 | 3.65 |
| Barry Latman | 8 | 5 | .615 | 37 | 0 | 156 | 72 | 97 | 3.75 |
| Ray Moore | 3 | 6 | .333 | 29 | 0 | 90 | 46 | 49 | 4.10 |
| Gerry Staley | 8 | 5 | .615 | 67 | 14 | 116 | 25 | 54 | 2.25 |
| Turk Lown | 9 | 2 | .818 | 60 | 15 | 93 | 42 | 63 | 2.90 |
| Ken McBride | 0 | 1 | .000 | 11 | 1 | 23 | 17 | 12 | 3.13 |
| Rudy Arias | 2 | 0 | 1.000 | 34 | 2 | 44 | 20 | 28 | 4.09 |
| Joe Stanka | 1 | 0 | 1.000 | 2 | 0 | 5 | 4 | 3 | 3.60 |
| Claude Raymond | 0 | 0 | | 3 | 0 | 4 | 2 | 1 | 9.00 |
| Don Rudolph | 0 | 0 | | 4 | 1 | 3 | 2 | 0 | 0.00 |
| Gary Peters | 0 | 0 | | 2 | 0 | 1 | 2 | 1 | 0.00 |

One of the fascinating things about this team is the extraordinary number of star players who played bit roles for them. Ted Kluszewski, Del Ennis, and Larry Doby had been huge stars in earlier years. Earl Battey, Norm Cash, Johnny Callison and Gary Peters would be stars later on. Earl Torgeson, Ray Boone, Don Mueller, Billy Goodman, Harry (Suitcase) Simpson and Gerry Staley had all been, if not quite stars, very well-respected players. John Romano, Dick Donovan and Claude Raymond would all become, if not stars, certainly very successful players. The White Sox that winter made a series of astonishingly bad trades, giving up Callison, Cash, Battey and Romano for basically nothing—and Don Mincher as well.

*One of the fascinating things about this team is the extraordinary number of star players who played bit roles for them.*

But this is dragging us afield from our purpose, which is to re-evaluate the contributions to victory of the 1959 members. Stated as wins and losses, this is what I have for the hitters on the 1959 White Sox:

## All 1959 CWS Batting Win Shares/Loss Shares

| Pos | Player | HR | RBI | AVG | SLG | OBA | OPS | Win Shares | Loss Shares |
|-----|--------|-----|-----|-----|-----|-----|-----|-----|-----|
| C | Sherm Lollar | 22 | 84 | .265 | .451 | .345 | .796 | 12 | 10 |
| | John Romano | 5 | 25 | .294 | .468 | .407 | .875 | 4 | 1 |
| | Earl Battey | 2 | 7 | .219 | .391 | .306 | .696 | 1 | 1 |
| | Cam Carreon | 0 | 0 | .000 | .000 | .000 | .000 | 0 | 0 |
| 1B | Earl Torgeson | 9 | 45 | .220 | .357 | .359 | .716 | 7 | 6 |
| | Norm Cash | 4 | 16 | .240 | .375 | .372 | .747 | 3 | 1 |
| | Ted Kluszewski | 2 | 10 | .297 | .396 | .351 | .747 | 2 | 2 |
| | Ray Boone | 1 | 5 | .238 | .381 | .400 | .781 | 1 | 0 |
| | Ron Jackson | 1 | 2 | .214 | .500 | .313 | .813 | 0 | 0 |
| 2B | Nellie Fox | 2 | 70 | .306 | .389 | .380 | .770 | 18 | 7 |
| 3B | Bubba Phillips | 5 | 40 | .264 | .380 | .319 | .699 | 7 | 8 |
| | Billy Goodman | 1 | 28 | .250 | .321 | .304 | .625 | 4 | 7 |
| | Sammy Esposito | 1 | 5 | .167 | .227 | .282 | .509 | 1 | 3 |
| | J.C. Martin | 0 | 1 | .250 | .250 | .250 | .500 | 0 | 0 |
| SS | Luis Aparicio | 6 | 51 | .257 | .332 | .316 | .647 | 12 | 15 |
| LF | Al Smith | 17 | 55 | .237 | .396 | .311 | .707 | 9 | 11 |
| | Johnny Callison | 3 | 12 | .173 | .288 | .271 | .560 | 1 | 4 |
| | Del Ennis | 2 | 7 | .219 | .344 | .250 | .594 | 1 | 3 |
| | Lou Skizas | 0 | 0 | .077 | .077 | .250 | .327 | 0 | 1 |
| CF | Jim Landis | 5 | 60 | .272 | .379 | .370 | .749 | 14 | 8 |
| | Joe Hicks | 0 | 0 | .429 | .429 | .500 | .929 | 0 | 0 |
| RF | Jim McAnany | 0 | 27 | .276 | .348 | .339 | .687 | 5 | 4 |
| | Jim Rivera | 4 | 19 | .220 | .384 | .266 | .650 | 3 | 5 |
| | Harry Simpson | 2 | 13 | .187 | .360 | .228 | .588 | 1 | 3 |
| | Larry Doby | 0 | 9 | .241 | .293 | .267 | .560 | 1 | 2 |
| PH | Don Mueller | 0 | 0 | .500 | .500 | .500 | 1.000 | 0 | 0 |
| P | Early Wynn | 2 | 8 | .244 | .389 | .317 | .706 | 3 | 0 |
| | Bob Shaw | 0 | 2 | .123 | .137 | .179 | .316 | 1 | 3 |
| | Billy Pierce | 0 | 7 | .191 | .265 | .267 | .531 | 2 | 1 |
| | Dick Donovan | 1 | 5 | .131 | .246 | .197 | .443 | 2 | 2 |
| | Barry Latman | 0 | 6 | .128 | .149 | .189 | .338 | 1 | 2 |
| | Ray Moore | 0 | 0 | .087 | .130 | .125 | .255 | 0 | 1 |
| | Gerry Staley | 0 | 0 | .154 | .154 | .313 | .466 | 1 | 0 |
| | Turk Lown | 0 | 0 | .250 | .250 | .308 | .558 | 0 | 0 |
| | Ken McBride | 0 | 0 | .167 | .167 | .167 | .333 | 0 | 0 |
| | Rudy Arias | 0 | 0 | .000 | .000 | .000 | .000 | 0 | 0 |
| | Joe Stanka | 0 | 1 | .333 | .333 | .333 | .667 | 0 | 0 |
| | **Total** | | | | | | | **119** | **112** |

We could summarize the performance of the White Sox hitters in seven points:

1) The catchers were very good, not only because Sherm Lollar was OK but because Romano was an exceptional hitter for a backup catcher.

2) The first basemen, while unimpressive, were in fact holding their own with the bat.

3) The second baseman/MVP Nellie Fox was a very good hitter.

4) The third basemen, left fielders and right fielders were not good hitters, but not horrible either.

5) Aparicio at short was not very good at the bat.

6) Jim Landis in center, with a .370 on-base percentage, was the second-best hitter on the team.

7) The pitchers hit pretty well for pitchers.

Turning now to the pitchers:

## All 1959 CWS Pitching Win Shares/Loss Shares

| Player | W | L | SV | ERA | Win Shares | Loss Shares |
|---|---|---|---|---|---|---|
| Early Wynn | 22 | 10 | 0 | 3.16 | 18 | 11 |
| Bob Shaw | 18 | 6 | 3 | 2.69 | 17 | 6 |
| Billy Pierce | 14 | 15 | 0 | 3.62 | 12 | 12 |
| Dick Donovan | 9 | 10 | 0 | 3.65 | 9 | 10 |
| Barry Latman | 8 | 5 | 0 | 3.75 | 9 | 9 |
| Ray Moore | 3 | 6 | 0 | 4.10 | 4 | 7 |
| Gerry Staley | 8 | 5 | 14 | 2.25 | 10 | 3 |
| Turk Lown | 9 | 2 | 15 | 2.90 | 11 | 4 |
| Ken McBride | 0 | 1 | 1 | 3.13 | 1 | 2 |
| Rudy Arias | 2 | 0 | 2 | 4.09 | 3 | 3 |
| Joe Stanka | 1 | 0 | 0 | 3.60 | 0 | 0 |
| Claude Raymond | 0 | 0 | 0 | 9.00 | 0 | 1 |
| Don Rudolph | 0 | 0 | 1 | 0.00 | 1 | 0 |
| Gary Peters | 0 | 0 | 0 | 0.00 | 0 | 0 |

So there was no hard-luck pitcher on the team, really, nor lucky pitcher. Almost every pitcher had a won-lost record that reflected his actual contribution to victory. Wynn was 22-10 (won-lost record) vs 18-11 (win shares and loss shares), but he was also 3-0 in win shares as a hitter, which makes his total win shares and loss 22-11—almost the same as his actual record. Most every pitcher on the team has the same close correlation of actual record to win shares and loss shares, a kind of remarkable occurrence.

And now we'll go to work on fielding. I will spare you all their defensive statistics; there is no warrant for that. This chart puts together the batting, fielding and pitching win shares for the 1959 White Sox:

### All 1959 CWS Total Win Shares/Loss Shares

| Pos | Player | Batting W | Batting L | Fielding W | Fielding L | Pitching W | Pitching L | Total W | Total L |
|-----|--------|----|----|----|----|----|----|----|----|
| C | Sherm Lollar | 12 | 10 | 5 | 2 | | | 18 | 11 |
| | John Romano | 4 | 1 | 1 | 0 | | | 6 | 1 |
| | Earl Battey | 1 | 1 | 1 | 0 | | | 2 | 1 |
| | Cam Carreon | 0 | 0 | 0 | 0 | | | 0 | 0 |
| 1B | Earl Torgeson | 7 | 6 | 1 | 3 | | | 8 | 9 |
| | Norm Cash | 3 | 1 | 0 | 1 | | | 4 | 2 |
| | Ted Kluszewski | 2 | 2 | 1 | 1 | | | 3 | 3 |
| | Ray Boone | 1 | 0 | 0 | 0 | | | 1 | 0 |
| | Ron Jackson | 0 | 0 | 0 | 0 | | | 0 | 0 |
| 2B | Nellie Fox | 18 | 7 | 5 | 3 | | | 23 | 10 |
| 3B | Bubba Phillips | 7 | 8 | 4 | 1 | | | 12 | 10 |
| | Billy Goodman | 4 | 7 | 3 | 1 | | | 7 | 7 |
| | Sammy Esposito | 1 | 3 | 1 | 0 | | | 1 | 3 |
| | J.C. Martin | 0 | 0 | 0 | 0 | | | 0 | 0 |
| SS | Luis Aparicio | 12 | 15 | 6 | 2 | | | 18 | 17 |
| LF | Al Smith | 9 | 11 | 4 | 2 | | | 14 | 13 |
| | Johnny Callison | 1 | 4 | 1 | 1 | | | 2 | 5 |
| | Del Ennis | 1 | 3 | 0 | 1 | | | 1 | 4 |
| | Lou Skizas | 0 | 1 | 0 | 0 | | | 0 | 1 |
| CF | Jim Landis | 14 | 8 | 6 | 1 | | | 20 | 9 |
| | Joe Hicks | 0 | 0 | 0 | 0 | | | 0 | 0 |
| RF | Jim McAnany | 5 | 4 | 2 | 1 | | | 7 | 5 |
| | Jim Rivera | 3 | 5 | 2 | 1 | | | 4 | 6 |
| | Harry Simpson | 1 | 3 | 0 | 1 | | | 1 | 3 |
| | Larry Doby | 1 | 2 | 0 | 0 | | | 1 | 2 |
| PH | Don Mueller | 0 | 0 | | | | | | |
| P | Early Wynn | 3 | 0 | | | 18 | 11 | 22 | 12 |
| | Bob Shaw | 1 | 3 | | | 17 | 6 | 19 | 8 |
| | Billy Pierce | 2 | 1 | | | 12 | 12 | 14 | 13 |
| | Dick Donovan | 2 | 2 | | | 9 | 10 | 10 | 11 |
| | Barry Latman | 1 | 2 | | | 9 | 9 | 10 | 10 |
| | Ray Moore | 0 | 1 | | | 4 | 7 | 4 | 8 |
| | Gerry Staley | 1 | 0 | | | 10 | 3 | 11 | 4 |
| | Turk Lown | 0 | 0 | | | 11 | 4 | 11 | 4 |
| | Ken McBride | 0 | 0 | | | 1 | 2 | 1 | 2 |
| | Rudy Arias | 0 | 0 | | | 3 | 3 | 3 | 3 |
| | Joe Stanka | 0 | 0 | | | 0 | 0 | 1 | 0 |
| | **Total** | **119** | **112** | **45** | **21** | **95** | **66** | **259** | **200** |

## Conclusions

1) The 1959 White Sox did overachieve, by a substantial but not historic margin. They played about seven games over their heads. Those seven games were critical to their success.

2) Several players on the team clearly deserve more credit than they usually receive for the success of the team, first among them Jim Landis. Landis, a brilliant center fielder who had a good year with the bat, comes in in this analysis at 20-9. Landis finished 7th in the MVP voting.

3) Other players who probably deserved more credit than they received included Bob Shaw (19-8), Sherm Lollar, and the relief twins of Gerry Staley and Turk Lown. Unlike modern relievers, Staley and Lown pitched more than 200 innings between them, were credited with 17 wins against 7 losses, and had extremely good ERAs.

4) It was an odd year, in that there was no obvious MVP; the MVP Award could have gone a lot of different directions. Nellie Fox was the White Sox MVP, but really, he ranks only a little bit ahead of Wynn, Landis and Bob Shaw. He doesn't stick out like an MVP

*The 1959 White Sox did overachieve, by a substantial but not historic margin.*

normally does. Mantle had his worst year since 1951, which is not to say that he wasn't still the best player in the league, but it's difficult to give the MVP Award to a player who had his worst season on a team that had their worst season. The MVP could have been Harvey Kuenn or Al Kaline or Eddie Yost of Detroit or Rocky Colavito or Tito Francona of Cleveland, or even Jackie Jensen or Pete Runnels of Boston. The best pitcher in the league—perhaps the best player in the league, I don't know—may have been Camilo Pascual. It's really difficult to say.

5) Cleveland had three outstanding outfielders (Colavito, Francona and Minoso) and probably had a better team than the White Sox, but they didn't win. We know from other research also in this book that Minnie Minoso was 22-9 in 1959, about the same as Fox, and he may have been the third-best outfielder on the Indians. But you can't really fault the MVP voters for discounting the individual accomplishments of a Cleveland team that didn't produce the wins that they should have had that year.

# Cincinnati Reds

## Key Players

| Pos | Player | G | AB | R | H | 2B | 3B | HR | RBI | SB | CS | BB | SO | Avg | OBP | SLG | OPS | WS |
|---|---|---|---|---|---|---|---|---|---|---|---|---|---|---|---|---|---|---|
| C | Ryan Hanigan | 90 | 251 | 22 | 66 | 6 | 1 | 3 | 11 | 0 | 0 | 37 | 31 | .263 | .361 | .331 | .692 | 8 |
| 1B | Joey Votto | 131 | 469 | 82 | 151 | 38 | 1 | 25 | 84 | 4 | 1 | 70 | 106 | .322 | .414 | .567 | .981 | 24 |
| 2B | Brandon Phillips | 153 | 584 | 78 | 161 | 30 | 5 | 20 | 98 | 25 | 9 | 44 | 75 | .276 | .329 | .447 | .776 | 18 |
| 3B | Adam Rosales | 87 | 230 | 23 | 49 | 10 | 1 | 4 | 19 | 1 | 2 | 26 | 46 | .213 | .303 | .317 | .620 | 3 |
| SS | Alex Gonzalez | 68 | 243 | 16 | 51 | 12 | 0 | 3 | 26 | 0 | 1 | 15 | 36 | .210 | .258 | .296 | .554 | 5 |
| LF | Laynce Nix | 116 | 309 | 42 | 74 | 26 | 1 | 15 | 46 | 0 | 1 | 22 | 81 | .239 | .291 | .476 | .767 | 6 |
| CF | Willy Taveras | 102 | 404 | 56 | 97 | 11 | 2 | 1 | 15 | 25 | 6 | 18 | 58 | .240 | .275 | .285 | .559 | 5 |
| RF | Jay Bruce | 101 | 345 | 47 | 77 | 15 | 2 | 22 | 58 | 3 | 3 | 38 | 75 | .223 | .303 | .470 | .773 | 9 |

## Key Pitchers

| Pos | Player | G | GS | W | L | SV | IP | H | R | ER | SO | BB | BR/9 | ERA | WS |
|---|---|---|---|---|---|---|---|---|---|---|---|---|---|---|---|
| SP | Bronson Arroyo | 33 | 33 | 15 | 13 | 0 | 220.1 | 214 | 101 | 94 | 127 | 65 | 11.76 | 3.84 | 13 |
| SP | Johnny Cueto | 30 | 30 | 11 | 11 | 0 | 171.1 | 172 | 90 | 84 | 132 | 61 | 12.97 | 4.41 | 7 |
| SP | Homer Bailey | 20 | 20 | 8 | 5 | 0 | 113.1 | 115 | 61 | 57 | 86 | 52 | 13.50 | 4.53 | 5 |
| SP | Aaron Harang | 26 | 26 | 6 | 14 | 0 | 162.1 | 186 | 82 | 76 | 142 | 43 | 12.92 | 4.21 | 7 |
| SP | Micah Owings | 26 | 19 | 7 | 12 | 1 | 119.2 | 126 | 75 | 71 | 68 | 64 | 14.74 | 5.34 | 4 |
| CL | Francisco Cordero | 68 | 0 | 2 | 6 | 39 | 66.2 | 58 | 21 | 16 | 58 | 30 | 11.88 | 2.16 | 13 |
| RP | Nick Masset | 74 | 0 | 5 | 1 | 0 | 76.0 | 54 | 22 | 20 | 70 | 24 | 9.24 | 2.37 | 10 |
| RP | Daniel Ray Herrera | 70 | 0 | 4 | 4 | 0 | 61.2 | 63 | 30 | 21 | 44 | 24 | 12.99 | 3.06 | 5 |

## Willy's Flat Bat

As always, Willy Taveras led the majors in bunt attempts in 2009. Taveras put 46 bunts in play in 2009, most in the majors, and now has 164 over the last three seasons.

## Nix Plus Nix Is More Than Naught

If you combine the 2009 stat lines for the two brothers, 29-year-old Laynce Nix of the Reds and 27-year-old Jayson Nix of the White Sox, you get a full season of play and some pretty nice power numbers (though not much of a batting average).

| Player | AB | R | H | 2B | 3B | HR | RBI | AVG |
|--------|-----|----|-----|----|----|----|-----|------|
| Laynce Nix | 309 | 42 | 74 | 26 | 1 | 15 | 46 | .239 |
| Jayson Nix | 255 | 36 | 57 | 11 | 0 | 12 | 32 | .224 |
| **Total** | **564** | **78** | **131** | **37** | **1** | **27** | **78** | **.232** |

## The Dusty Reds

In 2007 — the last year before Dusty Baker — Cincinnati leadoff men had a .368 on-base percentage, and the team scored 783 runs. In 2009, their leadoff men had a .302 on-base percentage, and the team scored 673 runs.

On the other hand, the Reds' defense has improved immensely. In 2007 the Reds' defense, carrying Adam Dunn, was -63 plays according to John Dewan's Plus/Minus System, meaning that they made 63 plays less than an average defense would make. They were -41 in the outfield, -29 on the corners of the infield, and got a little of that back at second base and short.

In 2009 they were +21 plays — +27 in the outfield, still good at short and second, still bad at first and third, but better than they were in 2007.

**Cincinnati Reds Team Totals and Rankings — 2007-2009**

| Year | Plus/Minus | | | | | Bunts | Throwing |
|------|-------------------|------------------|----------|-------|------|-------|----------|
| | Middle Infield | Corner Infield | Outfield | Total | Rank | Rank | Rank |
| 2007 | +7 | -29 | -41 | -63 | 27 | 21 | 11 |
| 2008 | +2 | -11 | -24 | -33 | 22 | 9 | 5 |
| 2009 | +8 | -14 | +27 | +21 | 9 | 1 | 1 |

## Fancy Fielding

And when you add it all up, the Reds had the best defense in the National League in 2009. The Reds defense saved an estimated 52 runs compared to an average defensive team, the best total in the National League. Defensive Runs Saved converts Dewan's Plus/Minus system into an estimate of the number of runs saved defensively. Seven other methods measuring various aspects of defense, such as turning double plays, controlling the running game, handling bunts, and throwing out runners from the outfield, are also converted to runs in Defensive Runs Saved.

### Team Defensive Runs Saved — National League 2009

| Team | P | C | 1B | 2B | 3B | SS | LF | CF | RF | Tot |
|------|---|---|----|----|----|----|----|----|----|----|
| Cincinnati | 12 | 1 | -3 | -3 | -3 | 10 | 17 | 14 | 7 | 52 |
| Arizona | -5 | 3 | -13 | 13 | -4 | 9 | 15 | 4 | 12 | 34 |
| San Francisco | 8 | -4 | 11 | -4 | -6 | -8 | 12 | 6 | 19 | 34 |
| Pittsburgh | 4 | 0 | -1 | -9 | 0 | 16 | 12 | 0 | 9 | 31 |
| St Louis | 11 | 5 | 12 | -8 | -8 | 14 | -5 | 4 | 6 | 31 |
| Los Angeles | 0 | 5 | 3 | 8 | 15 | 5 | -5 | -3 | 2 | 30 |
| New York | 13 | -1 | 13 | -12 | -11 | -6 | 5 | 11 | 8 | 20 |
| Philadelphia | -5 | 2 | -1 | 14 | 7 | -5 | -2 | -6 | 12 | 16 |
| Chicago | 3 | 7 | 3 | 0 | -4 | 2 | -2 | -1 | 8 | 16 |
| Colorado | 5 | -2 | -2 | 2 | 2 | 13 | 15 | -10 | -11 | 12 |
| Atlanta | 4 | 2 | 7 | -11 | 2 | 19 | -11 | -10 | 6 | 8 |
| Washington | 8 | -1 | -19 | 0 | 21 | -3 | -3 | 10 | -6 | 7 |
| San Diego | 5 | 2 | 12 | -20 | 1 | -14 | 0 | 17 | -4 | -1 |
| Houston | 3 | 2 | -2 | -4 | -12 | -15 | -3 | 10 | 19 | -2 |
| Milwaukee | -10 | -7 | -1 | 20 | -8 | 2 | -13 | 0 | -5 | -22 |
| Florida | -12 | -4 | -8 | -7 | -5 | 4 | -18 | 4 | 18 | -28 |

## Ryan and Ramon

Catcher Ryan Hanigan threw out 40.4% of base stealers in 2009, tied for the best in baseball. But now that veteran starting catcher Ramon Hernandez has been re-signed for 2010, Hanigan must be wondering what he has to do to win the starting job, given their respective 2009 performances.

| Player | Age | AB | OPS | Win Shares | Defensive Runs Saved | 2010 Salary |
|--------|-----|-----|-----|------------|----------------------|-------------|
| Ryan Hanigan | 28 | 251 | .692 | 8 | 2 | $400,000 |
| Ramon Hernandez | 33 | 287 | .699 | 10 | -3 | $3,000,000 |

### Barry Larkin, #11

This is not a case for Barry Larkin to make the Hall of Fame. That's for the BBWAA to decide. The statistics are in the history books. He'll make it on the second ballot, or the fourth, or he'll be elected by the Veteran's Committee, or he won't be elected at all. This is about Barry Larkin the ballplayer. A Cincinnati native who played baseball for a large, Catholic high school there, who was a first-round pick out of the University of Michigan in 1985. Who took over shortstop from another Reds great, Dave Concepcion, who also played his entire career with the Reds. If Cal Ripken redefined the position, Barry Larkin took it mainstream. He wore the white polyester uniform with dual red-racing stripes down the legs; his #11 wristbands ran from the bottom of his black glove halfway up his arm. He could just as easily flatten a catcher with the acceleration of a Tomahawk Missile (Mike Heath comes to mind) as turn a perfect pivot on a double play, seeming to hover like a toy glider above the outstretched arms of an incoming baserunner, his feet just a little too large for his jackrabbit legs. When finally elected as a starter to the All-Star Game in 1993,

*If Cal Ripken redefined the position, Barry Larkin took it mainstream.*

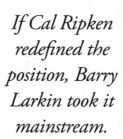

he ran out to his position and performed a flawless back-flip, because that's what Ozzie Smith always used to do. The torch had been passed. In truth, he should have been the All-Star starter long before that. He was cocky in a way that made other kids want to be him, to chomp bubblegum and wear their batting gloves in their back pocket. He was smooth in a way that could only have been considered smooth in the early-nineties … pre-grunge, pre-strike, pre-world-wide-web … when high fives weren't just cool, they were choreographed. The media sought him out. It wasn't until later, toward the end of his career … post-strike, mid-tech-bubble … when he said some things. He stripped the captain's C from his uniform and replaced it with the numbers of players who had been traded, along with the words "Who's next?" He wanted to play for a winner. But who doesn't? Barry Larkin retired in 2005. He's a studio analyst now, and was the bench coach for the United States in the 2009 World Baseball Classic. But the point is, you don't see him around Cincinnati much anymore. Maybe it's true what they say: You really can't go home again.

### Harangue Him Again, Harangue Him Again, Harder, Harder

Over the last two years the Reds are 23-32 in games started by Aaron Harang — 12-31 when Harang got the decision, but 11-1 when he did not. They provided him with 3.42 runs per game in 2009, the least of any Reds starting pitcher, and 3.52 in 2008, also the least of any Reds' starting pitcher. It may be a team-wide conspiracy: According to *The Hardball Times Baseball Annual 2010*, the Reds posted a woeful .659 defensive-efficiency ratio behind Harang in 2009, the lowest for any major-league pitcher with at least 162 innings pitched. Meaning that balls in play against Harang tended to become hits, rather than outs.

## A Cold Spell

On July 26, Joey Votto was hitting .352. He was a model of consistency for the season having posted batting averages of .346 in April, .378 in May, .321 in June, and .354 through that point in July. He then went into a month-and-a-half slump. From July 26 through August 8 he went 7-for-46 (.152) dropping his average down to .319. He hit his season low "temperature" of 45 degrees on that date, based on our formula to measure how hot and cold hitters are at any given time. But it didn't stop there. The skid continued until September 9, when his season average dropped all the way down to .295. From July 26 through September 9, Votto posted a .207 batting average in 150 at-bats.

He then finished the season with a bang. He hit his season-high temperature of 113 degrees on September 26 after an 11-game stretch where he went 22-for-40 (.550), lifting his season average to .318. He stayed hot and brought his average to .322 by season's end.

**Hot and Cold Summary — Joey Votto 2009**

| | |
|---|---|
| Season Ending Temperature | 101° |
| High Point of the Season (Sept. 26) | 113° |
| Low Point of the Season (Aug. 8) | 45° |
| Days Over 100° | 6 |
| Days Under 50° | 2 |
| Average Daily Temperature | 77.0° |

## Potential Realized?

Homer Bailey turned the corner in late August. In his first 11 starts, Bailey was 2-4 with a 7.53 ERA. It looked like a continuation of his first two partial years with the Reds in 2007 and 2008 when he went 4-8. 6.72 ERA. In his last 9 starts, he was 6-1, 1.70. He allowed fewer walks and hits, but it was his strikeout rate that really improved, from 5.4 to 8.2 strikeouts per nine innings.

**Homer Bailey**

| | GS | INN | H | SO | BB | SO/9 | W-L | ERA |
|---|---|---|---|---|---|---|---|---|
| 2007-2008 | 17 | 81.2 | 102 | 46 | 45 | 5.1 | 4-8 | 6.72 |
| First 11 Starts, 2009 | 11 | 55.0 | 62 | 33 | 28 | 5.4 | 2-4 | 7.53 |
| Last 9 Starts, 2009 | 9 | 58.1 | 53 | 53 | 24 | 8.2 | 6-1 | 1.70 |

## Holding Runners

Reds pitchers were remarkable in controlling the running game in 2009. Eight different pitchers contributed an estimated 10 runs saved compared to the average pitcher by preventing runners from attempting stolen bases as well as catching them when they tried. Certainly the 40% caught stealing percentage posted by catcher Ryan Hanigan helped, but nabbing nine runners with throws to first by these pitchers tells the main story leading to their overall 56% caught stealing rate.

### Reds Pitchers — 2009 Key Pitchers Controlling the Running Game

| Player | Stolen Base Attempts | Caught by Catcher | Caught by Pitcher | Caught Steal PCT | Runs Saved |
|---|---|---|---|---|---|
| Bronson Arroyo | 18 | 5 | 1 | 33% | 1 |
| Johnny Cueto | 7 | 3 | 2 | 71% | 2 |
| Francisco Cordero | 7 | 3 | 1 | 57% | 1 |
| Daniel Herrera | 3 | 2 | 0 | 67% | 1 |
| Arthur Rhodes | 4 | 1 | 1 | 50% | 1 |
| Carlos Fisher | 6 | 4 | * 1 | 83% | 2 |
| Matt Maloney | 5 | 2 | 1 | 60% | 1 |
| Mike Lincoln | 2 | 1 | 1 | 100% | 1 |
| **Total** | **52** | **21** | *** 8** | **56%** | **10** |

*Carlos Fisher also had a pickoff

## Hanigan, Janish, Gonzalez et al

Reds number eight hitters in 2009 combined for 41 runs and 46 RBI in 2009 — the worst productivity from the 8 spot in the major leagues. Even Reds #9 hitters scored 44 and drove in 41.

# Cleveland Indians

**2009 TEAM OVERVIEW**

**65-97**

**4** th place AL Central

| | RUNS | HOME RUNS | BATTING AVG. | WALKS | OPS | STOLEN BASES |
|---|---|---|---|---|---|---|
| **Opp.** | **865** | **183** | **.280** | **598** | **.793** | **111** |
| **ML RANK** | 26th | 21st | 29th | 20th | 26th | 17th |

## Key Players

| Pos | Player | G | AB | R | H | 2B | 3B | HR | RBI | SB | CS | BB | SO | AVG | OBP | SLG | OPS | WS |
|-----|--------|---|----|----|----|----|----|----|-----|----|----|----|----|-----|-----|-----|-----|-----|
| C | Kelly Shoppach | 89 | 271 | 33 | 58 | 14 | 0 | 12 | 40 | 0 | 0 | 33 | 98 | .214 | .335 | .399 | .734 | 7 |
| 1B | Victor Martinez | 99 | 377 | 56 | 107 | 21 | 1 | 15 | 67 | 0 | 0 | 51 | 51 | .284 | .368 | .464 | .832 | 13 |
| 2B | Luis Valbuena | 103 | 368 | 52 | 92 | 25 | 3 | 10 | 31 | 2 | 3 | 26 | 83 | .250 | .298 | .416 | .714 | 6 |
| 3B | Jhonny Peralta | 151 | 582 | 57 | 148 | 35 | 1 | 11 | 83 | 0 | 2 | 51 | 134 | .254 | .316 | .375 | .690 | 10 |
| SS | Asdrubal Cabrera | 131 | 523 | 81 | 161 | 42 | 4 | 6 | 68 | 17 | 4 | 44 | 89 | .308 | .361 | .438 | .799 | 18 |
| LF | Ben Francisco | 89 | 308 | 48 | 77 | 21 | 1 | 10 | 33 | 13 | 3 | 33 | 59 | .250 | .336 | .422 | .758 | 7 |
| CF | Grady Sizemore | 106 | 436 | 73 | 108 | 20 | 6 | 18 | 64 | 13 | 8 | 60 | 92 | .248 | .343 | .445 | .788 | 13 |
| RF | Shin-Soo Choo | 156 | 583 | 87 | 175 | 38 | 6 | 20 | 86 | 21 | 2 | 78 | 151 | .300 | .394 | .489 | .883 | 23 |
| DH | Travis Hafner | 94 | 338 | 46 | 92 | 19 | 0 | 16 | 49 | 0 | 0 | 41 | 67 | .272 | .355 | .470 | .826 | 8 |

## Key Pitchers

| Pos | Player | G | GS | W | L | SV | IP | H | R | ER | SO | BB | BR/9 | ERA | WS |
|-----|--------|---|----|----|----|----|-----|----|----|----|----|----|------|-----|-----|
| SP | David Huff | 23 | 23 | 11 | 8 | 0 | 128.1 | 159 | 82 | 80 | 65 | 41 | 14.10 | 5.61 | 3 |
| SP | Carl Pavano | 21 | 21 | 9 | 8 | 0 | 125.2 | 150 | 80 | 75 | 88 | 23 | 12.60 | 5.37 | 3 |
| SP | Cliff Lee | 22 | 22 | 7 | 9 | 0 | 152.0 | 165 | 53 | 53 | 107 | 33 | 11.90 | 3.14 | 11 |
| SP | Fausto Carmona | 24 | 24 | 5 | 12 | 0 | 125.1 | 151 | 97 | 88 | 79 | 70 | 16.44 | 6.32 | 0 |
| SP | Jeremy Sowers | 23 | 22 | 6 | 11 | 0 | 123.1 | 134 | 73 | 72 | 51 | 52 | 13.79 | 5.25 | 3 |
| CL | Kerry Wood | 58 | 0 | 3 | 3 | 20 | 55.0 | 48 | 26 | 26 | 63 | 28 | 12.93 | 4.25 | 6 |
| RP | Rafael Perez | 54 | 0 | 4 | 3 | 0 | 48.0 | 66 | 41 | 39 | 32 | 25 | 17.44 | 7.31 | 0 |
| RP | Jensen Lewis | 47 | 0 | 2 | 4 | 1 | 66.1 | 62 | 37 | 34 | 62 | 29 | 12.62 | 4.61 | 3 |

## Falling Behind Early

The 2009 Indians were ahead after one inning and ahead after two innings less often than any other major league team.

### Indians — Innings Ahead/Behind/Tied 2009

| Inning | 1 | 2 | 3 | 4 | 5 | 6 | 7 | 8 | 9 | Extra | Final |
|--------|----|----|----|----|----|----|----|----|----|-------|-------|
| Ahead | 29 | 35 | 55 | 61 | 58 | 56 | 61 | 58 | 61 | 4 | 65 |
| Behind | 41 | 65 | 72 | 77 | 81 | 88 | 87 | 91 | 88 | 8 | 97 |
| Tied | 92 | 62 | 35 | 24 | 23 | 18 | 14 | 12 | 12 | 15 | -- |

## Thank God the Pitchers Don't Bat

The ninth spot in the Indians' lineup was the most productive tail end of the order in the American League. Cleveland had the highest on-base percentage, .340, and slugging percentage, .394, in the league. The league averaged a .305 on-base percentage and slugging percentage of .349 from the ninth spot in the order.

| Pos | Players | AVG | OBP | SLG | OPS |
|-----|---------|-----|-----|-----|-----|
| 1 | Sizemore (77 G), Cabrera (32 G), Brantley (23 G) | .258 | .337 | .391 | .728 |
| 2 | Cabrera (58 G), Carroll (36 G), Sizemore (28 G) | .289 | .345 | .443 | .787 |
| 3 | Martinez (87 G), Choo (49 G), Cabrera (21 G) | .293 | .375 | .452 | .826 |
| 4 | Choo (85 G), Peralta (43 G), Hafner (18 G) | .277 | .359 | .448 | .808 |
| 5 | Peralta (73 G), Hafner (43 G), DeRosa (20 G) | .258 | .334 | .408 | .742 |
| 6 | Hafner (27 G), Valbuena (24 G), Peralta (21 G) | .240 | .314 | .385 | .699 |
| 7 | Garko (32 G), Shoppach (24 G), Valbuena (23 G) | .249 | .322 | .433 | .755 |
| 8 | Valbuena (31 G), Francisco (22 G), Crowe (19 G) | .250 | .322 | .391 | .713 |
| 9 | Shoppach (31 G), Crowe (26 G), Francisco (18 G) | .253 | .340 | .394 | .734 |
| **Total** | | **.264** | **.339** | **.417** | **.756** |

## Why Does This Always Happen to Cleveland?

The Indians lost their last 15 road games of the season, the most consecutive road losses by any major league team to end a season since the infamous 1899 Cleveland Spiders.

## Strikeout Famine

Among American League pitchers who faced 300 batters last season, four of the ten lowest strikeout rates per out were posted by Cleveland pitchers Jeremy Sowers, Aaron Laffey, Tomo Ohka and David Huff.

| Jeremy Sowers 2009 | |
| --- | --- |
| Batters Faced | 545 |
| Reached Base | 208 |
| Retired | 337 |

| Retired By | |
| --- | --- |
| Strikeout | 51 |
| Ground Out | 114 |
| Line Out | 9 |
| Fly Out | 132 |
| Pop Out | 31 |
| Other | 0 |

| Aaron Laffey 2009 | |
| --- | --- |
| Batters Faced | 539 |
| Reached Base | 220 |
| Retired | 319 |

| Retired By | |
| --- | --- |
| Strikeout | 58 |
| Ground Out | 135 |
| Line Out | 10 |
| Fly Out | 93 |
| Pop Out | 23 |
| Other | 0 |

| Tomo Ohka 2009 | |
| --- | --- |
| Batters Faced | 306 |
| Reached Base | 108 |
| Retired | 198 |

| Retired By | |
| --- | --- |
| Strikeout | 30 |
| Ground Out | 75 |
| Line Out | 4 |
| Fly Out | 61 |
| Pop Out | 28 |
| Other | 0 |

| David Huff 2009 | |
| --- | --- |
| Batters Faced | 574 |
| Reached Base | 221 |
| Retired | 353 |

| Retired By | |
| --- | --- |
| Strikeout | 65 |
| Ground Out | 116 |
| Line Out | 14 |
| Fly Out | 104 |
| Pop Out | 52 |
| Other | 0 |

## Ouch

Cleveland batters were hit by 81 pitches last season, 11 more than any other American League team, and 29 more times than the league average.

The main victims were Kelly Shoppach and Shin-Soo Choo, who finished first and second in the league in being hit by pitches with 18 and 17. Ryan Garko was tied for 7th most with 10 hit by pitches.

## Youth Is On Their Side

Cleveland had the youngest hitters in the American League last season.

Only 1,571 of the Indians 6,320 plate appearances were by players age 30 or older.

48% of the plate appearances by the older players were by Victor Martinez and Mark DeRosa.

## Can You Make One Home Run Count?

It is generally though imperfectly true that everybody wins 70% of the time when they hit 2 homers in a game and loses 70% of the time when they don't hit any. The difference is in the ability to win with one home run. The Indians in 2007 could do that. In 2009, they couldn't.

| Indians Record By Home Runs — 2007 | | Indians Record By Home Runs — 2009 | |
| --- | --- | --- | --- |
| HR | W-L | HR | W-L |
| 0 | 20-27 | 0 | 19-54 |
| 1 | 38-29 | 1 | 16-25 |
| 2 | 29-8 | 2 | 21-13 |
| 3 or more | 9-2 | 3 or more | 9-5 |

## Ground Ball to Short

Jhonny Peralta hit 147 ground balls to the left side in 2009 — more than any other major league player. Unfortunately, he averaged just .136 on those plays.

**Jhonny Peralta — Ground Balls to Left**

| GB to Left | Outs | H | AVG | 1B | 2B | 3B | HR |
| --- | --- | --- | --- | --- | --- | --- | --- |
| 147 | 127 | 20 | .136 | 16 | 4 | 0 | 0 |

## Jamey Carroll, Multi-Year Pitch Analysis

Jamey Carroll had the third highest percentage of pitches taken in the major leagues last season, 66%. This was the highest figure of his career, but since 2004 he has never taken fewer than 59% of the pitches he has seen.

| | 2004 | 2005 | 2006 | 2007 | 2008 | 2009 |
| --- | --- | --- | --- | --- | --- | --- |
| Pitches Seen | 1,119 | 1,457 | 2,215 | 1,077 | 1,623 | 1,520 |
| Taken | 695 | 858 | 1,371 | 650 | 1,000 | 1,006 |
| Take % | 62% | 59% | 62% | 60% | 62% | 66% |
| Swung At | 424 | 599 | 844 | 427 | 623 | 514 |
| Swing % | 38% | 41% | 38% | 40% | 38% | 34% |

## David vs. King Felix

What was the worst pitching mismatch of 2009? On August 23rd at Jacobs Field in Cleveland, the Indians sent Fausto Carmona to the mound against Felix Hernandez. Carmona finished the season 5-12 with a 6.32 ERA, a Season Score of -49. Hernandez finished the year 19-5 with a 2.49 ERA, a Season Score of 299 — the highest of the year. In terms of their starting pitchers, Seattle had a 348-point advantage.

Naturally, Cleveland won the game. Carmona pitched 7 innings, giving up just 5 hits and one run — his best start of the year. King Felix pitched 6 innings, giving up 9 hits and 6 runs — not his worst outing of the year, but one of his worst. Cleveland won 6-1. This is truly baseball.

OK, one game, anything can happen. The question I was trying to get to is this: How often does the team with the best pitcher on the mound actually win the game?

59%. 59.1% of the time, in 2009, the team with the better starting pitcher on the mound wound up winning the game.

I've wondered about that question for a long time, and, with Retrosheet and modern computers and a son who can write code to parse the data, I was finally able to get an answer. We determined "better pitcher on the mound" by the Season Score — a method which takes into account innings pitched, runs and earned runs allowed, wins, losses, strikeouts and walks (and also saves, although that's not a big factor for starting pitchers). These are some season scores for representative pitchers from 2009:

| | Player | G | W | L | IP | R | ER | SO | BB | ERA | Score |
|---|---|---|---|---|---|---|---|---|---|---|---|
| **300 Level** | Felix Hernandez | 34 | 19 | 5 | 238.2 | 81 | 66 | 217 | 71 | 2.49 | 299 |
| **250 Level** | Roy Halladay | 32 | 17 | 10 | 239.0 | 82 | 74 | 208 | 35 | 2.79 | 255 |
| | Justin Verlander | 35 | 19 | 9 | 240.0 | 99 | 92 | 269 | 63 | 3.45 | 245 |
| **200 Level** | Josh Beckett | 32 | 17 | 6 | 212.1 | 99 | 91 | 199 | 55 | 3.86 | 202 |
| | Jon Lester | 32 | 15 | 8 | 203.1 | 80 | 77 | 225 | 64 | 3.41 | 199 |
| **150 Level** | Tommy Hanson | 21 | 11 | 4 | 127.2 | 42 | 41 | 116 | 46 | 2.89 | 154 |
| | Jeff Niemann | 31 | 13 | 6 | 180.2 | 84 | 79 | 125 | 59 | 3.94 | 146 |
| **100 Level** | Jarrod Washburn | 28 | 9 | 9 | 176.0 | 77 | 74 | 100 | 49 | 3.78 | 104 |
| | Cole Hamels | 32 | 10 | 11 | 193.2 | 95 | 93 | 168 | 43 | 4.32 | 98 |
| **50 Level** | David Huff | 23 | 11 | 8 | 128.1 | 82 | 80 | 65 | 41 | 5.61 | 50 |
| | Trevor Cahill | 32 | 10 | 13 | 178.2 | 99 | 92 | 90 | 72 | 4.63 | 49 |
| **Zero Level** | Joe Martinez | 9 | 3 | 2 | 30.0 | 27 | 25 | 19 | 12 | 7.50 | 0 |
| | Micah Owings | 26 | 7 | 12 | 119.2 | 75 | 71 | 68 | 64 | 5.34 | 0 |
| **-50 Level** | Fausto Carmona | 24 | 5 | 12 | 125.1 | 97 | 88 | 79 | 70 | 6.32 | -49 |
| | Sidney Ponson | 14 | 1 | 7 | 58.2 | 50 | 48 | 32 | 25 | 7.36 | -51 |

So if Detroit was playing Cleveland and Justin Verlander was opposing Jon Lester, we would figure that Detroit had the better pitcher on the mound by a margin of 46 points, notwithstanding that Lester actually had a better ERA than Verlander. There is an argument either way, but to answer the question that we posed, we have to decide who is better, and our system decides that Verlander is better.

A little more than one-third of major league games in 2009 featured pitching matchups — like this one — that were essentially even; we have to decide who is better, so we do, but it's a fair fight. There were 2,430 regular-season games in 2009. In 844 of those, the difference in the season scores of the starting pitchers was less than 50 points — a small difference. When the difference was small, the team with the better pitcher on the mound won 435 times, lost 409 — a .515 percentage.

But when the difference in the quality of the starting pitchers was more than 50 points, the team with the better pitcher on the mound won more than 60% of the time.

When the difference was 50 to 100 points, the winning percentage of the team with the better pitcher was .602 (397-262).

When the difference was 100 to 150 points, the winning percentage of the team with the better starting pitcher was .623 (286-173).

When the difference was 150 to 200 points, the winning percentage of the team with the better starting pitcher was .645 (185-102).

When the difference was more than 200 points, the winning percentage of the team with the better starting pitcher was .729 (132-49).

Notwithstanding Fausto Carmona beating Felix Hernandez.

# What I Would Do with the All-Star Game If It Was Up To Me

by Bill James

FIRST OF ALL, I'D CUT THE ROSTERS TO 18 PLAYERS. I USED TO BE more radical on this, back when the managers had entirely lost track of trying to win the game and were just trying to make sure that everybody got one at-bat. I couldn't stand that…long strings of at-bats, the only purpose of which was to enable people to say that "I played in the All-Star game". When they were doing that I wanted to cut the rosters down to 14. I have since realized there might be actual problems with playing the game with a 14-man roster, so I'll agree to 18.

*The Pirates' fans would vote on which Pirates' player they wanted to send to the All-Star game; the Dodger fans would vote on which Dodger to send.*

The composition of the rosters would be largely determined by the fans' votes, in this way. Each city would be its own "precinct" for the voting, and each ballpark would vote only on the players who played there. In other words, the Pirates' fans would vote on which Pirates' player they wanted to send to the All-Star game; the Dodger fans would vote on which Dodger to send. Balloting would be only at the ballpark, and only for the players who played in that park.

The manager would pick the roster, within these limits:

1) That he must pick one player from each team,
2) That he must pick at least 8 players who finished first in the balloting in their precinct,
3) That he must pick at least 12 players who finished 1 or 2 in the balloting in their precinct,
4) That he must pick at least 16 players who finished 1, 2 or 3 in the balloting in their precinct, and
5) That he cannot pick more than two players from any team.

Four players from the host team or the closest team in the other league would be designated as injury backups, on hand to insure that the game can be completed.

## American League Team

There would never be a situation in which it would be difficult to choose an outstanding team within these rules, absolutely never. In 2010, the options in the American League might be something like this:

| Team | Player1 | Player 2 | Player 3 |
|------|---------|----------|----------|
| Bal | Nick Markakis | Brian Roberts | Adam Jones |
| Bos | Dustin Pedroia | Kevin Youkilis | Josh Beckett |
| CWS | Mark Buehrle | Carlos Quentin | Gordon Beckham |
| Cle | Grady Sizemore | Asdrubal Cabrera | Shin-Soo Choo |
| Det | Miguel Cabrera | Justin Verlander | Rick Porcello |
| KC | Zack Greinke | Billy Butler | Joakim Soria |
| LAA | Kendry Morales | Brian Fuentes | Jered Weaver |
| Min | Joe Mauer | Justin Morneau | Joe Nathan |
| NYY | Derek Jeter | Mark Teixeira | CC Sabathia |
| Oak | Kurt Suzuki | Brett Anderson | Ryan Sweeney |
| Sea | Ichiro Suzuki | Cliff Lee | Felix Hernandez |
| TB | Evan Longoria | Carl Crawford | Jason Bartlett |
| Tex | Ian Kinsler | Michael Young | Josh Hamilton |
| Tor | Adam Lind | Aaron Hill | Travis Snider |

You look at that as a manager, you've got to think "Wow. I get 18 of these guys? I'm going to be OK." You'd start by looking down the list of #1s that you would want on the team…Mauer, Greinke, Cabrera, Longoria. At second base I've got Pedroia or Kinsler; either one of them is OK, so I'll choose one of them later. I don't have a reliever who is a "1", so my options there are Nathan, Soria, Fuentes. Jeter gives me a shortstop, and I've got three outfielders who are #1s in Lind, Sizemore and Markakis, so that gives me 8 number one picks:

| | |
|------|------|
| Battery | Zack Greinke and Joe Mauer |
| Infield | Miguel Cabrera, Evan Longoria, Derek Jeter |
| Outfield | Adam Lind, Grady Sizemore and Nick Markakis |

I'm going to need a lot more pitching, so let's look at the pitchers who are "2's"—Verlander, Fuentes, Brett Anderson and Cliff Lee. Not crazy about Brett Anderson or Fuentes, but there's no rule against adding more #1s, so I'll add Buehrle and Pedroia, Verlander and Cliff Lee, and I've basically got a team:

| | |
|------|------|
| P | Zack Greinke, Justin Verlander, Cliff Lee, Mark Buehrle |
| C | Joe Mauer |
| INF | Miguel Cabrera, Dustin Pedroia, Evan Longoria and Derek Jeter |
| OUT | Adam Lind, Grady Sizemore and Nick Markakis |

At this point I need a DH and two or three relievers, and I've got to cover the A's, Angels and the Rangers. Kendry Morales can DH, and I'll pick Michael Young because he can play second, third or short if need be; that's 14. I've got four picks left, and I can choose anybody on the charts and two people not on the charts. I'll take Felix Hernandez and Mariano Rivera for the pitching staff; two left, but I can't pick any more from those three teams; can't take Sabathia or Teixeira or Ichiro. I'll take Kurt Suzuki as a backup catcher and Brian Roberts for the infield and to pinch run.

Now that's an All-Star team:

| Pos | Player | Pos | Player |
|-----|--------|-----|--------|
| C | Joe Mauer | P | Justin Verlander |
| 1B | Miguel Cabrera | P | Zack Greinke |
| 2B | Dustin Pedroia | P | Mark Buehrle |
| 3B | Evan Longoria | P | Cliff Lee |
| SS | Derek Jeter | P | Mariano Rivera |
| LF | Adam Lind | P | Felix Hernandez |
| CF | Grady Sizemore | C | Kurt Suzuki |
| RF | Nick Markakis | 2B | Brian Roberts |
| DH | Kendry Morales | SS | Michael Young |

You've got about a dozen Hall of Famers there, twelve #1 picks in the voting, four #2 picks, one #3 pick, and one other guy (Mariano Rivera). I'd pay to watch those guys play a baseball game. Brandon Inge taking his at-bat and getting congratulations for being an All-Star…I've seen enough of that. No city gets shorted in the voting, nobody gets to go to the All-Star game because his old manager owes him a favor and he's having a decent year. It's all stars. Almost everybody on the roster is going to get into the game. Los Angeles is the host city, so the Angels sends four guys to protect the roster in case of injuries.

## National League Team

That was kind of fun; let's do the NL. The voting might go something like this, depending on who is having a good year in 2010:

| Team | Player 1 | Player 2 | Player 3 |
|------|----------|----------|----------|
| Ari | Justin Upton | Dan Haren | Mark Reynolds |
| Atl | Yunel Escobar | Jair Jurrjens | Brian McCann |
| CHC | Carlos Zambrano | Ted Lilly | Ryan Theriot |
| Cin | Joey Votto | Brandon Phillips | Bronson Arroyo |
| Col | Troy Tulowitzki | Brad Hawpe | Todd Helton |
| Fla | Hanley Ramirez | Josh Johnson | Dan Uggla |
| Hou | Roy Oswalt | Carlos Lee | Hunter Pence |
| LAD | Matt Kemp | Jon. Broxton | Andre Ethier |
| Mil | Ryan Braun | Prince Fielder | Yovani Gallardo |
| NYM | David Wright | Carlos Beltran | Johan Santana |
| Phi | Chase Utley | Ryan Howard | Roy Halladay |
| Pit | And. McCutchen | Zach Duke | Andy LaRoche |
| SD | Adrian Gonzalez | Luke Gregerson | Heath Bell |
| SF | Tim Lincecum | Pablo Sandoval | Matt Cain |
| StL | Albert Pujols | Chris Carpenter | Adam Wainwright |
| Was | Ryan Zimmerman | Adam Dunn | John Lannan |

We'll start with the most obvious picks — Hanley Ramirez, Adrian Gonzalez and Albert Pujols. Brian McCann looks like the only catcher who made any list anywhere, so we'll include him:

| Pos | Player | | Pos | Player |
|-----|--------|---|-----|--------|
| C | Brian McCann | | SS | Hanley Ramirez |
| 1B | Albert Pujols | | DH | Adrian Gonzalez |

Chase Utley at second and Tim Lincecum for the mound are pretty obvious; that gives me five #1s on the list, need three more. Oswalt and Ryan Zimmerman:

| Pos | Player | | Pos | Player |
|-----|--------|---|-----|--------|
| C | Brian McCann | | SS | Hanley Ramirez |
| 1B | Albert Pujols | | DH | Adrian Gonzalez |
| 2B | Chase Utley | | P | Tim Lincecum |
| 3B | Ryan Zimmerman | | P | Roy Oswalt |

I've got no outfield, but Ryan Braun and Matt Kemp are #1s; that takes care of the #1s with one to spare. Right field is empty; I can use Justin Upton for that. Well…would I rather have Upton or Andrew McCutchen? I'll use McCutchen, and that way I can choose Dan Harren. That's 12:

| Pos | Player | | Pos | Player |
|-----|--------|---|-----|--------|
| C | Brian McCann | | CF | Matt Kemp |
| 1B | Albert Pujols | | RF | Andrew McCutchen |
| 2B | Chase Utley | | DH | Adrian Gonzalez |
| 3B | Ryan Zimmerman | | P | Tim Lincecum |
| SS | Hanley Ramirez | | P | Dan Haren |
| LF | Ryan Braun | | P | Roy Oswalt |

I need three more pitchers and I have to cover the Cubs, Reds, Rockies and the Mets. I'll go with Ubaldo Jimenez, Ted Lilly and Johan Santana. For bench players, how about Ryan Howard and Brandon Phillips? Who's the best player in the league who's not on my team? Whoever he is, I'll add him…let's say Pablo Sandoval. Could be Chris Carpenter or Chipper Jones; who knows:

| Pos | Player | | Pos | Player |
|-----|--------|---|-----|--------|
| C | Brian McCann | | P | Tim Lincecum |
| 1B | Albert Pujols | | P | Dan Haren |
| 2B | Chase Utley | | P | Roy Oswalt |
| 3B | Ryan Zimmerman | | P | Ubaldo Jimenez |
| SS | Hanley Ramirez | | P | Johan Santana |
| LF | Ryan Braun | | P | Ted Lilly |
| CF | Matt Kemp | | 1B | Ryan Howard |
| RF | Andrew McCutchen | | 2B | Brandon Phillips |
| DH | Adrian Gonzalez | | 3B | Pablo Sandoval |

*I'd pay to watch those guys play a baseball game.*

I think it's a better system; I think it makes a better game with stronger rosters, more meaningful participation from the fans, and it makes selection to the game a real honor. New York and Boston and LA fans can't swamp the voting because there are more of them; they can only vote for their own guys. Fans are not asked (or not allowed) to vote on hundreds of players, many of whom they probably haven't thought about all season. They're asked to sort out the players on their home team. Here's a few other rules I'd put in place to make it work:

1) Home-town injury backups can only be added to the active roster by the consent of the commissioner.

2) Starting pitchers are placed on the inactive list by the league for the Saturday and Sunday before the All-Star game. They can be replaced on the active roster for those games by minor league callups, *without placing those players on the 40-man roster in the normal way.* In other words, it's an "exceptional callup" — an exception to the normal rule that a player called to the majors must be placed on the 40-man roster. San Francisco loses two starting pitchers for Saturday and Sunday, but they can call up Kevin Pucetas and Ryan Sadowski for those two games if they want to.

3) Relief pitchers are placed on the inactive list by the league for the Sunday before the All-Star game, and can also be replaced on the roster for that day.

4) Players who are selected for the All-Star game and choose not to participate are replaced on the All-Star roster by hometown alternates, and are automatically ineligible to play for seven games following the All-Star break.

5) If the manager feels that he is unable to form a satisfactory roster from the players selected by the fans as the top three options on the team, he can petition the commissioner for an exemption from the rules requiring eight #1 fan selections, twelve #1 or #2 selections, and sixteen #1-2-3 selections.

It's not going to happen; there's never going to be a situation where you can't choose a representative roster from the top three players on each team. But just remembering Murphy's Law, you would need a plan in place in case it does…in case, for example, the top three players listed by American League fans include no shortstops and no catchers. Or in case the four first basemen available to the American League all pull up with actual injuries in the last week. (But remember — if you don't play in the All-Star game, you don't play in the seven games following the All-Star game. That's just the rule.)

*New York and Boston and LA fans can't swamp the voting because there are more of them. Fans are not asked (or not allowed) to vote on hundreds of players. They're asked to sort out the players on their home team.*

# Colorado Rockies

| | ML RANK | 6th | 6th | 16th | 2nd | 4th | 11th |
|---|---|---|---|---|---|---|---|
| **2009 TEAM OVERVIEW** | **Team** | **804** | **190** | **.261** | **660** | **.784** | **106** |
| **92-70** | | RUNS | HOME RUNS | BATTING AVG. | WALKS | OPS | STOLEN BASES |
| **2nd place NL West** | **Opp.** | **715** | **141** | **.261** | **528** | **.733** | **115** |
| | ML RANK | 7th | 5th | 14th | 8th | 7th | 19th |

## Key Players

| Pos | Player | G | AB | R | H | 2B | 3B | HR | RBI | SB | CS | BB | SO | AVG | OBP | SLG | OPS | WS |
|---|---|---|---|---|---|---|---|---|---|---|---|---|---|---|---|---|---|---|
| C | Chris Iannetta | 93 | 289 | 41 | 66 | 15 | 2 | 16 | 52 | 0 | 1 | 43 | 75 | .228 | .344 | .460 | .804 | 10 |
| 1B | Todd Helton | 151 | 544 | 79 | 177 | 38 | 3 | 15 | 86 | 0 | 1 | 89 | 73 | .325 | .416 | .489 | .904 | 23 |
| 2B | Clint Barmes | 154 | 550 | 69 | 135 | 32 | 3 | 23 | 76 | 12 | 10 | 31 | 121 | .245 | .294 | .440 | .734 | 13 |
| 3B | Ian Stewart | 147 | 425 | 74 | 97 | 19 | 3 | 25 | 70 | 7 | 4 | 56 | 138 | .228 | .322 | .464 | .785 | 11 |
| SS | Troy Tulowitzki | 151 | 543 | 101 | 161 | 25 | 9 | 32 | 92 | 20 | 11 | 73 | 112 | .297 | .377 | .552 | .930 | 24 |
| LF | Seth Smith | 133 | 335 | 61 | 98 | 20 | 4 | 15 | 55 | 4 | 1 | 46 | 67 | .293 | .378 | .510 | .889 | 14 |
| CF | Dexter Fowler | 135 | 433 | 73 | 115 | 29 | 10 | 4 | 34 | 27 | 10 | 67 | 116 | .266 | .363 | .406 | .770 | 15 |
| RF | Brad Hawpe | 145 | 501 | 82 | 143 | 42 | 3 | 23 | 86 | 1 | 3 | 79 | 145 | .285 | .384 | .519 | .903 | 19 |

## Key Pitchers

| Pos | Player | G | GS | W | L | SV | IP | H | R | ER | SO | BB | BR/9 | ERA | WS |
|---|---|---|---|---|---|---|---|---|---|---|---|---|---|---|---|
| SP | Jorge de la Rosa | 33 | 32 | 16 | 9 | 0 | 185.0 | 172 | 95 | 90 | 193 | 83 | 12.84 | 4.38 | 12 |
| SP | Ubaldo Jimenez | 33 | 33 | 15 | 12 | 0 | 218.0 | 183 | 87 | 84 | 198 | 85 | 11.48 | 3.47 | 19 |
| SP | Jason Marquis | 33 | 33 | 15 | 13 | 0 | 216.0 | 218 | 104 | 97 | 115 | 80 | 12.58 | 4.04 | 15 |
| SP | Aaron Cook | 27 | 27 | 11 | 6 | 0 | 158.0 | 175 | 76 | 73 | 78 | 47 | 12.76 | 4.16 | 11 |
| SP | Jason Hammel | 34 | 30 | 10 | 8 | 0 | 176.2 | 203 | 94 | 85 | 133 | 42 | 12.94 | 4.33 | 10 |
| CL | Huston Street | 64 | 0 | 4 | 1 | 35 | 61.2 | 43 | 22 | 21 | 70 | 13 | 8.17 | 3.06 | 15 |
| RP | Franklin Morales | 40 | 2 | 3 | 2 | 7 | 40.0 | 38 | 22 | 20 | 41 | 23 | 13.95 | 4.50 | 4 |
| RP | Matt Daley | 57 | 0 | 1 | 1 | 0 | 51.0 | 43 | 24 | 24 | 55 | 18 | 11.12 | 4.24 | 4 |

## Second-Half Surge

The Rockies had the best record in the National League after the All-Star break, 45-29.

| Split | W | L | PCT | RS | RA | RS/GM | RA/GM |
|---|---|---|---|---|---|---|---|
| First Half | 47 | 41 | .534 | 442 | 405 | 5.02 | 4.60 |
| Second Half | 45 | 29 | .608 | 362 | 310 | 4.89 | 4.19 |

## Wockies

The Rockies led the National League in walks drawn with 660, 102 more than the average team. Todd Helton, Brad Hawpe and Troy Tulowitzki all finished in the top 20 in the league in base on balls.

## More Walks than Strikeouts

Since 2002, 126 National Leaguers have had a season where they had more walks than strikeouts with at least 300 plate appearances. That equals about one per team per season.

2009 was the 8th straight season Todd Helton had more walks than strikeouts. Only two other Rockies have done this during Helton's streak.

## De la Rosa's Delight

Jorge de la Rosa had the best run-support of any starting pitcher in the National League who made more than 10 starts. The Rockies scored 5.78 runs per game when he started, and they went 20-12 in those games.

## Bases Loaded Bashing

The Rockies led all National League teams with a batting average of .311, an on-base percentage of .376, and slugging percentage of .529 with the bases loaded. Colorado scored 128 runs in 149 plate appearances with the bases loaded.

## Pinch Hitting Par Excellence

Seth Smith was 17 for 36 with a .472 batting average as a pinch-hitter. He also drew 10 walks and ended the season with a 1.436 on-base plus slugging percentage when pinch-hitting.

As a team the Rockies led the National League with a .287 batting average when pinch-hitting (60 of 209).

## Using the Hard Stuff to Set Up the Slow Stuff

Ubaldo Jimenez' fastball averaged 96.1 miles per hour, the highest average in the National League. Jorge de la Rosa's 93.3 mph fastball measured as the fifth-fastest in the league. Both pitchers ranked in the top five of the league in effectiveness with their changeup.

| Fastest Average Fastball (Minimum 162 IP) | | Opposition OPS vs. Changeups (Minimum 100 BF) | |
| --- | --- | --- | --- |
| Player | MPH | Player | OPS |
| Ubaldo Jimenez | 96.1 | Ubaldo Jimenez | .452 |
| Josh Johnson | 95.0 | Tim Lincecum | .483 |
| Clayton Kershaw | 93.9 | Javier Vazquez | .488 |
| Max Scherzer | 93.6 | Jorge de la Rosa | .550 |
| Jorge de la Rosa | 93.3 | John Lannan | .567 |

## Quality Rotation

The Rockies' starting pitchers had the best season in team history. Their 94 quality starts tied the Cubs for the second-most quality starts in the majors. The starters' 4.10 ERA was 48 points lower than their team's previous best. For the first time in club history they had five different starting pitchers reach ten wins in a season.

**Colorado Rockies — 2009 Performance by Starting Pitcher**

| Games Started | GS | Run Support | Runs Allowed | Won | Lost |
|---|---|---|---|---|---|
| Jason Marquis | 33 | 158 | 140 | 19 | 14 |
| Ubaldo Jimenez | 33 | 139 | 129 | 17 | 16 |
| Jorge de la Rosa | 32 | 185 | 165 | 20 | 12 |
| Jason Hammel | 30 | 150 | 136 | 18 | 12 |
| Aaron Cook | 27 | 139 | 119 | 14 | 13 |
| Jose Contreras | 2 | 9 | 2 | 2 | 0 |
| Franklin Morales | 2 | 18 | 8 | 2 | 0 |
| Esmil Rogers | 1 | 2 | 3 | 0 | 1 |
| Josh Fogg | 1 | 1 | 6 | 0 | 1 |
| Jhoulys Chacin | 1 | 3 | 7 | 0 | 1 |
| **Total** | **162** | **804** | **715** | **92** | **70** |

## Loooooooooooong At-Bats

If you watch Rockies games, the first thing you will notice is that Todd Helton's at-bats go on forever. Helton's at-bats last forever not because he is a modern Mike Hargrove (the Human Rain Delay); heck, the Mike Hargrove-type pointless delay of the game is now so ubiquitous that if Hargrove returned and did the same stuff, nobody would notice. Helton's at-bats go on forever because he fouls off approximately 27 pitches per at-bat. That's an estimate; I haven't checked the data.

Helton in 2009 had a batting average of .315 in long at-bats — the highest such average in the National League and the only player to hit .300.

**N.L. Batting Average in Long At-Bats**

| Player | Long AB | H | AVG |
|---|---|---|---|
| 1. Todd Helton, Col | 314 | 99 | .315 |
| 2. Luis Castillo, NYM | 307 | 88 | .287 |
| 3. Troy Tulowitzki, Col | 285 | 81 | .284 |
| 4. Angel Pagan, NYM | 191 | 54 | .283 |
| 5. Joey Votto, Cin | 277 | 78 | .282 |

## The Men Who Made Jim Tracy Famous

Troy Tulowitzki and Carlos Gonzalez helped fuel the Rockies' second half surge into the playoffs. Tulowitzki was good in the first half, but his on-base plus slugging percentage of 1.042 was the second-best in the National League after the All-Star break.

Gonzalez' first half was good too, batting .339, with a .630 slugging percentage — in Colorado Springs. His first month in the majors was rough, but after the All-Star game he started treating the National League like he did the Pacific Coast League. He hit .320 with a .608 slugging percentage, and also finished in the top 10 in the league in OPS in the second half of the season.

### Troy Tulowitzki

| Split | G | PA | AB | R | H | HR | RBI | BA | OBP | SLG | OPS |
|-------|---|----|----|----|----|----|-----|------|------|------|-------|
| 1st Half | 82 | 331 | 284 | 49 | 72 | 16 | 37 | .254 | .338 | .489 | .828 |
| 2nd Half | 69 | 297 | 260 | 52 | 89 | 16 | 55 | .342 | .421 | .619 | 1.040 |

### Carlos Gonzalez

| Split | G | PA | AB | R | H | HR | RBI | BA | OBP | SLG | OPS |
|-------|---|----|----|----|----|----|-----|------|------|------|------|
| 1st Half | 27 | 94 | 84 | 11 | 17 | 1 | 5 | .202 | .280 | .333 | .613 |
| 2nd Half | 62 | 223 | 194 | 42 | 62 | 12 | 24 | .320 | .384 | .608 | .992 |

### NL OPS Leaders in 2nd Half

| Rank | Player | Team | OPS |
|------|--------|------|-----|
| 1. | Derrek Lee | Cubs | 1.092 |
| 2. | Troy Tulowitzki | Rockies | 1.042 |
| 3. | Matt Holliday | Cardinals | 1.023 |
| 4. | Adrian Gonzalez | Padres | 1.018 |
| 5. | Albert Pujols | Cardinals | 1.009 |
| 6. | Ryan Howard | Phillies | 1.003 |
| 7. | Carlos Gonzalez | Rockies | .992 |
| 8. | Ryan Zimmerman | Nationals | .969 |
| 9. | Prince Fielder | Brewers | .967 |
| 10. | Chris Coghlan | Marlins | .966 |

Minimum 201 PA

## Protest, Appeal, Recount. . .Do Something

In 2002 the two best pitchers in baseball were Randy Johnson and Curt Schilling. Colorado pitcher Randy Flores made two starts that year, and the opposing starters in those two games were Randy Johnson and Curt Schilling.

On the other hand, in 2004 Gary Glover of the Brewers made three starts, and was matched up against Casey Fossum (4-15, 6.65 ERA), Peter Munro (4-7, 5.15 ERA), and Ryan Vogelson (6-13, 6.50 ERA).

## One Trick Pony

Aaron Cook threw his fastball 84.2% of the time last season. No other starting pitcher relied on a single pitch more, not even Tim Wakefield who throws his knuckleball 83.8% of the time.

| Aaron Cook — 2009 | | |
|---|---|---|
| Fastball | 2,023 | 84% |
| Curveball | 93 | 4% |
| Changeup | 21 | 1% |
| Slider | 244 | 10% |
| Not Charted | 23 | 1% |
| Total | 2,404 | |

| Tim Wakefield — 2009 | | |
|---|---|---|
| Fastball | 208 | 10% |
| Curveball | 93 | 5% |
| Knuckleball | 1,692 | 84% |
| Not Charted | 27 | 1% |
| Total | 2,020 | |

## Dexter's Room for Improvement

Dexter Fowler had a solid rookie season at bat, but ranked 34th of 35 center fielders in plays made. According to John Dewan's Plus/Minus System, he was 26 plays below average in center field.

### Dexter Fowler — 2009 Fielding Bible Plus/Minus

| Year | Inn | Outs Made | Basic | Shallow | Medium | Deep | Enhanced | Runs Saved | Rank |
|---|---|---|---|---|---|---|---|---|---|
| 2009 | 977.2 | 247 | -14 | -6 | -10 | -10 | -26 | -15 | 34 |

# Detroit Tigers

| 2009 TEAM OVERVIEW | ML RANK | 15th | 8th | 17th | 18th | 14th | 24th |
|---|---|---|---|---|---|---|---|
| **86-77** | **Team** | **743** | **183** | **.261** | **540** | **.747** | **72** |
| | | RUNS | HOME RUNS | BATTING AVG. | WALKS | OPS | STOLEN BASES |
| **2** nd place AL Central | **Opp.** | **745** | **182** | **.263** | **594** | **.759** | **88** |
| | ML RANK | 12th | 20th | 15th | 19th | 18th | 7th |

## Key Players

| Pos | Player | G | AB | R | H | 2B | 3B | HR | RBI | SB | CS | BB | SO | AVG | OBP | SLG | OPS | WS |
|---|---|---|---|---|---|---|---|---|---|---|---|---|---|---|---|---|---|---|
| C | Gerald Laird | 135 | 413 | 49 | 93 | 23 | 2 | 4 | 33 | 5 | 0 | 40 | 68 | .225 | .306 | .320 | .626 | 14 |
| 1B | Miguel Cabrera | 160 | 611 | 96 | 198 | 34 | 0 | 34 | 103 | 6 | 2 | 68 | 107 | .324 | .396 | .547 | .942 | 25 |
| 2B | Placido Polanco | 153 | 618 | 82 | 176 | 31 | 4 | 10 | 72 | 7 | 2 | 36 | 46 | .285 | .331 | .396 | .727 | 21 |
| 3B | Brandon Inge | 161 | 562 | 71 | 129 | 16 | 1 | 27 | 84 | 2 | 5 | 54 | 170 | .230 | .314 | .406 | .720 | 13 |
| SS | Adam Everett | 118 | 345 | 43 | 82 | 21 | 0 | 3 | 44 | 5 | 2 | 22 | 61 | .238 | .288 | .325 | .613 | 6 |
| LF | Carlos Guillen | 81 | 277 | 36 | 67 | 10 | 3 | 11 | 41 | 1 | 3 | 39 | 56 | .242 | .339 | .419 | .757 | 6 |
| CF | Curtis Granderson | 160 | 631 | 91 | 157 | 23 | 8 | 30 | 71 | 20 | 6 | 72 | 141 | .249 | .327 | .453 | .780 | 20 |
| RF | Magglio Ordonez | 131 | 465 | 54 | 144 | 24 | 2 | 9 | 50 | 3 | 1 | 51 | 65 | .310 | .376 | .428 | .804 | 13 |
| DH | Marcus Thames | 87 | 258 | 33 | 65 | 11 | 1 | 13 | 36 | 0 | 2 | 29 | 72 | .252 | .323 | .453 | .777 | 4 |

## Key Pitchers

| Pos | Player | G | GS | W | L | SV | IP | H | R | ER | SO | BB | BR/9 | ERA | WS |
|---|---|---|---|---|---|---|---|---|---|---|---|---|---|---|---|
| SP | Justin Verlander | 35 | 35 | 19 | 9 | 0 | 240.0 | 219 | 99 | 92 | 269 | 63 | 10.80 | 3.45 | 21 |
| SP | Edwin Jackson | 33 | 33 | 13 | 9 | 0 | 214.0 | 200 | 93 | 86 | 161 | 70 | 11.57 | 3.62 | 17 |
| SP | Rick Porcello | 31 | 31 | 14 | 9 | 0 | 170.2 | 176 | 81 | 75 | 89 | 52 | 12.18 | 3.96 | 13 |
| SP | Armando Galarraga | 29 | 25 | 6 | 10 | 0 | 143.2 | 158 | 93 | 90 | 95 | 67 | 14.47 | 5.64 | 3 |
| SP | Jarrod Washburn | 8 | 8 | 1 | 3 | 0 | 43.0 | 51 | 35 | 35 | 21 | 16 | 14.44 | 7.33 | 0 |
| CL | Fernando Rodney | 73 | 0 | 2 | 5 | 37 | 75.2 | 70 | 38 | 37 | 61 | 41 | 13.44 | 4.40 | 10 |
| RP | Bobby Seay | 67 | 0 | 6 | 3 | 0 | 48.2 | 46 | 23 | 23 | 37 | 17 | 12.21 | 4.25 | 6 |
| RP | Brandon Lyon | 65 | 0 | 6 | 5 | 3 | 78.2 | 56 | 25 | 25 | 57 | 31 | 10.18 | 2.86 | 11 |

## Balls in Play Average — Armando Galarraga

Armando Galarraga's record went from 13-7 with a 3.73 ERA in 2008, to 6-10 with a 5.64 ERA in 2009.

In 2008 Galarraga allowed a batting average on balls in play of .237, .067 below the Tigers' team average. His 7.7 hits allowed per nine innings pitched was the second-best rate in the American League.

Galarraga's batting average on balls in play returned to a more normal .298 in 2009, just .002 above the Detroit team average. That bumped his hits allowed to 9.9 per nine innings pitched.

## Tigers Ninth

The only American League team that improved their winning percentage more from the 8th inning to the 9th inning than the Tigers did was the Yankees. If baseball was an eight-inning game, the Tigers would have finished the year with a winning percentage of .493. They increased their winning percentage to .523 by playing the 9th inning.

**Detroit Tigers 2009**

| Inning | 1 | 2 | 3 | 4 | 5 | 6 | 7 | 8 | 9 | Extra | Final |
|--------|----|----|----|----|----|----|----|----|----|-------|-------|
| Ahead | 35 | 60 | 69 | 73 | 68 | 72 | 75 | 73 | 79 | 6 | 86 |
| Behind | 41 | 52 | 59 | 66 | 65 | 68 | 72 | 75 | 72 | 5 | 77 |
| Tied | 87 | 51 | 35 | 24 | 30 | 23 | 16 | 14 | 11 | 16 | -- |

## Making Contact

When Placido Polanco swung the bat in 2009 he put the ball in play 57% of the time, the highest rate among American League batters. This is typical for Polanco. His 57% career rate leads all active batters who have seen a minimum of 5,000 pitches.

**Placido Polanco**

| Season | Pitches Swung At | Put In Play | Pct |
|--------|------------------|-------------|-----|
| 2009 | 1,026 | 585 | 57% |
| Career | 7,122 | 4,082 | 57% |

## Hands in the Cookie Jar

Justin Verlander and his catchers combined to catch 16 baserunners stealing, while allowing only 9 successful steals. The last pitcher to catch that many basestealers in a single season was Tom Glavine, who caught 16 in 2002.

## Workhorse

Justin Verlander threw 3,937 pitches in 2009 — 300 more than any other pitcher in the majors, and more than any other American League pitcher in the last ten years.

## Gerald Laird

Gerald Laird has been in the majors four years now, not counting cameos. What do you notice about his records:

| Year | Team | Age | G | PA | AVG | OBP | SLG | OPS |
|------|------|-----|-----|-----|------|------|------|------|
| 2006 | TEX | 26 | 78 | 260 | .296 | .332 | .473 | .805 |
| 2007 | TEX | 27 | 120 | 448 | .224 | .278 | .349 | .627 |
| 2008 | TEX | 28 | 95 | 381 | .276 | .329 | .398 | .727 |
| 2009 | DET | 29 | 135 | 477 | .225 | .306 | .320 | .626 |

His OPS is in inverse order of his plate appearances. The years in which he has had the most plate appearances are 2009, 2007, 2008, 2006; the highest OPS is in the exact opposite order. The more plate appearances he gets, the less he hits.

Does he wear down? Well. . .yes. His career average in June is .293. In August, it's .200.

| Month | G | PA | AVG | OBP | SLG | OPS |
|-------|-----|-----|------|------|------|------|
| March/April | 88 | 321 | .266 | .328 | .374 | .702 |
| May | 95 | 325 | .255 | .337 | .360 | .698 |
| June | 67 | 245 | .293 | .332 | .467 | .799 |
| July | 62 | 226 | .262 | .315 | .381 | .697 |
| August | 87 | 324 | .200 | .245 | .319 | .563 |
| Sept./Oct. | 110 | 385 | .227 | .292 | .334 | .626 |

## Clutch Hitting

Tiger hitters in 2009 had 951 at-bats in clutch situations — the most in the American League, and almost 50% above the league average. The number for the Tigers was high because

1) They did play a lot of close games, as was reflected in our nugget about their 9th-inning wins, and

2) They were in a pennant race that lasted to the last day of the season and one day beyond — whereas many of the other teams were either never in the pennant race, or were in races that were over with two weeks to go.

### Detroit Tigers Clutch Totals 2009

| Player | AB | H | 2B | 3B | HR | RBI | BB | SO | GIDP | AVG | OBP | SLG |
|---|---|---|---|---|---|---|---|---|---|---|---|---|
| Totals | 951 | 248 | 41 | 5 | 26 | 190 | 94 | 223 | 27 | .261 | .329 | .396 |

The Royals had the fewest clutch at-bats, with just 473. If they had hit better in the clutch situations than they had, they would have had more of them.

### Kansas City Royals 2009

| Player | AB | H | 2B | 3B | HR | RBI | BB | SO | GIDP | AVG | OBP | SLG |
|---|---|---|---|---|---|---|---|---|---|---|---|---|
| Totals | 473 | 103 | 17 | 5 | 9 | 87 | 44 | 105 | 16 | .218 | .284 | .332 |

## Deadly Deadline Deals

On July 31 the Tigers received Jarrod Washburn in a deal with Seattle Mariners in exchange for Lucas French and a minor leaguer. Washburn slotted into French's spot in the rotation.

Having shored up their rotation, the Tigers decided to see if they could fix the disappointing production they were getting from the DH position. They traded a minor league pitcher to Baltimore for Aubrey Huff on August 17. They held a six-and-a-half-game lead over the Twins on that date.

Washburn made eight starts for the Tigers, posted a 7.33 ERA and a 1-3 record.

Huff started 28 of the team's final 46 games at DH, and he hit .189 with a .302 slugging percentage after joining Detroit.

## Finishing Strong

Magglio Ordonez was the hottest hitter in baseball when the season ended.  He ended the season with a 13-game hitting streak, hitting .490 during the streak, and driving his batting average from .288 to .310.

### Magglio Ordonez 2009

| | |
|---|---|
| Season Ending Temperature | 114° |
| High Point of the Season (Oct. 4) | 114° |
| Low Point of the Season (July 1) | 49° |
| Days Over 100° | 1 |
| Days Under 50° | 1 |
| Average Daily Temperature | 72.9° |

## Sliderfest

The Tigers in 2009 had both the pitcher who threw the most sliders in the American League and the pitcher who threw the highest percentage of sliders in baseball (among starting pitchers.)  Edwin Jackson threw 937 sliders, most in the league, and 27% of his total pitches.  Armando Galarraga was right behind him with 928 sliders, or 38% of his total. That was the highest percentage for a starting pitcher.

## Inge Fly Balls

Brandon Inge's ability to be an effective offensive player is highly dependent on his fly balls becoming home runs.

| Year | Fly Balls | HR | Pct | OPS |
|---|---|---|---|---|
| 2006 | 189 | 26 | 14% | .776 |
| 2007 | 147 | 12 | 8% | .688 |
| 2008 | 119 | 11 | 9% | .672 |
| 2009 | 175 | 27 | 15% | .720 |

## Hanley Grandley

The number of runs that a player will drive in can be predicted with a good deal of accuracy by the formula (HR + TB/4). In last year's book, we observed that the #1 RBI under-producer in the majors was Hanley Ramirez, who (because he batted leadoff in 2008) drove in only 67 runs, whereas this formula would have predicted that he would drive in 112. In 2009 Ramirez drove in 106 — about the number we said that he would drive in, were he not batting leadoff.

Based on that, we wondered who the "Hanley Ramirez of 2009" was — that is, the player who could be expected to drive in more runs. It's Curtis Granderson. Granderson hit 30 home runs in 2009, but, usually batting leadoff, drove in only 71 runs. We would expect, based on his numbers, that he would have driven in about 101.

Actually, the #1 RBI under-producer was not Granderson, but Ichiro. But Ichiro has been in that role for years and has been an RBI under-producer for years (because he bats leadoff), and we would have to expect that he will be the same in 2010. Granderson, not so much. If he hits in New York the way the Janquis expect him to, he should drive in around 100 runs. With a .327 on-base percentage and 30 homers, he is really *not* a leadoff man.

# The 300 Group Total

by Bill James

PITCHERS WINNING 300 GAMES IS ONE OF THOSE ISSUES, I AM AWARE, about which I write too often. However, while I generally pooh-pooh the idea that pitchers are going to stop winning 300 games, I do acknowledge that it is theoretically possible for this to happen. .400 hitters have become extinct. 30-game winners have become extinct. 300-inning pitchers have disappeared. It is possible for the same thing to happen to 300-game winners.

One method that I have used since the 1970s to track this issue is to look at the league-leading wins total…what we could call the "normal league-leading" number. The normal league-leading number, in any category, is the average of the last ten players to lead the league in that category. In wins, at the moment, this is 19.9:

| | | |
|---|---|---|
| 2005 American League | Bartolo Colon | 21 Wins |
| 2005 National League | Dontrelle Willis | 22 Wins |
| 2006 American League | 2 Tied with | 19 Wins |
| 2006 National League | 6 Tied with | 16 Wins |
| 2007 American League | Josh Beckett | 20 Wins |
| 2007 National League | Jake Peavy | 19 Wins |
| 2008 American League | Cliff Lee | 22 Wins |
| 2008 National League | Brandon Webb | 22 Wins |
| 2009 American League | 3 Tied with | 19 Wins |
| 2009 National League | Adam Wainwright | 19 Wins |

*While I generally pooh-pooh the idea that pitchers are going to stop winning 300 games, it is theoretically possible for this to happen.*

That adds up to 199 wins, an average of 19.9. Let's call it 20. If a league-leading pitcher wins 20 games, then 300 wins represents 15 years worth of league-leading performance.

If the league-leading numbers go up, then the number of years required go down. If the league-leading numbers go down, the number of years required goes up. We can track how difficult it is to win 300 games by tracking the league-leading totals.

It recently occurred to me, though, that one can track this change in a different and perhaps better way by looking at the data for just one season. In 1884, seven major league pitchers won a total of 329 games — 59 by Old Hoss Radbourn, 52 by Guy Hecker, 48 by Charlie Buffinton, 46 by Pud Galvin, 43 by Billy Taylor, 41 by Charlie Sweeney, and 40 by either Jim McCormick or Bill Sweeney. Eight pitchers won 40 or more games.

If seven pitchers can win 300 games in a season, then, how long would it take a top-flight pitcher to win 300 games? Seven years. You just have to remain one of those top seven pitchers for seven years.

Seven is the lowest "300 group total" in the history of baseball. In 1876, 1877, and 1878 there were fewer than 300 major league games played, thus there is no number of pitchers required to win 300 games. The first year in major league history in which 300 games were played was 1879, and in 1879 it required 13 pitchers to win a total of 300 games. This number dropped to 7 in 1884, and was 8 or 9 for most of the 1880s:

| | | | | | | | | | 1879 |
|---|---|---|---|---|---|---|---|---|---|
| | | | | | | | | | 13 |

| 1880 | 1881 | 1882 | 1883 | 1884 | 1885 | 1886 | 1887 | 1888 | 1889 |
|---|---|---|---|---|---|---|---|---|---|
| 11 | 14 | 11 | 8 | 7 | 8 | 8 | 9 | 10 | 9 |

They were still figuring out the rules then. Pitchers in 1880 were still required to throw underhand — and still did. By 1883 they were still required to throw underhand, but no longer did. By 1886 they were no longer required to. Pitchers in this era threw 500, 600 innings in a season. You could rack up a lot of wins in a few years.

In the 1890s pitchers began to develop sophisticated throwing motions, and to throw hard. Increases in velocity required the mound to be moved back to 60 feet, 6 inches beginning in 1893:

| 1890 | 1891 | 1892 | 1893 | 1894 | 1895 | 1896 | 1897 | 1898 | 1899 |
|---|---|---|---|---|---|---|---|---|---|
| 9 | 9 | 10 | 12 | 11 | 12 | 12 | 14 | 12 | 13 |

By the end of the decade, win totals were low enough that one had to remain a top-flight pitcher for 12 to 14 years to win 300 games. This remained the standard, generally speaking, into the early 1920s:

| 1900 | 1901 | 1902 | 1903 | 1904 | 1905 | 1906 | 1907 | 1908 | 1909 |
|---|---|---|---|---|---|---|---|---|---|
| 17 | 13 | 13 | 13 | 12 | 14 | 14 | 13 | 12 | 14 |

| 1910 | 1911 | 1912 | 1913 | 1914 | 1915 | 1916 | 1917 | 1918 | 1919 |
|---|---|---|---|---|---|---|---|---|---|
| 14 | 13 | 12 | 13 | 12 | 13 | 14 | 14 | 16 | 15 |

*Pitchers in 1880 were still required to throw underhand — and still did.*

During all of that period, the Dead Ball Era, the top pitchers won 30+ games, and a pitcher could get to 300 with a run of 12 to 14 years, excepting 1918, which was a war-shortened season, and 1919, when they chopped the schedule to 140 games. This snuck upward by two in the early 1920s, and then one or two more in the late 1930s:

| 1920 | 1921 | 1922 | 1923 | 1924 | 1925 | 1926 | 1927 | 1928 | 1929 |
|------|------|------|------|------|------|------|------|------|------|
| 13 | 14 | 14 | 14 | 16 | 16 | 16 | 15 | 14 | 16 |

| 1930 | 1931 | 1932 | 1933 | 1934 | 1935 | 1936 | 1937 | 1938 | 1939 |
|------|------|------|------|------|------|------|------|------|------|
| 16 | 16 | 15 | 16 | 15 | 15 | 15 | 17 | 18 | 16 |

By the late 1930s the "300 group total" was up to 18 pitchers. It stayed about there through the 1940s, and ticked upward again in the 1950s:

| 1940 | 1941 | 1942 | 1943 | 1944 | 1945 | 1946 | 1947 | 1948 | 1949 |
|------|------|------|------|------|------|------|------|------|------|
| 17 | 17 | 17 | 18 | 16 | 16 | 17 | 16 | 17 | 16 |

| 1950 | 1951 | 1952 | 1953 | 1954 | 1955 | 1956 | 1957 | 1958 | 1959 |
|------|------|------|------|------|------|------|------|------|------|
| 16 | 16 | 15 | 17 | 16 | 19 | 15 | 19 | 19 | 17 |

I would like to pause for a second to reflect on the uncanny steadiness of this number. In theory, this number *could* fluctuate wildly from year to year. In 1955 no American League pitcher won more than 18 games. In 1956 six American League pitchers won 20 or more, and Don Newcombe won 27 in the National League. The number, which was 19 in 1955, '57, and '58, was 15 in 1956 and dropped again to 17 in 1959.

It *could* fluctuate, but it normally doesn't. The era 1889-1891 is one of the wildest and most unstable eras in baseball history — but the numbers go 9, 9, 9. The numbers from 1901 to 1903 go 13, 13, 13. From 1921 to 1923 they go 14, 14, 14, followed by 16, 16, 16. From 1940 to 1942 they go 17, 17, 17.

The numbers are very stable, but there is, from 1900 to 1959, a gradual increase in them. In the Walter Johnson era a pitcher could win 300 games in 12 high-quality seasons. By the Whitey Ford era it was up to 19 years. If that number goes over 20 — even to 21 — if it is stable at 21, 300-game winners disappear. In the 1960s and 1970s, however, the number went back in time by 50 years:

| 1960 | 1961 | 1962 | 1963 | 1964 | 1965 | 1966 | 1967 | 1968 | 1969 |
|------|------|------|------|------|------|------|------|------|------|
| 18 | 17 | 15 | 15 | 16 | 15 | 16 | 17 | 15 | 15 |

| 1970 | 1971 | 1972 | 1973 | 1974 | 1975 | 1976 | 1977 | 1978 | 1979 |
|------|------|------|------|------|------|------|------|------|------|
| 15 | 15 | 15 | 15 | 15 | 16 | 16 | 16 | 15 | 17 |

By the mid-1970s, the number was stable at 15. Several things contributed to this — the addition of 8 extra games to the schedule, expansion, the Designated Hitter rule, other things. From 1962 to 1974, however, the number was usually 15.

We could predict, based on that, that there would be an explosion of 300-game winners — and in fact there was. Carlton, Sutton, Nolan Ryan, Phil Niekro, Gaylord Perry, Tom Seaver, all active in that period, all won 300 games. By the late 1970s, however, the number was beginning to work its way back up:

| 1980 | 1981 | 1982 | 1983 | 1984 | 1985 | 1986 | 1987 | 1988 | 1989 |
|---|---|---|---|---|---|---|---|---|---|
| 16 | 25 | 17 | 17 | 17 | 16 | 17 | 18 | 16 | 17 |

| 1990 | 1991 | 1992 | 1993 | 1994 | 1995 | 1996 | 1997 | 1998 | 1999 |
|---|---|---|---|---|---|---|---|---|---|
| 17 | 17 | 16 | 16 | 23 | 17 | 17 | 17 | 17 | 17 |

Basically, over-simplifying, during all of the 1980s and 1990s it required 17 top-flight seasons for a pitcher to win 300 games. Several pitchers still did. Then we come to the last decade, 2000-2009:

| 2000 | 2001 | 2002 | 2003 | 2004 | 2005 | 2006 | 2007 | 2008 | 2009 |
|---|---|---|---|---|---|---|---|---|---|
| 17 | 16 | 16 | 17 | 18 | 18 | 18 | 17 | 17 | 19 |

We started the decade back at 16, then stabilized at 18 (18, 18, 18), and then last year it took 19 pitchers to add together to get a total of 300 wins.

19 is a high number. 19 is the highest number ever, except for the strike-shortened seasons and the years 1876-1878. 19 is close to 21, and at 21, 300-game winners are gone.

There are two kinds of predictions. In the 1970s and early 1980s I could and did "predict" that there would be a flood of 300-game winners. But this was not *really* a prediction. It was an observation about the reality of the game *then*, and about how that would manifest itself in the future.

To say that this number will go on up from 19 to 21, however, would be an actual prediction. It went to 19 before, in the late 1950s, but then history turned a corner and went off in a different direction. Is it possible we could turn a corner now?

Sure it is. Pitchers don't *have* to come out of the game at the 100-pitch mark; it's just a choice that managers make. If the commissioner succeeds in speeding up the games, one result of that should be more complete games, which would drive this number down, thus making it easier to win 300 games. All I will really say is that it is still possible to win 300 games now. Ten years from now, if that number is 21, 22, 22, 22…it's over.

*We could predict that there would be an explosion of 300-game winners — and in fact there was.*

# Florida Marlins

| 2009 TEAM OVERVIEW | | | | | | | |
|---|---|---|---|---|---|---|---|
| **ML RANK** | | 13th | 14th | 8th | 15th | 13th | 22nd |
| **87-75** | **Team** | **772** | **159** | **.268** | **568** | **.756** | **75** |
| | | RUNS | HOME RUNS | BATTING AVG. | WALKS | OPS | STOLEN BASES |
| **2**nd place NL East | **Opp.** | **766** | **160** | **.258** | **601** | **.741** | **129** |
| **ML RANK** | | 18th | 9th | 8th | 22th | 11th | 23th |

## Key Players

| Pos | Player | G | AB | R | H | 2B | 3B | HR | RBI | SB | CS | BB | SO | AVG | OBP | SLG | OPS | WS |
|---|---|---|---|---|---|---|---|---|---|---|---|---|---|---|---|---|---|---|
| C | John Baker | 112 | 373 | 59 | 101 | 25 | 0 | 9 | 50 | 0 | 0 | 41 | 89 | .271 | .349 | .410 | .759 | 13 |
| 1B | Jorge Cantu | 149 | 585 | 67 | 169 | 42 | 0 | 16 | 100 | 3 | 1 | 47 | 81 | .289 | .345 | .443 | .788 | 17 |
| 2B | Dan Uggla | 158 | 564 | 84 | 137 | 27 | 1 | 31 | 90 | 2 | 1 | 92 | 150 | .243 | .354 | .459 | .813 | 18 |
| 3B | Emilio Bonifacio | 127 | 461 | 72 | 116 | 11 | 6 | 1 | 27 | 21 | 9 | 34 | 95 | .252 | .303 | .308 | .611 | 7 |
| SS | Hanley Ramirez | 151 | 576 | 101 | 197 | 42 | 1 | 24 | 106 | 27 | 8 | 61 | 101 | .342 | .410 | .543 | .954 | 34 |
| LF | Chris Coghlan | 128 | 504 | 84 | 162 | 31 | 6 | 9 | 47 | 8 | 5 | 53 | 77 | .321 | .390 | .460 | .850 | 21 |
| CF | Cody Ross | 151 | 559 | 73 | 151 | 37 | 1 | 24 | 90 | 5 | 2 | 34 | 122 | .270 | .321 | .469 | .790 | 16 |
| RF | Jeremy Hermida | 129 | 429 | 48 | 111 | 14 | 2 | 13 | 47 | 5 | 2 | 56 | 101 | .259 | .348 | .392 | .740 | 11 |

## Key Pitchers

| Pos | Player | G | GS | W | L | SV | IP | H | R | ER | SO | BB | BR/9 | ERA | WS |
|---|---|---|---|---|---|---|---|---|---|---|---|---|---|---|---|
| SP | Josh Johnson | 33 | 33 | 15 | 5 | 0 | 209.0 | 184 | 77 | 75 | 191 | 58 | 10.68 | 3.23 | 19 |
| SP | Ricky Nolasco | 31 | 31 | 13 | 9 | 0 | 185.0 | 188 | 111 | 104 | 195 | 44 | 11.38 | 5.06 | 6 |
| SP | Chris Volstad | 29 | 29 | 9 | 13 | 0 | 159.0 | 169 | 100 | 92 | 107 | 59 | 13.08 | 5.21 | 4 |
| SP | Sean West | 20 | 20 | 8 | 6 | 0 | 103.1 | 115 | 62 | 55 | 70 | 44 | 14.11 | 4.79 | 4 |
| SP | Anibal Sanchez | 16 | 16 | 4 | 8 | 0 | 86.0 | 84 | 39 | 37 | 71 | 46 | 13.71 | 3.87 | 5 |
| CL | Leo Nunez | 75 | 0 | 4 | 6 | 26 | 68.2 | 59 | 33 | 31 | 60 | 27 | 11.80 | 4.06 | 9 |
| RP | Renyel Pinto | 73 | 0 | 4 | 1 | 0 | 61.1 | 53 | 25 | 22 | 58 | 45 | 14.67 | 3.23 | 5 |
| RP | Dan Meyer | 71 | 0 | 3 | 2 | 2 | 58.1 | 47 | 24 | 20 | 56 | 21 | 10.65 | 3.09 | 6 |

## Loves to Pull

Jorge Cantu pulled 53.8% of the balls he put into play in 2009, second-highest among qualifying hitters. Over the past two years, 44 of his 45 home runs have been hit to left field.

### Jorge Cantu – 2008-2009

|  | Total | Home Runs |
|---|---|---|
| Balls Hit to Left | 551 | 44 |
| Balls Hit to Center | 282 | 1 |
| Balls Hit to Right | 200 | 0 |

## Needs to Pull

For his career, Cody Ross has batted .453 with 52 home runs on 162 fly balls to left, and .133 with four home runs on 169 fly balls to right.

## Coming Through in the Clutch

Cody Ross hit 7 home runs and drove in 28 runs in clutch at-bats in 2009. It was his worst clutch performance in the four years he's spent in the majors. He now has a career average of .321 and a slugging percentage of .632 in clutch at-bats.

### Cody Ross — Clutch Hitting

| Year | AB | H | 2B | 3B | HR | RBI | BB | SO | GIDP | AVG | OBP | SLG |
|---|---|---|---|---|---|---|---|---|---|---|---|---|
| 2003 | 1 | 0 | 0 | 0 | 0 | 0 | 0 | 1 | 0 | .000 | .000 | .000 |
| 2005 | 2 | 0 | 0 | 0 | 0 | 0 | 0 | 1 | 1 | .000 | .000 | .000 |
| 2006 | 26 | 9 | 3 | 0 | 2 | 11 | 0 | 4 | 0 | .346 | .370 | .692 |
| 2007 | 23 | 10 | 3 | 0 | 2 | 10 | 3 | 8 | 0 | .435 | .500 | .826 |
| 2008 | 70 | 24 | 4 | 1 | 5 | 24 | 4 | 15 | 2 | .343 | .373 | .643 |
| 2009 | 87 | 24 | 3 | 1 | 7 | 28 | 4 | 19 | 5 | .276 | .315 | .575 |
| Totals | 209 | 67 | 13 | 2 | 16 | 73 | 11 | 48 | 8 | .321 | .359 | .632 |

## Love That First One

Hanley Ramirez had the most one-pitch plate appearances in baseball (122), and once again, he was one of the most dangerous first-pitch hitters in baseball, batting .470 with a major league-high 55 hits. He now is a career .428 hitter on the first pitch.

## Ground Ball Success

Hanley Ramirez led the majors with a .389 batting average on ground balls. Ichiro Suzuki was the next-highest qualifying hitter at .353. Among active players, Ramirez has the second-highest career average on ground balls (minimum 1,000 at-bats).

**Career Average on Ground Balls**

| Player | AVG |
|---|---|
| 1. Rocco Baldelli | .321 |
| 2. Hanley Ramirez | .318 |
| 3. Justin Upton | .318 |
| 4. Matt Kemp | .315 |
| 5. Akinori Iwamura | .313 |

## Hit Happy

Hanley Ramirez had 3 or more hits in 24 games, the most in baseball. In those games, the Marlins went 19-5 and scored an average of 6.5 runs.

**Hanley Ramirez — 2009 Games With X Hits**

| | G | AB | R | H | 2B | 3B | HR | RBI | AVG |
|---|---|---|---|---|---|---|---|---|---|
| 0 Hits | 36 | 117 | 6 | 0 | 0 | 0 | 0 | 2 | .000 |
| 1 Hits | 59 | 215 | 27 | 59 | 13 | 0 | 6 | 26 | .274 |
| 2 Hits | 32 | 133 | 36 | 64 | 18 | 1 | 10 | 41 | .481 |
| 3 Hits | 22 | 100 | 27 | 66 | 10 | 0 | 7 | 32 | .660 |
| 4 Hits | 2 | 11 | 5 | 8 | 1 | 0 | 1 | 5 | .727 |

## Maybe He'd Do Better in a Higher League

Chris Volstad in his career is 11-9 with a 3.58 ERA against winning teams but only 4-8 with a 6.24 ERA against losing teams.

### Chris Volstad — Career Records Against Quality of Opposition

| Opponent | G | IP | W | L | SO | BB | ERA |
|---|---|---|---|---|---|---|---|
| .600 teams | 3 | 18.0 | 1 | 0 | 13 | 6 | 3.50 |
| .500 - .599 teams | 25 | 150.1 | 10 | 9 | 94 | 42 | 3.59 |
| .400 - .499 teams | 11 | 55.1 | 3 | 6 | 34 | 30 | 5.86 |
| sub .400 teams | 5 | 19.2 | 1 | 2 | 18 | 17 | 7.32 |

## Dinkers and Doinkers Only

Kiko Calero faced 239 batters and allowed only 7 extra-base hits, one per every 34.1 batters faced. It was the best ratio in baseball for a pitcher with 50 innings pitched. At the other end of the spectrum was Angels rookie Sean O'Sullivan, who faced 227 batters and allowed 33 extra-base hits, one every 6.9 batters.

## Damage Control

Rick VandenHurk made 11 starts and never allowed more than two runs in a single inning. No other major league starter threw as many innings without giving up at least three runs in an inning.

## You Can't Catch Me

Brett Carroll has participated in 141 major league games and has yet to be thrown out on the bases. He hasn't been caught stealing, doubled off or tagged out advancing.

**Brett Carroll — Baserunning Analysis**

| Year | 1st to 3rd | | 2nd to Home | | 1st to Home | | Double Play | | Bases Taken | BR Outs | BR Gain | SB Gain | Net Gain |
| | Adv | Opp | Adv | Opp | Adv | Opp | Opp | GIDP | | | | | |
|---|---|---|---|---|---|---|---|---|---|---|---|---|---|
| 2007 | 2 | 2 | 2 | 4 | 0 | 0 | 12 | 1 | 4 | 0 | +5 | 0 | +5 |
| 2008 | 1 | 1 | 2 | 3 | 0 | 0 | 3 | 0 | 4 | 0 | +5 | 0 | +5 |
| 2009 | 0 | 3 | 2 | 6 | 2 | 2 | 32 | 2 | 8 | 0 | +7 | 0 | +7 |
| **Totals** | **3** | **6** | **6** | **13** | **2** | **2** | **47** | **3** | **16** | **0** | **+18** | **0** | **+17** |
| | | 50% | | 46% | | 100% | | 6% | | | | | |

## Going the Other Way

John Baker may be the best opposite-field hitter in baseball. In 2009, he hit .512 when he hit the ball to the opposite field, highest in baseball among batters who batted 300 times. The year before, he'd hit .543 on balls to the opposite field.

## Bunt Happy

Emilio Bonifacio had 15 bunt hits in 2009, third-highest in the majors. They accounted for 13.8% of his hits, the highest percentage in baseball among players who batted 300 times.

## Can He Run or What?

In 2009, Emilio Bonifacio was on first base when a double was hit 10 times, and scored all 10 times. No one in the majors scored from first on a double more often; Chase Utley also did it 10 times, but needed 13 opportunities to do it. Bonifacio also scored from second base on a single 17 times in 19 opportunities, the fourth-best percentage in the majors.

### Emilio Bonifacio — Baserunning Analysis

| Year | 1st to 3rd Adv | 1st to 3rd Opp | 2nd to Home Adv | 2nd to Home Opp | 1st to Home Adv | 1st to Home Opp | Double Play Opp | Double Play GIDP | Bases Taken | BR Outs | BR Gain | SB Gain | Net Gain |
|------|-----|-----|-----|-----|-----|-----|-----|-----|-----|-----|-----|-----|-----|
| 2007 | 2 | 3 | 0 | 1 | 0 | 0 | 0 | 0 | 1 | 0 | +1 | -2 | -1 |
| 2008 | 2 | 5 | 6 | 6 | 1 | 1 | 23 | 2 | 5 | 0 | +8 | -1 | +7 |
| 2009 | 11 | 27 | 17 | 19 | 10 | 10 | 87 | 5 | 16 | 4 | +21 | +3 | +24 |
| **Totals** | **15** | **35** | **23** | **26** | **11** | **11** | **110** | **7** | **22** | **4** | **+30** | **0** | **+30** |
| | | 43% | | 88% | | 100% | | 6% | | | | | |

## Who's the Better Leadoff Man?

Emilio Bonifacio batted leadoff in 53 games for the Marlins in 2009, and Chris Coghlan hit first in 106 games. Bonifacio's on-base percentage batting first in the order was .299, and Coghlan's was nearly 100 points better, at .397. This was reflected in the team's record in the games each of them led off.

| Leadoff Hitter | W-L | Pct | R/G |
|----------------|-----|-----|-----|
| Emilio Bonifacio | 23-30 | .434 | 4.51 |
| Chris Coghlan | 62-44 | .585 | 4.95 |

## Well, He *Can* Hit

Chris Coghlan was installed as the regular left fielder in mid-May. At the time, he had a total of one game of pro experience at the position. His inexperience was reflected by his subsequent performance there. The Defensive Runs Saved metric rated his range 16 runs worse than the average left fielder, which tied him with Ryan Braun for worst at the position. He was especially weak on balls hit deep, where his Plus/Minus mark of -19 was second-worst at the position after Braun. His defensive shortcomings helped to drag down the team's overall defensive performance from roughly average in 2008 to the worst in the National League in 2009, as rated by Team Defensive Runs Saved. The club compiled a major league-worst mark of -18 Runs Saved at the left field position, a decline of 25 runs over the previous year which was responsible for the bulk of the team's 37-run defensive decline.

# Houston Astros

### 2009 TEAM OVERVIEW

## 74-88

## 5th place NL Central

| | ML RANK | 27th | 20th | 18th | 28th | 24th | 9th |
|---|---|---|---|---|---|---|---|
| **Team** | | **643** | **142** | **.260** | **448** | **.719** | **113** |
| | | RUNS | HOME RUNS | BATTING AVG. | WALKS | OPS | STOLEN BASES |
| **Opp.** | | **770** | **176** | **.275** | **546** | **.784** | **65** |
| | ML RANK | 21st | 17th | 26th | 12th | 24th | 2nd |

## Key Players

| Pos | Player | G | AB | R | H | 2B | 3B | HR | RBI | SB | CS | BB | SO | AVG | OBP | SLG | OPS | WS |
|---|---|---|---|---|---|---|---|---|---|---|---|---|---|---|---|---|---|---|
| C | Ivan Rodriguez | 93 | 327 | 41 | 82 | 15 | 2 | 8 | 34 | 0 | 2 | 13 | 74 | .251 | .280 | .382 | .662 | 4 |
| 1B | Lance Berkman | 136 | 460 | 73 | 126 | 31 | 1 | 25 | 80 | 7 | 4 | 97 | 98 | .274 | .399 | .509 | .907 | 22 |
| 2B | Kaz Matsui | 132 | 476 | 56 | 119 | 20 | 2 | 9 | 46 | 19 | 3 | 34 | 85 | .250 | .302 | .357 | .659 | 16 |
| 3B | Geoff Blum | 120 | 381 | 34 | 94 | 14 | 1 | 10 | 49 | 0 | 1 | 33 | 61 | .247 | .314 | .367 | .681 | 6 |
| SS | Miguel Tejada | 158 | 635 | 83 | 199 | 46 | 1 | 14 | 86 | 5 | 2 | 19 | 48 | .313 | .340 | .455 | .795 | 22 |
| LF | Carlos Lee | 160 | 610 | 65 | 183 | 35 | 1 | 26 | 102 | 5 | 3 | 41 | 51 | .300 | .343 | .489 | .831 | 18 |
| CF | Michael Bourn | 157 | 606 | 97 | 173 | 27 | 12 | 3 | 35 | 61 | 12 | 63 | 140 | .285 | .354 | .384 | .738 | 23 |
| RF | Hunter Pence | 159 | 585 | 76 | 165 | 26 | 5 | 25 | 72 | 14 | 11 | 58 | 109 | .282 | .346 | .472 | .818 | 17 |

## Key Pitchers

| Pos | Player | G | GS | W | L | SV | IP | H | R | ER | SO | BB | BR/9 | ERA | WS |
|---|---|---|---|---|---|---|---|---|---|---|---|---|---|---|---|
| SP | Wandy Rodriguez | 33 | 33 | 14 | 12 | 0 | 205.2 | 192 | 77 | 69 | 193 | 63 | 11.38 | 3.02 | 16 |
| SP | Roy Oswalt | 30 | 30 | 8 | 6 | 0 | 181.1 | 183 | 83 | 83 | 138 | 42 | 11.56 | 4.12 | 9 |
| SP | Brian Moehler | 29 | 29 | 8 | 12 | 0 | 154.2 | 187 | 101 | 94 | 91 | 51 | 14.08 | 5.47 | 2 |
| SP | Mike Hampton | 21 | 21 | 7 | 10 | 0 | 112.0 | 128 | 71 | 66 | 74 | 46 | 14.14 | 5.30 | 4 |
| SP | Felipe Paulino | 23 | 17 | 3 | 11 | 0 | 97.2 | 126 | 73 | 68 | 93 | 37 | 15.39 | 6.27 | 0 |
| CL | Jose Valverde | 52 | 0 | 4 | 2 | 25 | 54.0 | 40 | 15 | 14 | 56 | 21 | 10.50 | 2.33 | 11 |
| RP | Tim Byrdak | 76 | 0 | 1 | 2 | 0 | 61.1 | 39 | 23 | 22 | 58 | 36 | 11.45 | 3.23 | 5 |
| RP | LaTroy Hawkins | 65 | 0 | 1 | 4 | 11 | 63.1 | 60 | 16 | 15 | 45 | 16 | 11.08 | 2.13 | 10 |

## Wandy

In 2009, Wandy Rodriguez threw a curveball 37% of the time, more often than any other major league pitcher.

| Year | Curve |
|------|-------|
| 2006 | 21% |
| 2007 | 24% |
| 2008 | 30% |
| 2009 | 37% |

## The Tough Get Going When...

Wandy Rodriguez has a better career ERA against good teams than bad:

**Wandy Rodriguez Records against Quality of Opposition**

| Opponent | G | IP | W | L | SO | BB | ERA |
|----------|---|-----|----|----|-----|-----|------|
| .500 - .599 teams | 66 | 368.1 | 22 | 24 | 297 | 136 | 3.98 |
| .400 - .499 teams | 69 | 371.1 | 26 | 24 | 318 | 136 | 4.39 |

As a matter of principle, we should acknowledge that Wandy has a career ERA of 8.41 against .600+ teams, but that's just 4 games, and his overall ERA is still better against good teams.

## Win Shares Age

The Astros were the oldest team in baseball last year, as measured by their "Win Shares Age" — the average age of the team weighted by the Win Shares contributed by each player.

| Team | Win Shares Age |
|------|----------------|
| 1. Astros | 31.2 |
| 2. Yankees | 30.7 |
| 3. Phillies | 30.7 |
| 4. White Sox | 29.8 |
| 5. Mets | 29.8 |

## Speed Kills

Michael Bourn scored nine times after hitting a triple — as many as any other major league hitter — and scored 48 times after hitting a single, the third-highest total in the majors.

**Michael Bourn — 2009 Runs Scored Analysis**

| Reached on | | Runs Scored After | |
|---|---|---|---|
| Home Runs | 3 | | 3 |
| Triples | 12 | Scored after Triple | 9 |
| Doubles | 27 | Scored after Double | 10 |
| Singles | 131 | Scored after Single | 48 |
| Walk/HBP | 65 | Scored after Walk/HBP | 22 |
| Reached on Error | 8 | Scored after ROE | 1 |
| Reached on Forceout | 21 | Vultured Runs | 3 |
| Inserted as Pinch Runner | 2 | Runs as pinch runner | 1 |
| | | Total Runs Scored | 97 |

## Bourn By Himself

Despite having the major league's best baserunner in their lineup, Michael Bourn, the Astros were the third-worst baserunning team in the majors.    The Astros were 55 bases below average as baserunners — +55 for Bourn, but -110 for the rest of the team.    The worst major league baserunning team was Kansas City, at -67.

## Leadoff Effectiveness

The Astros started the year with Kaz Matsui in the leadoff position, but switched to Michael Bourn after their 39th game.  When Matsui led off an inning, the Astros averaged 0.48 runs; with Bourn leading off, they averaged 0.52 runs.

**Kaz Matsui — 2009 Performance as Leadoff Man**

| | Times | Team Runs | Runs/ Inning |
|---|---|---|---|
| Innings Led Off | 141 | 68 | .48 |
| Reached Base Leading Off | 43 | 45 | 1.05 |
| Did Not Reach | 98 | 23 | .23 |
| Other Innings for Team | 1,302 | 575 | .44 |

**Michael Bourn — 2009 Performance as Leadoff Man**

| | Times | Team Runs | Runs/ Inning |
|---|---|---|---|
| Innings Led Off | 273 | 142 | .52 |
| Reached Base Leading Off | 106 | 85 | .80 |
| Did Not Reach | 167 | 57 | .34 |
| Other Innings for Team | 1,170 | 501 | .43 |

### Great Defense By Pence

Hunter Pence "saved" 10 more runs than the average right fielder with his arm, second-best in the majors. He "saved" 9 runs more than the average right fielder with his glove and range afield, third-best in the majors. His total of 19 runs saved led the next-best right fielder by five runs.

**Right Field — 2009 Total Runs Saved**

| Player | Runs Saved |
|---|---|
| 1. Hunter Pence, Hou | 19 |
| 2. Ryan Church, NYM-Atl | 14 |
| 3. Ryan Sweeney, Oak | 14 |
| 4. Ichiro Suzuki, Sea | 12 |
| 5. Justin Upton, Ari | 11 |
| 6. Nelson Cruz, Tex | 11 |
| 7. Randy Winn, SF | 11 |
| 8. Jay Bruce, Cin | 11 |
| 9. Jayson Werth, Phi | 10 |
| 10. Brandon Moss, Pit | 9 |

### Hampton's Hitting

Mike Hampton's .324 batting average in 2009 was the fourth time in his career he has hit .300. He also hit .311 in 1999, .344 in 2002, and .320 in 2005. His best year with the bat was actually 2001, when he hit "just" .291, but with 7 homers, 16 RBI.

His career average is now .246, with 16 homers, 79 RBI in 725 at-bats.

### Putting the Ball in Play

Miguel Tejada struck out 7% of the time and walked 3% of the time. All in all, he put the ball in play in 88% of his plate appearances. That was the highest "ball in play" rate in the majors.

## Oswalt's Slider

Over the last five years, Roy Oswalt has gradually mixed in more sliders and fewer fastballs.

| Season | Fastball | Slider |
|--------|----------|--------|
| 2005 | 70% | 9% |
| 2006 | 68% | 8% |
| 2007 | 65% | 11% |
| 2008 | 66% | 12% |
| 2009 | 61% | 15% |

## It Just Didn't Matter

The Astros averaged about one home run in each game they won and 0.76 home runs in each game they lost. The difference of .24 home runs was the lowest in the majors.

**Houston Astros 2009**

| | Wins | Losses |
|---|------|--------|
| Games | 74 | 88 |
| Runs Scored | 411 | 232 |
| Runs Allowed | 188 | 582 |
| Batting Average | .295 | .230 |
| On-Base Percentage | .356 | .286 |
| Slugging Percentage | .460 | .348 |
| Home Runs | 75 | 67 |
| Home Runs Allowed | 54 | 122 |
| ERA | 2.42 | 6.43 |

## Poor Paulino

The Astros scored only 40 runs in the 17 games started by Felipe Paulino, or 2.35 runs per start — the worst run support for any major league pitcher.   They were outscored in Paulino's games, 89 to 40.

# Bourn To Run

## by Bill James

A GENERATION AGO THERE WAS A PLAYER NAMED GARY PETTIS; his name appears four times on the chart that accompanies this article. Pettis was not only fast, he was also a very good outfielder. Even had he had just ordinary speed, Pettis would still have been a good outfielder; he had excellent instincts in the field, and a better arm than most of those fast singles hitters, most of whom can't throw. Pettis won five Gold Gloves, which is pretty good considering that he was only really a regular one year.

Why wasn't he a regular, then?

He struck out. He struck out a lot. Pettis never hit more than 5 home runs in a season, but he struck out 100+ times six different seasons — and remember, he wasn't playing every day. Typically he would strike out 120 times a season in about 420 at-bats.

*He struck out. He struck out a lot.*

Gary Pettis held the record for most strikeouts by a player hitting 5 home runs or fewer from 1986 until 2009. The record was broken last year by Houston Astros outfielder Michael Bourn. Bourn hit 3 homers, but struck out 140 times. Bourn doesn't actually strike out quite as often as Pettis did, but he had 600+ at-bats, which Pettis never did. Pettis and Bourn are similar players; not identical, but similar. Bourn stole 61 bases last year; Pettis never stole more than 56, but that was with 443 at-bats. If he had been able to stay in the lineup, he'd have stolen 75 a year.

I always liked Gary Pettis, and I always defended him. When people would complain about his strikeouts — which was basically whenever his name was mentioned — I would always say that we needed to focus not on his strikeouts, but on his walks. In 1989 Pettis batted just 444 times but drew 84 walks, giving him a .375 on-base percentage despite a low average. My argument was that Pettis, with his speed, his defense and his ability to get on base, was a valuable man despite the high strikeout/low power combination.

Whereas with Michael Bourn, I tend to look at it like "If he's only going to hit 3 homers a year, why does he need to strike out so much?" Unlike home runs and stolen bases, which are simple phenomenon, strikeouts are a complex phenomenon. Many, many different things can cause a player to strike out, but those things can be summarized into three areas: Power, Patience, and Incompetence.

If you or I were somehow given the opportunity to play major league baseball we would strike out 250 or

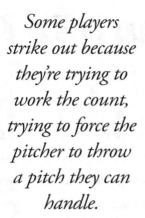

*Some players strike out because they're trying to work the count, trying to force the pitcher to throw a pitch they can handle.*

300 times a year, simply because we would be unable to consistently put the bat on a 95 MPH fastball or an 86 MPH slider. That's incompetence. Wily Mo Pena struck out in a third of his at-bats because he could not learn to lay off of a slider down and away, out of the strike zone. That's incompetence, too, but in his case he was trying to hit home runs; he was trying to jerk the slider out of the park, if not out of the universe. That's incompetence mixed with power. Power hitters strike out because they're trying to generate enough bat speed to get the ball to fly a long way, and the harder you swing the less control of the bat head you have, unless you're a freak of nature like Dustin Pedroia or Albert Pujols.

And the third element is patience. Some players strike out because they're trying to work the count, trying to force the pitcher to throw a pitch they can handle. Manny Ramirez might not strike out 15 times a year, except that he drives every at-bat to 2-2 or 3-2. He is always hitting with two strikes on him, and this leads to a

## Most Strikeouts with 5 or Less Homers

| Rank | Player | Year | HR | RBI | AVG | OPS | SB | K |
|---|---|---|---|---|---|---|---|---|
| 1. | Michael Bourn | 2009 | 3 | 35 | .285 | .738 | 61 | 140 |
| 2. | Gary Pettis | 1986 | 5 | 58 | .258 | .683 | 50 | 132 |
| 3. | Ken Hubbs | 1962 | 5 | 49 | .260 | .646 | 3 | 129 |
| t-4. | Bobby Knoop | 1968 | 3 | 39 | .249 | .625 | 3 | 128 |
| t-4. | Damian Jackson | 2001 | 4 | 38 | .241 | .660 | 23 | 128 |
| 6. | Vince Coleman | 1987 | 3 | 43 | .289 | .721 | 109 | 126 |
| 7. | Gary Pettis | 1985 | 1 | 32 | .257 | .670 | 56 | 125 |
| t-8. | Pat Listach | 1992 | 1 | 47 | .290 | .701 | 54 | 124 |
| t-8. | Gary Pettis | 1987 | 1 | 17 | .208 | .561 | 24 | 124 |
| t-8. | Delino DeShields | 1996 | 5 | 41 | .224 | .585 | 48 | 124 |
| t-11. | Omar Moreno | 1982 | 3 | 44 | .245 | .606 | 60 | 121 |
| t-11. | Brian L. Hunter | 1997 | 4 | 45 | .269 | .687 | 74 | 121 |
| 13. | Gus Williams | 1914 | 4 | 47 | .253 | .647 | 35 | 120 |
| 14. | Gary Pettis | 1990 | 3 | 31 | .239 | .668 | 38 | 118 |
| 15. | Cito Gaston | 1969 | 2 | 28 | .230 | .585 | 4 | 117 |

certain number of strikeouts. Gary Pettis struck out in part because he was a selective hitter who would gladly take a walk if you wanted to give him one.

Actually, what you could say about Gary Pettis is that he would gladly take two bases if you wanted to give him one. Growing up, Pettis was no doubt able to steal second — and third — any time he wanted to. Even in the major leagues in 1985, he stole 56 bases in 65 attempts. After his mid-twenties he started to get the inevitable leg twinges that gradually sap your speed, and...major league catchers are major league catchers for a reason. Still, he was able to get into scoring position after a walk quite a few times.

I understand Adam Dunn and Ryan Howard and Mark Reynolds striking out 200 times a year, because they're trading strikeouts for power. I understand Gary Pettis and Manny Ramirez striking out, because they're looking for their pitch. I understand Wily Mo Pena striking out, because he's made a bad bargain with a slider. What I do not understand is why Michael Bourn needs to strike out so much. He's not really a bad hitter, doesn't appear to be anyway. He hit .285. If Gary Pettis could have hit .285, he'd have won 15 Gold Gloves instead of 5.

One suspects that Bourn is over-swinging, that he is trying to hit the ball harder than he ought to be trying to hit the ball, given his speed and his lack of power. There have been hitters in baseball history who made dramatic mid-career improvements in their strikeout

*Bourn needs to make significant gains, if he is going to be the player he was Bourn to be.*

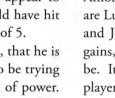

rate — not many of them, but it has happened. Doc Lavan struck out 83 times in 1915. The rest of his career, including years as a regular, he never struck out more than 38 times. Lou Boudreau struck out 57 times in 1941. In 1948, in basically the same number of at-bats, he struck out 9 times (10 times in '47 and '49). Jerry Grote in 1964-1965 struck out 156 times in 615 at-bats. In 1975-76 he struck out only 42 times in more than 700 at-bats. Carney Lansford struck out 115 times in 1979, 93 times in 1980. In 1989, still a regular, he struck out only 25 times. Bill Russell struck out in 14% of his plate appearances through 1972, 7% after that. Wally Pipp eliminated two-thirds of his strikeouts. Jorge Orta struck out 87 times in 425 at-bats in 1973, 88 times in 525 at-bats in 1974. After 1976 he never struck out 50 times in a season, and he was around for a long time. Ron Jackson, a hitting coach in the Astros' system, eliminated most of his strikeouts as his career went on.

Many players make some improvement in their strikeout rate as they mature. Among recent players who have made significant gains are Luis Castillo, Scott Rolen, Carlos Lee, Randy Winn and Jimmy Rollins. Bourn needs to make significant gains, if he is going to be the player he was Bourn to be. It's not impossible for that to happen, but as many players see their strikeout rate go up as see it come down. If Bourn's rate goes up, he'll be out of the game by the time he is 32.

# Kansas City Royals

**2009 TEAM OVERVIEW**

**65-97**

**4**th place **AL Central**

| | ML RANK | 23rd | 19th | 20th | 27th | 23rd | 16th |
|---|---|---|---|---|---|---|---|
| **Team** | | **686** | **144** | **.259** | **457** | **.724** | **88** |
| | | RUNS | HOME RUNS | BATTING AVG. | WALKS | OPS | STOLEN BASES |
| **Opp.** | | **842** | **166** | **.269** | **600** | **.765** | **114** |
| | ML RANK | 25th | 10th | 22nd | 21st | 21st | 18th |

## Key Players

| Pos | Player | G | AB | R | H | 2B | 3B | HR | RBI | SB | CS | BB | SO | AVG | OBP | SLG | OPS | WS |
|---|---|---|---|---|---|---|---|---|---|---|---|---|---|---|---|---|---|---|
| C | Miguel Olivo | 114 | 390 | 51 | 97 | 15 | 5 | 23 | 65 | 5 | 2 | 19 | 126 | .249 | .292 | .490 | .781 | 9 |
| 1B | Billy Butler | 159 | 608 | 78 | 183 | 51 | 1 | 21 | 93 | 1 | 0 | 58 | 103 | .301 | .362 | .492 | .853 | 18 |
| 2B | Alberto Callaspo | 155 | 576 | 79 | 173 | 41 | 8 | 11 | 73 | 2 | 1 | 52 | 51 | .300 | .356 | .457 | .813 | 17 |
| 3B | Mark Teahen | 144 | 524 | 69 | 142 | 34 | 1 | 12 | 50 | 8 | 1 | 37 | 123 | .271 | .325 | .408 | .734 | 9 |
| SS | Yuniesky Betancourt | 71 | 246 | 25 | 59 | 10 | 5 | 4 | 27 | 0 | 2 | 11 | 26 | .240 | .269 | .370 | .639 | 4 |
| LF | David DeJesus | 144 | 558 | 74 | 157 | 28 | 9 | 13 | 71 | 4 | 9 | 51 | 87 | .281 | .347 | .434 | .781 | 16 |
| CF | Mitch Maier | 127 | 341 | 42 | 83 | 15 | 3 | 3 | 31 | 9 | 2 | 43 | 76 | .243 | .333 | .331 | .665 | 9 |
| RF | Jose Guillen | 81 | 281 | 30 | 68 | 8 | 0 | 9 | 40 | 1 | 0 | 22 | 50 | .242 | .314 | .367 | .681 | 4 |
| DH | Mike Jacobs | 128 | 434 | 46 | 99 | 16 | 1 | 19 | 61 | 0 | 0 | 41 | 132 | .228 | .297 | .401 | .698 | 5 |

## Key Pitchers

| Pos | Player | G | GS | W | L | SV | IP | H | R | ER | SO | BB | BR/9 | ERA | WS |
|---|---|---|---|---|---|---|---|---|---|---|---|---|---|---|---|
| SP | Zack Greinke | 33 | 33 | 16 | 8 | 0 | 229.1 | 195 | 64 | 55 | 242 | 51 | 9.81 | 2.16 | 26 |
| SP | Kyle Davies | 22 | 22 | 8 | 9 | 0 | 123.0 | 122 | 76 | 72 | 86 | 66 | 14.05 | 5.27 | 5 |
| SP | Brian Bannister | 26 | 26 | 7 | 12 | 0 | 154.0 | 161 | 94 | 81 | 98 | 50 | 12.56 | 4.73 | 6 |
| SP | Gil Meche | 23 | 23 | 6 | 10 | 0 | 129.0 | 144 | 81 | 73 | 95 | 58 | 14.30 | 5.09 | 5 |
| SP | Luke Hochevar | 25 | 25 | 7 | 13 | 0 | 143.0 | 167 | 109 | 104 | 106 | 46 | 13.91 | 6.55 | 1 |
| CL | Joakim Soria | 47 | 0 | 3 | 2 | 30 | 53.0 | 44 | 14 | 13 | 69 | 16 | 10.53 | 2.21 | 12 |
| RP | Juan Cruz | 46 | 0 | 3 | 4 | 2 | 50.1 | 46 | 34 | 32 | 38 | 29 | 13.59 | 5.72 | 2 |
| RP | Jamey Wright | 65 | 0 | 3 | 5 | 0 | 79.0 | 73 | 51 | 38 | 60 | 44 | 14.13 | 4.33 | 4 |

## Tracking the Season by Segments

The Royals opened the season 12-11, with Zack Greinke winning his first five starts. The team then put together a six-game winning streak, including sweeping back-to-back series at home against the White Sox and Mariners, May 4 through 7.

Kansas City's 18-11 record was good for first place in the Central giving them a three-game lead over the Tigers. They had allowed the fewest runs in the league, and were tied with the Red Sox for the second-best record in the league.

The wheels fell off the Royals' wagon at that point. They followed up their hot start with a 0-5 road trip, which was the beginning of a 20-48 stretch. After a 1-8 home stand in mid-July, they were 38-59 overall and had the worst record in the American League.

The Royals came into September with a 50-81 record, the second-worst in baseball. They rallied to finish the remainder of the season 15-16, when their offense finally began to click. They batted .278 and averaged 4.9 runs per game in September/October.

### Tracking the Season by Segments — 2009 Kansas City Royals

| | Dates | W-L | Runs | Runs/ Game | AVG | Opp Runs | Opp Runs/ Game | ERA | Season Record |
|---|---|---|---|---|---|---|---|---|---|
| Road | Apr 7-9 | 2-1 | 6 | 2.0 | .214 | 5 | 1.7 | 1.73 | 2-1 |
| Home | Apr 10-15 | 3-3 | 25 | 4.2 | .217 | 24 | 4.0 | 4.00 | 5-4 |
| Road | Apr 17-23 | 3-3 | 30 | 5.0 | .294 | 22 | 3.7 | 3.53 | 8-7 |
| Home | Apr 24- 30 | 4-3 | 36 | 5.1 | .250 | 31 | 4.4 | 4.14 | 12-10 |
| Road | May 1-3 | 2-1 | 22 | 7.3 | .297 | 19 | 6.3 | 4.82 | 14-11 |
| Home | May 4-7 | 4-0 | 23 | 5.8 | .321 | 9 | 2.3 | 2.13 | 18-11 |
| Road | May 8-13 | 0-5 | 9 | 1.8 | .201 | 28 | 5.6 | 3.83 | 18-16 |
| Home | May 14-21 | 3-4 | 36 | 5.1 | .281 | 36 | 5.1 | 4.86 | 21-20 |
| Road | May 22-24 | 1-2 | 3 | 1.0 | .188 | 12 | 4.0 | 4.32 | 22-22 |
| Home | May 25-31 | 1-5 | 19 | 3.2 | .235 | 45 | 7.5 | 6.50 | 23-27 |
| Road | Jun 2-11 | 2-7 | 29 | 3.2 | .227 | 45 | 5.0 | 4.80 | 25-34 |
| Home | Jun 12-21 | 4-5 | 44 | 4.9 | .275 | 59 | 6.6 | 5.67 | 29-39 |
| Road | Jun 23-28 | 3-3 | 18 | 3.0 | .218 | 22 | 3.7 | 3.74 | 32-42 |
| Home | Jun 29-Jul 5 | 3-4 | 19 | 2.7 | .277 | 25 | 3.6 | 3.00 | 35-46 |
| Road | July 6 -12 | 2-5 | 27 | 3.9 | .242 | 42 | 6.0 | 6.05 | 37-51 |
| Home | Jul 17-26 | 1-8 | 33 | 3.7 | .248 | 55 | 6.1 | 5.33 | 38-59 |
| Road | Jul 27-Aug 3 | 3-5 | 26 | 3.3 | .242 | 46 | 5.8 | 5.74 | 41-64 |
| Home | Aug4-9 | 2-4 | 39 | 6.5 | .330 | 41 | 6.8 | 6.83 | 43-68 |
| Road | Aug 11-19 | 4-5 | 40 | 4.4 | .234 | 46 | 5.1 | 5.12 | 47-73 |
| Home | Aug 21-26 | 1-5 | 28 | 4.7 | .297 | 39 | 6.5 | 6.22 | 48-78 |
| Road | Aug 27-Sep 2 | 3-4 | 31 | 4.4 | .237 | 39 | 5.6 | 5.49 | 51-82 |
| Home | Sep 4-10 | 4-3 | 29 | 4.1 | .305 | 24 | 3.4 | 3.18 | 55-85 |
| Road | Sep 11-20 | 6-3 | 54 | 6.0 | .268 | 35 | 3.9 | 3.67 | 61-88 |
| Home | Sep 21-27 | 3-4 | 36 | 5.1 | .289 | 50 | 7.1 | 5.57 | 64-92 |
| Road | Sep 28-Oct 4 | 1-5 | 24 | 4.0 | .255 | 43 | 7.2 | 7.61 | 65-97 |

## Pitching Well in Losses

Zack Greinke had the lowest ERA in the American League among qualifiers in Wins at 1.00. Felix Hernandez ranked third at 1.43.

Felix had the lowest ERA in the league in No-Decisions, 2.15, Zack was second, 2.35.

Greinke ranked second in ERA in Losses with a 4.62 ERA.

Hernandez' ERA in Losses was 8.89, 29th of the 30 league qualifiers.

### Zack Greinke 2009

| Group | G | IP | W | L | Pct | H | R | SO | BB | ERA |
|---|---|---|---|---|---|---|---|---|---|---|
| Wins | 16 | 117.1 | 16 | 0 | 1.000 | 82 | 14 | 122 | 21 | 1.00 |
| Losses | 8 | 50.2 | 0 | 8 | .000 | 56 | 32 | 59 | 13 | 4.62 |
| No-Decisions | 9 | 61.1 | 0 | 0 | ---- | 57 | 18 | 61 | 17 | 2.35 |

Quality Starts: 14 in Wins, 4 in Losses, 8 in No-Decisions

### Felix Hernandez 2009

| Group | G | IP | W | L | Pct | H | R | SO | BB | ERA |
|---|---|---|---|---|---|---|---|---|---|---|
| Wins | 19 | 144.1 | 19 | 0 | 1.000 | 98 | 30 | 124 | 37 | 1.43 |
| Losses | 5 | 27.1 | 0 | 5 | .000 | 47 | 31 | 22 | 7 | 8.89 |
| No-Decisions | 10 | 67.0 | 0 | 0 | ---- | 55 | 20 | 71 | 27 | 2.15 |

Quality Starts: 19 in Wins, 1 in Losses, 9 in No-Decisions

Although I am a huge Zack Greinke fan, this chart illustrates why I was not logically convinced that Greinke actually deserved the Cy Young Award, rather than Hernandez. Greinke was clearly above the usual standard of a Cy Young pitcher — but so was Hernandez. Greinke's "advantage" over Hernandez, such as it was, was in games that were lost. What is the value in pitching well in a loss? Minimal, marginal, or none. Greinke won the Cy Young Award essentially because he gave up fewer runs than Hernandez in the games that he lost. I'm not sure that's a good way to define value.

## Fan Favorite

Zack Greinke started the season 5-0, with a 0.50 ERA. On May 4 he appeared on the cover of *Sports Illustrated* and started at home that night before a crowd of 21,827. His starts became an event in Kansas City and in his 14 home starts after April the team averaged 25,953 fans. In the 54 home games after May 4, the team averaged 21,828 in non-Greinke starts.

That's a gain of 4,000 fans a game, but having attended most of those games, the actual effect was much larger than that. The 21,828 average includes tickets sold but not used, or used only for a couple of innings at the start of the game. The Royals have a strong season-ticket program, but the actual crowd count for some of the non-Greinke games was more like 12,000 than 22,000.

## Working Out of a Jam

Zack Greinke allowed the leadoff man to reach 73 times in 2009, but gave up only 41 runs in those innings. This is a rate of 5.05 runs per nine innings — by far the lowest in the American League. The only other American Leaguer below 6.50 in that situation (162 or more innings) was Felix Hernandez, at 5.76.

**Innings Analysis**
**Zack Greinke — 2009**

| | |
|---|---|
| Innings Pitched | 229.1 |
| Runs Allowed | 64 |
| Innings Started | 232 |
| Runs in Those Innings | 64 |
| | |
| Shutout Innings | 188 |
| One-Run Innings | 30 |
| Two-Run Innings | 10 |
| Three-Run Innings | 2 |
| Four-Run Innings | 2 |
| | |
| Got First Man Out | 159 |
| Runs Scored in Those Innings | 23 |
| Runs/9 Innings | 1.30 |
| | |
| First Man Reached | 73 |
| Runs Scored in Those Innings | 41 |
| Runs/9 Innings | 5.05 |
| | |
| 1-2-3 Innings | 91 |
| 10-pitch Innings (or less) | 45 |
| Long Innings (20 or more pitches) | 39 |
| Failed to Finish Inning | 4 |

## How Do You Solve a Problem Like Alberto?

Alberto Callaspo, the Royals' second baseman in 2009, is not a bad hitter. Callaspo hit safely in 119 games, which was the most by any Royal since 2001, when Carlos Beltran hit safely in 119. He hit .300, hit 41 doubles, and walked more often than he struck out. On a team starving for offense, he was one of three or four guys who could pretty reliably hit.

So he lost his job over the winter; the Royals traded for Chris Getz, and apparently intend to use Getz at second base. Which, if you had seen Callaspo play second, you would understand. According to John Dewan's Fielding Bible Plus/Minus, Callaspo ranked 35th among major league second basemen in range, and was 19 plays below average. It seems generous, but then, John didn't rank the outfielders as second basemen; I'm sure there are lots of outfielders who could play second base better than Callaspo, too. I've seen umpires get to more balls than Callaspo does.

So what do you do with Callaspo? I don't know. I would compare him to Jorge Orta, for those of you who are old enough to remember Jorge Orta; like Callaspo, he was an ersatz second baseman but a very good line-drive hitter. He became a DH/pinch hitter/first baseman/left fielder. The Royals can't play Alberto at first; they've got Billy Butler at first. They won't play him in left field; they've got David DeJesus in left (although honestly, DeJesus is no better a hitter than Callaspo). It's hard to DH him because, although he's a good hitter, he's not going to put up the power numbers that most of the other DHs do. They can't trade him because everybody else has seen him play second base, too. It's a tough one.

**Games With 1 Hit — 2009**

| Player | Games |
|---|---|
| Alberto Callaspo | 73 |
| Michael Cuddyer | 72 |
| Kurt Suzuki | 70 |
| Brandon Inge | 69 |
| Aaron Hill | 67 |

## Mom Would Not Be Happy

Royal Cleanup Hitters — let me repeat, Cleanup Hitters — in 2009 had a lower collective batting average than any major league regular in the last five years except Nick Punto in 2007. Their cleanup hitters hit .211. Punto in 2007 hit .210.

Their cleanup OPS was .596. This is lower than any regular player in 2009, and lower than any regular player in the last five years with four exceptions: Punto, Angel Berroa in 2006, Brad Ausmus in 2006, and Michael Bourn in 2008.

## Another Two-Bagger for Butler

Billy Butler in 2009 became the eighth player in history to hit 50 doubles in a season by age 23. The other seven: Hank Greenberg, Enos Slaughter, Stan Musial, Alex Rodriguez, Albert Pujols, Miguel Cabrera and Grady Sizemore.

## Luke Hochevar

One of the biggest keys to the 2010 Royals is whether Luke Hochevar's other stats can catch up to his strikeout-to-walk-ratio.

The Royals in 2009 struck out 1,153 batters, 68 more than the previous team record of 1,085, which was set in 2008. Comparing the Royals to the Mariners (who led the league in ERA), the Royals had 110 more strikeouts, and allowed 6 fewer home runs. The Royals were fourth in the league in strikeouts, and they allowed the second-fewest home runs in the league.

The Royals did lead the league in walks, yes, but with 600 walks they were only 66 behind the Mariners. Based on the theory of three true outcomes for the pitcher (Strikeout, Walk and Home Run), the Royals' pitching was about as good as the Mariners' was.

Luke Hochevar struck out 106 batters and walked only 46 — a better-than-league average strikeout-to-walk ratio. His ERA was 6.55. In all the history of baseball, there is only one other pitcher with a 2-to-1 strikeout-to-walk ratio and an ERA that bad in 100 or more innings (Ryan Rupe, 2001).

The reason, of course, was defense: the Royals didn't have a second baseman, a shortstop, a third baseman, a center fielder, a right fielder or a catcher. Zack Greinke was able to overcome that. Luke Hochevar and Brian Bannister, although they pitched pretty well, just couldn't.

## Defense Is Lacking

Team Defensive Runs Saved compiles all of the defensive ratings into a single number that estimates the number of actual runs saved or allowed by the fielder, compared to average.

For the second consecutive season the Royals were last in the American League in this category.

Pitcher and left field were the only positions where they were not below average.

### Team Defensive Runs Saved By Position — American League 2009

| Team | P | C | 1B | 2B | 3B | SS | LF | CF | RF | Tot |
|------|----|----|----|----|----|----|----|----|----|-----|
| Seattle | 12 | 12 | 1 | 6 | 27 | -6 | 8 | 36 | 14 | 110 |
| Los Angeles | -1 | -3 | 10 | 14 | 28 | -4 | 23 | -1 | -1 | 65 |
| Tampa Bay | -11 | -4 | -11 | 13 | 15 | 5 | 26 | -1 | 25 | 57 |
| Toronto | 6 | 6 | -1 | 22 | 11 | 14 | -4 | -10 | 8 | 52 |
| Texas | 2 | 3 | -8 | 20 | -16 | 18 | 5 | 5 | 13 | 42 |
| Detroit | -3 | 2 | -2 | 5 | 8 | 4 | 13 | 15 | -5 | 37 |
| New York | 4 | -7 | 1 | 6 | -13 | 2 | -1 | 3 | 7 | 2 |
| Cleveland | -4 | -9 | 5 | 2 | -7 | 4 | -7 | -1 | 13 | -4 |
| Chicago | 16 | 0 | -4 | 1 | -11 | 2 | -8 | 5 | -10 | -9 |
| Baltimore | 7 | -8 | -12 | -5 | -5 | 14 | 0 | -2 | -3 | -14 |
| Oakland | 1 | 2 | -8 | -10 | -7 | -32 | 19 | 12 | 8 | -15 |
| Minnesota | -4 | -5 | 2 | -22 | 9 | -24 | -1 | 17 | -5 | -33 |
| Boston | -17 | -8 | 10 | 11 | -18 | -19 | -2 | -11 | 2 | -52 |
| Kansas City | 4 | -5 | -2 | -13 | -12 | -17 | 6 | -2 | -21 | -62 |

## They Can Steal, but Can They Run?

The Royals in 2009 were pretty good base stealers, stealing 88 bases with only 29 caught stealing. We credit them with +30 bases for that (88 − 29 * 2 = 30).

As base runners, rather than base stealers, they were by far the worst in the major leagues. In terms of things like going from first to third on a single, grounding into double plays, running into outs on the bases and moving up on passed balls and wild pitches, the Royals were 97 bases below average — minus 97 in the chart below. The Astros were second-worst in the majors, at -79, and the Angels were the best, at +77.

| Year | 1st to 3rd | | 2nd to Home | | 1st to Home | | DP Opp | GIDP | Total Bases | BR Outs | BR Gain | SB Gain | Net Gain |
|------|-----|-----|-----|-----|-----|-----|------|------|-------|------|------|------|------|
| | Adv | Opp | Adv | Opp | Adv | Opp | | | | | | | |
| 2009 | 74 | 307 | 105 | 177 | 40 | 88 | 1128 | 136 | 100 | 48 | -97 | +30 | -67 |

### And They Did It Without Knuckleballs!

The Royals broke their team record for wild pitches in a season, with 89. That was 22 more than any other team in the American League last season. They had the second-most wild pitches in the league in 2008, and tied for the league lead in 2006.

The Royals over the winter let go of both of their catchers (John Buck and Miguel Olivo), bringing in the aged Jason Kendall. We're sure that will correct that problem, and won't cause any others.

### The Crown Jewels

We credit a starting pitcher with throwing a "gem" whenever he has a Game Score of 65 or higher, or whenever he pitches six shutout innings. The Royals benefitted from 40 pitching gems — the second-highest total in the American League.

In their 40 Gems starts, the Royals were 31-9, with a 0.71 ERA from the starting pitching. In the other 122 games they were 34-88, with a 6.49 ERA from their starters.

### Tejeda in September

After spending the first five months of the season in the bullpen, Robinson Tejeda made six starts for the Royals in September. His Game Scores in the first four — against good teams in every case — were excellent: 70, 72, 60 and 65.

### Royals Walks Allowed

The Royals in 2009 led the American League in walks allowed (600) — but actually missed by less than one walk per game of leading the league in fewest walks allowed. It was kind of a fluke year in that regard; the American League standard deviation of team walks was very low. All the teams walked about the same number of men, except of course that Minnesota walked fewer.

## Historic Impatience

Miguel Olivo had his best strikeout-to-walk ratio in 2009 since 2004 — 126 to 19. These are the ten worst strikeout-to-walk ratios of the last ten years (minimum, 250 plate appearances):

| Player | Year | BB | SO | SO/BB |
|---|---|---|---|---|
| Miguel Olivo | 2008 | 7 | 82 | 11.71 |
| Miguel Olivo | 2006 | 9 | 103 | 11.44 |
| Ivan Rodriguez | 2007 | 9 | 96 | 10.67 |
| Miguel Olivo | 2005 | 8 | 80 | 10.00 |
| Chris Truby | 2002 | 10 | 98 | 9.80 |
| Tomas Perez | 2006 | 5 | 44 | 8.80 |
| Miguel Olivo | 2007 | 14 | 123 | 8.79 |
| Ivan Rodriguez | 2005 | 11 | 93 | 8.45 |
| Eliezer Alfonzo | 2006 | 9 | 74 | 8.22 |
| Tony Pena Jr. | 2007 | 10 | 78 | 7.80 |

Olivo's career strikeout-to-walk ratio (683 to 98) is the worst of any player in major league history (2,000 or more plate appearances), with the exceptions of Pud Galvin, a 19th-century pitcher, and Silver Flint, a 19th-century catcher. There are 15 other pitchers who batted 2,000 or more times — but (with the exception of Galvin) even they had better strikeout-to-walk ratios than Olivo.

## Timing (Not Everything)

The Kansas City Royals in 2009 were 46-23 in games in which they had more hits than their opponents. Was this, would you guess:

a) a very good record,

b) a normal record,

c) a very poor record, or

d) a stupid record that nobody could possibly care about except the authors of this book.

The answer is (c); it is a very poor record for games in which a team out-hits their opponents — in fact, it was the worst in the American League.

We have heard since the invention of radio that it isn't how many hits you get that counts, it's when you get 'em. It turns out that how many you get is pretty important, too. In 2009 there were 2,430 regular-season games. In 231 of those games, the two teams had the same number of hits, and the won-lost record in those games, obviously, was 231-231. But when one team had more hits than the other, the team with more hits was 1,766-433 — an .803 winning percentage. The Royals were one of just five American League teams with a winning percentage under .800 when they out-hit their opponents.

On September 4 at Kaufmann Stadium, the Royals out-hit the Angels 11 to 3 — and lost the game. This was the only major league game in 2009 in which one team out-hit the other by 8 hits, but still lost. The major league record of all teams that out-hit their opponents in a game by 9 or more was 197-0:

| Hit Difference | W | L | Pct |
|---|---|---|---|
| 9 hits or more | 197 | 0 | 1.000 |
| 8 hits | 95 | 1 | .990 |
| 7 hits | 119 | 4 | .967 |
| 6 hits | 156 | 7 | .957 |
| 5 hits | 186 | 16 | .921 |
| 4 hits | 222 | 50 | .816 |
| 3 hits | 241 | 63 | .793 |
| 2 hits | 278 | 112 | .713 |
| 1 hit | 272 | 180 | .602 |
| No difference | 231 | 231 | .500 |

# Greinke, Felix, Lincecum, Carpenter

by Bill James

THE CY YOUNG CONTESTS LAST YEAR, TO JUDGE FROM MY mailbag at Bill James Online (BJOL), seemed to occasion more than the usual amount of discussion. "I'm probably not the first person who's asked this question since Greinke's award was announced," asked Rob T. on November 17 — actually he was the first person to ask it — "but do you think it's a slight 'victory' for yourself and every other sabermetrician? I honestly thought CC was going to get it. But maybe at least the writers are starting to get it…."

"Let's hope," I responded. "By now, I've declared victory more often than Casanova." Which was a lousy answer; I was in smart-ass mode rather than thoughtful mode. The thoughtful answer is that we should resist invitations to personalize the discussion, even when the invitations come in attractive envelopes. It's not about "my side" of the argument and "your side"; it's about what's true. We'll close in on the truth more quickly if we resist projecting personalities into the discussion.

*By now, I've declared victory more often than Casanova.*

Then the Pope of Chili Town pointed out that Bryan Burwell wrote in the *St. Louis Post–Dispatch*;

*What was my greatest fear in the past is now upon us. Armed with their "advanced metrics" and clutching their spread sheets, the new-age baseball voters have officially taken over the sport both in the front offices and behind the scenes.*

Really, Mr. Burwell? Your *greatest* fear? Because you know, honestly, I think I could find bigger things for you to be afraid of. Spiders, serial murderers, terrorists, global warming, venereal disease…pick your poison; I'm sure you can do better than this.

Again, this is personalizing the debate, but I don't think Burwell has mixed feelings about it. Writing for a St. Louis audience, he is trying to smear sabermetrics by saying, in essence, that we were responsible for taking the award away from St. Louis pitchers. Setting aside the position that it may be better not to personalize the debate, is that even what happened? Isn't what happened here more like two St. Louis pitchers split the vote and allowed the San Francisco pitcher to win it?

Maybe, but there was something else going on that I didn't know at the time: Will Carroll voted. According to Carroll (November 16, *Baseball Prospectus*), "Later on in awards season, I'll touch on the other award I had a vote for, and explain my selections and criticize the picks if you want, but in a year where the BBWAA opened up its voting to members they knew might think a little different, I have to feel like it's a step forward. Now about those Gold Gloves…."

Ooooooooooh. Oh, I had missed that entirely; I didn't realize the BBWAA had granted us the vote. Sabermetric suffrage has arrived. Susan B. Anthony and me, we're tight. Now I understand what Burwell was raving about.

Then Matthew Namee weighed in, more with a comment than a question:

*Some people are obviously upset that two writers left Carpenter off of their NL Cy Young ballots, thus allegedly depriving him of the award. He only threw 192.2 innings, though. Excluding strike years, the fewest innings pitched by a Cy Young-winning starter was Sutcliffe in '84 (150.1 IP, but before that he was in the AL, and his total was 244.2). Nobody else won with fewer than 213 innings (Pedro in '99). In other words, had Carpenter won, he would have had, by far, the fewest innings pitched of any Cy Young starter, by a wide margin.*

I'm not sure that I get the logic for excluding Sutcliffe there. Sutcliffe won the National League Award while pitching only 150 innings in the National League. Doesn't that pretty well cover Carpenter winning the award while pitching only 193 innings? Next, Rcberlo commented that:

*What I've read about the NL Cy Young vote seems to indicate that the decision between Lincecum and Carpenter hinged mainly on the value of Lincecum's 30 "extra" innings. Does it make sense to estimate that value by looking at who occupied Carpenter's slot in the rotation when he was gone and, in effect, add 30 innings worth of that pitcher's record to Carpenter's stats?*

Which doesn't *quite* make sense, to me, because isn't that saying that if the guy who filled in for Carpenter when Carpenter was out was good, then Carpenter deserves the award, but if the guy who filled in for him was lousy, then Carpenter shouldn't get the award?

I'm not sure I buy the theory that Lincecum's extra innings are the deciding factor here. I think I might stick with the explanation that two St. Louis players split the vote and allowed the San Francisco guy to win — exactly like the American League MVP Award in 1954, when two Cleveland Indians split the vote (Larry Doby and Bobby Avila) and allowed a Yankee to win, or in the National League in 1965, when two Dodgers split the vote and allowed Willie Mays to win, or the American League Cy Young vote in 1970, when three Baltimore Orioles split twelve first-place votes and allowed a Minnesota Twin to win with six. Et cetera.

Finally, Ventboys wrote:

*To amplify on the Cy Young voting, I found it encouraging that CC finished 4th, behind Felix and Verlander. Up here in the northwest we are celebrating Felix' 2nd place finish like he won. We weren't sure that the writers had heard of him. Wilbon and Kornheiser couldn't even name the teams that the two Rookies of the Year played on.*

I was even getting questions from *non*-subscribers, like Cy Morong:

*On page 448 of the new Handbook, you have both Greinke and Hernandez with 26 win shares. How did they come out equal when most other evaluations give Greinke a substantial advantage? For instance, Fangraphs has Greinke with 9.4 wins above replacement, when Hernandez has only 6.9.*

*Sabermetric suffrage has arrived. Susan B. Anthony and me, we're tight.*

## Getting to the Real Issue

OK, setting aside the reader comments and getting to the issue itself. I have long been a huge fan of Zack Greinke. When he first came to the Royals in 2004 he was 20 years old, but he was a lot of fun to watch. At that time he was one of those pitchers, like Sabathia and El Duque and Randy Johnson and Lincecum and Tiant and Fernando Valenzuela, who was instantly recognizable as something different, something outside the ordinary. He took an epic detour between then and 2008, as has been well documented, but when I returned to the Kansas City area in late summer 2008 I saw him pitch three or four times, and I was just blown away. He's a very different pitcher now than he was in 2004. He has morphed from a guy who makes pitching look interesting to a guy who makes it look easy. I've never seen anybody have so many easy innings. I told everybody who would listen a year ago that Greinke was as good a pitcher as anybody in baseball.

Greinke, in important ways, saved last season for Royals fans. He enabled Royals fans to go to the game every fifth day and forget that the team stunk on the other four days. Four days in five, being a Royals fan might be painful, but when Greinke took the mound, they were more than the equal of whomever it was they were facing. We got drunk every weekend on ZG power.

But having said that, I still don't see that the contest between Greinke and Felix Hernandez is a mismatch, and I was surprised that Greinke dominated the voting the way that he did. Yes, Greinke was sensational, but so was Felix. It seemed to me that both Greinke and Felix were well above the median standard of a modern Cy Young pitcher, and I really wouldn't have been upset if Hernandez had won.

The first two things I look at are the pitcher's Season Score and his Win Shares. These are the Season Scores for the top American League pitchers this year:

| Rank | Player | Score |
|---|---|---|
| 1. | Felix Hernandez, Sea | 299 |
| 2. | Zack Greinke, KC | 283 |
| 3. | Roy Halladay, Tor | 255 |
| 4. | Justin Verlander, Det | 245 |
| 5. | CC Sabathia, NYY | 236 |
| 6. | Mariano Rivera, NYY | 232 |
| 7. | Joe Nathan, Min | 230 |
| 8. | Andrew Bailey, Oak | 206 |
| 9. | Josh Beckett, Bos | 202 |
| 10. | Jonathan Papelbon, Bos | 201 |
| 11. | Jon Lester, Bos | 199 |

Had to go to 11 to get Jon Lester in there. And here are the top Season Scores in the National League:

| Rank | Player | Score |
|---|---|---|
| 1. | Adam Wainwright, Sea | 281 |
| 2. | Chris Carpenter, StL | 276 |
| 3. | Tim Lincecum, SF | 263 |
| 4. | Javier Vazquez, Atl | 228 |
| 5. | Josh Johnson, Fla | 223 |
| 6. | Matt Cain, SF | 215 |
| 7. | Jonathan Broxton, LAD | 215 |
| 8. | Dan Haren, Ari | 214 |
| 9. | Jair Jurrjens, Atl | 208 |
| 10. | Heath Bell, SD | 207 |
| 11. | Ryan Franklin, StL | 205 |

*Greinke enabled Royals fans to go to the game every fifth day and forget that the team stunk on the other four days.*

The second thing I looked at was Win Shares. These are the 2009 Win Shares for the top Cy Young contenders:

| American League | | National League | |
|---|---|---|---|
| **Player** | **WS** | **Player** | **WS** |
| Zack Greinke | 26 | Tim Lincecum | 22 |
| Felix Hernandez | 26 | Adam Wainwright | 21 |
| Roy Halladay | 21 | Chris Carpenter | 21 |
| Justin Verlander | 21 | Dan Haren | 20 |
| CC Sabathia | 18 | Matt Cain | 20 |
| Jon Lester | 17 | Ubaldo Jimenez | 19 |
| Edwin Jackson | 17 | Josh Johnson | 19 |
| Jered Weaver | 17 | Jair Jurrjens | 17 |
| Andrew Bailey | 17 | Javier Vazquez | 16 |
| Josh Beckett | 16 | Wandy Rodriguez | 16 |
| Mark Buehrle | 16 | Jonathan Broxton | 16 |
| John Danks | 16 | | |
| Joe Nathan | 16 | | |
| David Aardsma | 16 | | |

Season Scores are just a method of making simple comparisons of what the value *appears* to be, rather than what it really *is*, and Win Shares are not a way of comparing two seasons, but rather a system of very carefully comparing *groups* of players or groups of seasons such as careers. What these systems do is not resolve the Cy Young or MVP debate, but rather make it apparent who the leading contenders are.

Very often these systems make it apparent that there is only one serious contender for an award — the Cy Young Award in the American League in 2008, for example, when Cliff Lee outdistanced the field by 57 points in the Season Score. The Season Score predicts the Cy Young voting a high percentage of the time, but it doesn't *prove* anything, and isn't intended to.

2009 is not one of those years when these two systems will end the debate. What these systems do in 2009 is make it apparent who the serious candidates are — Greinke and Hernandez in the American League; Wainwright, Carpenter and Lincecum in the National. Which, of course, we knew anyway; we're spinning our wheels here.

Sometime last summer I introduced the Strike Zone won-lost record, which is a way of stating a pitcher's strikeouts and walks as if they were wins and losses. These are the top strike zone winning percentages of 2009. "KS" stands for "Strike Zone Wins" and "KL" for "Strike Zone Losses":

| Player | G | W | L | KS | KL | K PCT |
|---|---|---|---|---|---|---|
| Mariano Rivera, NYY | 66 | 3 | 3 | 5 | 2 | .748 |
| Roy Halladay, Tor | 32 | 17 | 10 | 15 | 5 | .746 |
| Dan Wheeler, TB | 69 | 4 | 5 | 3 | 1 | .712 |
| Kevin Slowey, Min | 16 | 10 | 3 | 5 | 2 | .712 |
| Zack Greinke, KC | 33 | 16 | 8 | 18 | 8 | .701 |
| Mike Wuertz, Oak | 74 | 6 | 1 | 7 | 3 | .686 |
| Matt Thornton, CWS | 70 | 6 | 3 | 6 | 3 | .682 |
| Joakim Soria, KC | 47 | 3 | 2 | 5 | 2 | .680 |
| Alfredo Aceves, NYY | 43 | 10 | 1 | 5 | 2 | .680 |
| Justin Verlander, Det | 35 | 19 | 9 | 20 | 9 | .678 |
| Joe Nathan, Min | 70 | 2 | 2 | 6 | 3 | .666 |
| Koji Uehara, Bal | 12 | 2 | 4 | 3 | 2 | .664 |
| Andrew Bailey, Oak | 68 | 6 | 3 | 7 | 4 | .652 |
| Carl Pavano, Min | 33 | 14 | 12 | 11 | 6 | .650 |
| Brandon League, Tor | 67 | 3 | 6 | 6 | 3 | .641 |
| Josh Beckett, Bos | 32 | 17 | 6 | 14 | 8 | .641 |
| Jon Lester, Bos | 32 | 15 | 8 | 16 | 9 | .634 |
| Jason Frasor, Tor | 61 | 7 | 3 | 4 | 2 | .633 |
| Phil Hughes, NYY | 51 | 8 | 3 | 7 | 4 | .628 |
| Russ Springer, TB | 74 | 1 | 4 | 4 | 3 | .627 |
| Scott Baker, Min | 33 | 15 | 9 | 12 | 7 | .625 |
| Brett Anderson, Oak | 30 | 11 | 11 | 11 | 7 | .622 |
| Jake Peavy, CWS | 16 | 9 | 6 | 8 | 5 | .615 |
| James Shields, TB | 33 | 11 | 12 | 12 | 8 | .613 |
| Jon. Papelbon, Bos | 66 | 1 | 1 | 6 | 4 | .610 |
| Darren O'Day, Tex | 68 | 2 | 1 | 4 | 3 | .606 |
| Freddy Garcia, CWS | 9 | 3 | 4 | 3 | 2 | .603 |
| Bobby Jenks, CWS | 52 | 3 | 4 | 4 | 2 | .602 |
| Felix Hernandez, Sea | 34 | 19 | 5 | 16 | 10 | .601 |

Greinke's strike zone won-lost record is 18-8, a little better than his actual record of 16-8, and Hernandez' strike zone won-lost record is 16-10, which is significantly worse than his actual record of 19-5.

Of course, again, a great pitcher doesn't *have* to have a great strikeout to walk ratio; it merely often happens that he does. 95% of Cy Young Award winners have strike zone winning percentages over .500 — but there are other elements to the game. I am always amazed at how many pitchers have about the same strike zone won-lost record as actual won-lost record. These are the National League leaders:

| Player | G | W | L | KS | KL | K PCT |
|---|---|---|---|---|---|---|
| Chad Qualls, Ari | 51 | 2 | 2 | 3 | 1 | .761 |
| Dan Haren, Ari | 33 | 14 | 10 | 16 | 5 | .744 |
| Javier Vazquez, Atl | 32 | 15 | 10 | 17 | 6 | .728 |
| Huston Street, Col | 64 | 4 | 1 | 5 | 2 | .728 |
| Ricky Nolasco, Fla | 31 | 13 | 9 | 14 | 6 | .687 |
| Cliff Lee, Phi | 34 | 14 | 13 | 13 | 6 | .676 |
| Ted Lilly, CHC | 27 | 12 | 9 | 11 | 5 | .675 |
| John Smoltz, StL | 15 | 3 | 8 | 5 | 3 | .668 |
| Edward Mujica, SD | 67 | 3 | 5 | 5 | 3 | .665 |
| Jon. Broxton, LAD | 73 | 7 | 2 | 8 | 4 | .661 |
| Cole Hamels, Phi | 32 | 10 | 11 | 12 | 6 | .660 |
| Joel Pineiro, StL | 32 | 15 | 12 | 7 | 4 | .659 |
| Tim Lincecum, SF | 32 | 15 | 7 | 18 | 10 | .656 |
| Chris Carpenter, StL | 28 | 17 | 4 | 10 | 5 | .653 |
| Rafael Soriano, Atl | 77 | 1 | 6 | 7 | 4 | .652 |
| Hiroki Kuroda, LAD | 21 | 8 | 7 | 6 | 3 | .643 |
| Ryan Madson, Phi | 79 | 5 | 5 | 5 | 3 | .637 |
| Trevor Hoffman, Mil | 55 | 3 | 2 | 3 | 2 | .630 |
| Aaron Harang, Cin | 26 | 6 | 14 | 10 | 6 | .621 |
| Josh Johnson, Fla | 33 | 15 | 5 | 13 | 8 | .620 |
| Heath Bell, SD | 68 | 6 | 4 | 6 | 3 | .620 |
| Roy Oswalt, Hou | 30 | 8 | 6 | 10 | 6 | .620 |
| Pedro Feliciano, NYM | 88 | 6 | 4 | 4 | 3 | .619 |
| Adam Wainwright, StL | 34 | 19 | 8 | 15 | 9 | .614 |
| Mark DiFelice, Min | 59 | 4 | 1 | 3 | 2 | .613 |
| Johan Santana, NYM | 25 | 13 | 9 | 10 | 7 | .611 |
| Jor. Zimmermann, Was | 16 | 3 | 5 | 6 | 4 | .611 |
| Jason Hammel, Col | 34 | 10 | 8 | 9 | 6 | .611 |
| Todd Coffey, Mil | 78 | 4 | 4 | 5 | 3 | .606 |
| Brian Wilson, SF | 68 | 5 | 6 | 6 | 4 | .604 |
| Wandy Rodriguez, Hou | 33 | 14 | 12 | 14 | 9 | .603 |
| Matt Daley, Col | 57 | 1 | 1 | 4 | 3 | .602 |
| Rafael Betancourt, Col | 61 | 4 | 3 | 4 | 3 | .602 |

I think the data for Cliff Lee and John Smoltz here includes the data from both leagues. At this point in the analysis I understand something about the Cardinals that I didn't previously understand. Throughout history there have been several teams that, working in a pitcher's park, were able to make good finesse-type pitchers appear to be as dominant as power pitchers. The Orioles of the 1960s and 1970s are the classic team of this type, but there have been others: the Oakland A's of the 1970s and 1980s, the Dodgers of the 1970s and 1980s, the Reds of 1939/1940, the Milwaukee Braves of the late 1950s, and others. If you work in a pitcher's park and you don't walk anybody and you have a good defense behind you, you're likely to have a winning record and a low ERA. You're going to look a lot better than you really are. The situation favors a finesse pitcher.

The Cardinals, I now understand, have become one of those teams that makes low strikeout/low walk pitchers look better than they really are. Wainwright, Carpenter, Pineiro — these guys are all low strikeout/low walk pitchers. It's not that they're not *good*; it's just that they're not as good as their records look. I didn't get that a half-hour ago.

Stripping those charts down to the relevant contenders:

| Player | G | W | L | KS | KL | K PCT |
|---|---|---|---|---|---|---|
| Zack Greinke, KC | 33 | 16 | 8 | 18 | 8 | .701 |
| Justin Verlander, Det | 35 | 19 | 9 | 20 | 9 | .678 |
| Felix Hernandez, Sea | 34 | 19 | 5 | 16 | 10 | .601 |
| Tim Lincecum, SF | 32 | 15 | 7 | 18 | 10 | .656 |
| Chris Carpenter, StL | 28 | 17 | 4 | 10 | 5 | .653 |
| Adam Wainwright, Stl | 34 | 19 | 8 | 15 | 9 | .614 |

This still is not how we find the deserving Cy Young winners; it is merely another thing that is worth looking at. Probably 70% of a pitcher's value is centered in the strikeout and walk categories. Looking at that 70%, Greinke and Lincecum are ahead.

## Toward an Actual Answer

Starting now along the path toward an actual answer, let us begin with Runs Saved. Greinke pitched 229.1 innings with an ERA 2.29 runs better than the league average (2.16 versus 4.45). That makes him 58 runs better than an average pitcher. Felix pitched 238.2 innings with an ERA 1.96 runs better than the league average. That makes him 52 runs better than an average pitcher. Advantage, Greinke.

This, however, is without making park adjustments. Kauffman Stadium was re-modeled between 2007 and 2009, and is, in essence, a new park. The new park played in 2009 as the best hitter's park in the American League. The Royals scored and allowed 805 runs in Kauffman Stadium, 723 on the road. Adjusting for that, Greinke is not 58 runs better than an average pitcher, but 64 runs better.

Puget Sound Park in Seattle had a park effect of .95 — a pitcher's park. Adjusting for that, Hernandez is not 52 runs better than average, but 49 runs better. Greinke is now ahead, 64-49.

OK, Greinke is well ahead now, and I'm happy that Greinke won, and nobody seems to be too unhappy about it, so let's set that one aside for now and concentrate on the National League race. In the National League, without park effects, Lincecum is 42 runs better than the league average, Carpenter 41 runs better, and Wainwright 40 runs better.

Departing from this point, one can construct a sabermetric argument that Carpenter is the best pitcher in the league. Lincecum leads Carpenter by a razor-thin margin, but this is without considering:

1) Un-earned runs,
2) Pitcher's hitting, and
3) Efficient use of the runs.

Carpenter gave up 48 earned runs, but gave up only 1 un-earned run. Lincecum gave up 61 earned runs, plus 7 un-earned runs. Much analytical thinking proceeds from the assumption that only earned runs are relevant, but clearly this is untrue. The first un-earned run that Lincecum gave up came about when Juan Pierre was on first for the Dodgers and Lincecum tried to pick him off. Lincecum threw the ball away — E-1 — putting Pierre on third base.

I won't argue about it being an "earned" as opposed to "un-earned" run — but it is clearly and absolutely a run for which Lincecum is responsible. Even setting that aside, it seems to me more reasonable to hold a pitcher 50% responsible for un-earned runs, rather than to say that he is totally absolved of responsibility for any run that is tainted by fielding malfeasance. So let's hold Lincecum totally responsible for the Juan Pierre run and hold the pitchers 50% responsible for other un-earned runs. Carpenter goes from 1 run behind to 2 ½ ahead:

| Lincecum | |
| --- | --- |
| Earned runs versus average | 42 |
| Juan Pierre run | -1 |
| Other un-earned runs | -3 |
| **New total** | **38** |

| Carpenter | |
| --- | --- |
| Earned runs versus average | 41 |
| Un-earned run | -0.5 |
| **New total** | **40.5** |

*Of course, a great pitcher doesn't have to have a great strikeout to walk ratio; it merely often happens that he does.*

Next, let's consider the pitcher's own contributions to the offense. Runs created formulas don't work well when the totals get close to zero; what works better there is just to assume that every 4 bases is a run and every 7 outs are a negative run. Lincecum, with a .386 OPS, had 11 total bases and 6 walks, contributed 17 bases with 57 outs, not counting sacrifice hits and flies, which are sort of "justified outs". Carpenter, with a .482 OPS, had 17 total bases, 2 walks and a hit by pitch, contributed 20 bases with 53 outs. Figuring 4 bases is a run, that's 3/4 of a run for Carpenter plus 4/7 of a run for having fewer outs; Carpenter gains another 1.3 runs:

**Lincecum**

| | |
|---|---|
| Old total | 38 |
| Batting plus | 4.25 |
| Batting minus | 8.14 |
| **New total** | **34.1** |

**Carpenter**

| | |
|---|---|
| Old total | 40.5 |
| Batting plus | 5 |
| Batting minus | 7.57 |
| **New total** | **37.9** |

Carpenter is now ahead by almost 4 runs.

But this now gets Wainwright back into the discussion; Wainwright was the best hitter of the three. Wainwright hit 5 doubles, a triple and 2 homers. His total bases plus hits are 30, with 73 outs. Going back a step to include him, he also allowed 7 un-earned runs:

**Wainwright**

| | |
|---|---|
| Earned runs versus average | 40 |
| Un-earned runs | -3.5 |
| Batting plus | 7.5 |
| Batting minus | -10.4 |
| **New total** | **33.6** |

But we haven't yet dealt with the "efficient use of the runs" stat. Stating the traditionalists' argument in its best form, Carpenter had, among these three pitchers, both the best winning percentage (.810) and the best ERA (2.24). Carpenter was 17-4, 2 ½ games better than Lincecum. This has *usually* been enough, in the history of Cy Young voting, to sway the decision. If you have the best record and the best ERA, you win; end of discussion. One can look at strikeouts and walks, but, as we showed earlier, Lincecum doesn't *really* have better strikeout and walk data than Carpenter; he merely has more strikeouts. Lincecum's strike zone winning percentage is .656; Carpenter's is .653. It's not a meaningful difference.

The bottom line is winning. Look at it this way: the Cardinals scored 125 runs in Carpenter's 28 starts — 4.46 runs per start — and Carpenter was 17-4. The Giants scored 146 runs in Lincecum's 32 starts — 4.56 per start — yet Lincecum was "just" 15-7. The Cardinals scored 125 runs in Carpenter's starts, and won 18 games. That's 1 win for each 6.94 runs. The Giants scored 146 runs in Lincecum's starts, and won 19 games. That's 1 win for each 7.68 runs. Carpenter simply made more efficient use of his runs.

At this point, however, the pro-Carpenter argument begins to collapse. There are four issues here we haven't fully examined:

1) Park Effects,

2) Durability,

3) Quality of Competition, and

4) Systematic as opposed to testimonial study of "Run efficiency."

I carefully dodged the park effects data before I departed on the pro-Carpenter argument because, if I hadn't, there's no pro-Carpenter argument. Busch Stadium is a pitcher's park, with a 2009 Park Effect of .919. Willie Mays Park in San Francisco is a hitter's park, with a 2009 Park Effect of 1.052. If you adjust for that, Lincecum isn't 42 runs better than average, he's 45 runs better than average, and Carpenter isn't 41 runs better than average, he's 38 runs better than average. The difference between them isn't 1 run; it's 7 runs.

It's 7 runs versus an *average* pitcher, but value does not consist of being better than average; it consists of being better than replacement level. No one can say *exactly* what the replacement level is, but let's say the replacement level is a pitcher 35% worse than the league average (an ERA of about 5.66 in the National League, 6.01 in the American League, without park adjustments).

If you compare the pitcher to a replacement level pitcher, Lincecum's advantage over Carpenter isn't 45-38; it's 83-68. The advantage for Lincecum grows because by pitching 30 additional innings he is taking innings away from a bad pitcher, which is the real situation that baseball teams face. When your quality pitchers go out, the guys you have to put on the mound are usually pretty awful. You don't win too many of those games.

Then let's look at the issue of quality of competition. Chris Carpenter made 28 starts in 2009. Eighteen of those starts were against teams with losing records. Carpenter started only 3 times against teams with 90 or more wins. Lincecum started 11 times against teams with 90 or more wins. That looks like a huge difference, although, as we'll see in a moment, it really isn't. Carpenter had only 3 starts all year in which it was a fair fight. Lincecum had 11. Let's chart it:

|  | Carpenter | Lincecum |
| --- | --- | --- |
| 90-Win Teams | 3 | 11 |
| Winning Teams | 10 | 16 |
| Losing Teams | 18 | 16 |
| 90-Loss Teams | 7 | 7 |

The aggregate won-lost record of the 28 teams that Carpenter faced was 2,193-2,341, a .484 winning percentage. The aggregate won-lost record of Lincecum's opponents was 2,603-2,579, a .502 percentage.

Let's see...an average National League team this year allowed 4.49 runs per game. To cause an 18-point difference (.018) in winning percentage would require almost exactly 1/6 of a run per game. Assuming 24 games — 216 innings — that's 4 runs. To offset his disadvantage in facing tougher competition, we need to credit Lincecum with an additional 4 runs.

Four runs isn't a huge difference, but it's a difference. Lincecum was ahead 83-68; he's now ahead about 87-68. You can give Carpenter a run for being a better hitter, 3 or 4 runs for the un-earned runs...it doesn't matter as much if Lincecum starts out 19 runs ahead.

Carpenter's defense collapses completely when we take a more systematic look at the issue of Run Efficiency. The Cardinals with Carpenter got 1 win for each 6.94 runs versus 1 win for each 7.68 with Lincecum. True, but you know what that is? That's just the Park Effect again — the Park Effect, combined with the fact that Carpenter was a little bit more effective per inning pitched. When you have fewer runs, each run has more impact in the win column, independent of the issue of run/win efficiency. A better way to look at the issue of run/win efficiency is to look at the runs scored, runs allowed and won-lost record in the pitcher's starts, which can be found in our system at BJOL under Statistics/Team Profiles/Performance by Starting Pitcher.

In Carpenter's starts this year the Cardinals scored 125 runs, allowed 68 runs, and finished 18-10. If you score 125 runs and allow 68 runs, what should your

*Lincecum was the best pitcher in the National League and deserved the award.*

winning percentage be? Sabermetrics 101: it's .772. (In Sabermetrics 413 you'll learn that it's actually not .772, but more like .750, but let's keep it simple; Burwell might be listening at the door.) At 18-10, their actual winning percentage in these games was .643.

Far from being *efficient* in his use of runs, Chris Carpenter was actually one of the most *in*-efficient pitchers in the major leagues, by this method. He was short by 3.6 wins, making him the sixth most inefficient pitcher in the majors.

Lincecum was short by 2.6 wins as well. The Giants winning percentage in Lincecum's starts should have been .676 but was actually .594. This doesn't help Lincecum a lot, but he doesn't need the help. At this point in the analysis it is Carpenter who is grasping at straws, and this particular straw isn't going to hold him up.

That isn't a perfect analysis, either; the run/win efficiency method that I just outlined has three serious problems:

1) That it treats runs scored after the pitcher has left the game the same as runs scored while he was in the game,

2) That it treats offensive support of 11-1-1 in three games the same as offensive support of 4-5-4, when in reality they are very different,

3) That it uses the Pythagorean approach in a very low-run context, where the Pythagorean method becomes less accurate.

One never gets perfect answers. I have been doing post-award analysis like this for 30 years, actually more than 30 years. The analysis that we can do now is much, much more sophisticated and more accurate than the analysis that we could do 30 years ago, but we are no closer to perfect methods now than we were then. We have introduced many more factors into the analysis, and much more available data. These new benefits give us better answers — but they also expose flaws in the old reasoning, requiring us to think more deeply about some of the issues.

There is no end to the argument, but I am now satisfied that, at the end of the argument, Lincecum is still going to be ahead. Tim Lincecum won the award; Tim Lincecum deserved the award. I am satisfied that

that is true.

Let's go back now to Greinke versus Felix, and look at some of the same issues. Hitting…we can skip that; American league hitters don't hit very often. Greinke had a double and Felix didn't, but we'll skip it.

Greinke allowed 9 un-earned runs, Felix allowed 15. Holding the pitcher 50% responsible for those gives Greinke an additional 3-run edge, which puts him ahead by 18 runs, a probably impossible advantage for Felix to overcome.

To get to durability, let's back up and look at runs vs. replacement pitcher, rather than runs versus average. Greinke was 106 runs better than a replacement-level pitcher; Hernandez was 89 runs better — but remember, each run has less impact as more runs are scored. Greinke was pitching in a hitter's park; Hernandez, a pitcher's park. If you normalize for that, the advantage isn't 106-89, but 101-92. It's close.

Then we look at run/win efficiency. You remember, Chris Carpenter was minus 3.6, Lincecum minus 2.6. Felix Hernandez was plus 2.3. Greinke was minus 1.6. Let me chart the data:

| Hernandez | |
|---|---|
| Runs Scored | 150 |
| Runs Allowed | 106 |
| Expected W Pct. | .667 |
| Expected Wins | 22.7 |
| Actual Wins (25-9) | 25 |
| **Net Gain** | **2.3** |

| Greinke | |
|---|---|
| Runs Scored | 123 |
| Runs Allowed | 108 |
| Expected W Pct. | 0.565 |
| Expected Wins | 18.6 |
| Actual Wins (17-16) | 17 |
| **Net Gain** | **-1.6** |

Putting this in plain English: The Mariners were 25-9 with Hernandez on the mound. The Royals were 17-16 with Greinke — and the difference *cannot* be fully explained by run support. There is something else going on.

There's a problem with that method, as I said before; Greinke's bullpen was awful, and we can't hold him personally accountable for that. On the other hand, if we *did* hold him personally responsible for all of it, a difference of 3.9 wins is a difference of roughly 39 runs. Hernandez would vault far ahead in the overall analysis.

Then we get to the issue of Quality of Competition, the quality of the opposition or whatever you want to call it. Hernandez started 22 times against teams with winning records; Greinke started 15 times. Let's do the chart that we did before, with Lincecum and Carpenter:

|  | Greinke | Hernandez |
| --- | --- | --- |
| 90-Win Teams | 3 | 7 |
| Winning Teams | 15 | 22 |
| Losing Teams | 18 | 12 |
| 90-Loss Teams | 9 | 5 |

The 33 teams faced by Greinke had an aggregate record of 2,599-2,733, a .487 winning percentage. The 34 teams faced by Hernandez had an aggregate record of 2,840-2,674, a .515 percentage. Greinke had an advantage of .028 (winning percentage), based simply on facing weaker opposition.

Stating that as runs, to offset an advantage of .028 winning percentage, at the level of offense in the American League in 2009, requires about .275 runs per game. Given that they each pitched about 26 full games (234 innings), it's a difference of about seven runs.

Well, I'm not here to argue that Greinke didn't deserve the award. Greinke very much deserved the award, very richly deserved the award. But whether he was actually better than Felix Hernandez...I don't know. It comes down to the issue of how much weight is given to the differences in run/win efficiency, and our methods on that specific issue are crude and un-convincing.

But here's what I would say. In the National League, the vote was split three ways, it was a very close vote, and it's been a controversial vote. In the American League Greinke won easily, and this vote has been uncontroversial, and this vote has been celebrated by the analytical community as a victory for reason and logic.

But actually it seems pretty clear to me, under the most careful analysis that I can do, that Lincecum was the best pitcher in the National League and deserved the award — whereas in the American League, under the most careful analysis that I can do, it is unclear to me whether Greinke or Hernandez is more deserving. They are both very deserving, but I can't say which is *more* deserving. Ask me again in another 30 years, I'll have a better answer for you.

# Los Angeles Angels of Anaheim

## Key Players

| Pos | Player | G | AB | R | H | 2B | 3B | HR | RBI | SB | CS | BB | SO | AVG | OBP | SLG | OPS | WS |
|---|---|---|---|---|---|---|---|---|---|---|---|---|---|---|---|---|---|---|
| C | Mike Napoli | 114 | 382 | 60 | 104 | 22 | 1 | 20 | 56 | 3 | 3 | 40 | 103 | .272 | .350 | .492 | .842 | 10 |
| 1B | Kendry Morales | 152 | 566 | 86 | 173 | 43 | 2 | 34 | 108 | 3 | 7 | 46 | 117 | .306 | .355 | .569 | .924 | 23 |
| 2B | Howie Kendrick | 105 | 374 | 61 | 109 | 21 | 3 | 10 | 61 | 11 | 4 | 20 | 71 | .291 | .334 | .444 | .778 | 15 |
| 3B | Chone Figgins | 158 | 615 | 114 | 183 | 30 | 7 | 5 | 54 | 42 | 17 | 101 | 114 | .298 | .395 | .393 | .789 | 26 |
| SS | Erick Aybar | 137 | 504 | 70 | 157 | 23 | 9 | 5 | 58 | 14 | 7 | 30 | 54 | .312 | .353 | .423 | .776 | 20 |
| LF | Juan Rivera | 138 | 529 | 72 | 152 | 24 | 1 | 25 | 88 | 0 | 1 | 36 | 57 | .287 | .332 | .478 | .810 | 16 |
| CF | Torii Hunter | 119 | 451 | 74 | 135 | 26 | 1 | 22 | 90 | 18 | 4 | 47 | 92 | .299 | .366 | .508 | .873 | 20 |
| RF | Bobby Abreu | 152 | 563 | 96 | 165 | 29 | 3 | 15 | 103 | 30 | 8 | 94 | 113 | .293 | .390 | .435 | .825 | 23 |
| DH | Vladimir Guerrero | 100 | 383 | 59 | 113 | 16 | 1 | 15 | 50 | 2 | 1 | 19 | 56 | .295 | .334 | .460 | .794 | 7 |

## Key Pitchers

| Pos | Player | G | GS | W | L | SV | IP | H | R | ER | SO | BB | BR/9 | ERA | WS |
|---|---|---|---|---|---|---|---|---|---|---|---|---|---|---|---|
| SP | Jered Weaver | 33 | 33 | 16 | 8 | 0 | 211.0 | 196 | 91 | 88 | 174 | 66 | 11.35 | 3.75 | 17 |
| SP | Joe Saunders | 31 | 31 | 16 | 7 | 0 | 186.0 | 202 | 102 | 95 | 101 | 64 | 13.16 | 4.60 | 11 |
| SP | John Lackey | 27 | 27 | 11 | 8 | 0 | 176.1 | 177 | 84 | 75 | 139 | 47 | 11.89 | 3.83 | 12 |
| SP | Ervin Santana | 24 | 23 | 8 | 8 | 0 | 139.2 | 159 | 83 | 78 | 107 | 47 | 13.92 | 5.03 | 6 |
| SP | Matt Palmer | 40 | 13 | 11 | 2 | 0 | 121.1 | 105 | 55 | 53 | 69 | 55 | 12.16 | 3.93 | 10 |
| CL | Brian Fuentes | 65 | 0 | 1 | 5 | 48 | 55.0 | 53 | 24 | 24 | 46 | 24 | 13.42 | 3.93 | 9 |
| RP | Darren Oliver | 63 | 1 | 5 | 1 | 0 | 73.0 | 61 | 22 | 22 | 65 | 22 | 10.85 | 2.71 | 9 |
| RP | Jason Bulger | 64 | 0 | 6 | 1 | 1 | 65.2 | 46 | 26 | 26 | 68 | 30 | 10.55 | 3.56 | 7 |

## A New Vlad

The clearest evidence yet that Vlad is slipping: After having been the least-pitched-to hitter in the majors for four years running, Vladimir Guerrero finally was dethroned last year. Only 42.7% of the pitches thrown to him were in the strike zone, but he was out-Vlad-ed by Pablo Sandoval (40.6%), who also exhibits a compulsion to crush any spheroid thrown in his general direction. You have to give Vlad credit, though — he didn't cede the crown without a fight, continuing to give thorough consideration to pitches in just about all locations. He swung at 41.1% of the non-strikes he saw, topping the majors in that department for the second consecutive year.

### Vladimir Guerrero — 2009 Pitch Analysis

| Overall | | | Swung At by Pitch Location | | |
|---|---|---|---|---|---|
| Pitches Seen | 1305 | | In Strike Zone | 459 | 59% |
| Taken | 526 | 40% | High | 24 | 3% |
| Swung At | 779 | 60% | Low | 117 | 15% |
| | | | Inside | 99 | 13% |
| | | | Outside | 80 | 10% |

## Another 20 or 30 Years of This and He'll be Rickey Henderson

You might not have noticed, but last year Howie Kendrick was considerably more patient at the plate. He swung at only 47% of the pitches he saw, after having swung at 52-53% during each of his first three seasons in the league. This helped him more than double his unintentional walk total — all the way from 9 to 19 (which may explain why you'd failed to notice).

| Year | Pitches | Swung At | |
|---|---|---|---|
| 2006 | 923 | 482 | 52% |
| 2007 | 1,133 | 594 | 52% |
| 2008 | 1,233 | 652 | 53% |
| 2009 | 1,526 | 723 | 47% |
| **Total** | **4,815** | **2,451** | **51%** |

## Fighting the Erosion of Traditional Values — and Winning

For the second time in three years, the Angels had the majors' best record in games in which they were held homerless. In 2008, when the Red Sox had the best record in such games, the Angels were only second-best. Over the three-year span, the Angels' record when held homerless is a full 21 games better than any other team's.

### Angels — 2009 Record By Home Runs

| Home Runs | W-L |
|---|---|
| 0 | 29-30 |
| 1 | 32-25 |
| 2 | 22-8 |
| 3 or more | 14-2 |

## Bobby Abreu

Bobby Abreu drove in 103 runs, and 35 of them — more than one-third — were scored by Chone Figgins. No player drove in a single teammate more often, and the only other hitter who equaled it was Mark Teixeira, who drove in Derek Jeter 35 times.

### Bobby Abreu — 2009 RBI Analysis

| Drove In | Times |
|---|---|
| Erick Aybar | 17 |
| Chone Figgins | 35 |
| Vladimir Guerrero | 1 |
| Maicer Izturis | 12 |
| Howie Kendrick | 9 |
| Jeff Mathis | 4 |
| Gary Matthews Jr. | 2 |
| Mike Napoli | 5 |
| Juan Rivera | 1 |
| Reggie Willits | 2 |
| His Own Bad Self | 15 |
| **Total** | **103** |

## Picky, Picky

Bobby Abreu took 688 called strikes, most in the majors, and seven times as many as Vlad Guerrero (98). He swung at less than half of the pitches in the strike zone that he saw (49.4%). Luis Castillo was the only major league regular who swung at a lower percentage (48.6%).

### Bobby Abreu

#### Overall

| | | |
|---|---|---|
| Pitches Seen | 2,787 | |
| Taken | 1,873 | 67% |
| Swung At | 914 | 33% |

#### Pitches Taken

| | | |
|---|---|---|
| Taken for a Strike | 688 | 37% |
| Called a ball | 1,185 | 63% |

#### By Pitch Location

| | | |
|---|---|---|
| In Strike Zone | 688 | 37% |
| High | 136 | 7% |
| Low | 425 | 23% |
| Inside | 151 | 8% |
| Outside | 410 | 22% |

#### Swung At

| | | |
|---|---|---|
| Missed | 157 | 17% |
| Fouled Off | 298 | 33% |
| Put in Play | 459 | 50% |

## Playing the Park?

In 2008, playing in Old Yankee Stadium, the great Bobby Abreu hit 201 balls to right field, 131 to left. In 2009, without the short porch beckoning him, Abreu hit 150 to right, 153 to left.

Abreu is among the most remarkable players of this generation, and sometimes it's hard to figure out what he's doing. It could be that this has nothing to do with Yankee Stadium. It could be that, as Abreu is aging, he is less able to turn on an inside pitch, and is compensating for this by hitting the opposite way. It could be that this is a difference in the Angel philosophy vs. the Yankee philosophy. Something is different, and, as Abreu is so much in command of what he is doing at the plate, we have to assume this was deliberate.

## Angels Batting Order

The Angels' OPS from the #5 spot in their batting order (.951) was by far the best in the majors, 69 points better than any other team. Angels' fifth-place hitters hit 42 home runs and drove in 129 runs — but the Angels didn't have a regular #5 hitter. Four different hitters saw considerable action there: Juan Rivera and Kendry Morales each started there about one-third of the time, Torii Hunter was there about 20% of the time, and Mike Napoli hit fifth about 10% of the time. All four hitters — and especially Rivera — were more productive when batting fifth than when hitting somewhere else.

| Player | Hitting Fifth | | | Hitting in other spots | | |
|---|---|---|---|---|---|---|
| | AVG | OBP | SLG | AVG | OBP | SLG |
| Juan Rivera | .316 | .358 | .609 | .268 | .334 | .389 |
| Kendry Morales | .322 | .376 | .584 | .295 | .369 | .560 |
| Torii Hunter | .303 | .366 | .569 | .298 | .403 | .488 |
| Mike Napoli | .379 | .486 | .621 | .253 | .352 | .469 |

## Tough Competition

You might assume that 30-year-old rookie Matt Palmer owed much of his 11-2 record (including a 9-1 record in 13 starts) to having been spotted against weaker teams. Not so; in fact it was very much the opposite, as it turned out. Ten of his 13 starts came against teams that wound up with a winning record, and five of them came against teams that ultimately went to the postseason. He beat three of the five playoff teams he faced.

### Matt Palmer — Career Records Against Quality of Competition

| Opponent | G | IP | W | L | SO | BB | ERA |
|---|---|---|---|---|---|---|---|
| .600 teams | 3 | 9.1 | 1 | 1 | 4 | 3 | 1.93 |
| .500 - .599 teams | 19 | 73.0 | 6 | 1 | 45 | 33 | 4.32 |
| .400 - .499 teams | 18 | 45.2 | 4 | 2 | 20 | 30 | 5.32 |
| Sub .400 teams | 3 | 6.0 | 0 | 0 | 3 | 2 | 1.50 |

## Angels, Team Baserunning Analysis

The Angels in 2009 advanced from first to third on a single 128 times — twenty more than any other major league team. The only three major league players who have gone from first to third on a single more than 50% of the time in their careers (50 or more opportunities) are Torii Hunter, Chone Figgins and Erick Aybar — all Angels in 2009.

| Year | 1st to 3rd | | 2nd to Home | | 1st to Home | |
|---|---|---|---|---|---|---|
| | Adv | Opp | Adv | Opp | Adv | Opp |
| 2002 | 80 | 269 | 139 | 244 | 26 | 66 |
| 2003 | 74 | 233 | 124 | 192 | 20 | 52 |
| 2004 | 78 | 272 | 122 | 199 | 26 | 60 |
| 2005 | 74 | 244 | 130 | 217 | 27 | 53 |
| 2006 | 82 | 243 | 135 | 204 | 30 | 57 |
| 2007 | 100 | 277 | 139 | 219 | 37 | 86 |
| 2008 | 85 | 235 | 121 | 202 | 14 | 61 |
| 2009 | 128 | 367 | 161 | 223 | 41 | 88 |
| Totals | 701 | 2,140 | 1,071 | 1,700 | 221 | 523 |
| | | 33% | | 63% | | 42% |

## Defensive Decline

Gary Matthews Jr.'s defense has declined right along with his offense since coming to LA. In his last three years with Texas, his estimated defensive runs saved (at all three outfield spots combined) were +10, +14 and +11. In his three years with Anaheim they have been -11, -6 and -10.

### Gary Matthews Jr. — Defensive Runs Saved By Position

| Year | Team | Left Field | | | | Center Field | | | | Right Field | | | | Tot |
|------|------|-----|-----------|-----------|-----|-----|-----------|-----------|-----|-----|-----------|-----------|-----|-----|
| | | +/- | OF Arm | HR Save | Tot | +/- | OF Arm | HR Save | Tot | +/- | OF Arm | HR Save | Tot | |
| 2004 | TEX | 1 | 1 | 0 | 2 | 4 | 1 | 0 | 5 | 1 | 2 | 0 | 3 | 10 |
| 2005 | TEX | -1 | 1 | 0 | 0 | 6 | 0 | 0 | 6 | 5 | 1 | 2 | 8 | 14 |
| 2006 | TEX | -- | -- | -- | -- | 4 | 2 | 6 | 12 | -2 | 1 | 0 | -1 | 11 |
| 2007 | TEX | -- | -- | -- | -- | -13 | 0 | 2 | -11 | -- | -- | -- | -- | -11 |
| 2008 | LAA | -7 | 0 | 0 | -7 | 3 | 2 | 0 | 5 | -5 | 1 | 0 | -4 | -6 |
| 2009 | LAA | -1 | -1 | 0 | -2 | -8 | -1 | 0 | -9 | 1 | 0 | 0 | 1 | -10 |

Note: Runs saved by outfield position are estimated based on the Plus/Minus System (+/-), throwing arm performance (OF ARM), and home run saving catches (HR SAV.)

## Catching Fire in the Fifth

Although they ultimately finished with the second-best record in the majors, the Angels were eleven games under .500 after one inning — ahead 33 times, behind 44. Through four innings they were only three games over .500 — ahead 65 times, behind 62. But they took the game over in the second four innings.

### Angels — 2009 Innings Ahead/Behind/Tied

| Inning | 1 | 2 | 3 | 4 | 5 | 6 | 7 | 8 | 9 | Extra | Final |
|--------|----|----|----|----|----|----|----|----|----|-------|-------|
| Ahead | 33 | 54 | 64 | 65 | 73 | 81 | 90 | 91 | 90 | 7 | 97 |
| Behind | 44 | 52 | 58 | 62 | 65 | 58 | 60 | 57 | 61 | 4 | 65 |
| Tied | 85 | 56 | 40 | 35 | 24 | 23 | 12 | 14 | 11 | 7 | |

## Scooting Around the Bases

Maicer Izturis reached base (not including Home Runs) 163 times in 2009, and scored 66 of those times, which is a little over 40%. This was the highest percentage in baseball. Geovany Soto reached base 127 times, not including homers, but scored only 16 times, or 13%.

**Maicer Izturis — 2009 Runs Scored Analysis**

| Reached on | | Runs Scored After | |
|---|---|---|---|
| Home Runs | 8 | Home runs | 8 |
| Triples | 3 | Scored after Triple | 3 |
| Doubles | 22 | Scored after Double | 12 |
| Singles | 83 | Scored after Single | 27 |
| Walk/HBP | 40 | Scored after Walk/HBP | 14 |
| Reached on Error | 6 | Scored after ROE | 5 |
| Reached on Forceout | 8 | Vultured Runs | 4 |
| Other | 1 | Other | 1 |
| | | **Total Runs** | **74** |

## Yin and Yang

Last year the Angels' catching chores were almost evenly divided between Mike Napoli and Jeff Mathis — Napoli started behind the plate in 84 games, and Mathis started the other 78. As players, the two are polar opposites, with Napoli being one of the best-hitting catchers in baseball but a below-average defender, and Mathis being one of the weakest hitters in the majors as well as one of the better receivers. Each one's particular contributions were reflected perfectly in the team's performance in the games they started.

With Napoli starting behind the dish, the Angels were one of the most dangerous offensive clubs in baseball. They scored 5.80 runs per game — more than the Yankees (5.65 R/G), the majors' highest-scoring team — but allowed 5.01 runs per game. With Mathis, they turned into a club that was among the best at *preventing* runs. They scored far fewer runs (5.08 per game), but allowed only 4.36 per game, a figure that would have ranked second-best in the AL. And while they took two very different paths to success, they were almost exactly as good with Napoli (51-33, .607) as they were with Mathis (46-32, .590).

# Los Angeles Dodgers

| 2009 TEAM OVERVIEW | ML RANK | 11th | 18th | 4th | 7th | 11th | 8th |
|---|---|---|---|---|---|---|---|
| **95-67** | **Team** | **780** | **145** | **.270** | **607** | **.758** | **116** |
| | | RUNS | HOME RUNS | BATTING AVG. | WALKS | OPS | STOLEN BASES |
| **1** st place NL West | **Opp.** | **611** | **127** | **.233** | **584** | **.673** | **89** |
| | ML RANK | 1st | 3rd | 1st | 17th | 1st | 8th |

## Key Players

| Pos | Player | G | AB | R | H | 2B | 3B | HR | RBI | SB | CS | BB | SO | AVG | OBP | SLG | OPS | WS |
|---|---|---|---|---|---|---|---|---|---|---|---|---|---|---|---|---|---|---|
| C | Russell Martin | 143 | 505 | 63 | 126 | 19 | 0 | 7 | 53 | 11 | 6 | 69 | 80 | .250 | .352 | .329 | .680 | 16 |
| 1B | James Loney | 158 | 576 | 73 | 162 | 25 | 2 | 13 | 90 | 7 | 3 | 70 | 68 | .281 | .357 | .399 | .756 | 18 |
| 2B | Orlando Hudson | 149 | 551 | 74 | 156 | 35 | 6 | 9 | 62 | 8 | 1 | 62 | 99 | .283 | .357 | .417 | .774 | 20 |
| 3B | Casey Blake | 139 | 485 | 84 | 136 | 25 | 6 | 18 | 79 | 3 | 4 | 63 | 116 | .280 | .363 | .468 | .832 | 19 |
| SS | Rafael Furcal | 150 | 613 | 92 | 165 | 28 | 5 | 9 | 47 | 12 | 6 | 61 | 89 | .269 | .335 | .375 | .711 | 17 |
| LF | Manny Ramirez | 104 | 352 | 62 | 102 | 24 | 2 | 19 | 63 | 0 | 1 | 71 | 81 | .290 | .418 | .531 | .949 | 18 |
| CF | Matt Kemp | 159 | 606 | 97 | 180 | 25 | 7 | 26 | 101 | 34 | 8 | 52 | 139 | .297 | .352 | .490 | .842 | 26 |
| RF | Andre Ethier | 160 | 596 | 92 | 162 | 42 | 3 | 31 | 106 | 6 | 4 | 72 | 116 | .272 | .361 | .508 | .869 | 21 |

## Key Pitchers

| Pos | Player | G | GS | W | L | SV | IP | H | R | ER | SO | BB | BR/9 | ERA | WS |
|---|---|---|---|---|---|---|---|---|---|---|---|---|---|---|---|
| SP | Randy Wolf | 34 | 34 | 11 | 7 | 0 | 214.1 | 178 | 81 | 77 | 160 | 58 | 10.16 | 3.23 | 14 |
| SP | Chad Billingsley | 33 | 32 | 12 | 11 | 0 | 196.1 | 173 | 94 | 88 | 179 | 86 | 12.19 | 4.03 | 9 |
| SP | Clayton Kershaw | 31 | 30 | 8 | 8 | 0 | 171.0 | 119 | 55 | 53 | 185 | 91 | 11.11 | 2.79 | 12 |
| SP | Hiroki Kuroda | 21 | 20 | 8 | 7 | 0 | 117.1 | 110 | 59 | 49 | 87 | 24 | 10.36 | 3.76 | 5 |
| SP | Eric Stults | 10 | 10 | 4 | 3 | 0 | 50.0 | 51 | 27 | 27 | 33 | 26 | 14.58 | 4.86 | 2 |
| CL | Jonathan Broxton | 73 | 0 | 7 | 2 | 36 | 76.0 | 44 | 24 | 22 | 114 | 29 | 8.76 | 2.61 | 16 |
| RP | Ramon Troncoso | 73 | 0 | 5 | 4 | 6 | 82.2 | 83 | 30 | 25 | 55 | 34 | 13.06 | 2.72 | 8 |
| RP | Ronald Belisario | 69 | 0 | 4 | 3 | 0 | 70.2 | 52 | 21 | 16 | 64 | 29 | 11.08 | 2.04 | 7 |

## Games Played by Opening Day Starters

If your eight opening day starters all played every game, that would be 1,296 games — 162 times eight. The Dodgers' opening day starters played 1,102 games, the third-most in baseball. Were it not for the suspension of Manny Ramirez, the Dodgers would likely have led the majors in keeping their lineup on the field.

Los Angeles' opening day starters accounted for 85% of their regular season starting lineups.

| | Player | Starts |
|---|---|---|
| C | Russell Martin | 136 |
| 1B | James Loney | 147 |
| 2B | Orlando Hudson | 143 |
| 3B | Casey Blake | 131 |
| SS | Rafael Furcal | 141 |
| LF | Manny Ramirez | 99 |
| CF | Matt Kemp | 155 |
| RF | Andre Ethier | 150 |

## Juan being Manny

The Dodgers' winning percentage while Manny Ramirez was suspended for 50 games (.580) was essentially the same as it was the rest of the year (.589). Juan Pierre started all 50 games in left field while Manny was being Manny, hitting .318 with a very good .381 on-base percentage, 32 runs scored and 21 stolen bases. Projected to a full schedule: 104 runs, 68 steals. Manny last played on May 6, and returned to the lineup on July 3rd.

## First-Inning Fireworks

The 2009 Dodgers outscored their opponents in the first inning 121 to 54. They were ahead after the first inning in 55 games, behind only 26 times — 29 games over .500, after the first inning. Had they played at the same level all game, they would likely have finished the season with a record of about 135-27.

### Innings Ahead/Behind/Tied

| Inning | 1 | 2 | 3 | 4 | 5 | 6 | 7 | 8 | 9 | Extra | Final |
|---|---|---|---|---|---|---|---|---|---|---|---|
| Ahead | 55 | 63 | 57 | 69 | 75 | 76 | 83 | 81 | 83 | 12 | 95 |
| Behind | 26 | 43 | 53 | 56 | 58 | 58 | 58 | 62 | 58 | 9 | 67 |
| Tied | 81 | 56 | 52 | 37 | 29 | 28 | 21 | 19 | 21 | 27 | -- |

## Solid at Every Position

There are two theories of how to spend your money effectively in baseball — one, to attract superstars, and two, to make sure that the team is solid at every position. The Mets represent one approach; the Dodgers, the other. In the world of Win Shares, a player who earns 15 Win Shares in a season is a solid regular. At 15 Win Shares you won't win an MVP Award, and you won't make an all-star team, but you won't lose your job, either. Fifteen Win Shares is solid.

A bad team will normally have only one or two players who earn 15 Win Shares. The Pirates in 2009 had only one; the Dodgers in 2005, when they lost 91 games, had only one. The 2009 Dodgers were the first major league team since the 2003 Red Sox to have a player with 15 Win Shares at each everyday lineup position:

| Pos | Player | WS | | Pos | Player | WS |
|-----|--------|----|---|-----|--------|----|
| C | Russell Martin | 16 | | SS | Rafael Furcal | 17 |
| 1B | James Loney | 18 | | LF | Manny Ramirez | 18 |
| 2B | Orlando Hudson | 20 | | CF | Matt Kemp | 26 |
| 3B | Casey Blake | 19 | | RF | Andre Ethier | 21 |

Actually, the Dodgers had at least sixteen Win Shares at every position, which is even more rare. The Dodgers were only the seventh team in major league history to have at least 16 Win Shares at every slot. The other six were the 1906 Cubs, the 1910 New York Giants, the 1962 San Francisco Giants, the 1974 Dodgers, and the 1975 and 1976 Cincinnati Reds.

## Productivity by Batting Order Position

The Dodgers got fairly ordinary productivity from each spot in the lineup, with two huge exceptions: the seventh and eighth spots. Their .842 OPS from the seventh spot was better than any other team except the Yankees, and their .798 OPS from the eighth spot was the best in baseball.

It wasn't that they had a good hitter who hit seventh or a good hitter who hit eighth. They rotated hitters at both spots. But, as the Dodgers put out a lineup without an easy out, their bottom-of-the-order hitters tended to be the best in the game.

| Pos | Players | AVG | OBP | SLG | OPS |
|-----|---------|-----|-----|-----|-----|
| 1 | Furcal (105 G), Pierre (53 G) | .291 | .351 | .397 | .748 |
| 2 | Hudson (57 G), Furcal (32 G), Ethier (28 G) | .273 | .341 | .421 | .762 |
| 3 | Ramirez (73 G), Ethier (46 G), Hudson (39 G) | .277 | .369 | .486 | .855 |
| 4 | Blake (43 G), Ethier (42 G), Kemp (27 G) | .265 | .347 | .422 | .769 |
| 5 | Loney (60 G), Blake (40 G), Martin (26 G) | .253 | .343 | .361 | .704 |
| 6 | Loney (49 G), Martin (36 G), Kemp (24 G) | .290 | .362 | .441 | .803 |
| 7 | Kemp (46 G), Martin (34 G) | .291 | .375 | .467 | .842 |
| 8 | Blake (30 G), Castro (26 G), Hudson (25 G) | .297 | .360 | .438 | .798 |
| 9 | Wolf (30 G), Billingsley (27 G), Kershaw (27 G) | .184 | .249 | .255 | .503 |

## Andre Ethier, Clutch Hitting

Andre Ethier had 43 RBI in clutch situations in 2009, second-most in the major leagues. His OPS in clutch situations was a pitiful .471 as a rookie in 2006, but has gone up by at least 120 points in each of the past three seasons.

| Year | AB | H | 2B | 3B | HR | RBI | BB | SO | GIDP | AVG | OBP | SLG | OPS |
|------|-----|----|----|----|----|-----|----|----|------|------|------|------|-------|
| 2006 | 72 | 11 | 1 | 1 | 1 | 9 | 7 | 22 | 2 | .153 | .235 | .236 | .471 |
| 2007 | 62 | 12 | 1 | 0 | 5 | 14 | 10 | 13 | 4 | .194 | .301 | .452 | .753 |
| 2008 | 83 | 26 | 3 | 2 | 2 | 20 | 16 | 20 | 0 | .313 | .422 | .470 | .892 |
| 2009 | 109 | 33 | 10 | 0 | 7 | 43 | 22 | 20 | 2 | .303 | .425 | .587 | 1.112 |
| **Totals** | **326** | **82** | **15** | **3** | **15** | **86** | **55** | **75** | **8** | **.252** | **.362** | **.454** | **.816** |

## Improved Defense

One of the keys to the Dodgers' eleven-game improvement in 2009 was not so much the acquisition of Orlando Hudson, but the retirement of Jeff Kent. In 2008 the Dodger second basemen, primarily the 40-year-old Kent, were an estimated 17 runs worse than an average major league second baseman. Late in the free agent period they signed 2009 Gold Glove winner Orlando Hudson, and the Dodgers were 8 runs better than an average second baseman. The 25-run improvement in defense at second base helped move the Dodgers from +4 runs (defensively) to +32 — which helped them move from 84 wins to 95.

**Dodgers Defensive Runs Saved by Position**

| Year | P | C | 1B | 2B | 3B | SS | LF | CF | RF | Tot |
|------|---|----|----|-----|----|----|----|----|----|-----|
| 2008 | 3 | -2 | 0 | -17 | 14 | 1 | 5 | 5 | -5 | 4 |
| 2009 | 0 | 5 | 3 | 8 | 15 | 6 | -4 | -3 | 2 | 32 |

## The Best Bullpen in the Majors

The Dodgers' bullpen in 2008 was very good. Over the winter and in the spring the Dodgers lost most of their main bullpen contributors, and emerged with. . .the best bullpen in the majors.

The Dodgers' bullpen ERA in 2008 was 3.34, third-best in the majors. That winter they lost to free agency Chan Ho Park, Takashi Saito and Joe Beimel, three relievers who'd combined for almost 200 innings with an ERA of 2.82. They lost or essentially lost a fourth, Cory Wade, to shoulder problems, and a fifth, Hong-Chih Kuo, to elbow miseries.

But equally effective replacements were found for all five pitchers. Rookie Ronald Belisario posted a 2.04 ERA in 70.2 innings. Another rookie, James McDonald, compiled a 2.72 ERA in 49.2 innings of relief — plus, if you put the two of them together, you always had a friend wearing big red shoes. Holdover Ramon Troncoso stepped into a more prominent role and posted a 2.72 ERA in 82.2 innings; and Guillermo Mota returned as a free agent and enjoyed his best season in years, with a 3.44 ERA. George Sherrill was acquired at the trade deadline and allowed only two earned runs in 27.2 innings.

With Big Jon Broxton emerging as a dominant closer, it added up to the best bullpen in the majors by far. The Dodgers' bullpen ERA was 3.14, best in the majors by more than one-third of a run.

### 2009 Dodgers Bullpen

| Player | Pos | T | G | Saves | | | Relief Results | | | | | |
|---|---|---|---|---|---|---|---|---|---|---|---|---|
| | | | | Easy | Reg | Tough | Saves | Opps | Holds | SV/HLD PCT | OPP OPS | ERA |
| Jonathan Broxton | CL | R | 73 | 19 - 22 | 15 - 17 | 2 - 3 | 36 | 42 | 1 | .86 | .479 | 2.61 |
| George Sherrill | CL | L | 72 | 13 - 14 | 8 - 10 | 0 - 2 | 21 | 26 | 11 | .86 | .588 | 1.70 |
| Hong-Chih Kuo | SU | L | 35 | 0 - 1 | 0 - 0 | 0 - 0 | 0 | 1 | 14 | .93 | .599 | 3.00 |
| Cory Wade | SU | R | 27 | 0 - 0 | 0 - 4 | 0 - 2 | 0 | 6 | 7 | .54 | .735 | 5.53 |
| Brent Leach | LT | L | 38 | 0 - 0 | 0 - 0 | 0 - 0 | 0 | 0 | 4 | 1.00 | .783 | 5.75 |
| Will Ohman | LT | L | 21 | 1 - 1 | 0 - 0 | 0 - 1 | 1 | 2 | 4 | .83 | .979 | 5.84 |
| Scott Elbert | LT | L | 19 | 0 - 0 | 0 - 0 | 0 - 0 | 0 | 0 | 3 | 1.00 | .784 | 5.03 |
| Jeff Weaver | LM | R | 21 | 0 - 0 | 0 - 0 | 0 - 0 | 0 | 0 | 0 | .00 | .803 | 3.99 |
| Ramon Troncoso | UR | R | 73 | 3 - 4 | 2 - 2 | 1 - 1 | 6 | 7 | 14 | .95 | .675 | 2.72 |
| Ronald Belisario | UR | R | 69 | 0 - 1 | 0 - 4 | 0 - 2 | 0 | 7 | 12 | .63 | .580 | 2.04 |
| Guillermo Mota | UR | R | 61 | 0 - 0 | 0 - 1 | 0 - 1 | 0 | 2 | 2 | .50 | .671 | 3.44 |
| James McDonald | UR | R | 41 | 0 - 0 | 0 - 0 | 0 - 0 | 0 | 0 | 5 | 1.00 | .695 | 2.72 |

## Performance by Starting Pitcher

Although Hiroki Kuroda's ERA was 3.76 and Clayton Kershaw's was 2.79, the Dodgers actually gave up fewer runs per game with Kuroda starting than with Kershaw. The bullpen ERA for Kuroda was 1.55. For Kershaw, it was 4.31.

| Starter | GS | Run Support | Runs Allowed | W | L |
|---|---|---|---|---|---|
| Randy Wolf | 34 | 167 | 125 | 22 | 12 |
| Chad Billingsley | 32 | 143 | 133 | 17 | 15 |
| Clayton Kershaw | 30 | 123 | 108 | 14 | 16 |
| Hiroli Kuroda | 20 | 98 | 71 | 12 | 8 |
| Eric Stults | 10 | 67 | 45 | 7 | 3 |
| Jeff Weaver | 7 | 28 | 25 | 4 | 3 |
| Vicente Padilla | 7 | 39 | 25 | 6 | 1 |
| Jon Garland | 6 | 26 | 17 | 3 | 3 |
| Eric Milton | 5 | 23 | 17 | 3 | 2 |
| Jason Schmidt | 4 | 19 | 17 | 2 | 2 |
| James McDonald | 4 | 32 | 21 | 3 | 1 |
| Charlie Haeger | 3 | 15 | 7 | 2 | 1 |
| **Total** | **162** | **780** | **611** | **95** | **67** |

## Hiroki Kuroda

Hiroki Kuroda's career ERA is 3.14 against winning teams, 4.22 against losing teams.

### Hiroki Kuroda, Career Records Against Quality of Competition

| Opponent | G | IP | W | L | SO | BB | ERA |
|---|---|---|---|---|---|---|---|
| .600 teams | 3 | 21.2 | 1 | 2 | 19 | 5 | 1.66 |
| .500 - .599 teams | 19 | 110.1 | 5 | 5 | 80 | 21 | 3.43 |
| .400 - .499 teams | 23 | 132.0 | 7 | 8 | 74 | 29 | 4.23 |
| Sub .400 teams | 7 | 36.2 | 4 | 2 | 30 | 11 | 4.17 |

## Smokin'

Jonathan Broxton in 2009 was the first major league pitcher since 2004 — and only the 12th pitcher in major league history — to record one-half of his outs by strikeouts. The first pitcher ever to do that, pitching 50 or more innings, was Rob Dibble in 1991. Dibble did it again in 1992, and was joined in the feat by Billy Wagner (three times), and also Armando Benitez (1999), Matt Mantei (1999), Byung-Hyun Kim (2000), the Big Unit (2001), Eric Gagne (2003) and Brad Lidge (2004). Randy Johnson is the only starting pitcher ever to do this, the only pitcher to do it while pitching more than 100 innings, and the only pitcher to do it later than the age of 28.

No pitcher has ever done this in the American League.

| Player | Year | Age | G | W | L | IP | SO | BB | ERA |
|--------|------|-----|---|---|---|-----|-----|----|------|
| Rob Dibble, Cin | 1991 | 27 | 67 | 3 | 5 | 82.1 | 124 | 25 | 3.17 |
| Rob Dibble, Hou | 1992 | 28 | 63 | 3 | 5 | 70.1 | 110 | 31 | 3.07 |
| Billy Wagner, Hou | 1997 | 25 | 62 | 7 | 8 | 66.1 | 106 | 30 | 2.85 |
| Billy Wagner, Hou | 1998 | 26 | 58 | 4 | 3 | 60.0 | 97 | 25 | 2.70 |
| Armando Benitez, NYM | 1999 | 26 | 77 | 4 | 3 | 78.0 | 128 | 41 | 1.85 |
| Billy Wagner, Hou | 1999 | 27 | 66 | 4 | 1 | 74.2 | 124 | 23 | 1.57 |
| Matt Mantei, Fla-Ari | 1999 | 25 | 65 | 1 | 3 | 65.0 | 99 | 44 | 2.77 |
| Byung-Hyun Kim, Ari | 2000 | 21 | 61 | 6 | 6 | 70.2 | 111 | 46 | 4.46 |
| Randy Johnson, Ari | 2001 | 37 | 35 | 21 | 6 | 249.2 | 372 | 71 | 2.49 |
| Eric Gagne, LAD | 2003 | 27 | 77 | 2 | 3 | 82.1 | 137 | 20 | 1.20 |
| Brad Lidge, Hou | 2004 | 27 | 80 | 6 | 5 | 94.2 | 157 | 30 | 1.90 |
| Jonathan Broxton, LAD | 2009 | 25 | 73 | 7 | 2 | 76.0 | 114 | 29 | 2.61 |

## Clayton Kershaw, Decision Analysis

In 2008, left-handed hitters had a .475 slugging percentage against Clayton Kershaw. In 2009, Kershaw dominated lefties, limiting them to a .173 batting average, with one home run in 139 at-bats. Slugging percentage: .252.

In the 15 games in which he did not have a decision (including one relief appearance), Clayton Kershaw had an ERA of 1.38. This was the lowest in the majors among starting pitchers with six or more no-decisions.

| Group | G | IP | W | L | PCT | H | R | SO | BB | ERA |
|-------|---|-----|---|---|-----|----|----|-----|----|------|
| Wins | 8 | 50.0 | 8 | 0 | 1 | 25 | 8 | 47 | 24 | 1.44 |
| Losses | 8 | 36.1 | 0 | 8 | 0 | 43 | 33 | 37 | 30 | 7.93 |
| No-Decisions | 15 | 84.2 | 0 | 0 | -- | 51 | 14 | 101 | 37 | 1.38 |

Quality Starts: 7 in Wins, 1 in Losses, 8 in No-Decisions

## Chad Billingsley, Pitch Type Analysis

In 2007 Chad Billingsley threw his fastball 64% of the time — one of the highest percentages in baseball. In 2009 he was one of only 14 ERA qualifiers who threw his fastball less than half the time.

|  | 2007 | | 2009 | |
| --- | --- | --- | --- | --- |
| Fastball | 1,611 | 64% | 1,541 | 47% |
| Curveball | 361 | 14% | 717 | 22% |
| Changeup | 75 | 3% | 17 | 1% |
| Slider | 85 | 3% | 110 | 3% |
| Cut Fastball | 354 | 14% | 719 | 22% |
| Pitchout | 8 | 0% | 0 | 0% |
| Not Charted | 24 | 1% | 146 | 4% |
| **Total** | **2,518** | | **3,250** | |

## Rafael Furcal vs. Pitchers with ERA over 5.25

At Bill James Online, we like to keep track of whether hitters do well against quality pitchers, and vice versa. Unfortunately, most of what this shows is just random variation; hitters hit .150 against quality pitchers one year, .350 the next. And vice versa.

But occasionally it works. As long as we have been keeping track of this, Rafael Furcal has ripped it up against pitchers with ERAs over 5.25.

| Year | AB | H | HR | RBI | AVG | OPS |
| --- | --- | --- | --- | --- | --- | --- |
| 2002 | 120 | 39 | 0 | 7 | .325 | .738 |
| 2003 | 129 | 46 | 8 | 21 | .357 | 1.083 |
| 2004 | 104 | 32 | 4 | 15 | .308 | .899 |
| 2005 | 112 | 37 | 2 | 17 | .330 | .891 |
| 2006 | 143 | 49 | 5 | 22 | .343 | .969 |
| 2007 | 116 | 29 | 1 | 8 | .250 | .696 |
| 2008 | 43 | 15 | 2 | 9 | .349 | 1.068 |
| 2009 | 108 | 40 | 2 | 12 | .370 | .932 |

## Rafael Furcal vs. Pitchers with ERA <= 3.50

But he has had difficulty keeping his head above water versus pitchers with good ERAs.

You may well ask "Doesn't everybody?" No, they don't. Everybody hits better against weaker pitchers, over time, but not usually this much better or this consistently.

| Year | AB | H | HR | RBI | AVG | OPS |
| --- | --- | --- | --- | --- | --- | --- |
| 2002 | 204 | 50 | 2 | 15 | .245 | .631 |
| 2003 | 161 | 34 | 2 | 7 | .211 | .594 |
| 2004 | 102 | 21 | 0 | 7 | .206 | .564 |
| 2005 | 146 | 36 | 1 | 5 | .247 | .655 |
| 2006 | 105 | 26 | 0 | 8 | .248 | .612 |
| 2007 | 144 | 34 | 1 | 9 | .236 | .605 |
| 2008 | 29 | 10 | 0 | 1 | .345 | .940 |
| 2009 | 189 | 45 | 0 | 10 | .238 | .601 |

# Notes on the 1974 World Series

by Bill James

AS I WRITE THIS, MLB-TV IS BROADCASTING GAME ONE OF THE 1974 World Series, which I am much enjoying watching.

1) The pace of the game is unmistakably better. The pitchers just get the ball, take the sign, and fire. Nobody steps out to break the pitcher's rhythm…not clear whether the umpires would allow it or not. I don't believe the catcher goes to the mound to talk to the pitcher once, on either team. I could have missed it or it could have been edited out of the tape, I guess.

2) The umpiring is bad, and the announcers don't say anything about it. I would speculate that instant replay, along with training programs implemented by MLB in the late 1990s, have sharpened the umpiring more than we realize.

*I don't believe the catcher goes to the mound to talk to the pitcher once, on either team.*

3) Second inning, Joe Rudi on first, Ray Fosse hits a ground ball to third. The play goes 5-4, but it is way late. Rudi slides into second far ahead of the throw, is called out. Nobody says anything about it. Rudi just runs off the field.

4) But that's nothing compared to a double play in the bottom of the inning. Runners on first and second, Cey grounds to shortstop for a 6-4-3 Double Play.

But neither runner is anywhere *near* being out. On the play at second Dick Green is 3 to 4 feet off of second base, and hasn't *been* on second base anytime recently. I would have thought the "in the neighborhood" call at second was getting worse, rather than better, but…I haven't seen anything like that in years. There is *no* question that if you did that now, the umpire would not give you the call.

And then Cey beats the throw to first, and they call him out as well.

5) You may remember an article I did earlier about the great Dodger infield of the 1970s. I noticed that Bill Russell had defensive won-lost records that read, beginning in 1972: 5-1, 8-1, 4-4, 3-1, 7-2, 8-0, 8-1. The 4-4 record, which seems out of place, is in 1974, so I speculated that Russell must have had an injury that season. Sure enough, Vin Scully (broadcasting the series for NBC in 1974) talks repeatedly about Russell having an elbow injury that has interfered with his performance in the field.

6) Pre-game interview with Steve Garvey. The "con man" aspect of Garvey's personality seems really evident, and I wonder how I could have missed this at the time. Perhaps we should call it the "salesman" element of Garvey's personality, just to be polite. Garvey, for those of you not old enough to remember, projected a strong, conservative, values-driven personality, and talked from early in his career about running for political office after his playing career. This was undermined when it was revealed that he was involved in sexual adventures with a fair percentage of the population of southern California.

But just watching the pre-game interview (or am I reading what I know now into it?), there is something in Garvey's voice that tips you off immediately to the problem. The cadence, the timbre of his voice is so obviously calculated to ooze sincerity that it comes off as perversely phony. He smiles on cue and refers to Tony Kubek as "Tony" in almost every sentence.

My memory of this at the time is that some people I knew picked up on this element of Garvey and distrusted him from the start—but I didn't; I liked Garvey, and defended him as a person until the early 1980s. But just watching that interview, I wonder how I could possibly have missed it. Watch it if you get a chance, and let me know what you think.

7) Joe Ferguson in 1974 hit .252 with 16 homers and 75 walks with just 349 at-bats — an excellent power rate, a phenomenal walk rate — about which Vin Scully observes early in the game, "The experts say he takes too many pitches", and re-iterates this throughout the game.

*The "con man" aspect of Garvey's personality seems really evident, and I wonder how I could have missed this at the time.*

Scully is congenitally nice but a genius at making his points, and, boiling off the good manners, he has nothing good to say about Ferguson. "He is a gentle big man. They say he is too nice, too passive." (Quote is from memory…can't re-wind this to check the words.) Anyway, Ferguson's career unravels from that point, posing the question: Is Scully observing real failings in Ferguson? Or is it that the criticism of Ferguson forces him away from what he does best, and undermines his career?

Ferguson makes an absolutely magnificent throw from the outfield in the eighth inning. Jimmie Wynn is set up to make the catch in right center; Ferguson cuts him off and guns a strike to home plate to nail the runner. There aren't three players in the majors today who could make that throw.

8) Rollie Fingers, A's closer, enters the game in the fifth inning, with the starting pitcher exiting, having given up only one un-earned run.

9) Camera angles for the game often show the pitch from behind home plate, behind the umpire. They'll use the center field camera for a few pitches, then switch to behind the plate. You can't see where the pitch is. You lose the pitch as it leaves the pitcher's hand, pick it up on contact, and then only if the pitch is outside. I think the center field camera angle, which we now take for granted, didn't become dominant until the late 1970s.

10) Casey Stengel is at the game, and Cary Grant. I wouldn't have guessed either of them was still alive at that time, but they both look good.

11) Tony Kubek repeatedly kisses up to Vin Scully by praising his scouting insights into the Dodger players, but the scouting reports are really not good. The Dodger starter, Andy Messersmith, was second in the National League in strikeouts with 221, but Scully says, "Forget that; he hasn't been a strikeout pitcher for some time", and talks about Messersmith having trouble throwing his curve, and cites several late-season games in which Messersmith has had low strikeout totals.

But Messersmith struck out 36 batters in 49 innings in September 1974 — not really much different than his full-season strikeout rate. I think he's one strikeout off his season rate for September. He strikes out 8 batters in the game.

It's a three-man team — Curt Gowdy, Tony Kubek and Scully. Curt Gowdy interjects a quote from a conversation with Messersmith, in which Messersmith mentions "perfecting" his changeup. But Scully barely seems to realize that Messersmith throws a change, and talks constantly about his curveball, about his curveball not being as sharp as it was earlier in the season, etc. — totally missing the fact that Messersmith has switched from the curveball to the changeup as his strikeout pitch.

12) Scully says early in the game that Ron Cey has the most accurate arm he's ever seen at third base. Ron Cey then makes a throwing error later in the game.

13) Scully says that, in all his years broadcasting, he has never seen any player make as many dramatic and spectacular plays at any position as Bill Buckner has made that year in left field. Quite a comment…and we don't usually think of Buckner that way. Not suggesting Scully is wrong.

14) The A's are wearing green hats, but Alvin Dark is wearing a white hat, while the Dodgers (of course) are wearing blue hats, but Walter Alston is wearing a red hat. Huh?

15) The A's stole 164 bases in 1974, the Dodgers 149, but Scully observes that, apart from Bill North and

*Casey Stengel is at the game, and Cary Grant. I wouldn't have guessed either of them was still alive at that time, but they both look good.*

Bert Campaneris, the Dodgers appear "to have much more speed up and down the lineup". It's a real head-scratching comment. Yes, the A's have Ray Fosse, Gene Tenace, Sal Bando, Dick Green, and Joe Rudi in the lineup, but then the Dodgers have Steve Yeager, Steve Garvey, Ron Cey, Bill Russell, and Joe Ferguson.

16) Scully refers to Rollie Fingers as "Roland" Fingers, throughout the game. I don't believe he ever says "Rollie".

17) Mike Marshall throws a lot of screwballs, and Scully quotes a comment from early in the season, when the famously impolitic Marshall was asked to compare his screwball to Jim Brewer's and Tug McGraw's. "Their screwballs," Marshall replies, "are in the infantile stage."

Marshall's screwball is not what we think of as a screwball in the Mike Cuellar/Tug McGraw/Scottie McGregor/Fernando Valenzuela tradition. Kubek says that it is "not like anybody else's screwball", and it really isn't; it's much closer to what we would think of as a knuckle curve. He throws it different speeds, so that sometimes it almost looks like a slider, other times like a knuckleball. It often starts out high, above the strike zone, and almost always breaks *away* from a right-handed hitter, like a normal breaking pitch. The slow one comes in high and darts down and away from a right-handed hitter at a very late moment. One can see that it's a tough pitch, but it's hard to see how it's a screwball.

# Milwaukee Brewers

## Key Players

| Pos | Player | G | AB | R | H | 2B | 3B | HR | RBI | SB | CS | BB | SO | AVG | OBP | SLG | OPS | WS |
|---|---|---|---|---|---|---|---|---|---|---|---|---|---|---|---|---|---|---|
| C | Jason Kendall | 134 | 452 | 48 | 109 | 19 | 2 | 2 | 43 | 7 | 2 | 46 | 58 | .241 | .331 | .305 | .636 | 9 |
| 1B | Prince Fielder | 162 | 591 | 103 | 177 | 35 | 3 | 46 | 141 | 2 | 3 | 110 | 138 | .299 | .412 | .602 | 1.014 | 36 |
| 2B | Felipe Lopez | 66 | 259 | 44 | 83 | 20 | 2 | 3 | 32 | 0 | 3 | 37 | 41 | .320 | .407 | .448 | .855 | 13 |
| 3B | Casey McGehee | 116 | 355 | 58 | 107 | 20 | 1 | 16 | 66 | 0 | 2 | 34 | 67 | .301 | .360 | .499 | .859 | 17 |
| SS | J.J. Hardy | 115 | 414 | 53 | 95 | 16 | 2 | 11 | 47 | 0 | 1 | 43 | 85 | .229 | .302 | .357 | .659 | 6 |
| LF | Ryan Braun | 158 | 635 | 113 | 203 | 39 | 6 | 32 | 114 | 20 | 6 | 57 | 121 | .320 | .386 | .551 | .937 | 36 |
| CF | Mike Cameron | 149 | 544 | 78 | 136 | 32 | 3 | 24 | 70 | 7 | 3 | 75 | 156 | .250 | .342 | .452 | .795 | 17 |
| RF | Corey Hart | 115 | 419 | 64 | 109 | 24 | 3 | 12 | 48 | 11 | 6 | 43 | 92 | .260 | .335 | .418 | .753 | 9 |

## Key Pitchers

| Pos | Player | G | GS | W | L | SV | IP | H | R | ER | SO | BB | BR/9 | ERA | WS |
|---|---|---|---|---|---|---|---|---|---|---|---|---|---|---|---|
| SP | Braden Looper | 34 | 34 | 14 | 7 | 0 | 194.2 | 226 | 123 | 113 | 100 | 64 | 13.64 | 5.22 | 5 |
| SP | Yovani Gallardo | 30 | 30 | 13 | 12 | 0 | 185.2 | 150 | 78 | 77 | 204 | 94 | 12.07 | 3.73 | 10 |
| SP | Manny Parra | 27 | 27 | 11 | 11 | 0 | 140.0 | 179 | 108 | 99 | 116 | 77 | 16.52 | 6.36 | 0 |
| SP | Jeff Suppan | 30 | 30 | 7 | 12 | 0 | 161.2 | 200 | 106 | 95 | 80 | 74 | 15.87 | 5.29 | 2 |
| SP | David Bush | 22 | 21 | 5 | 9 | 0 | 114.1 | 131 | 84 | 81 | 89 | 37 | 14.41 | 6.38 | 0 |
| CL | Trevor Hoffman | 55 | 0 | 3 | 2 | 37 | 54.0 | 35 | 11 | 11 | 48 | 14 | 8.33 | 1.83 | 11 |
| RP | Mitch Stetter | 71 | 0 | 4 | 1 | 1 | 45.0 | 37 | 19 | 18 | 44 | 27 | 13.80 | 3.60 | 4 |
| RP | Todd Coffey | 78 | 0 | 4 | 4 | 2 | 83.2 | 76 | 28 | 27 | 65 | 21 | 10.76 | 2.90 | 7 |

## Swinging Low

Through 2006, Jason Kendall was a career .301 hitter coming off a .295 season. The following year his average plunged 53 points. Three years later, it still hasn't recovered. What changed? Simple. All of a sudden, he started hitting way more fly balls, and fewer ground balls and line drives.

| Year | Ground Balls | Line Drives | Fly Balls |
|------|--------------|-------------|-----------|
| 2004 | 50.4% | 21.9% | 27.5% |
| 2005 | 51.2% | 21.9% | 26.5% |
| 2006 | 49.9% | 23.5% | 25.6% |
| 2007 | 43.3% | 18.3% | 37.0% |
| 2008 | 44.9% | 17.3% | 35.9% |
| 2009 | 43.2% | 19.8% | 35.1% |

That's a hell of a change. In 2004, '05 and '06, he hit about as many ground balls and line drives as anyone in baseball. Then, in 2007, 40 or 50 of them turned into fly balls, and it's been that way ever since.

That kind of thing wouldn't necessarily cripple the numbers of your typical hitter, but Kendall is far from typical. He has as little home-run power as anyone in today's game. His fly balls, almost without exception, stay in the park, and therefore tend to fall safely as seldom as just about anyone's. Last year he batted .102 on fly balls, second-lowest in the majors. This was not atypical for him.

His batting average on fly balls has been about the same over the past three years as it had been from 2004-06. So has his batting average on ground balls and line drives. The only thing that's changed is the distribution. If he'd been able to maintain his old ground/liner/fly ratios over the past three years, his yearly batting averages would have been .290, .294 and .295, instead of .242, .246 and .241.

## Pulling Off an Upset

Among hitters who batted at least 300 times, Casey McGehee had the highest average when he pulled the ball.

| Player | AVG |
|--------|-----|
| 1. Casey McGehee, Mil | .504 |
| 2. Mark Reynolds, Ari | .503 |
| 3. Hanley Ramirez, Fla | .487 |
| 4. Kevin Youkilis, Bos | .485 |
| 5. Derrek Lee, ChC | .469 |

## J.J.'s Newfound Basepath Savvy

In 2009, J.J. Hardy dropped off both at the plate and in the field, but he did improve his game in at least one area: baserunning. In almost every category we track, he advanced almost exactly as often, and almost exactly as effectively, as he had the year before. The difference is that in 2008, he was doubled off or thrown out advancing a total of six times, while in 2009 he wasn't caught a single time either way. In fact, the only time he was thrown out on the bases in 2009 was a single caught-stealing. That helped him improve his net gain by 18 bases and put him in positive territory for the first time since his rookie season of 2005.

### J.J. Hardy — 2009 Baserunning Analysis

| Year | 1st to 3rd | | 2nd to Home | | 1st to Home | | Opp | GIDP | Bases Taken | BR Outs | BR Gain | SB Gain | Net Gain |
|---|---|---|---|---|---|---|---|---|---|---|---|---|---|
| | Adv | Opp | Adv | Opp | Adv | Opp | | | | | | | |
| 2005 | 6 | 16 | 11 | 12 | 1 | 2 | 83 | 10 | 6 | 1 | +6 | 0 | +6 |
| 2006 | 1 | 5 | 2 | 5 | 0 | 1 | 22 | 4 | 2 | 1 | -5 | -1 | -6 |
| 2007 | 4 | 21 | 8 | 14 | 2 | 6 | 100 | 13 | 14 | 6 | -12 | -4 | -16 |
| 2008 | 4 | 23 | 5 | 10 | 3 | 5 | 132 | 18 | 10 | 6 | -17 | 0 | -17 |
| 2009 | 5 | 30 | 5 | 11 | 3 | 6 | 104 | 14 | 12 | 0 | +3 | -2 | +1 |
| **Totals** | **20** | **95** | **31** | **52** | **9** | **20** | **441** | **59** | **44** | **14** | **-25** | **-7** | **-32** |
| | | 21% | | 60% | | 45% | | 13% | | | | | |

## Hitting Ground Balls

Alcides Escobar hit .304 in 38 games last year, but there was a ton of luck in that. He did it by hitting .375 on his ground balls. To hit .375 on your ground balls, consistently, is totally impossible. There are a handful of hitters who can consistently hit CLOSE to .300 on ground balls, like Hanley Ramirez, Matt Holliday, Carl Crawford and Ichiro. Escobar will not be one of those guys. Normal hitters hit more like .250 on ground balls. If Escobar had hit .250 on ground balls, his average would have been .248.

### Alcides Escobar

| | Times | Outs | Hits | Avg | Hit Type | | | |
|---|---|---|---|---|---|---|---|---|
| | | | | | 1B | 2B | 3B | HR |
| Ground Balls | 56 | 35 | 21 | .375 | 21 | 0 | 0 | 0 |
| Line Drives | 18 | 7 | 11 | .611 | 9 | 2 | 0 | 0 |
| Fly Balls | 33 | 27 | 6 | .188 | 3 | 1 | 1 | 1 |
| All Balls in Play | 110 | 72 | 38 | .355 | 33 | 3 | 1 | 1 |

### Out-Homered

Despite having the majors' second-leading home run hitter, Prince Fielder, and another, Ryan Braun, who just missed the NL top ten, the Brewers were out-homered 207-182. Braun and Fielder, the team's No. 3 hitter and cleanup hitter, combined for 78 home runs; Brewers pitchers gave almost all of it back by allowing a total of 74 home runs to opponents' number-3 and -4 hitters. (note: This is NOT a park effect. Miller Park is not a home run park.)

### Yeah, But In-Between, He Was Brilliant

Ryan Braun's plus/minus rating was worst among left fielders on balls hit shallow (-10) *and* on balls hit deep (-22).

### Like Mariano — Part I

Trevor Hoffman started 51 innings and completed a shutout inning in 45 of them, 88.2%. Mariano Rivera (90.3%) was the only pitcher who started 50 innings and compiled a higher percentage.

### Like Mariano — Part II

Mark DiFelice threw 79% cutters. Mariano Rivera (92%) was the only other pitcher (min. 50 IP) who threw more than 51% cutters.

## Plastered

Brewers starting pitchers posted a game score below 30 — which is to say, the starting pitcher got plastered — a major league-high 37 times, nearly once every four games. The Braves and Dodgers had only 7 such games.

In those 37 games the Brewers scored 200 runs — more than five runs a game — but finished 7-30. The pitchers who contributed to this list included Manny Parra (8 games), Jeff Suppan (8 games), Braden Looper (7 games), Dave Bush (6 games), Mike Burns (3 games), Carlos Villanueva (2 games), Yovani Gallardo (only 2 in 30 starts), and Seth McClung (1 game).

This is the record of their starting pitchers in those 37 games:

| G | IP | W | L | WPct | Hits | R | ER | SO | BB | ERA |
|---|-----|---|----|------|------|-----|-----|----|-----|-------|
| 37 | 150.2 | 4 | 27 | .130 | 312 | 241 | 228 | 79 | 101 | 13.65 |

## Parra's ERA

Manny Parra had a 4.61 ERA in 2009 in the games that he won. Of the other 76 pitchers who won 10 games or more, none had an ERA in his wins higher than 4.13.

**Manny Parra — 2009 Decision Anaylsis**

| Group | G | IP | W | L | Pct | H | R | SO | BB | ERA |
|-------|----|------|----|----|-------|----|----|----|----|-------|
| Wins | 11 | 68.1 | 11 | 0 | 1.000 | 81 | 37 | 59 | 32 | 4.61 |
| Losses | 11 | 47.0 | 0 | 11 | .000 | 73 | 61 | 35 | 34 | 10.34 |
| No Decisions | 5 | 24.2 | 0 | 0 | ---- | 25 | 10 | 22 | 11 | 3.65 |

Quality Starts: 6 in Wins, 3 in Losses, 2 in No Decisions

## No Need to Signal

The typical lefty specialist comes in and throws sliders to left-handed hitters, but no one throws as many of them as Mitch Stetter. In 2009, 70% of the pitches he threw to left-handed hitters were sliders. No other lefty specialist threw more than 52%.

## Slow Motion

The cinematic equivalent of the last five years of Jeff Suppan's career would be the boxer who's felled by the slo-mo knockout punch.

| Year | Wins | Opposing Hitters' | | | |
|------|------|------|------|------|------|
| | | ERA | AVG | OPS | SLG |
| 2005 | 16 | 3.57 | .275 | .335 | .428 |
| 2006 | 12 | 4.12 | .277 | .343 | .440 |
| 2007 | 12 | 4.62 | .298 | .356 | .445 |
| 2008 | 10 | 4.96 | .298 | .361 | .483 |
| 2009 | 7 | 5.29 | .309 | .387 | .512 |

## Serving Up Crooked Numbers

Braden Looper gave up multiple runs in 35 separate innings, three more than anyone else in baseball.

## More Runs Please

Braden Looper went 14-7 despite a 5.22 ERA, while Yovani Gallardo went only 13-12 despite an ERA that was nearly a run-and-a-half lower. The reason for the discrepancy, of course, was run support. The Brewers scored 5.71 runs per game in Looper's starts, but only 4.33 runs per game in Gallardo's. If the run support had been reversed, Looper's record probably would have been closer to 7-14, and Gallardo's would have been 19-6.

One of two things will happen to Yovani Gallardo:

a) He'll hurt his arm, or

b) He'll be a great pitcher.

I believe that we're a little better now at protecting pitcher's arms than we were in the past — but (a) is still much more likely than (b). Since 1960 there have been 71 pitchers who struck out 200 batters in a season at the age of 24 or earlier — actually 54 pitchers who have done it 71 times by the age of 24. Only six of those pitchers are in the Hall of Fame; only three or four more of them are likely to make the Hall of Fame (Clemens, Pedro Martinez, Blyleven).

Even if you look at the last decade, the pitchers who rung up big strikeout numbers at a young age mostly have had a hard time following through. From 1998 to 2008 the pitchers who were added to this list were Kerry Wood, Kevin Millwood, Ryan Dempster, Barry Zito, Javier Vazquez, Roy Oswalt, Mark Prior, Carlos Zambrano, Jake Peavy, Brett Myers, Jeremy Bonderman, Scott Kazmir, Edinson Volquez, Tim Lincecum and Chad Billingsley. There's only one pitcher on that list who is a good candidate for immortality, and he won't be 26 until June. The great pitchers that you might think would be on that list, like Santana and Sabathia, actually aren't.

**Milwaukee Brewers — 2009 Performance By Starting Pitcher**

| Games Started | GS | RS | RA | Won | Lost |
|---|---|---|---|---|---|
| Braden Looper | 34 | 194 | 180 | 20 | 14 |
| Jeff Suppan | 30 | 128 | 159 | 13 | 17 |
| Yovani Gallardo | 30 | 130 | 109 | 16 | 14 |
| Manny Parra | 27 | 132 | 157 | 11 | 16 |
| David Bush | 21 | 104 | 107 | 10 | 11 |
| Mike Burns | 8 | 42 | 43 | 4 | 4 |
| Carlos Villanueva | 6 | 27 | 34 | 2 | 4 |
| Chris Narveson | 4 | 16 | 14 | 3 | 1 |
| Seth McClung | 2 | 12 | 15 | 1 | 1 |
| **Team Totals** | 162 | 785 | 818 | 80 | 82 |

# Minnesota Twins

## Key Players

| Pos | Player | G | AB | R | H | 2B | 3B | HR | RBI | SB | CS | BB | SO | AVG | OBP | SLG | OPS | WS |
|---|---|---|---|---|---|---|---|---|---|---|---|---|---|---|---|---|---|---|
| C | Joe Mauer | 138 | 523 | 94 | 191 | 30 | 1 | 28 | 96 | 4 | 1 | 76 | 63 | .365 | .444 | .587 | 1.031 | 32 |
| 1B | Justin Morneau | 135 | 508 | 85 | 139 | 31 | 1 | 30 | 100 | 0 | 0 | 72 | 86 | .274 | .363 | .516 | .878 | 18 |
| 2B | Nick Punto | 125 | 359 | 56 | 82 | 15 | 1 | 1 | 38 | 16 | 3 | 61 | 70 | .228 | .337 | .284 | .621 | 11 |
| 3B | Joe Crede | 90 | 333 | 42 | 75 | 16 | 1 | 15 | 48 | 0 | 0 | 29 | 56 | .225 | .289 | .414 | .703 | 6 |
| SS | Brendan Harris | 123 | 414 | 44 | 108 | 22 | 1 | 6 | 37 | 0 | 2 | 29 | 78 | .261 | .310 | .362 | .672 | 7 |
| LF | Delmon Young | 108 | 395 | 50 | 112 | 16 | 2 | 12 | 60 | 2 | 5 | 12 | 92 | .284 | .308 | .425 | .733 | 7 |
| CF | Denard Span | 145 | 578 | 97 | 180 | 16 | 10 | 8 | 68 | 23 | 10 | 70 | 89 | .311 | .392 | .415 | .807 | 21 |
| RF | Michael Cuddyer | 153 | 588 | 93 | 162 | 34 | 7 | 32 | 94 | 6 | 1 | 54 | 118 | .276 | .342 | .520 | .862 | 17 |
| DH | Jason Kubel | 146 | 514 | 73 | 154 | 35 | 2 | 28 | 103 | 1 | 1 | 56 | 106 | .300 | .369 | .539 | .907 | 19 |

## Key Pitchers

| Pos | Player | G | GS | W | L | SV | IP | H | R | ER | SO | BB | BR/9 | ERA | WS |
|---|---|---|---|---|---|---|---|---|---|---|---|---|---|---|---|
| SP | Scott Baker | 33 | 33 | 15 | 9 | 0 | 200.0 | 190 | 99 | 97 | 162 | 48 | 10.89 | 4.37 | 12 |
| SP | Nick Blackburn | 33 | 33 | 11 | 11 | 0 | 205.2 | 240 | 103 | 92 | 98 | 41 | 12.43 | 4.03 | 12 |
| SP | Kevin Slowey | 16 | 16 | 10 | 3 | 0 | 90.2 | 113 | 50 | 49 | 75 | 15 | 13.20 | 4.86 | 5 |
| SP | Glen Perkins | 18 | 17 | 6 | 7 | 0 | 96.1 | 120 | 64 | 63 | 45 | 23 | 13.45 | 5.89 | 2 |
| SP | Francisco Liriano | 29 | 24 | 5 | 13 | 0 | 136.2 | 147 | 93 | 88 | 122 | 65 | 14.36 | 5.80 | 2 |
| CL | Joe Nathan | 70 | 0 | 2 | 2 | 47 | 68.2 | 42 | 16 | 16 | 89 | 22 | 8.65 | 2.10 | 16 |
| RP | Matt Guerrier | 79 | 0 | 5 | 1 | 1 | 76.1 | 58 | 23 | 20 | 47 | 16 | 9.20 | 2.36 | 11 |
| RP | Jose Mijares | 71 | 0 | 2 | 2 | 0 | 61.2 | 50 | 17 | 16 | 55 | 23 | 10.95 | 2.34 | 8 |

## How Hot Was He?

We have a system which tracks the "temperature" of every hitter after every at-bat. The hottest hitter in the American League, at any point in the season, was Joe Mauer on May 25 — 120 degrees.

Mauer's hot streak really started on May 7. On May 7 at Baltimore he had three hits. In his next four games (May 8, 9, 10 and 12) he had two hits in every game, with homers in three of the four. From May 13th to the 20th he was usually down to one hit a game, but he hit safely in every game, giving him a 13-game streak at that point, and he homered three more times.

On May 21 he had two doubles and a homer, driving in 6 runs. On May 22 he was held hitless, ending the hitting streak at 14, but walked twice, scored two runs, and drove in two runs. On May 23 against Milwaukee he was 3-for-3 with a homer. On May 24 he was 2-for-3 with a homer. On May 25 against Boston he had the day off, but was called in to pinch hit against Jonathan Papelbon with two out in the ninth inning. He homered.

In the 18 games beginning May 7 and ending May 25, Mauer hit .453 with 10 homers, 28 RBI.

**Joe Mauer — 2009**
**Hot and Cold Summary**

| | |
|---|---|
| Season Ending Temperature | 73° |
| High Point of the Season (May 25) | 120° |
| Low Point of the Season (July 19) | 46° |
| Days Over 100° | 18 |
| Days Under 50° | 1 |
| Average Daily Temperature | 82.3° |

## Ghost RBI

Here is one more talking point for the people that say Joe Mauer doesn't get enough credit for the little things he does. A Ghost RBI is credited to a batter who advances a runner who later scores, and who would not or might not have scored had the batter not advanced him. Joe Mauer led the American League with 24 Ghost RBI.

## The Next Guy Must Be Easier

The Twins benefitted from 46 Intentional Walks, most in the American League. Joe Mauer's 14 were second in the league, while Justin Morneau and Jason Kubel finished fourth and eighth.

## Be My Guest and Take Two

Carl Pavano's 33 stolen bases allowed were the most in the major leagues in 2009. With the Indians Pavano pitched 126 innings, allowing 20 stolen bases with 6 runners caught stealing. With Minnesota he pitched 74 innings, allowing 13 stolen bases with nobody caught stealing.

14 of the 39 runners who attempted to steal against Pavano eventually scored. The stolen bases allowed probably cost Pavano about two runs.

## When It Counts

Carl Pavano has always pitched his best ball against quality opponents.

### Carl Pavano — Career Record Against Quality of Competition

| Opp | G | IP | W | L | SO | BB | ERA |
|---|---|---|---|---|---|---|---|
| .600 teams | 15 | 78.1 | 3 | 5 | 41 | 17 | 4.37 |
| .500 - .599 teams | 67 | 380.1 | 25 | 21 | 247 | 104 | 4.19 |
| .400 - .499 teams | 70 | 412.1 | 28 | 23 | 276 | 87 | 4.50 |
| sub .400 teams | 8 | 33.1 | 3 | 2 | 22 | 4 | 5.67 |

## He Popped Him Up

Jered Weaver and Scott Baker led the majors in batters retired on pop outs last season with 92 and 91. No other big leaguer had more than 70. Sixteen percent of Baker's outs came on pop ups. He has consistently recorded a high percentage of outs in this way — 13% in 2008, 14% in 2007.

| Scott Baker | | Jared Weaver | |
|---|---|---|---|
| Batters Retired | 577 | Batters Retired | 596 |

| Retired by | | Retired by | |
|---|---|---|---|
| Strikeout | 162 | Strikeout | 173 |
| Ground Out | 150 | Ground Out | 141 |
| Line Out | 19 | Line Out | 15 |
| Fly Out | 155 | Fly Out | 175 |
| Pop Out | 91 | Pop Out | 92 |
| Other | 0 | Other | 0 |

## Year after Year of Control

Twins pitchers in 2009 issued the fewest free passes in the American League for the fifth time in six years — 2004, 2005, 2006, 2008 and 2009. In 2007 they missed by ten walks.

## At That Level, Is It Really a Slugging Percentage?

Alexi Casilla's 2009 slugging percentage was .259. The last American Leaguer with a slugging percentage that low (250 or more plate appearances) was Jermaine Dye in 2003.

## Swinging at Everything

Delmon Young has swung at 61% of the pitches he has seen in the major leagues — the highest percentage of anyone who has seen more than 2,500 pitches.

### Delmon Young — 2009 Pitch Analysis

| Season | Pitches Seen | Pitches Taken | | Swung At | |
|--------|-------------|---------------|-----|----------|-----|
| 2006 | 374 | 117 | 31% | 257 | 69% |
| 2007 | 2,380 | 895 | 38% | 1,485 | 62% |
| 2008 | 2,190 | 915 | 42% | 1,275 | 58% |
| 2009 | 1,456 | 600 | 41% | 856 | 59% |
| **Total** | **6,400** | **2,527** | **39%** | **3,873** | **61%** |

## The Wheels of Carlos

Carlos Gomez was used as a pinch runner 22 times in 2009 — the most of any major league player.

## Bunting That Makes Sense

Denard Span bunted 27 times in 2009, the most bunts in play of any American League player. Twelve of those were Sacrifice Bunts. Of the other 15, ten were singles — a .667 batting average on efforts to bunt for a hit, or .370 if you include the 12 sacrifices.

Sabermetricians are often critical of the bunt, arguing that the sac bunt, even when successful, reduces the number of runs the team can expect to score. But this misses a critical point: that the "Denard Span" bunt, where you're really bunting for a hit but you'll take the sacrifice as a by-product of failure, is a very good play. If there's a runner on first and nobody out and you try to bunt for a hit, you only have to bunt about .275 to make it a good play — assuming that you'll get the sac bunt even if the effort for a hit doesn't work. A good bunter can bunt much more than .275 — making it a good play.

## Spanning the Bases

We credit a baserunner with a "Base Taken" whenever he moves up a base on a Wild Pitch, a Passed Ball, a Sacrifice Fly, a Balk or Defensive Indifference.

Denard Span had 31 Bases Taken, tying David Wright for the major league lead.

## Making His Three-Baggers Count

Denard Span's ten triples in 2009 drove in a whopping 13 runs. He was the only major league player to have a double-digit RBI count on his triples.

## As Luck Would Have It

When Francisco Liriano took the mound for his first start in 2009 (April 6, Twins vs. Mariners), the opposing starting pitcher was Felix Hernandez.

Liriano should have taken that as a warning.

On April 16, Liriano started against the Blue Jays. Roy Halladay.

On April 28, Liriano started against the Rays. James Shields.

On May 9, Liriano started again against the Mariners. Felix Hernandez.

On June 5, he started against the Mariners again. Felix Hernandez, once again.

On September 27, he started against the Royals. Guess who.

Among all major league pitchers, Liriano had the toughest luck in terms of drawing difficult pitching matchups — by far. Liriano actually had the highest average Season Score by his pitching opponents since Jon Lieber in 2005. In addition to starting five times against the three best pitchers in the league (Hernandez, Greinke and Halladay), Liriano was also matched up against Joel Pineiro, Edwin Jackson (twice), John Danks, John Lackey, James Shields, Brad Penny (twice) and Tommy Hunter. He had only two starts all year in

which he was matched against pitchers having genuinely bad seasons.

On the other end of that scale: Tommy Hanson of Atlanta. Hanson finished the season 11-4, in part because he pitched really well, and in part because he pitched a lot of games against pitchers who were struggling. Hanson pitched only three times against pitchers having good seasons — Yovani Gallardo (July 25), Wandy Rodriguez (September 9) and Cliff Lee (September 20). The Braves lost all three of those games.

In his first four starts, the Braves won all four games. On the other hand, his pitching opponents in those games were Manny Parra (11-11, 6.36 ERA), Jason Berken (6-12, 6.54 ERA), Matt Maloney (2-4, 4.87 ERA) and Chien-Ming Wang (1-6, 9.54 ERA). He pitched once against the Dodgers; he drew Jason Schmidt (2-2, 5.60 ERA). He pitched once against the Padres; he drew Chad Gaudin (6-10, 4.64 ERA). In his first start against the Marlins he drew Chris Volstad (9-13, 5.21 ERA). He pitched once against the Mets, and drew Pat Misch (3-4, 4.48). In his last two starts of the year he faced the Nationals, and drew Garrett Mock (3-10, 5.62 ERA). Both times.

## Rally Killers

The Twins grounded into 147 double plays in 2009, most in the American League. The leading offenders were Michael Cuddyer, Brendan Harris, Delmon Young and Orlando Cabrera.

| Player | GIDP | Situations | PCT |
|---|---|---|---|
| Michael Cuddyer | 22 | 138 | 16% |
| Brendan Harris | 16 | 85 | 19% |
| Delmon Young | 17 | 79 | 22% |
| Orlando Cabrera | 9 | 53 | 17% |

# On the Move

by Bill James

DO PLAYERS JUMP FROM TEAM TO TEAM MORE OFTEN NOW, because of free agency, than they did before free agency?

In early May I read somewhere a debate on this issue, in which some of my old research was cited. X and Y were debating the issue; X said that free agency has led to players changing teams more often than they used to, and Y responded that Bill James showed that this was untrue. Uh oh.

Well, yes, I *did* study that issue, but it's been a while. It's been fifteen years or more since I did research on the issue, and, since those kind of studies can only look backward in time, that pushes it back 25 years at least. The free agency era is less than 35 years old. The research is pretty dated, and…how good was it to begin with?

> *The research is pretty dated, and…how good was it to begin with?*

As an aside, we do hear media and fans comment now that the players don't stay with the same team now the way they did years ago — but then, I very clearly remember hearing the same comment several times 45 years ago. As we age, our perception of time changes, so that things around us seem to be moving more rapidly. When you were in the fourth grade, the period between the start of the fall semester and Christmas seemed like an eternity. At my age, it seems like a weekend. Our minds proportion time compared to the span of our memories, so that six years to a 60-year-old seems about the same as one year to a 10-year-old. This creates the illusion, as we age, that the world is losing permanence.

I decided that I should do some good, thorough research about this subject. The way that I studied this issue before was to pick a moment as a starting point and then look at how many players remained where they were x years later. In other words, let's take the regulars of 1970; 24 times 8 is 192 regulars. How many of those 192 regulars were still with the same team one year later? Two years later? Three years later? What is the "decay rate"? How does the decay rate from 1970 compare to that from 1960, or 1950?

That isn't a bad way to study the issue, but there are some problems with it. It focuses only on regulars (and regular pitchers), ignoring part-time players and ignoring players who may have been regulars in other seasons but weren't in the base season. It produces results so close to 100%, for the first two years, that differences may not be meaningful or apparent, and so close to zero after eight or ten years that one has the same problem. It is subject to fluctuation due to changes in the game like expansion (which impacted the data for the 1960s), World War II (which impacted the data for the 1940s), and even the DH Rule (the 1970s). It is hard to find a starting point from which to measure the decay rate.

There must be a better way to measure it.

OK, here's what I came up with. Suppose that we look at all players in history who have played 1,000 games, and we ask this question: When this player played in his 1,000th major league game, how many major league teams had he played for? What is the figure for players who played their 1,000th game in the 1920s, the 1930s, the 1940s? What about the 1,500th game, or the 2,000th?

That's a lot more work, but it is a better way to study the issue. If players change teams more rapidly than they did in the past, then, by the time they have played 1,000 games, they have to have played for more teams, right? I don't see how the study can fail. I started with a list of all players in history who have played 1,000 games, 1,500 games or 2,000 games, and the year in which the player passed that marker. By my count there were, through 2008:

*When this player played in his 1,000th major league game, how many major league teams had he played for?*

- 217 players who had played 2,000 games,
- 606 players who had played 1,500 games, and
- 1,378 players who had played 1,000 games.

Then I looked up each of those players in the Encyclopedia, manually, and counted how many teams he had played for at the moment of his 1,000th, 1,500th and 2,000th games.

I wish I had studied computer programming.

Anyway, let's use 1,000 games as our "base number" here, since there are far more players at that level, and thus we get a truer read more rapidly.

The first player to get to 1,000 games played in his career, I was surprised to learn, was *not* Cap Anson. It was actually a fairly obscure player named John Morrill. (I started the counts in 1876.) Morrill, Anson and Paul Hines played almost the same number of games every year from 1876 on, and were neck-and-neck in terms of career totals. However, because of an injury to Anson in 1879, Morrill was a little bit ahead, and he was the first player to get to 1,000 games in his career.

Barely. Morrill, Anson, Hines, Jim O'Rouke and Ezra Sutton all crossed the 1,000-game barrier in 1887. We'll consider the first "decade" here to be the 19th century, since there were no players who played in 1,000 games prior to 1887…our first "decade" is a little over a decade, 1887-1899.

By the end of the 19th century 93 players had played in 1,000 games in their careers. Of those 93 players:

- 8 had played for only one team at the time of their 1,000th game,
- 16 had played for two teams,
- 24 had played for three teams,
- 18 had played for four teams,
- 15 had played for five teams,
- 4 had played for six teams,
- 5 had played for seven teams,
- 1 had played for eight teams,
- 1 had played for nine teams, and
- 1, a middle infielder named Pop Smith, had played for ten different teams.

Pop Smith's 10 teams in 1,000 games remains the major league record — in fact, until the last few years, there had not been another player reaching nine. Greg Myers and John Mabry, in recent years, played for nine teams in their first 1,000 games, and someone else did in the 19th century, but no one did that in the 20th century.

I did not count playing for another organization in the minor leagues. Jeff Bagwell is a one-team player (the Astros) even though he was drafted and signed by a different team. Also, I was counting the number of team changes, not the number of teams involved, so if a player left a team and then went back to them, it counts as another team. Harold Baines went from the White Sox to the Rangers to the A's to the Orioles to the White Sox to the Orioles to the Indians to the Orioles to the White Sox; that's nine teams, although there are only five franchises involved. He played for the White Sox and the Orioles three times each.

Also, if a player stayed with a franchise when the franchise moved…no team change. One can see it either way. We are looking at the issue of stability, as perceived by the fans. If Hank Aaron plays for one franchise in three different cities, is that perceived by the fans as his being with the same team all those years, or not? I decided to count it as all the same team, but certainly there is another kind of "location instability" that could be measured there.

I did not include pitchers in the study, even if they played 1,000 games in their careers.

Anyway, the 93 players from the 19th century had played for an average of 3.71 teams at the time of their 1,000th major league game. That's 270 games per team (1000 divided by 3.71). This is a chart summary of the 19th century data:

| Decade | 1,000-Game Players | One-Team Players | One-Team Pct | Avg Teams | Games Per Team |
|---|---|---|---|---|---|
| 1876-1899 | 93 | 8 | 9% | 3.71 | 270 |

*If Hank Aaron plays for one franchise in three different cities, is that perceived by the fans as his being with the same team all those years, or not?*

Now let's compare that to the data from the three following decades:

| Decade | 1,000-Game Players | One-Team Players | One-Team Pct | Avg Teams | Games Per Team |
|---|---|---|---|---|---|
| 1876-1899 | 93 | 8 | 9% | 3.71 | 270 |
| 1900-1909 | 56 | 5 | 9% | 3.48 | 287 |
| 1910-1919 | 86 | 35 | 41% | 2.26 | 442 |
| 1920-1929 | 86 | 27 | 31% | 2.53 | 395 |

The 1920s were not quite as stable as the 1910s, but in general the trend line here is toward more roster stability — toward players staying longer with their first team.

We romanticize one-team players. "In my day," says Old Joe Blowhard, "if you were any good, you stayed with the team that signed you. You lived in that city. You married a girl from that city, raised your kids there, bought a business there and stayed there after your playing career. Those people knew you, and you became a part of that community. That was the way it was." Of course, that was never *exactly* the way it was; neither Babe Ruth nor Ty Cobb nor Honus Wagner nor Cy Young nor Willie Mays nor Hank Aaron was a one-team player. But my idea was that, while one-team players are so rare that it is difficult to measure the frequency of them reliably, we could get at the same issue by looking at the precursors to that. To play his entire career with one team, the player must be on his first team when he plays his 1,000th game. He must be there when he plays his 1,500th game, and his 2,000th. When the number of precursors increases, we can assume the number of one-team players is increasing, and vice versa.

Adding now the 1930s and 1940s:

| Decade | 1,000-Game Players | One-Team Players | One-Team Pct | Avg Teams | Games Per Team |
|---|---|---|---|---|---|
| 1876-1899 | 93 | 8 | 9% | 3.71 | 270 |
| 1900-1909 | 56 | 5 | 9% | 3.48 | 287 |
| 1910-1919 | 86 | 35 | 41% | 2.26 | 442 |
| 1920-1929 | 86 | 27 | 31% | 2.53 | 395 |
| 1930-1939 | 85 | 30 | 35% | 2.14 | 467 |
| 1940-1949 | 70 | 29 | 41% | 2.23 | 448 |

The length of time players stayed with a team took a great leap forward about 1910, and then flattened out. Let's add the 1950s and 1960s:

| Decade | 1,000-Game Players | One-Team Players | One-Team Pct | Avg Teams | Games Per Team |
|---|---|---|---|---|---|
| 1876-1899 | 93 | 8 | 9% | 3.71 | 270 |
| 1900-1909 | 56 | 5 | 9% | 3.48 | 287 |
| 1910-1919 | 86 | 35 | 41% | 2.26 | 442 |
| 1920-1929 | 86 | 27 | 31% | 2.53 | 395 |
| 1930-1939 | 85 | 30 | 35% | 2.14 | 467 |
| 1940-1949 | 70 | 29 | 41% | 2.23 | 448 |
| 1950-1959 | 104 | 42 | 40% | 2.29 | 437 |
| 1960-1969 | 116 | 42 | 36% | 2.38 | 420 |

There may have been a slight downturn in the 1960s, probably attributable to side-effects of expansion, but the data is essentially stable. We now enter the free agent era, which began in the mid-1970s:

| Decade | 1,000-Game Players | One-Team Players | One-Team Pct | Avg Teams | Games Per Team |
|---|---|---|---|---|---|
| 1876-1899 | 93 | 8 | 9% | 3.71 | 270 |
| 1900-1909 | 56 | 5 | 9% | 3.48 | 287 |
| 1910-1919 | 86 | 35 | 41% | 2.26 | 442 |
| 1920-1929 | 86 | 27 | 31% | 2.53 | 395 |
| 1930-1939 | 85 | 30 | 35% | 2.14 | 467 |
| 1940-1949 | 70 | 29 | 41% | 2.23 | 448 |
| 1950-1959 | 104 | 42 | 40% | 2.29 | 437 |
| 1960-1969 | 116 | 42 | 36% | 2.38 | 420 |
| 1970-1979 | 159 | 57 | 36% | 2.24 | 446 |

The game average for the 1970s is the third-highest of all time, a hair behind the 1940s and some small distance behind the 1930s. Studying data from the 1970s, I thus concluded — correctly, I believe — that the 1970s rosters were not more unstable than previous generations. Now the 1980s:

| Decade | 1,000-Game Players | One-Team Players | One-Team Pct | Avg Teams | Games Per Team |
|---|---|---|---|---|---|
| 1970-1979 | 159 | 57 | 36% | 2.24 | 446 |
| 1980-1989 | 176 | 57 | 32% | 2.47 | 405 |

Beginning immediately with the onset of free agency, the number of games per team began to go down. This trend continued in the 1990s:

| Decade | 1,000-Game Players | One-Team Players | One-Team Pct | Avg Teams | Games Per Team |
|---|---|---|---|---|---|
| 1970-1979 | 159 | 57 | 36% | 2.24 | 446 |
| 1980-1989 | 176 | 57 | 32% | 2.47 | 405 |
| 1990-1999 | 175 | 40 | 23% | 2.78 | 360 |

And it has continued in the 21st century:

| Decade | 1,000-Game Players | One-Team Players | One-Team Pct | Avg Teams | Games Per Team |
|---|---|---|---|---|---|
| 1970-1979 | 159 | 57 | 36% | 2.24 | 446 |
| 1980-1989 | 176 | 57 | 32% | 2.47 | 405 |
| 1990-1999 | 175 | 40 | 23% | 2.78 | 360 |
| 2000-2008 | 172 | 31 | 18% | 3.18 | 314 |

That seems like fairly compelling data, but, to be on the safe side, let's look at the data for players playing 1,500 games:

| Decade | 1,600-Game Players | One-Team Players | One-Team Pct | Avg Teams | Games Per Team |
|---|---|---|---|---|---|
| 1876-1899 | 20 | 3 | 15% | 4.50 | 333 |
| 1900-1909 | 32 | 1 | 3% | 4.72 | 318 |
| 1910-1919 | 23 | 7 | 30% | 2.17 | 691 |
| 1920-1929 | 42 | 8 | 19% | 2.60 | 577 |
| 1930-1939 | 36 | 14 | 39% | 2.28 | 658 |
| 1940-1949 | 31 | 7 | 23% | 2.71 | 554 |
| 1950-1959 | 38 | 19 | 50% | 2.18 | 688 |
| 1960-1969 | 51 | 15 | 29% | 2.45 | 612 |
| 1970-1979 | 64 | 25 | 39% | 2.53 | 593 |
| 1980-1989 | 99 | 17 | 17% | 2.99 | 502 |
| 1990-1999 | 76 | 15 | 20% | 3.07 | 489 |
| 2000-2008 | 94 | 11 | 12% | 3.85 | 390 |

One might ask why the games-per-team average is so much higher here than it was before. The reason is that those players who play 1,500 games in their careers are much, much better players than those whose careers end in the 1,000-1,499 game range. As they are better players, their teams are more inclined to keep them, and so the average games per team is much higher.

In any case, here again we see that there has been a quite dramatic decrease in the length of time that players stay with a team, beginning with the onset of the free agent era. The percentage of players who were still with their first major league team at the 1,500-game mark has dropped, over the last three decades, from 39% to 12% — the lowest it has been in 100 years.

The numbers of 2,000-game players are so small that, looked at by decade, we would have unstable numbers. Let's group them into three-decade packages:

| Time Period | 2,000-Game Players | One-Team Players | One-Team Pct | Avg Teams | Games Per Team |
|---|---|---|---|---|---|
| 1876-1919 | 18 | 2 | 11% | 3.83 | 522 |
| 1920-1949 | 34 | 10 | 29% | 2.62 | 763 |
| 1950-1979 | 50 | 20 | 40% | 2.14 | 935 |
| 1980-2008 | 115 | 21 | 18% | 3.37 | 593 |

First of all, we can see here that there has been a stunning increase, in the last 30 years, in the number of players having long careers. But the central data is consistent with the data from the 1,000-game and 1,500-game studies.

In short, there is no question whatsoever that the rate at which players move from team to team has in fact increased, and increased quite dramatically, during the free agent era. The data could not be any more clear or any more definitive:

• The length of time that a moderately talented player typically spends with one team has decreased, since free agency began, from 446 games to 314 games.

• The number of games that a more talented player typically spends with one team has decreased from 593 to 390.

• The number of games that the most talented player typically spends with one team has decreased, over the last 30 years, from 935 games to 593.

*There is no question whatsoever that the rate at which players move from team to team has in fact increased, and increased quite dramatically, during the free agent era.*

# New York Mets

| 2009 TEAM OVERVIEW | ML RANK | 25th | 25th | 5th | 23rd | 21st | 6th |
|---|---|---|---|---|---|---|---|
| **70-92** | **Team** | **671** | **95** | **.270** | **526** | **.729** | **122** |
| **4** th place NL East | | RUNS | HOME RUNS | BATTING AVG. | WALKS | OPS | STOLEN BASES |
| | **Opp.** | **757** | **158** | **.264** | **616** | **.759** | **66** |
| | ML RANK | 15th | 8th | 17th | 25th | 19th | 3rd |

## Key Players

| Pos | Player | G | AB | R | H | 2B | 3B | HR | RBI | SB | CS | BB | SO | AVG | OBP | SLG | OPS | WS |
|---|---|---|---|---|---|---|---|---|---|---|---|---|---|---|---|---|---|---|
| C | Omir Santos | 96 | 281 | 28 | 73 | 14 | 1 | 7 | 40 | 0 | 0 | 15 | 44 | .260 | .296 | .391 | .688 | 7 |
| 1B | Daniel Murphy | 155 | 508 | 60 | 135 | 38 | 4 | 12 | 63 | 4 | 2 | 38 | 69 | .266 | .313 | .427 | .741 | 10 |
| 2B | Luis Castillo | 142 | 486 | 77 | 147 | 12 | 3 | 1 | 40 | 20 | 6 | 69 | 58 | .302 | .387 | .346 | .732 | 16 |
| 3B | David Wright | 144 | 535 | 88 | 164 | 39 | 3 | 10 | 72 | 27 | 9 | 74 | 140 | .307 | .390 | .447 | .837 | 20 |
| SS | Alex Cora | 82 | 271 | 31 | 68 | 11 | 1 | 1 | 18 | 8 | 3 | 25 | 28 | .251 | .320 | .310 | .630 | 5 |
| LF | Gary Sheffield | 100 | 268 | 44 | 74 | 13 | 2 | 10 | 43 | 2 | 1 | 40 | 46 | .276 | .372 | .451 | .823 | 8 |
| CF | Carlos Beltran | 81 | 308 | 50 | 100 | 22 | 1 | 10 | 48 | 11 | 1 | 47 | 43 | .325 | .415 | .500 | .915 | 14 |
| RF | Jeff Francoeur | 75 | 289 | 40 | 90 | 20 | 2 | 10 | 41 | 1 | 3 | 11 | 46 | .311 | .338 | .498 | .836 | 6 |

## Key Pitchers

| Pos | Player | G | GS | W | L | SV | IP | H | R | ER | SO | BB | BR/9 | ERA | WS |
|---|---|---|---|---|---|---|---|---|---|---|---|---|---|---|---|
| SP | Johan Santana | 25 | 25 | 13 | 9 | 0 | 166.2 | 156 | 67 | 58 | 146 | 46 | 11.07 | 3.13 | 14 |
| SP | Mike Pelfrey | 31 | 31 | 10 | 12 | 0 | 184.1 | 213 | 112 | 103 | 107 | 66 | 13.96 | 5.03 | 4 |
| SP | Livan Hernandez | 23 | 23 | 7 | 8 | 0 | 135.0 | 164 | 83 | 82 | 75 | 51 | 14.40 | 5.47 | 2 |
| SP | John Maine | 15 | 15 | 7 | 6 | 0 | 81.1 | 67 | 42 | 40 | 55 | 38 | 12.06 | 4.43 | 4 |
| SP | Tim Redding | 30 | 17 | 3 | 6 | 0 | 120.0 | 122 | 72 | 68 | 76 | 50 | 13.05 | 5.10 | 2 |
| CL | Francisco Rodriguez | 70 | 0 | 3 | 6 | 35 | 68.0 | 51 | 34 | 28 | 73 | 38 | 11.91 | 3.71 | 10 |
| RP | Pedro Feliciano | 88 | 0 | 6 | 4 | 0 | 59.1 | 51 | 25 | 20 | 59 | 18 | 10.47 | 3.03 | 7 |
| RP | Sean Green | 79 | 0 | 1 | 4 | 1 | 69.2 | 64 | 37 | 35 | 54 | 36 | 14.08 | 4.52 | 3 |

## Fadin' Away, Fadin' Away

On May 29th, the New York Mets were in first place with a 27-20 record in the midst of completing a 5-1 homestand. After that date, they had eight more road trips and eight more homestands. They did not win another homestand or road trip until they swept their last three games at home against the Astros in the final weekend of the season. That's 15 straight non-winning road trips or homestands.

**Tracking the Season by Segments — 2009 New York Mets**

| | Date | W-L | Runs | Runs/Game | AVG | Opp Runs | Opp R/GM | ERA | Season Record |
|---|---|---|---|---|---|---|---|---|---|
| Road | Apr 6-12 | 3-3 | 30 | 5.0 | .288 | 27 | 4.5 | 4.01 | 3-3 |
| Home | Apr 13-19 | 3-3 | 25 | 4.2 | .277 | 22 | 3.7 | 3.50 | 6-6 |
| Road | Apr 21-23 | 0-3 | 14 | 4.7 | .295 | 23 | 7.7 | 8.63 | 6-9 |
| Home | Apr 24-29 | 3-3 | 27 | 4.5 | .274 | 25 | 4.2 | 4.00 | 9-12 |
| Road | May 1-5 | 3-1 | 22 | 5.5 | .283 | 17 | 4.3 | 3.68 | 12-13 |
| Home | May 6-13 | 6-2 | 47 | 5.9 | .304 | 32 | 4.0 | 2.84 | 18-15 |
| Road | May 14-24 | 5-5 | 43 | 4.3 | .267 | 45 | 4.5 | 4.12 | 23-20 |
| Home | May 25-31 | 5-1 | 26 | 4.3 | .266 | 17 | 2.8 | 2.57 | 28-21 |
| Road | Jun 1-7 | 2-4 | 23 | 3.8 | .242 | 30 | 5.0 | 4.94 | 30-25 |
| Home | Jun 9-11 | 1-2 | 13 | 4.3 | .307 | 16 | 5.3 | 4.20 | 31-27 |
| Road | Jun 12-18 | 2-4 | 28 | 4.7 | .282 | 41 | 6.8 | 6.88 | 33-31 |
| Home | Jun 19-28 | 4-6 | 35 | 3.5 | .225 | 43 | 4.3 | 3.90 | 37-37 |
| Road | Jun 29-Jul 5 | 2-5 | 22 | 3.1 | .250 | 37 | 5.3 | 5.34 | 39-42 |
| Home | Jul 7-12 | 3-3 | 20 | 3.3 | .261 | 33 | 5.5 | 5.33 | 42-45 |
| Road | Jul 16-26 | 4-6 | 38 | 3.8 | .245 | 44 | 4.4 | 4.39 | 46-51 |
| Home | Jul 27-Aug 5 | 5-5 | 54 | 5.4 | .291 | 39 | 3.9 | 3.76 | 51-56 |
| Road | Aug 6-12 | 2-5 | 23 | 3.3 | .247 | 35 | 5.0 | 5.12 | 53-61 |
| Home | Aug 14-24 | 4-7 | 38 | 3.5 | .272 | 60 | 5.5 | 5.40 | 57-68 |
| Road | Aug 25-Sep 3 | 3-6 | 37 | 4.1 | .283 | 43 | 4.8 | 4.92 | 60-74 |
| Home | Sep 4-10 | 2-4 | 22 | 3.7 | .271 | 32 | 5.3 | 5.17 | 62-78 |
| Road | Sep 11-17 | 1-6 | 24 | 3.4 | .283 | 38 | 5.4 | 5.62 | 63-84 |
| Home | Sep 18-23 | 2-4 | 20 | 3.3 | .262 | 29 | 4.8 | 4.33 | 65-88 |
| Road | Sep 25-30 | 2-4 | 24 | 4.0 | .243 | 27 | 4.5 | 4.62 | 67-92 |
| Home | Oct 2-4 | 3-0 | 16 | 5.3 | .333 | 2 | 0.7 | 0.67 | 70-92 |

## All Smoke, No Fire

The Mets' offense in 2009 had the bases loaded, two out 68 times, and scored only 19 runs from those situations. This is 32 runs below the major league average — just in those 68 situations.

The Mets' offense was also very poor in bases-loaded, none-out situations and bases-loaded, one-out situations, granting that this is double-counting because if you make an out in a bases-loaded, none-out situation, it often leads to a bases-loaded, one-out situation, and if you make an out there. . .you've probably got my point. An average major league team scored 2.28 runs per opportunity after they had the bases loaded with no one out; the Mets were next-to-last in the majors at 1.84. An average major league team scored 1.56 runs per opportunity when they had the bases loaded with one out; the Mets were next-to-last at 1.12. With the bases loaded and two out, they were dead last by far.

| Situation | Occurred | Runs | AVG | MLB AVG |
|---|---|---|---|---|
| Bases Loaded, none out | 25 | 46 | 1.840 | 2.279 |
| Bases Loaded, one out | 67 | 75 | 1.119 | 1.558 |
| Bases Loaded, two out | 68 | 19 | .279 | .750 |

## Sheffield Grounders

Forty-year-old Gary Sheffield, who hit .225 in 2008, gave the Mets' offense a lift after he was acquired in early April, batting .276 with ten home runs in 312 plate appearances. The secret to his 2009 success, however, was that his ground balls got through the infield. Sheffield hit .349 on grounders, almost 100 points higher than a normal batting average with the ball on the ground.

**Gary Sheffield on Ground Balls**

| Year | At-Bats | AVG |
|---|---|---|
| 2007 | 175 | .269 |
| 2008 | 144 | .257 |
| 2009 | 106 | .349 |

## A Change to the Change

There is some question as to whether Francisco Rodriguez throws a slider or hard curveball. Whatever it is, K-Rod throws it a little bit less often every year than he did the year before, switching gradually to the changeup — and his OPS allowed is going up by 10 points a year.

| Year | Fastball | Slider/ Curve | Change | OPS Against |
|------|----------|---------------|--------|-------------|
| 2005 | 50% | 48% | 0% | .591 |
| 2006 | 55% | 42% | 2% | .610 |
| 2007 | 51% | 39% | 10% | .605 |
| 2008 | 50% | 33% | 16% | .630 |
| 2009 | 54% | 19% | 21% | .644 |

## Lot of Classical Gas in the Tank

Mets lefty Pedro Feliciano has led the majors in games pitched in each of the last two years — 86 games in 2008, 88 in 2009 — and also has led the majors both years in games pitched after having pitched the previous day — 34 both years. As a lefty assigned to get out lefties and then get out, he averages less than three batters faced per outing.

Feliciano had a better year in 2009 than 2008, in part perhaps because the manager did a better job of spotting him against left-handed batters. In 2008 he faced essentially as many right-handed hitters as lefties. In 2009, almost two-thirds of the hitters he faced were the ones that nature intended for him to pitch to.

| **Batters Faced** | | |
|------|------|------|
| Year | LHB | RHB |
| 2008 | 119 | 118 |
| 2009 | 156 | 86 |

## Lack of Runs

Johan Santana was the Mets' best starting pitcher of 2009 by far, with an ERA of 3.13. However, the Mets were only 13-12 in his starts, primarily because they scored just 3.52 runs per game with Santana on the mound. Only two major league starters, Aaron Harang and Barry Zito, had worse run support last year.

**Performance by Starting Pitcher**

| Games Started | GS | Run Support | Runs Allowed | W | L |
|---|---|---|---|---|---|
| Mike Pelfrey | 31 | 126 | 155 | 15 | 16 |
| Johan Santana | 25 | 88 | 94 | 13 | 12 |
| Livan Hernandez | 23 | 104 | 122 | 9 | 14 |
| Tim Redding | 17 | 63 | 83 | 6 | 11 |
| John Maine | 15 | 76 | 59 | 8 | 7 |
| **Team Totals** | **162** | **671** | **757** | **70** | **92** |

## But Fortunately, the Players Who Were Missing Were Minor Contributors

The Mets' opening-day lineup accounted for 50% of the team's total games; only Arizona (41%) and Washington (48%) had lower percentages among all major league teams.

**Games Played by Opening Day Starters**

| Pos | Player | Starts |
|---|---|---|
| C | Brian Schneider | 52 |
| 1B | Carlos Delgado | 25 |
| 2B | Luis Castillo | 135 |
| 3B | David Wright | 142 |
| SS | Jose Reyes | 35 |
| LF | Daniel Murphy | 124 |
| CF | Carlos Beltran | 80 |
| RF | Ryan Church | 58 |
| | **Total** | **651** |

## Twilight Zone Pennant Race

As pointed out elsewhere in this book, the team which has more hits in a game will win the game more than 80% of the time. Suppose, then, that the team which had more hits in the game always won the game. Would the standings then be about the same as they are, or very different?

Very different.

If the team that had more hits *always* won the game, the only two teams that would still have won their division (and did win their division) were the Yankees and the Dodgers. The Dodgers would have gone 102-60 if the team with more hits had won every game (splitting evenly the games in which the two teams had the same number of hits), and the Yankees would have gone 99-63. Those two teams would still have won their divisions.

On the other hand:

1) The Mariners would have won the AL West, at 95-67,

2) The White Sox would have won the Central, with 80 or 81 wins,

3) The Cubs would have won the NL Central, with 87 or 88 wins, and

4) The Phillies would have finished fourth in the NL East, only four-and-a-half games ahead of the Nationals.

The Phillies in 2009 were 58-8 in games in which they out-hit their opponents, and 11-9 when the hits were even. If the team that had more hits won every game, the Phillies would have been 66-0 and 10-10 in those games — but 0-76 when they were out-hit, thus 76-86 overall.

The Phillies in 2009 were out-hit by their opponents more often than not. What makes them a great team is that, with their power and walks (their pitchers have very good control), they were able to win 24 games in which they were out-hit — the most of any major league team.

The Mets, on the other hand, were able to win only *six* games in which they were out-hit — the fewest of any major league team. These are the won-lost records of the five NL East teams:

1) In games with more hits,

2) In games with fewer hits than their opponents, and

3) In games in which each team had the same number of hits.

The right-hand column re-creates the standings as they would have been if the team with more hits had won every game.

| Opponent | With More Hits | | | With Fewer Hits | | | With Same Hits | | | Twilight Zone | | | |
|---|---|---|---|---|---|---|---|---|---|---|---|---|---|
| | W | L | PCT | W | L | PCT | W | L | PCT | W | L | PCT | GB |
| Marlins | 59 | 14 | .808 | 13 | 48 | .213 | 15 | 13 | .536 | 87.0 | 75.0 | .537 | 0.0 |
| Braves | 61 | 14 | .813 | 12 | 52 | .188 | 13 | 10 | .565 | 86.5 | 75.5 | .534 | 0.5 |
| Mets | 54 | 21 | .720 | 6 | 58 | .094 | 10 | 13 | .435 | 86.5 | 75.5 | .534 | 0.5 |
| Phillies | 58 | 8 | .879 | 24 | 52 | .316 | 11 | 9 | .550 | 76.0 | 86.0 | .469 | 11.0 |
| Nationals | 39 | 22 | .639 | 15 | 65 | .188 | 5 | 16 | .238 | 71.5 | 90.5 | .441 | 15.5 |

## Power Outage – The New York Mets

In 2009 the New York Mets hit 27 fewer homers than any other major league team — 95 for the Mets, 122 or more for everybody else. While Citi Field would be the obvious, pre-analytical explanation for this, the fact is that the Mets both hit and allowed more home runs at home than they did on the road. They hit 49 at Citi Field, 46 on the road, and allowed 81 at home, 77 on the road. The park doesn't really seem to have anything to do with the lack of power.

The real explanation: the Mets don't hit the ball in the air. With Delgado and Beltran out of action much of the year, only 33% of the balls put in play by the Mets were fly balls. This was the lowest percentage in the major leagues.

**Percent of Batted Balls**
**(Five Lowest Fly Ball Percentages)**

| Team | Fly Ball | Ground Ball | Line Drive |
|---|---|---|---|
| 1. Mets | 33% | 47% | 20% |
| 2. Dodgers | 34% | 45% | 21% |
| 3. Astros | 34% | 48% | 18% |
| 4. Giants | 36% | 45% | 19% |
| 5. Twins | 36% | 46% | 18% |

## Power Outage – David Wright

David Wright had one of the strangest years I have ever seen a major league player have.

1) After hitting a steady 30 homers a year since he came to the major leagues, he hit only 10.

2) He seems convinced that the new park played a big role in this, but there is no direct evidence of this. The previous four years he had hit 12 to 15 homers a year on the road, and a similar number at home. In 2009 he was at 5 and 5.

3) He struck out far more than he has ever struck out before, which probably was a park effect.

4) But his batting average remained essentially the same because his in-play batting average was the highest in the majors (.400).

I would be willing to bet that there is no other player in major league history who had a sudden loss of homers and an increase in strikeouts at an early age (26), but who continued to hit for the same average as before. But I'm interrupting the list here.

5) Despite the injuries to all the other power hitters in the Met lineup, which should have encouraged pitchers to pitch around Wright, his walk total dropped by 20.

6) His defensive plus/minus went to hell in a handbasket. In 2007 he ranked as the 6th best defensive third baseman in the majors; in 2008 he was above average. In 2009 he was one of the worst in the majors.

It's just a very weird season, and we're not even going to get in to what happened to his girlfriend. I did a search of players who had large drop-offs in home runs at an early age. This essentially confirmed that no one has ever had a season like this before. The greatest drop-off ever (considering youth as a factor) was Hank Greenberg,

1935-36, who dropped from 36 homers to 1 due to an injury. He was 25 years old.

Most of the greatest drop-offs in power at an early age resulted from injuries, but some of them were just bad years. George Bell in 1988, for example, dropped from 47 homers to 24, aged 28, although he was healthy or at least in the lineup all year. Bell, however, did not have an increase in strikeouts, and he DID have a sharp drop in batting average, so that's not comparable to Wright in any Wrespect.

Adrian Beltre in 2005 dropped from 48 homers to 19, same age as Wright, and his strikeouts increased, but his batting average dropped by 79 points. Johnny Mize had a vaguely similar season in 1941.

I'm trying to get a line on what we should expect from Wright in 2010. We would expect him to recover his power if similar players did recover their power. But since there are no similar players, guesswork will have to do.

Wright probably made inappropriate adjustments to a difficult and complicated situation. Realizing that he was having trouble picking up the ball in Citi Field, he apparently cut down his stroke to try to keep his strikeout rate from exploding. With injuries to all the other good hitters in the lineup, he may have put pressure on himself to carry the team, which could have led to a further degeneration of his strikeout to walk ratio. Most likely these things will straighten out in 2010.

I would guess that David Wright will recover his power stroke, and perhaps even his defense, in 2010 — but there is this difference. Before, we might have projected that his best seasons were still ahead of him. Twenty-five years old in 2008, consistent 30-homer power, extraordinarily well-rounded game; we might have projected 40-homer, MVP seasons yet to come. Now, we're looking for him to get back to where he used to be.

*I would be willing to bet that there is no other player in major league history who had a sudden loss of homers and an increase in strikeouts at an early age, but who continued to hit for the same average as before.*

# New York Yankees

## Key Players

| Pos | Player | G | AB | R | H | 2B | 3B | HR | RBI | SB | CS | BB | SO | AVG | OBP | SLG | OPS | WS |
|---|---|---|---|---|---|---|---|---|---|---|---|---|---|---|---|---|---|---|
| C | Jorge Posada | 111 | 383 | 55 | 109 | 25 | 0 | 22 | 81 | 1 | 0 | 48 | 101 | .285 | .363 | .522 | .885 | 19 |
| 1B | Mark Teixeira | 156 | 609 | 103 | 178 | 43 | 3 | 39 | 122 | 2 | 0 | 81 | 114 | .292 | .383 | .565 | .948 | 26 |
| 2B | Robinson Cano | 161 | 637 | 103 | 204 | 48 | 2 | 25 | 85 | 5 | 7 | 30 | 63 | .320 | .352 | .520 | .871 | 18 |
| 3B | Alex Rodriguez | 124 | 444 | 78 | 127 | 17 | 1 | 30 | 100 | 14 | 2 | 80 | 97 | .286 | .402 | .532 | .933 | 23 |
| SS | Derek Jeter | 153 | 634 | 107 | 212 | 27 | 1 | 18 | 66 | 30 | 5 | 72 | 90 | .334 | .406 | .465 | .871 | 28 |
| LF | Johnny Damon | 143 | 550 | 107 | 155 | 36 | 3 | 24 | 82 | 12 | 0 | 71 | 98 | .282 | .365 | .489 | .854 | 21 |
| CF | Melky Cabrera | 154 | 485 | 66 | 133 | 28 | 1 | 13 | 68 | 10 | 2 | 43 | 59 | .274 | .336 | .416 | .752 | 14 |
| RF | Nick Swisher | 150 | 498 | 84 | 124 | 35 | 1 | 29 | 82 | 0 | 0 | 97 | 126 | .249 | .371 | .498 | .869 | 18 |
| DH | Hideki Matsui | 142 | 456 | 62 | 125 | 21 | 1 | 28 | 90 | 0 | 1 | 64 | 75 | .274 | .367 | .509 | .876 | 18 |

## Key Pitchers

| Pos | Player | G | GS | W | L | SV | IP | H | R | ER | SO | BB | BR/9 | ERA | WS |
|---|---|---|---|---|---|---|---|---|---|---|---|---|---|---|---|
| SP | CC Sabathia | 34 | 34 | 19 | 8 | 0 | 230.0 | 197 | 96 | 86 | 197 | 67 | 10.68 | 3.37 | 18 |
| SP | Andy Pettitte | 32 | 32 | 14 | 8 | 0 | 194.2 | 193 | 101 | 90 | 148 | 76 | 12.62 | 4.16 | 11 |
| SP | A.J. Burnett | 33 | 33 | 13 | 9 | 0 | 207.0 | 193 | 99 | 93 | 195 | 97 | 13.04 | 4.04 | 12 |
| SP | Joba Chamberlain | 32 | 31 | 9 | 6 | 0 | 157.1 | 167 | 94 | 83 | 133 | 76 | 14.59 | 4.75 | 6 |
| SP | Sergio Mitre | 12 | 9 | 3 | 3 | 0 | 51.2 | 71 | 45 | 39 | 32 | 13 | 15.15 | 6.79 | 0 |
| CL | Mariano Rivera | 66 | 0 | 3 | 3 | 44 | 66.1 | 48 | 14 | 13 | 72 | 12 | 8.28 | 1.76 | 15 |
| RP | Phil Coke | 72 | 0 | 4 | 3 | 2 | 60.0 | 44 | 34 | 30 | 49 | 20 | 9.75 | 4.50 | 5 |
| RP | David Robertson | 45 | 0 | 2 | 1 | 1 | 43.2 | 36 | 19 | 16 | 63 | 23 | 12.37 | 3.30 | 3 |

## Thunder at the Top of the Order

The Yankees' 1 to 3 hitters in 2009 scored 365 runs and drove in 307 — both figures were the highest in baseball.

The Red Sox led the majors in runs scored by the heart of the order (4-5-6); the Angels led in RBI by the heart of the order.

The Angels led in runs scored by the bottom of the order, and the Red Sox led in RBI by the bottom of the order.

### Yankees 2009 — Productivity by Batting Order Position

| Pos | Players | Runs | RBI |
|-----|---------|------|-----|
| 1 | Jeter (147 G) | 121 | 73 |
| 2 | Damon (127 G), Swisher (20 G) | 128 | 104 |
| 3 | Teixeira (154 G) | 116 | 130 |
| 4 | Rodriguez (122 G), Matsui (21 G) | 103 | 127 |
| 5 | Matsui (63 G), Cano (50 G), Posada (29 G) | 103 | 101 |
| 6 | Posada (59 G), Swisher (46 G), Cano (45 G) | 94 | 103 |
| 7 | Cano (61 G), Cabrera (34 G), Matsui (27 G) | 90 | 92 |
| 8 | Cabrera (57 G), Swisher (29 G) | 84 | 82 |
| 9 | Molina (37 G), Gardner (32 G), Cabrera (31 G) | 76 | 69 |
| | **Total** | **915** | **881** |

## Fortunately, a Limited Sample

The Yankees were just 12-23 in games in which they did not hit a home run. Their winning percentage without a homer was basically the same as the Mets'; it's just that the Mets played 92 games without hitting a home run.

### New York Yankees — 2009 Record by Home Runs

| Home Runs | W-L |
|-----------|-----|
| 0 homers | 12-23 |
| 1 homer | 34-19 |
| 2 homers | 35-10 |
| 3 or more | 22-7 |

## The Durability of Yankee Starters

The Yankees led the American League with 139 starts by their first five starters.

### 2009 Starts Made by First Five Starters — American League

| Team | Apr | May | June | July | Aug | Sept | Total |
|------|-----|-----|------|------|-----|------|-------|
| Yankees | 21 | 22 | 26 | 23 | 23 | 24 | 139 |
| Rays | 23 | 28 | 21 | 19 | 22 | 20 | 133 |
| Tigers | 21 | 24 | 22 | 18 | 22 | 22 | 129 |
| White Sox | 21 | 24 | 22 | 21 | 24 | 16 | 128 |
| Red Sox | 20 | 25 | 24 | 17 | 16 | 19 | 121 |
| Athletics | 19 | 24 | 20 | 17 | 12 | 13 | 105 |
| Blue Jays | 19 | 13 | 13 | 12 | 15 | 24 | 96 |
| Twins | 19 | 22 | 18 | 15 | 10 | 7 | 91 |
| Mariners | 19 | 17 | 12 | 17 | 12 | 13 | 90 |
| Royals | 20 | 19 | 14 | 11 | 15 | 9 | 88 |
| Rangers | 20 | 20 | 14 | 8 | 6 | 11 | 79 |
| Indians | 19 | 23 | 12 | 10 | 6 | 6 | 76 |
| Angels | 17 | 13 | 11 | 11 | 10 | 12 | 74 |
| Orioles | 20 | 17 | 8 | 5 | 6 | 10 | 66 |

## A.J. Burnett Curveballs

A.J. Burnett threw more curveballs (1,067) than the entire pitching staffs of the Cubs (963) and Indians (508).

### A.J. Burnett — 2009 Pitch Type Analysis

| | vs. RHB | | vs. LHB | | Overall | |
|------|------|------|------|------|------|------|
| Outs Recorded | 275 | | 346 | | | |
| Fastball | 1,118 | 70% | 1,152 | 62% | 2,270 | 66% |
| Curveball | 464 | 29% | 605 | 33% | 1,069 | 31% |
| Changeup | 11 | 1% | 96 | 5% | 107 | 3% |
| Slider | 2 | 0% | 0 | 0% | 2 | 0% |
| Not Charted | 9 | 1% | 7 | 0% | 16 | 0% |
| **Total Pitches** | **1,604** | | **1,860** | | **3,464** | |

## The New Cutter

Phil Hughes was a much different pitcher this year, pitching out of the bullpen, than he was last year as a starter. Part of the reason for his success was the development of a cutter. This year, Hughes threw a cutter for 16% of his pitches as opposed to not throwing a single cutter last season, and opponents' batting average against Hughes went from .314 to .217. Hanging out with Mariano Rivera has its benefits.

### Phil Hughes — Pitch Type Analysis

| 2008 | vs. RHB | | vs. LHB | | Overall | |
|---|---|---|---|---|---|---|
| Outs Recorded | 60 | | 42 | | | |
| Fastball | 208 | 63% | 177 | 59% | 385 | 61% |
| Curveball | 73 | 22% | 68 | 23% | 141 | 22% |
| Changeup | 1 | 0% | 32 | 11% | 33 | 5% |
| Slider | 40 | 12% | 18 | 6% | 58 | 9% |
| Pitchout | 4 | 1% | 0 | 0% | 4 | 1% |
| Not Charted | 6 | 2% | 3 | 1% | 9 | 1% |
| Total | 332 | | 298 | | 630 | |

| 2009 | vs. RHB | | vs. LHB | | Overall | |
|---|---|---|---|---|---|---|
| Outs Recorded | 145 | | 113 | | | |
| Fastball | 438 | 59% | 470 | 66% | 908 | 62% |
| Curveball | 137 | 18% | 161 | 23% | 298 | 20% |
| Changeup | 0 | 0% | 8 | 1% | 8 | 1% |
| Cut Fastball | 167 | 22% | 66 | 9% | 233 | 16% |
| Not Charted | 3 | 0% | 9 | 1% | 12 | 1% |
| Total | 745 | | 714 | | 1,459 | |

## Jeter's Defense

Derek Jeter was recognized as having improved defensively in 2009. If you look at his plus/minus numbers, he was virtually the same player in 2008 as he was in 2009 on balls hit right to him (+9 to +6) and balls to his left (-1 to +2). The big improvement came on balls hit in the hole, where Jeter improved 15 plays, from -18 to -3.

### Derek Jeter — 2009 Fielding Bible Plus/Minus

| Year | Inn | Outs Made | To his Right | Straight On | To His Left | GB | Air | Total | Runs Saved | Rank |
|---|---|---|---|---|---|---|---|---|---|---|
| 2004 | 1341.2 | 456 | -24 | +5 | -5 | -25 | +9 | -16 | -12 | 32 |
| 2005 | 1352.2 | 526 | -18 | +3 | -25 | -39 | +5 | -34 | -26 | 34 |
| 2006 | 1292.1 | 450 | -10 | +1 | -10 | -19 | -3 | -22 | -17 | 34 |
| 2007 | 1318.1 | 420 | -14 | -6 | -14 | -33 | -1 | -34 | -26 | 34 |
| 2008 | 1258.2 | 430 | -18 | +9 | -1 | -10 | -1 | -11 | -8 | 31 |
| 2009 | 1260.2 | 398 | -3 | +6 | +2 | +5 | +1 | +6 | 5 | 14 |

## Gardner's Great Patience

Brett Gardner took 66% of the pitches he saw in 2009, trailing the major league leader (Bobby Abreu) by only two percent.  It didn't work great for him, in part perhaps because he was a rookie, and rookies sometimes don't get the corners called in their favor.  In the minors, though, Gardner did have very high walk rates.  I would suspect that, in his second season, Gardner might get more calls, and his walk rate might go way up.

On the other hand, with the Yankees trading for Granderson, we may never know.

**Brett Gardner — 2009 Pitch Analysis**

**Overall**

| | | |
|---|---|---|
| Pitches Seen | 1149 | |
| Taken | 753 | 66% |
| Swung At | 396 | 34% |

**Pitches Taken**

| | | |
|---|---|---|
| Taken for a Strike | 319 | 42% |
| Called a ball | 434 | 58% |

**Pitches Taken by Pitch Location**

| | | |
|---|---|---|
| In Strike Zone | 319 | 43% |
| High | 78 | 10% |
| Low | 154 | 21% |
| Inside | 58 | 8% |
| Outside | 141 | 19% |

**Swung At**

| | | |
|---|---|---|
| Missed | 47 | 12% |
| Fouled Off | 134 | 34% |
| Put in Play | 215 | 54% |

**Swung At by Pitch Location**

| | | |
|---|---|---|
| In Strike Zone | 296 | 75% |
| High | 19 | 5% |
| Low | 23 | 6% |
| Inside | 22 | 6% |
| Outside | 35 | 9% |

## The Javier Vazquez Saga

Who in the majors has had a more interesting career than Javier Vazquez? In the decade we have just finished, the first decade of the 21st century, only three major league pitchers pitched 2,000 innings: Mark Buehrle, Livan Hernandez and Javier Vazquez.

Only two pitchers in those ten years struck out 2,000 batters. Randy Johnson, Javier Vazquez.

Vazquez' strikeout to walk ratio, in those ten years, was 3.79 to 1, which is outstanding. Among the 105 pitchers who pitched 1,000 or more innings over the decade, Vazquez' strikeout to walk ratio was the 11th best.

And yet, despite these accomplishments, on some level Vazquez has always been perceived as a failure. Not early in the decade; early in the decade, pitching for the old Montreal Expos, Vazquez was regarded by insiders as a hidden star. Nobody was going to the Expos' games then, expectations were low, Vazquez won 16 games in 2001. Life was good. He was the Felix Hernandez of 2001. In 2003 Vazquez struck out 241 batters, walked only 57, and was traded to the Yankees.

Expectations skyrocketed. Cy Young, man; he's Cy Young. He'll win 20 easy. The first half of the season he pitched well, made the All-Star team, pitched a 1-2-3 inning in the All-Star game with two strikeouts.

Then things fell apart. He had ERAs of 6.61 in July, 7.43 in August, 6.29 in September, and 9.53 in the post-season. People started to say that he couldn't handle New York, he couldn't handle the pennant race, couldn't handle the pressure. His reputation was ruined.

He became a journeyman. He spent a year in Arizona, had a losing record. He moved on to the White Sox, the defending World Champions at that time. He had a losing record. He had a good year in 2007, but followed it up with another bad one in 2008: 12-16, 4.67 ERA. What up with that, dude? You're better than that.

The strikeout to walk ratios remained great, but the other stuff never caught up. Why?

*People started to say that he couldn't handle New York, he couldn't handle the pennant race, couldn't handle the pressure. His reputation was ruined.*

With Atlanta in 2009 Vazquez had the best year he has had yet: 15-10, 2.87 ERA, basically the same strikeout to walk ratio as Zack Greinke. OK, a little better than Greinke. Greinke was 242-51; Vazquez was 238-44.

What do we say about this? Has he finally turned the corner? Has he finally matured?

What the talk show hosts still say is that he can't handle pressure. He had a good year in Atlanta; cool. The Braves weren't really in the pennant race.

A more tolerant explanation is: the changeup. When you see a pitcher with a great strikeout to walk ratio but numbers not as good across the board, what you normally find is a changeup; sometimes a slow curve, but normally a changeup. The changeup is the pitch that gets both strikeouts and hard contact — strikeouts from the batters who don't read it, hard contact from those who do.

Vazquez is an unusual pitcher, in that he does throw a lot of changeups, and he does have a deep pitch mix. He's been throwing about 20% changeups as long as we've been charting it, sometimes as high as 23-24%. Last year the number was down to 13%.

Whether he has been getting beat with the changeup and has finally figured this out. . .I don't know. It's possible. 23% changeups is a huge number. It's not like he doesn't have other pitches. He throws both a slider and a curve, and they are distinct pitches. He threw each of them over 500 times last year. There aren't many pitchers who throw 500 curves AND 500 sliders in a season.

For the decade as a whole Vazquez was "just" 128-116, but he was also "just" 98 runs better than the league average ERA, without park adjustments. The ERA and the won-lost record actually do match up, within a few games anyway.

Is it too late for Vazquez to stick it up his critics' you-know-what? No, it is not. He was 32 years old in

2009. His career record is 142-139. At the same age, Gaylord Perry's career record was 134-109, Luis Tiant was 118-93, Randy Johnson was 104-64, Curt Schilling was 99-83, Phil Niekro was 81-72, David Wells was 79-61, and Mike Cuellar was 65-52. Jamie Moyer was 59-76. Warren Spahn had 145 wins at the same age. Vazquez has more wins at that age than Bob Lemon, Jim Bunning, Joe McGinnity, Red Faber or Jesse Haines, all of whom are in the Hall of Fame.

I would never say that Vazquez couldn't handle the pressure, because I don't believe in making judgments about players' character based on their on-field performance. If it is said that Vazquez has gone a long time without ever really succeeding, it must also be said that he has gone a long time without ever really failing. He could have ten more years ahead of him. If he pitches the way he did last year, the October sun will surely shine in his face once more.

### Chien-Ming Wang – Ground Ball Pitcher

One of the unanswered riddles of baseball is why there are so few successful ground ball pitchers. As you may know, those of us in sabermetrics are suspicious of successful pitchers who don't record strikeouts. Low-strikeout pitchers simply don't succeed, season to season.

In any season there will be a handful of pitchers who pitch very well despite low strikeout totals. In 2009 this group included David Huff, Matt Palmer, Rick Porcello, Joel Pineiro and Scott Feldman. These are, in general, ground ball pitchers.

And, in general, all of them are going to implode sometime in the next two years.

There are also a few pitchers who get both strikeouts and ground balls, like Roy Halladay and Felix Hernandez. That's not what I'm talking about; those guys are great. I'm talking about ... well, Chien-Ming Wang and Fausto Carmona.

Chien-Ming Wang won 19 games in 2006 with only 76 strikeouts, and 19 games in 2007 with only 104 strikeouts. These are very unusual ratios, and ordinarily we would predict that a pitcher with that kind of ratio would have difficulty sustaining his success.

Oh, but Chien-Ming Wang is going to be an exception, because he gets so many ground balls. He's a wonderfully-conditioned athlete, and he throws that tremendous sinker that gets quick outs. Fausto Carmona is going to be an exception, because he's tremendously strong and he throws hard sinkers that are impossible to get into the air. Rick Porcello is going to be an exception, and Joel Pineiro is going to be an exception, and Matt Palmer is going to be an exception.

No, he's not. There are *some* successful ground ball pitchers with relatively low strikeout rates — a few. Derek Lowe has had a very nice career living off the ground ball, and Mark Buehrle has. Tim Hudson was good for several years living off the ground ball, and Brandon Webb was, although Hudson and Webb were more in the Roy Halladay mold than the Derek Lowe mold. But there are a few.

What I have never understood is why there aren't more of them. The fact is that the overwhelming majority of the pitchers who are consistently successful — the Andy Pettitte's, Josh Becketts, Johan Santanas, Roger Clemenses, CC Sabathias, Tim Lincecums and Pedro Martinezes — the overwhelming majority of them are *not* ground ball pitchers. The great majority of pitchers who have a good year living off the ground ball *will* self-destruct within two years. As far as I know, no one can explain why that is true.

# The Right Place for an RBI Man

by Bill James

HOW OFTEN DOES THE PLAYER WHO LEADS THE LEAGUE IN RBI do so simply because he has the most at-bats with runners in scoring position? And, extending the issue…since we know the league leader in RBI is often the MVP, how often does it happen that somebody wins the MVP Award, in essence, simply because he has more RBI opportunities than anybody else?

Due to the miracle of Retrosheet we can actually study this now. Retrosheet has play by play, occasionally missing a plate appearance, for both leagues back to 1954 and for the National League in 1953. That gives us 111 leagues to look at — both leagues 1954-2008, plus 1953 in the National.

*80% of the time, the player who leads the league in at-bats with runners in scoring position does not lead the league in RBI.*

In 2004, the league leaders in RBI were Miguel Tejada (150) and Vinny Castilla (131). The league leaders in at-bats with runners in scoring position were Miguel Tejada (208) and Vinny Castilla (203). This also happened in 1965. In 1965 the league leaders in RBI were Deron Johnson (130) and Rocky Colavito (108). The league leaders in at-bats with runners in scoring position were Deron Johnson (180) and Rocky Colavito (171).

The real answer, though, is that it happens less often than I would have guessed. Since 1953 there have been 22 players who led the league both in RBI and at-bats with runners in scoring position. Thus, 80% of the time, the player who leads the league in at-bats with runners in scoring position does *not* lead the league in RBI.

In fact, over half the time the player who leads the league in RBI does not finish among the top four in the league in at-bats with runners in scoring position. I count 50 times since 1953 that the league leader in RBI has been among the top four in at-bats with runners in scoring position, but 61 times that he has not, or 45%. This is a little bit artificially high because of ties…ties in who leads the league in RBI, ties in who leads the league in at-bats with runners in scoring position.

Occasionally two players tie for the league lead in RBI, and if *either* of them was in the top four in the league in RBI, I counted it as an occurrence. I would have assumed that if two players tied for the league lead in RBI one of them would have to be among the league leaders in the other category, but not so. In 1995, for example, Albert Belle and Mo Vaughn (founder of MoVaughn.org) tied for the American League lead in RBI with 126, although neither of them was among the league leaders in at-bats with runners in scoring position.

### MVP Consideration

And as to the other thing — winning the MVP Award because you have a huge number of at-bats with runners in scoring position — that basically never happens. There is only one time since 1953 that you can make an argument that this happened. There are only six times since 1953 that the player who led the league in at-bats with runners in scoring position has won the MVP Award, and five of them are pretty legit:

• Henry Aaron led the league in at-bats with runners in scoring position in 1957 (156), but he hit .322 with 44 homers, 132 RBI, and it's really hard to argue with his MVP selection.

• Roberto Clemente led the NL in at-bats with runners in scoring position in 1966 (163), and this did help him win the MVP Award in one of the rare seasons that he *didn't* lead the league in hitting, but again, it's hard to argue that the RBI opportunities made him the MVP. I probably wouldn't have voted for Clemente as the MVP, but his at-bats with runners in scoring position weren't that large (163), and, given his defensive skills and the fact that two or three of the nation's leading sportswriters had been lobbying to get him an MVP Award for several years before then, I don't think you can draw a strong line between the two.

• Joe Torre led the NL in at-bats with runners in scoring position in 1971 (190) and did win the MVP Award, but then, Torre hit .363 and had 230 hits, so it's not really a questionable MVP Award, although Willie Stargell also had a great year.

*The one player who probably did get an MVP Award in large measure because of an unusual number of at-bats with runners in scoring position was Don Baylor in 1979.*

• George Foster led the NL in at-bats with runners in scoring position in 1977 (197), and did win the MVP, but again, appears to be the legitimate MVP. He hit .320, and his 52 homers and 149 RBI were both the highest totals in the major leagues between 1966 and 1995. He would obviously have led the league in RBI even had he not led in at bats with runners in scoring position.

• A-Rod led the American League in at-bats with runners in scoring position in 2005 (186), and did win the MVP Award, but again, it's not an especially questionable selection. And it's impossible to argue that leading the league in at-bats with runners in scoring position that one year manufactured A-Rod's aura.

The one player who probably did get an MVP Award in large measure because of an unusual number of at-bats with runners in scoring position was Don Baylor in 1979. Baylor led the league in at-bats with runners in scoring position with one of the highest totals ever, 215, and drove in 139 runs in part because of that. Baylor was a player who was well liked by the press and perceived as a leader and a winner, even before the MVP Award, but he was also a halftime outfielder/halftime DH. He couldn't throw, and he wasn't a great outfielder when he could throw, and he wasn't the best hitter in the league even in 1979, which was his best year. It is unlikely that he would have been an MVP contender had he not had an unusual number of RBI opportunities.

Here's a story about Baylor, though the story is told in anecdotal form without references, so dock me three points for accuracy. When Baylor was a rookie in 1972 he was struggling, and, on the advice of a coach, he cut down his stroke to try to make better contact. Earl Weaver immediately pulled him aside and told him not to do that. "You're going to be the American League MVP in 1978," Weaver told him, "and I don't want you up there slapping at the ball." Weaver missed his MVP season by one year.

Anyway, other than Aaron, Clemente, Torre, Foster, A-Rod and Baylor, no one has ever led the league in at-bats with runners in scoring position and also won the MVP Award. I'm surprised that there isn't more of a connection.

## Most Chances and Best Ever

If my notes are correct, the highest number of at-bats with runners in scoring position on record is 218, by Derek Bell in the National League in 1996. Bell hit .263 with 17 homers, 113 RBI, but still missed leading the league in RBI by 37.

Not a lot of players have gotten to hit 200 times in a season with runners in scoring position. In the first 20 years of the data, 1953-1973, the only player to bat 200 times in the situation was Tommy Davis in 1962, the year Maury Wills stole 104 bases and Davis hit .346 with 27 homers, 153 RBI. Davis had 213. Since 1974 this situation has been more common, but still, no one has batted more than 200 times with runners in scoring position since 2004. Castilla, Tejada and Miguel Cabrera were all over 200 in 2004, though. I believe Baylor's 215 is the highest known total in the American League.

Frank Malzone had fantastic numbers of at-bats with runners in scoring position the first half of his career. Malzone led the majors in at-bats with runners in scoring position in 1957, his first year as a regular, with 176, and also hit .347 with runners in scoring position. He led the majors again in 1958, with 181 — he led the majors by a whopping 30 — and he again hit .320 with runners in scoring position. He led the American league in at-bats with runners in scoring position in 1959 (170), led the majors again in 1960 (172), and finished second in the American League in 1961 (157), and third in 1962 (165).

He stopped hitting notably well with runners in scoring position after the first two years, though, (.347, .320, .253, .250, .293, .291, .293, career average of .290). The question is why Malzone, among all players in history, would have such remarkable at-bat totals with runners in scoring position.

Part of it is doubles. The Red Sox in that era almost always led the league in doubles. But I wonder if, after Malzone hit so well with runners in scoring position in 1957, his first year, the Red Sox didn't start bunting to get him to the plate with men in scoring position, perhaps actually believing that he became a better hitter in RBI situations?

*There is more randomness than I would have expected in who finishes at (and near) the top of the league in at-bats with runners in scoring position.*

The NL equivalent to Malzone was Kenny Boyer. Boyer was a similar player to Malzone, except that he had a little more power (and was also a step quicker as a young player, but that may be just that he got to the majors at a younger age.) Anyway, similar players, but Boyer was better.

Boyer led the majors in at-bats, runners in scoring position in 1956 (173), led the National League in 1958 (151), finished second in the National League in 1959 (163), tied for second in 1961 (160), fourth in 1962 (169), led again in 1963 (181), and missed by one of leading the league in 1964, his MVP year, when he had a career-high 193 at-bats with runners in scoring position, and a career-high 119 RBI.

Brooks Robinson, another similar player, also has very high totals. He led the American League in 1962 (178), finished third in 1964 (165), led again in 1971 (172), and is near the league lead in some other seasons.

### (Lack of) Conclusion

In general, however, there is more randomness than I would have expected in who finishes at (and near) the top of the league in at-bats with runners in scoring position. Obviously there are predictable elements. You need to be a middle-of-the-order hitter who stays healthy to lead the league in this category, and it helps if you bat behind a base stealer. If you are *too* good a hitter — Mickey Mantle or Barry Bonds — you may lead the league in plate appearances with runners in scoring position, but not at-bats, because of walks. But a lot of it doesn't make intuitive sense, and appears to be just random. Quite a few players from not-very-good teams with not-very-good offenses have led the league in at-bats with runners in scoring position. Bill Mazeroski led the National League in 1967. Bob Oliver of the expansion Royals led the American League in 1970 — and led again in 1972, when he was playing for the Angels. Butch Wynegar led his league in 1977; Enos Cabell in 1979; Willie Upshaw in 1984; Keith Moreland and Julio Franco in 1985; Nick Esasky in 1989. Ron Gant and Benito Santiago tied for the National League lead in 1991.

Todd Zeile led his league in 1993; J. T. Snow in 1995; Derek Bell set the all-time record in 1996. Players from the Kansas City Royals led the American League in 1998 and 2000 (different players). Preston Wilson led the National League in 2000 and 2003; Ryan Zimmerman of the Nationals led the NL in 2006. It's not always the people you would expect.

Don Mattingly, although I have tended to diminish his RBI counts as being created by hitting behind Rickey Henderson, actually never led his league in at-bats with runners in scoring position. Steve Garvey led only once, which ties him with Bobby Tolan; Tolan led the National League in 1972. He hit .283 with 8 homers that year, and hit .236 with runners in scoring position — 47 for 199.

In 1957, when he first led the American League in this category, Frank Malzone batted all over the lineup — 15 games batting leadoff, 26 games batting second, 31 batting cleanup, 15 batting fifth, 65 batting sixth, and one batting seventh. His high at-bat total with runners in scoring position can't be a function of his position in the batting order, because he didn't really have one.

On the other side of this issue is Willie Mays. Mays had 84 at-bats with runners in scoring position in 1956, and 79 (!!) in 1957. How do you construct your lineup so badly that you're getting Willie Mays 80 at-bats a year with runners in scoring position?

In 1956, Johnny Temple was a leadoff man who batted 436 times with the bases empty — but still had 117 at-bats with runners in scoring position. He had 113 more in 1957. Who would have guessed that, in 1956 and 1957, Johnny Temple was batting far more times with runners in scoring position than Willie Mays was? And it's not walks…even if you added in Mays' walks with runners in scoring position, he still wouldn't have caught Temple.

This may be a function of the fact that Temple was batting leadoff, and the pitchers usually bunted when there was a man on first. Mays never led the league in at-bats with runners in scoring position, nor did

*How do you construct your lineup so badly that you're getting Willie Mays 80 at-bats a year with runners in scoring position?*

Mantle. For his career, as much as has been documented by Retrosheet, 23.4% of Mays' plate appearances were with runners in scoring position; 24.4% for Mantle…as opposed to 27.5% for Malzone; 28.1% for Ken Boyer; and 27.7% for Brooks Robinson.

### "Scoring Position"

About three or four years ago…I probably shouldn't do things like this from memory, but I am unable to locate my research, so what the hell. Three or four years ago, when SABR was providing searchable access to millions of old newspaper files, I tried to work out the origin of the phrase "in scoring position", which somebody had suggested was a 1970s phrase. I knew that wasn't right because I remember it from when I became a baseball fan.

I concluded that the phrase was originated or popularized by a Chicago sportswriter about 100 years ago; I believe it was Warren Brown, although I couldn't swear to that. Of the first 25 instances in which I could find this phrase being used, this one sportswriter was using it — and in different publications — about 15 to 20 times.

But in the first 40 years of its use, the expression was used with almost equal frequency in different sports. I found hundreds of examples of the phrase "in scoring position" being used in reporting on basketball, football, hockey, tennis, golf, bowling, wrestling, automobile racing and — with surprising frequency — polo. I found it used in basically every sport, including those which don't exactly "score", like foot races.

After World War II — about 1948 to 1958 — the phrase became an exclusively baseball expression. I suspect that it settled into baseball because, in baseball, the phrase had a definite and specific meaning, whereas in the other sports its use was somewhat ill-defined. When exactly is a basketball player "in scoring position"? One can't say…or one can say when he is in scoring position, but not necessarily when he *isn't*. I think this caused the expression to be gradually taken over by baseball.

# Oakland Athletics

## Key Players

| Pos | Player | G | AB | R | H | 2B | 3B | HR | RBI | SB | CS | BB | SO | AVG | OBP | SLG | OPS | WS |
|---|---|---|---|---|---|---|---|---|---|---|---|---|---|---|---|---|---|---|
| C | Kurt Suzuki | 147 | 570 | 74 | 156 | 37 | 1 | 15 | 88 | 8 | 2 | 28 | 59 | .274 | .313 | .421 | .734 | 17 |
| 1B | Jason Giambi | 83 | 269 | 39 | 52 | 13 | 0 | 11 | 40 | 0 | 0 | 50 | 72 | .193 | .332 | .364 | .697 | 5 |
| 2B | Mark Ellis | 105 | 377 | 52 | 99 | 23 | 0 | 10 | 61 | 10 | 3 | 23 | 54 | .263 | .305 | .403 | .708 | 11 |
| 3B | Adam Kennedy | 129 | 529 | 65 | 153 | 29 | 1 | 11 | 63 | 20 | 6 | 45 | 86 | .289 | .348 | .410 | .758 | 18 |
| SS | Orlando Cabrera | 101 | 414 | 41 | 116 | 23 | 0 | 4 | 41 | 11 | 4 | 25 | 39 | .280 | .318 | .365 | .683 | 9 |
| LF | Matt Holliday | 93 | 346 | 52 | 99 | 23 | 1 | 11 | 54 | 12 | 3 | 46 | 58 | .286 | .378 | .454 | .831 | 12 |
| CF | Rajai Davis | 125 | 390 | 65 | 119 | 27 | 5 | 3 | 48 | 41 | 12 | 29 | 70 | .305 | .360 | .423 | .784 | 13 |
| RF | Ryan Sweeney | 134 | 484 | 68 | 142 | 31 | 3 | 6 | 53 | 6 | 5 | 40 | 67 | .293 | .348 | .407 | .755 | 12 |
| DH | Jack Cust | 149 | 513 | 88 | 123 | 16 | 0 | 25 | 70 | 4 | 1 | 93 | 185 | .240 | .356 | .417 | .773 | 14 |

## Key Pitchers

| Pos | Player | G | GS | W | L | SV | IP | H | R | ER | SO | BB | BR/9 | ERA | WS |
|---|---|---|---|---|---|---|---|---|---|---|---|---|---|---|---|
| SP | Brett Anderson | 30 | 30 | 11 | 11 | 0 | 175.1 | 180 | 94 | 79 | 150 | 45 | 11.70 | 4.06 | 8 |
| SP | Trevor Cahill | 32 | 32 | 10 | 13 | 0 | 178.2 | 185 | 99 | 92 | 90 | 72 | 13.15 | 4.63 | 7 |
| SP | Dallas Braden | 22 | 22 | 8 | 9 | 0 | 136.2 | 144 | 63 | 59 | 81 | 42 | 12.38 | 3.89 | 8 |
| SP | Gio Gonzalez | 20 | 17 | 6 | 7 | 0 | 98.2 | 113 | 68 | 63 | 109 | 56 | 15.51 | 5.75 | 2 |
| SP | Vin Mazzaro | 17 | 17 | 4 | 9 | 0 | 91.1 | 120 | 61 | 54 | 59 | 39 | 16.06 | 5.32 | 2 |
| CL | Andrew Bailey | 68 | 0 | 6 | 3 | 26 | 83.1 | 49 | 17 | 17 | 91 | 24 | 7.88 | 1.84 | 17 |
| RP | Mike Wuertz | 74 | 0 | 6 | 1 | 4 | 78.2 | 52 | 25 | 23 | 102 | 23 | 8.58 | 2.63 | 10 |
| RP | Brad Ziegler | 69 | 0 | 2 | 4 | 7 | 73.1 | 82 | 27 | 25 | 54 | 28 | 13.62 | 3.07 | 7 |

## Pitch to Them

The Oakland A's, as a team, were issued only 16 intentional walks in 2009. That's not very many. Barry Bonds, as an individual, was issued 18 intentional walks in 2004 — in April. He drew 18 more in May, 23 in June, etc.; for the season Bonds drew 120 intentional walks, 47 clear and 73 cream. Of course, Barry Bonds is an exception to normalcy, and at that point probably had a better chance of winning the Kentucky Derby than of being allowed to bat in a game situation, but in any case, 16 intentional walks was the lowest total for a team since the 1981 White Sox, who also drew 16. But that was a strike-shortened season; the White Sox played only 106 games. The last team to draw as few as 16 intentional walks in a real season was the 1961 Kansas City A's.

## Costly Defense

In 2008 Oakland was the best defensive team in the American League by our measurements, totaling 64 Runs Saved versus an average defensive team. In 2009 they fell off to -15 Runs Saved — the largest defensive decline in baseball. Orlando Cabrera had a horrible defensive season. According to Runs Saved, Cabrera cost the A's 20 runs compared to an average shortstop. Add in his time with Minnesota, and Cabrera (at -33 Runs Saved) had the worst defensive season of any major league player dating back to 2003.

**Defensive Runs Saved – Oakland 2008-2009**

| Year | P | C | 1B | 2B | 3B | SS | LF | CF | RF | Total |
|------|---|---|----|----|----|----|----|----|----|-------|
| 2008 | 14 | 5 | 6 | 23 | 10 | -17 | -9 | 17 | 15 | 64 |
| 2009 | 1 | 2 | -8 | -10 | -7 | -32 | 19 | 12 | 8 | -15 |

## Struggling with Control

Trevor Cahill had the worst strikeout-to-walk ratio of any major league starting pitcher in 2009: 90 to 72. (Minimum, 162 innings.)

### Wuertz Best

With Andrew Bailey holding the closer duties, former Cub Michael Wuertz moved into the setup role, where he had the best season of his career and quietly became one of the most dominant relievers in baseball. Wuertz was one of three relievers to rack up 100 strikeouts, the other two being closers. The A's rewarded Wuertz with a multi-year deal before the 2010 season.

### Starting Off on the Right Foot

Andrew Bailey became the second reliever ever to make the All-Star team and win the Rookie of the Year in the same season. The other was Scott Williamson of the 1999 Reds.

### Home Run Drought

The A's allowed the fewest home runs in the American League in 2009, with 156. Unfortunately, they also hit the fewest home runs in the American League, with 135. It's not really a park factor; they probably would have hit and allowed only about five more home runs in another park.

### Young Arms

The 2009 A's had the youngest pitching staff in the major leagues. The average 2009 age of an Oakland pitcher, weighted by innings pitched, was 25.3 years.

## Top of the Order Pop Guns

The weakest two positions in Oakland's lineup were the leadoff spot — OPS, .687 — and the three spot — OPS, .683. The .683 OPS of their #3 hitters was the worst in baseball. Even their 7th, 8th and 9th place hitters did better:

| Pos | AB | R | H | 2B | 3B | HR | RBI | BB | SO | GDP | SB | CS | AVG | OBP | SLG |
|-----|-----|----|-----|----|----|----|-----|----|-----|-----|----|----|------|------|------|
| 1st | 695 | 89 | 186 | 37 | 1 | 10 | 65 | 54 | 110 | 19 | 23 | 7 | .268 | .321 | .367 |
| 2nd | 676 | 96 | 202 | 41 | 2 | 13 | 75 | 43 | 94 | 15 | 38 | 10 | .299 | .345 | .423 |
| 3rd | 645 | 96 | 153 | 32 | 2 | 17 | 88 | 66 | 123 | 14 | 13 | 2 | .237 | .311 | .372 |

It wasn't really a matter of having their worst hitters at those positions. It was more an issue of whoever they hit there, didn't hit. Kurt Suzuki hit .221 when he hit third, .287 when he didn't.

## How to Gain 16 Games Without Really Trying

The A's in 2009 scored 759 runs and allowed 761, which should have made them a .500 team. Their timing was a little off. The A's scored seven runs in a game 17 times in 2009 (exactly 7 runs, not 7 or more), which was the most of any team in baseball — but lost seven of those games.

Seattle — with whom the A's hope to be competing in 2010 — was outscored by 52 runs, but won 85 games. If those ratios return to normal, which they almost always do, Oakland gains 16 games versus Seattle, with nothing else changing.

### Oakland Athletics — 2009 Record by Runs Scored and Allowed

| | Scored | Allowed |
|-----------|--------|---------|
| 10 runs+ | 9-0 | 2-11 |
| 9 runs | 10-1 | 0-4 |
| 8 runs | 6-1 | 1-12 |
| 7 runs | 10-7 | 0-7 |
| 6 runs | 12-2 | 2-14 |
| 5 runs | 11-6 | 8-16 |
| 4 runs | 8-10 | 12-9 |
| 3 runs | 7-16 | 14-10 |
| 2 runs | 2-23 | 14-1 |
| 1 run | 0-12 | 12-3 |
| 0 runs | 0-9 | 10-0 |
| **Total** | **75-87** | **75-87** |

## Brett's Change

Brett Anderson in 2009 threw 237 changeups — NONE of them to a left-handed hitter.

**Brett Anderson — 2009 Pitch Type Analysis**

| Overall | | |
| --- | --- | --- |
| Total Pitches | 2,816 | |
| Fastball | 1467 | 52% |
| Curveball | 187 | 7% |
| Changeup | 237 | 8% |
| Slider | 896 | 32% |
| Not Charted | 29 | 1% |

| | vs. RHB | | vs. LHB | |
| --- | --- | --- | --- | --- |
| Total Pitches | 2,073 | | 743 | |
| Outs Recorded | 393 | | 133 | |
| Fastball | 1,037 | 50% | 430 | 58% |
| Curveball | 160 | 8% | 27 | 4% |
| Changeup | 237 | 11% | 0 | 0% |
| Slider | 622 | 30% | 274 | 37% |
| Not Charted | 17 | 1% | 12 | 2% |

## Oakland's Best Player in 2009

Who led the Oakland A's in Win Shares in 2009? Andrew Bailey with his 26 saves and 1.84 ERA? Nope, he had 17 Win Shares. Jack Cust and his 25 home runs? No, only 14 Win Shares. Matt Holliday before he left? Only 12 Win Shares. It was third baseman Adam Kennedy with 18 Win Shares, the lowest team-leading Win Share total in baseball in 2009 (tied with Paul Konerko of the White Sox and Andrew McCutchen of the Pirates).

## Team Runs Scored and Allowed

The A's allowed 761 runs in 2009, their highest team total since 2000 (when they allowed 813). The 2000 A's, however, were carried by an offense that produced 947 runs en route to winning 91 games and the AL West. By comparison, the 2009 team scored only 759 and finished 22 games out of first.

# *Whiff 7*

by Bill James

IN THE NATIONAL LEAGUE IN 2009, FOR THE FIRST TIME in history, there were more than seven strikeouts per nine innings pitched. Prior to 2009 the record for a league was 6.99, by the National in 2001 and again in 2008. All hail Mark Reynolds; we've shattered the seven-strikeout barrier. The magic seven.

In the first year of the National League (1876) the league averaged 1.12 strikeouts per nine innings. In the 133 years since then the strikeout average has gone up 73 years, down 60. The average gains are slightly larger (0.26) than the average losses (0.21). In the American League the data is similar. Since 1901 the league strikeout rate has gone up 61 times, and down 47 times, with the gains being slightly larger than the losses.

*Expanding the strike zone is exactly what baseball does not need.*

In recent years these increases have been larger than normal. In both leagues, the league ERA in 2009 was about the same as it was in 2005. But in the American League in those years, the strikeout rate has increased from 6.16 to 6.86. In the National League, it has increased from 6.57 to 7.09.

Strikeout rates have increased in the majors in every decade since 1920, except for the 1970s. The first league to average 5.00 strikeouts per nine innings was the National League in 1958; the first to average 6.00 was the American League in 1964. Strikeout rates went down in the 1970s — but they went up in the 1960s more than twice as much as they went down in the 1970s, so that the 1970s rate was still much higher than the 1950s. In the 1980s the major league strikeout rate was 5.38 per nine innings. In the 1990s it was 6.18, and, in the decade just completed, 6.63.

We have here a trend line which

a) Has been in motion for 130-plus years, and

b) Has tremendous momentum at the present time.

Such a trend is not likely to stop suddenly. I think we have to expect strikeout rates in the next ten years to average over 7.00 per nine innings, and there is a very real possibility that, by the end of the coming decade, we may be near 8.00.

Why does the strikeout rate always go up? Essentially for this reason: If you look at pitchers, strikeout pitchers are successful. Strikeout pitchers are more successful than non-strikeout pitchers.

But if you look at-batters, the obverse is not true. Batters who strike out are not less successful than batters who don't strike out. They are, if anything, a little more successful.

This unusual asymmetry in the game creates asymmetrical pressures on the strikeout rate. Teams are always looking for strikeout pitchers — but there is very little or no pressure to find batters who strike out less often. We accept strikeouts for hitters, value them for pitchers. This drives strikeout rates up. It always has.

Is there any end to this in sight?

Well, yes, depending on how you define "in sight". Strikeouts are not a practical negative for hitters because they correlate with power. Hitters who strike out tend also to hit home runs. When you increase your bat speed you increase your home runs, but you also increase your strikeouts. But this depends on there being a variation in home run rates. If every hitter had the same home run rate, then strikeouts would certainly be a negative.

We will never reach the point at which every player has the same home run rate — but the variation in home run rates is contracting at a meaningful pace. In 1954 Ted Kluszewski led the major leagues in Home Runs and RBI with 49 and 141. In 2008 Ryan Howard led the majors in the same two categories, with almost the same totals — 48 and 143. In 2009 the leaders in those categories had 47 and 141.

But in 1954, 39% of major league regulars (450 or more at-bats) hit less than 10 home runs, and 62% hit

*We accept strikeouts for hitters, value them for pitchers. This drives strikeout rates up. It always has.*

less than 15 home runs. In 2009, only 22% of major league regulars (450 or more at-bats) hit less than 10 home runs, and only 39% hit less than 15 home runs. We are transitioning to a game in which everyone is a power hitter, more or less.

In 1960 Mickey Mantle and Roger Maris led the American League in home runs, with 40 and 39. In 2009 Carlos Pena and Mark Teixeira tied for the American League lead in home runs, with 39 each.

But in 1960 an average American League team hit 136 home runs. In 2009 the average was 183. As before, the totals for the top players are back where they were decades ago — but the team totals are very different, because there are many more players hitting home runs.

If we were to reach a point at which every hitter was in the same range of power, then the advantage would go to the one who struck out less often. We will never reach the point at which all players' power is the same, but we are moving in that direction — and have been moving in that direction since 1920.

Eventually, this trend would kill off the other one. In a world in which every player was a power hitter, strikeouts would be as bad for hitters as they were good for pitchers. That's the good news.

The bad news is that we're at least 50 years away from the point at which that trend negates the other one, maybe 100 years away.

Strikeouts, observed that great philosopher Crash Davis, are boring — and they're fascist. Strikeouts minimize the need for defensive play, thus taking the fielders out of the game. If we want to live to see the end of the Dave Kingman generation, we need to take deliberate actions to bring about the end of it.

I hope you all know that I greatly admire Royals broadcaster Denny Matthews. I always have. But Mr. Matthews, at the moment, is selling a book which advocates expanding the strike zone. Expanding the strike zone is exactly what baseball does not need. Strikeouts are rising and rising and rising. Expanding the strike zone would cause them to explode. You expand the strike zone by one inch, you're going to have ten strikeouts per team per game.

Look, this is what I never understood, until about three years ago. Until the K zones started on TV, the PitchFx and the QuesTec, I had no idea how good major league pitchers were at hitting the corners of the strike zone. You sum up the pitches made by any good major league pitcher in a typical game, you've got 40 pitches on the edge of the strike zone, 40 pitches just off the edge of the strike zone, 15 pitches way out of the strike zone, and 5 pitches that are somewhere near the heart of the zone. At most 5. And a high percentage of those get crushed.

Maybe you always knew that — but I didn't. I remember Jim Bouton, in *Ball Four,* talking about pitching coaches telling him to hit the black. He thought it was impossible. What I always thought is this: that pitchers tried to hit the edges of the plate, but that, throwing 90+ miles an hour and spinning the ball, it was impossible to do this consistently. Pitchers would get behind, and they'd have to throw the pitch over the center of the plate.

Whenever a home run is hit, the announcer will usually say that it was a bad pitch, it was right out over the middle of the plate. I always thought that was BS; there's lots of pitches out over the middle of the plate, he just happened to hit that one.

What I understand now, and did not understand until we had the K zones, is that it is not BS. Good pitchers can and do trace the outlines of the strike zone — and pitches that go over the heart of the plate do get crushed. Even bad pitchers with bad control throw many more pitches on the edges of the strike zone than they do in the heart of the zone.

The key fact is not that pitchers have fantastic control. The key fact is that major league hitters do crush baseballs in the heart of the zone. Pitchers know that batters crush balls in the heart of the zone, so they are very careful not to throw the ball there. They aim pitches — 70% of the pitches — to be just outside the zone. Sometimes they miss, but usually they miss by a few inches. If you aim two inches off the strike zone and miss by four inches, you're two inches into the zone. If

*We will never reach the point at which all players' power is the same, but we are moving in that direction — and have been moving in that direction since 1920.*

you aim a pitch two inches inside the strike zone and miss by four inches, you're in the heart of the zone. Therefore, most pitchers aim most pitches just outside the zone.

Well, if pitchers can trace the outlines of the strike zone with their pitches, and you expand the strike zone, what happens? They trace the outlines of the expanded strike zone, of course. All you've done, by expanding the strike zone, is reduce further the number of hittable pitches.

The problem with baseball now is that the batter/pitcher confrontations drag on, and the batter/pitcher confrontations drag on because the hitter is trying to force the pitcher to throw him something he can hit, and the pitcher is very good at avoiding doing that. If you expand the strike zone, you make the problem worse. You're going to have no hittable pitches at all, and you're going to have batter/pitcher confrontations that drag on forever and wind up with ten strikeouts a game. This is not a solution to our problems.

What you need to do is, shrink the strike zone. Take the edges of the plate away from the pitcher, and force him to throw the ball where the hitter can put some wood on it.

Of course, if you do that, then you also have to do some other things to help the pitcher, or the league ERA will go to 6.14. You have to do other things to help the pitcher — but that's easy.

Here's what you can do.

First, deaden the baseball a little bit. Major League Baseball tests the resiliency of the baseballs, and has for many years. The problem is, they never do anything about it. The only reason they test them is so that, whenever some nitwit complains about the balls being too lively and too many home runs being hit, they can say that they test the baseballs, and they're no more lively than they ever were.

That's true; the liveliness of the baseballs is not the reason for the high number of home runs. But if you need to help the pitchers out, it's easy: Just reduce the resiliency of the baseballs.

Second, put the batters back in the batter's box, and move the batter's box back about three inches. If a hitter wipes out a line of the batter's box, call time out, call out the grounds crew, re-draw the line, and tell him not to do it again. If he does it again, you throw him out of the game.

If you keep the batter in the batter's box and back the batter's box up just a few inches, it becomes harder to get to the outside pitch, and it becomes easier for the pitcher to pitch inside. It will make a huge difference.

Third, get rid of the thin-handled bats and the multiple coats of shellac on the bats. We don't want to drive any hitter out of the game. Just set a minimum thickness for the handle of a bat — I'd suggest 0.90 inches to start with — and then increase that by .05 inches every other year until the bat handles have a minimum thickness of 1.60 inches. It will take about 30 years to get there, and hitters will adjust gradually and barely notice the differences.

At the same time, this will a) eliminate 95% of the broken bats, b) reduce the risk of someone being killed by a flying bat shard, and c) reduce the cost of using wooden bats, thus making it more practical to use wooden bats in college or other amateur venues.

The whip-handled bats have taken over for a reason: they're better for the hitter. They have a larger hitting surface, and the thin handle with the large head enables the hitter to generate more bat speed. It's good for the individual hitter — but it's bad for the game. It is one of the factors driving the game toward more home runs and more strikeouts. If you gradually go back to bats more like the bats that were used 30 years ago, you can then restore the resiliency of the baseballs, without having another 70-homer season.

Fourth, move a few fences back about ten feet.

My general point is, if you want to help the pitcher, it is really, really easy to do that, and to do that in ways that are all but invisible to the fan. You could keep the strike zone where it is now, keep the parks the same, and reduce the league ERA to 1.80 by just deadening the baseballs and moving the hitters off the plate. There is no reason to do anything radical and stupid like expanding the strike zone or, God forbid, raising the mound. Just deaden the balls a tiny bit, back the batters off the plate, and regulate the bats a little bit. The pitchers will be fine.

> *The key fact is not that pitchers have fantastic control. The key fact is that major league hitters do crush baseballs in the heart of the zone.*

# Philadelphia Phillies

| | | | | | | |
|---|---|---|---|---|---|---|
| ML RANK | 4th | 2nd | 22nd | 10th | 6th | 7th |
| **Team** | **820** | **224** | **.258** | **589** | **.781** | **119** |
| | RUNS | HOME RUNS | BATTING AVG. | WALKS | OPS | STOLEN BASES |
| **Opp.** | **709** | **189** | **.265** | **489** | **.757** | **95** |
| ML RANK | 6th | 24th | 18th | 3rd | 16th | 11th |

**2009 TEAM OVERVIEW**

**93-69**

**1**st place
NL East

## Key Players

| Pos | Player | G | AB | R | H | 2B | 3B | HR | RBI | SB | CS | BB | SO | AVG | OBP | SLG | OPS | WS |
|---|---|---|---|---|---|---|---|---|---|---|---|---|---|---|---|---|---|---|
| C | Carlos Ruiz | 107 | 322 | 32 | 82 | 26 | 1 | 9 | 43 | 3 | 2 | 47 | 39 | .255 | .355 | .425 | .780 | 13 |
| 1B | Ryan Howard | 160 | 616 | 105 | 172 | 37 | 4 | 45 | 141 | 8 | 1 | 75 | 186 | .279 | .360 | .571 | .931 | 26 |
| 2B | Chase Utley | 156 | 571 | 112 | 161 | 28 | 4 | 31 | 93 | 23 | 0 | 88 | 110 | .282 | .397 | .508 | .905 | 32 |
| 3B | Pedro Feliz | 158 | 580 | 62 | 154 | 30 | 2 | 12 | 82 | 0 | 1 | 35 | 68 | .266 | .308 | .386 | .694 | 18 |
| SS | Jimmy Rollins | 155 | 672 | 100 | 168 | 43 | 5 | 21 | 77 | 31 | 8 | 44 | 70 | .250 | .296 | .423 | .719 | 19 |
| LF | Raul Ibanez | 134 | 500 | 93 | 136 | 32 | 3 | 34 | 93 | 4 | 0 | 56 | 119 | .272 | .347 | .552 | .899 | 17 |
| CF | Shane Victorino | 156 | 620 | 102 | 181 | 39 | 13 | 10 | 62 | 25 | 8 | 60 | 71 | .292 | .358 | .445 | .803 | 22 |
| RF | Jayson Werth | 159 | 571 | 98 | 153 | 26 | 1 | 36 | 99 | 20 | 3 | 91 | 156 | .268 | .373 | .506 | .879 | 26 |

## Key Pitchers

| Pos | Player | G | GS | W | L | SV | IP | H | R | ER | SO | BB | BR/9 | ERA | WS |
|---|---|---|---|---|---|---|---|---|---|---|---|---|---|---|---|
| SP | Joe Blanton | 31 | 31 | 12 | 8 | 0 | 195.1 | 198 | 89 | 88 | 163 | 59 | 12.21 | 4.05 | 11 |
| SP | Cole Hamels | 32 | 32 | 10 | 11 | 0 | 193.2 | 206 | 95 | 93 | 168 | 43 | 11.80 | 4.32 | 10 |
| SP | J.A. Happ | 35 | 23 | 12 | 4 | 0 | 166.0 | 149 | 55 | 54 | 119 | 56 | 11.39 | 2.93 | 15 |
| SP | Jamie Moyer | 30 | 25 | 12 | 10 | 0 | 162.0 | 177 | 91 | 89 | 94 | 43 | 12.78 | 4.94 | 6 |
| SP | Cliff Lee | 12 | 12 | 7 | 4 | 0 | 79.2 | 80 | 35 | 30 | 74 | 10 | 10.39 | 3.39 | 6 |
| CL | Brad Lidge | 67 | 0 | 0 | 8 | 31 | 58.2 | 72 | 51 | 47 | 61 | 34 | 17.03 | 7.21 | 0 |
| RP | Ryan Madson | 79 | 0 | 5 | 5 | 10 | 77.1 | 73 | 29 | 28 | 78 | 22 | 11.41 | 3.26 | 10 |
| RP | Chad Durbin | 59 | 0 | 2 | 2 | 2 | 69.2 | 56 | 38 | 34 | 62 | 47 | 14.21 | 4.39 | 3 |

## Clutch Home Runs

On Bill James Online, we have a method of identifying "clutch" at-bats, based on the score, the inning, the runners on base, the opponent, and other factors.

Ryan Howard in 2009 led the majors in clutch home runs (12) and clutch RBI (48). Howard had more clutch home runs all by himself than the Indians, Mets or Royals did. In part, this is because bad teams don't have all that many clutch at-bats, since they play a lot of meaningless games. There are a lot more "clutch" situations in a pennant race than there are in Kansas City. These are the 2009 major league leaders in clutch home runs and RBI:

**Clutch Home Runs and RBI Leaders**

| Player | Homers | Player | Ribbies |
|---|---|---|---|
| 1. Ryan Howard | 12 | 1. Ryan Howard | 48 |
| 2. Raul Ibanez | 8 | 2. Andre Ethier | 43 |
| 3. Nick Swisher | 8 | 3. Jason Bay | 37 |
| 4. Mark Reynolds | 8 | 4. Matt Holliday | 36 |
| 5. Many tied with | 7 | 5. Albert Pujols | 35 |

Nick Swisher also led the majors in "being called out for leaving the base too early on sacrifice flies in clutch situations when he actually didn't but the umpire blew it and thought he did." Two.

## Leading Off

Jimmy Rollins led off 293 innings in 2009, in which the Phillies scored 209 runs, or 6.42 runs per nine innings. This was the best in the National League for any player who regularly batted leadoff.

**Jimmy Rollins — 2009 Performance as Leadoff Man**

| | Times | Team Runs | Runs/ Inning |
|---|---|---|---|
| Innings Led Off | 293 | 209 | .71 |
| Reached Base Leading Off | 85 | 125 | 1.47 |
| Did Not Reach | 208 | 84 | .40 |
| Other Innings for Team | 1,153 | 611 | .53 |

## Werth Waiting For

Jayson Werth in 2009 had 94 plate appearances that lasted 7 pitches or more. This was 10 more than anyone else in the majors.

Shane Victorino, Carlos Ruiz and Pedro Feliz, all put together, had 87 such plate appearances.

## No Need to Hurry

Shane Victorino scored 29 runs on other players' home runs — five more than anyone else in baseball.

### Shane Victorino — 2009 Runs Scored Analysis

| Reached on | | Runs Scored After | |
|---|---|---|---|
| Home Runs | 10 | | 10 |
| Triples | 13 | Scored after Triple | 9 |
| Doubles | 39 | Scored after Double | 16 |
| Singles | 119 | Scored after Single | 47 |
| Walk/HBP | 66 | Scored after Walk/HBP | 17 |
| Reached on Error | 8 | Scored after ROE | 2 |
| Reached on Forceout | 17 | Vultured Runs | 1 |
| Inserted as Pinch Runner | 1 | Runs as pinch runner | 0 |
| | | Total Runs Scored | 102 |

| Brought in by | | Driven in by | |
|---|---|---|---|
| Single | 21 | Ryan Howard | 30 |
| Double | 20 | Chase Utley | 24 |
| Triple | 1 | Jayson Werth | 15 |
| His own home run | 10 | Raul Ibanez | 11 |
| Other home run | 29 | Himself | 10 |
| Sac Fly | 11 | No RBI | 6 |
| Walk, Error, or Other | 10 | Greg Dobbs | 3 |
| | | Pedro Feliz | 2 |
| | | John Mayberry | 1 |

## Nibbling

Pitchers threw 630 pitches to Ryan Howard that were down and out of the strike zone — more than any other hitter. Chase Utley was second on the list, with 590.

## Damage Control

Cliff Lee gave up 175 singles, 10 more than anyone else, but minimized the damage by allowing only 34 of them to score. Fausto Carmona and Luke Hochevar each allowed only 99 singles but also allowed 34 of them to score.

## Squirt Gun Instead of a Hose

For the 37 pitchers who saved 10 or more games in 2009, the overall ERA in the games that they saved was 1.09. Brad Lidge's ERA, in the games that he saved, was 3.68.

Need more Lidge? Here's another one. Through eight innings, the Phillies were 30 games over .500 and the Yankees were 29. The Yankees wound up with 103 wins; the Phillies, 93. The Yankees beat the Phillies by eleven full games in the ninth inning.

### Brad Lidge — 2009 Decision Anaylsis

| Group | G | IP | W | L | PCT | H | R | SO | BB | ERA |
|---|---|---|---|---|---|---|---|---|---|---|
| Losses | 8 | 4.1 | 0 | 8 | .000 | 19 | 19 | 5 | 10 | 33.23 |
| Saves | 31 | 29.1 | 0 | 0 | ---- | 24 | 13 | 37 | 13 | 3.68 |
| Blown Saves | 11 | 7.1 | 0 | 7 | .000 | 23 | 23 | 9 | 11 | 24.55 |
| Holds | 1 | 0.1 | 0 | 0 | ---- | 1 | 0 | 0 | 1 | 0.00 |
| No Decisions | 23 | 20.2 | 0 | 0 | ---- | 22 | 14 | 15 | 8 | 6.10 |

## Chaserunning

By the method we use to measure this, Chase Utley was the second-best baserunner in the major leagues, behind Houston's Michael Bourn. Utley — not stunningly fast — was excellent in almost all of the baserunning categories that we track:

He went first-to-third on a single 57.6% of the time, the fourth-best percentage in the majors.

He scored from second 13 times in 15 opportunities, one of the best percentages in the majors.

He scored from first on a double 10 times, tied for the most in baseball.

He advanced 24 bases on wild pitches, passed balls, balks, sacrifice flies and defensive indifference, which is a high total.

He grounded into only five double plays in 134 opportunities, which is a very low GIDP rate, and

He established a major league record for stolen bases with zero caught stealing, with 23.

His only baserunning negative was that he was doubled off five times, which accounted for five of his seven baserunning outs.

The best baserunners in the major leagues in 2009:

| Player | Net Gain |
|---|---|
| 1. Michael Bourn, Hou | +55 |
| 2. Chase Utley, Phi | +50 |
| 3. Jacoby Ellsbury, Bos | +43 |
| 4. Ian Kinsler, Tex | +37 |
| 5. Rajai Davis, Oak | +36 |
| 6. Ryan Braun, Mil | +35 |
| 7. Chone Figgins, LAA | +35 |
| 8. Ichiro Suzuki, Sea | +32 |
| 9. Carl Crawford, TB | +32 |
| 10. Jason Bartlett, TB | +30 |

## Staying Healthy and Productive

The Phillies' eight opening-day starters started a total of 1,145 games, the highest total for a National League team in the eight years we've been keeping track of this stuff.

**Philadelphia Phillies —
2009 Games Played by Opening
Day Starter At Each Position**

| Pos | Player | Starts |
|---|---|---|
| C | Carlos Ruiz | 100 |
| 1B | Ryan Howard | 158 |
| 2B | Chase Utley | 154 |
| 3B | Pedro Feliz | 150 |
| SS | Jimmy Rollins | 152 |
| LF | Raul Ibanez | 129 |
| CF | Shane Victorino | 150 |
| RF | Jayson Werth | 152 |
| | **Total** | **1,145** |

## Chicks Dig It

The Phillies in 2009 scored 45.1% of their runs by home runs — easily the highest percentage in baseball. No other team was above 42.1%.

## Messing with Their Timing

The Phillies led the league in changeups. They threw it 15.5% of the time; no other team's pitchers threw it more than 14.0%. It was a key pitch for almost all of their starters. Cole Hamels threw the most changes in the majors, 933 — 141 more than any other pitcher. Joe Blanton threw it 17.3% of the time, second only to his fastball. Jamie Moyer you know about. The changeup was Cliff Lee and Pedro Martinez's #2 pitch, and J.A. Happ's #3 offering.

## Halladay and Lee

In each of the last two years, the batting record of all hitters facing Roy Halladay and all hitters facing Cliff Lee are surprisingly similar. In 2008 the on-base plus slugging percentage against Halladay was .621; against Lee, .633. In 2009 the OPS against Halladay was .667; against Lee, .696. These are really good numbers for the pitchers. The walks allowed are similar. Halladay gives up a few more bombs but gets more strikeouts, which gives him a lower batting average allowed. Halladay is a lot easier to run on. These records are a lot more similar than they are different.

### Cliff Lee and Roy Halladay — Record of Opposing Batters

#### Roy Halladay

| Season | AB | R | H | 2B | 3B | HR | RBI | BB | SO | SB | CS | GIDP | AVG | OBP | SLG | OPS |
|--------|-----|----|-----|----|----|----|-----|----|-----|----|----|------|------|------|------|------|
| 2008 | 927 | 88 | 220 | 34 | 6 | 18 | 84 | 39 | 206 | 15 | 5 | 21 | .237 | .276 | .345 | .621 |
| 2009 | 913 | 82 | 234 | 47 | 1 | 22 | 79 | 35 | 208 | 18 | 6 | 21 | .256 | .285 | .382 | .667 |

#### Cliff Lee

| Season | AB | R | H | 2B | 3B | HR | RBI | BB | SO | SB | CS | GIDP | AVG | OBP | SLG | OPS |
|--------|-----|----|-----|----|----|----|-----|----|-----|----|----|------|------|------|------|------|
| 2008 | 847 | 68 | 214 | 33 | 6 | 12 | 66 | 34 | 170 | 3 | 0 | 27 | .253 | .285 | .348 | .633 |
| 2009 | 900 | 88 | 245 | 51 | 2 | 17 | 84 | 43 | 181 | 7 | 3 | 14 | .272 | .306 | .390 | .696 |

# The 2009 Clutch Hitter of the Year

by Bill James

TODD HELTON HIT .397 IN CLUTCH SITUATIONS IN 2009, and Miguel Tejada hit .389. These men have long had reputations as clutch hitters. Casey Blake had a fine year in clutch situations, and Raul Ibanez, and Derek Jeter and Albert Pujols. Brad Hawpe had another fine year in the clutch, and Jason Bay drove in 37 runs in 65 clutch at-bats — an astonishing number.

Still, there is no question who was the major league Clutch Hitter of the Year in 2009, and, in the six or seven years that we have been doing this, the decision has never been so easy. Ryan Howard led the majors in clutch home runs (12) — more than many teams — and in clutch RBI with 48. His batting average in clutch at-bats was .357; his slugging percentage was .810.

Ryan Howard has always been a great hitter, and we take no position on whether he is actually better when the chips are down. In what we identify as Clutch Plate Appearances, Howard now has 48 career home runs, in 435 at-bats. It's a lot, even for him. In 15 post-season games, he drove in 17 more runs. He was by far the best clutch hitter of the 2009 season.

> *There is no question who was the major league Clutch Hitter of the Year in 2009.*

## Past Clutch Hitters of the Year

| Year | Player | Team |
| --- | --- | --- |
| 2008 | Manny Ramirez | Red Sox/Dodgers |
| 2007 | Brad Hawpe | Colorado Rockies |
| 2006 | Albert Pujols | St. Louis Cardinals |
| 2005 | Andruw Jones | Atlanta Braves |
| 2004 | David Ortiz | Boston Red Sox |
| 2003 | David Ortiz | Boston Red Sox |

# Pittsburgh Pirates

| 2009 TEAM OVERVIEW | ML RANK | 30th | 23rd | 27th | 25th | 27th | 14th |
|---|---|---|---|---|---|---|---|
| **62-99** | **Team** | **636** | **125** | **.252** | **499** | **.705** | **90** |
| | | RUNS | HOME RUNS | BATTING AVG. | WALKS | OPS | STOLEN BASES |
| **6**th place NL Central | **Opp.** | **768** | **152** | **.276** | **563** | **.788** | **107** |
| | ML RANK | 19th | 6th | 27th | 14th | 25th | 16th |

## Key Players

| Pos | Player | G | AB | R | H | 2B | 3B | HR | RBI | SB | CS | BB | SO | AVG | OBP | SLG | OPS | WS |
|---|---|---|---|---|---|---|---|---|---|---|---|---|---|---|---|---|---|---|
| C | Ryan Doumit | 75 | 280 | 31 | 70 | 16 | 0 | 10 | 38 | 4 | 0 | 20 | 49 | .250 | .299 | .414 | .714 | 4 |
| 1B | Adam LaRoche | 87 | 324 | 46 | 80 | 25 | 1 | 12 | 40 | 2 | 2 | 41 | 81 | .247 | .329 | .441 | .770 | 6 |
| 2B | Freddy Sanchez | 86 | 355 | 45 | 105 | 28 | 3 | 6 | 34 | 5 | 1 | 20 | 60 | .296 | .334 | .442 | .776 | 11 |
| 3B | Andy LaRoche | 150 | 524 | 64 | 135 | 29 | 5 | 12 | 64 | 3 | 1 | 50 | 84 | .258 | .330 | .401 | .731 | 12 |
| SS | Jack Wilson | 75 | 266 | 26 | 71 | 18 | 1 | 4 | 31 | 2 | 1 | 15 | 31 | .267 | .304 | .387 | .691 | 7 |
| LF | Nyjer Morgan | 71 | 278 | 39 | 77 | 6 | 5 | 2 | 27 | 18 | 10 | 29 | 49 | .277 | .351 | .356 | .707 | 7 |
| CF | Andrew McCutchen | 108 | 433 | 74 | 124 | 26 | 9 | 12 | 54 | 22 | 5 | 54 | 83 | .286 | .365 | .471 | .836 | 18 |
| RF | Brandon Moss | 133 | 385 | 47 | 91 | 20 | 4 | 7 | 41 | 1 | 5 | 34 | 84 | .236 | .304 | .364 | .668 | 5 |

## Key Pitchers

| Pos | Player | G | GS | W | L | SV | IP | H | R | ER | SO | BB | BR/9 | ERA | WS |
|---|---|---|---|---|---|---|---|---|---|---|---|---|---|---|---|
| SP | Ross Ohlendorf | 29 | 29 | 11 | 10 | 0 | 176.2 | 165 | 80 | 77 | 109 | 53 | 11.46 | 3.92 | 11 |
| SP | Paul Maholm | 31 | 31 | 8 | 9 | 0 | 194.2 | 221 | 102 | 96 | 119 | 60 | 13.27 | 4.44 | 8 |
| SP | Zach Duke | 32 | 32 | 11 | 16 | 0 | 213.0 | 231 | 101 | 96 | 106 | 49 | 11.96 | 4.06 | 12 |
| SP | Charlie Morton | 18 | 18 | 5 | 9 | 0 | 97.0 | 102 | 49 | 49 | 62 | 40 | 13.64 | 4.55 | 4 |
| SP | Ian Snell | 15 | 15 | 2 | 8 | 0 | 80.2 | 87 | 50 | 48 | 52 | 44 | 14.73 | 5.36 | 1 |
| CL | Matt Capps | 57 | 0 | 4 | 8 | 27 | 54.1 | 73 | 36 | 35 | 46 | 17 | 15.40 | 5.80 | 2 |
| RP | John Grabow | 45 | 0 | 3 | 0 | 0 | 47.1 | 43 | 19 | 18 | 41 | 28 | 13.88 | 3.42 | 5 |
| RP | Jesse Chavez | 73 | 0 | 1 | 4 | 0 | 67.1 | 69 | 33 | 30 | 47 | 22 | 12.30 | 4.01 | 4 |

### Zach Duke

Zach Duke led the National League with 16 losses in 2009, but also, the Pirates lost all five of his no-decisions. Thus, the Pirates' record with their best pitcher on the mound was 11-21 — the largest number of losses behind any one pitcher in the major leagues.

| Group | G | IP | W | L | PCT | H | R | SO | BB | ERA |
|---|---|---|---|---|---|---|---|---|---|---|
| Wins | 11 | 81.2 | 11 | 0 | 1.000 | 66 | 20 | 42 | 15 | 1.98 |
| Losses | 16 | 96.2 | 0 | 16 | .000 | 129 | 68 | 49 | 28 | 6.14 |
| No Decisions | 5 | 34.2 | 0 | 0 | ---- | 36 | 13 | 15 | 6 | 3.12 |

Zach Duke 2009

Quality Starts: 10 in Wins, 7 in Losses, 4 in No-Decisions

### Efficient Pitching

Zach Duke started 218 innings and in 29 of those innings he used 20 pitches or more. Duke's 13% ratio of long innings was the lowest rate of any pitcher in the majors.

| Player | Innings Started | Long Innings | Pct |
|---|---|---|---|
| Zach Duke | 218 | 29 | 13.3% |
| Joel Pineiro | 219 | 31 | 14.2% |
| Roy Halladay | 240 | 35 | 14.6% |
| Chris Carpenter | 194 | 29 | 14.9% |
| Ted Lilly | 181 | 28 | 15.5% |

## Cannon Arms

Pittsburgh outfielders in 2009 threw out 45 runners on the bases — eight more than any other major league team. The last time the Pirates led the majors in outfield assists, the outfielders were Willie Stargell, Matty Alou and Roberto Clemente.

## Strong Team Defense

The 2009 Pirates led the National League in fielding percentage, setting new team records with just 73 errors and a .988 fielding percentage. By team Defensive Runs Saved they were average or better at every position except second base. Delwyn Young's defensive issues at second probably kept the Pirates from ranking as the second-best defensive team in the National League.

### Team Defensive Runs Saved — 2009 National League

| Team | P | C | 1B | 2B | 3B | SS | LF | CF | RF | TOT |
|------|---|---|----|----|----|----|----|----|----|-----|
| 1. Cincinnati | 12 | 1 | -3 | -3 | -3 | 10 | 17 | 14 | 7 | 52 |
| 2. Arizona | -5 | 3 | -13 | 13 | -4 | 9 | 15 | 4 | 12 | 34 |
| 3. San Francisco | 8 | -4 | 11 | -4 | -6 | -8 | 12 | 6 | 19 | 34 |
| 4. Pittsburgh | 4 | 0 | -1 | -9 | 0 | 16 | 12 | 0 | 9 | 31 |
| 5. St. Louis | 11 | 5 | 12 | -8 | -8 | 14 | -5 | 4 | 6 | 31 |

## Turning Two

For the third straight season the Pirates led the National League in double plays turned. Jack Wilson and Freddy Sanchez were the Pirates' primary keystone combination in all of those seasons, but they will have new defenders there in 2010. The Pirates' rotation is primarily made up of ground ball pitchers so the new defenders should have plenty of opportunity to keep the streak alive.

## Falling Behind

The Pirates fell behind in the first inning 54 times in 2009, more often than any other team in the National League. First-inning hitters facing the Pirates in 2009 had a .311 batting average, .361 on-base percentage, and a .531 slugging percentage — about the same as the career batting numbers of Nomar Garciaparra.

**Pittsburgh Pirates 2009**

| Inning | 1 | 2 | 3 | 4 | 5 | 6 | 7 | 8 | 9 | Extra | Final |
|--------|----|----|----|----|----|----|----|----|----|-------|-------|
| Ahead  | 40 | 46 | 61 | 65 | 63 | 62 | 61 | 57 | 60 | 2 | 62 |
| Behind | 54 | 59 | 70 | 78 | 79 | 84 | 82 | 88 | 89 | 9 | 99 |
| Tied   | 67 | 56 | 30 | 18 | 19 | 15 | 17 | 15 | 11 | 16 | -- |

## Making a Good First Impression

Minor league journeyman Garrett Jones was called to the majors on July 1, 2009, and hit 7 home runs in his first 12 games. For the month of July he hit 10 home runs — the most of any major league player. The last Pirate to lead the majors in home runs in a month was Willie Stargell in 1971.

## Offensive Deficiency

The Pirates in 2009 had 42 games — a little more than one in four — in which they were either shut out or scored just one run. They lost all 42 of those games. The other National League teams averaged 26 games with zero or one runs.

## Not Manufactured to Standard

The Pirates in 2009 manufactured only 121 runs, the smallest number in the majors, and exactly 100 less than the Angels. A manufactured run is a run that is created by small offensive elements put together by pro-active measures. The average National League team averaged 152 manufactured runs.

## Lineup Changes

Is there a point at which a team wears out their re-set button?

Of the Pirates' eight opening-day starters, only one — third baseman Andy LaRoche — would appear in 100 games for the Pirates in 2009. Veterans Adam LaRoche, Freddy Sanchez, Nate McLouth and Jack Wilson were all traded to contending teams in mid-summer, while Nyjer Morgan went to Washington. Catcher Ryan Doumit missed a couple of months with a scaphoid injury, which. . .you know, who even knew that Ryan Doumit was keeping a scaphoid? Right fielder Brandon Moss just wasn't really good. The 665 games started by the Pirates opening-day starters were their fewest in the eight years that we have been tracking this.

| Games Played by Opening Day Starter at Each Position | | |
|---|---|---|
| Pos | Player | Starts |
| C | Ryan Doumit | 71 |
| 1B | Adam LaRoche | 86 |
| 2B | Freddy Sanchez | 84 |
| 3B | Andy LaRoche | 142 |
| SS | Jack Wilson | 74 |
| LF | Nyjer Morgan | 69 |
| CF | Nate McLouth | 44 |
| RF | Brandon Moss | 95 |
| | **Total** | **665** |

## Tip-Top Top Spot

Pittsburgh leadoff men Nyjer Morgan and Andrew McCutchen combined for an excellent season in the leadoff spot, with 106 runs scored, 78 walks, 34 steals and some power.

| G | AB | R | H | 2B | 3B | HR | RBI | BB | SO | SB | AVG | OBP | SLG | OPS |
|---|---|---|---|---|---|---|---|---|---|---|---|---|---|---|
| 162 | 651 | 106 | 186 | 32 | 13 | 13 | 78 | 78 | 127 | 34 | .286 | .364 | .435 | .799 |

## Lefty Specialist

Paul Maholm is extremely tough on left-handed batters.

| Split | AB | R | H | 2B | 3B | HR | BB | SO | BA | OBP | SLG | OPS |
|-------|-----|----|-----|----|----|----|----|----|------|------|------|------|
| vs RHB | 614 | 82 | 194 | 45 | 4 | 13 | 51 | 82 | .316 | .370 | .466 | .836 |
| vs LHB | 148 | 12 | 27 | 7 | 1 | 1 | 9 | 37 | .182 | .247 | .264 | .510 |

## John Grabow's Changeup

John Grabow uses his changeup more than any other National League reliever, but he rarely throws it to left-handed batters. While he throws his fastball just short of half the time to everyone, against right-handers he uses the changeup, but against lefties he uses his slider.

### John Grabow 2009

|  | vs. RHB | | vs. LHB | |
|--|---------|--|---------|--|
| Total Pitches | 823 | | 333 | |
| Outs Recorded | 155 | | 62 | |
| Fastball | 381 | 46% | 143 | 43% |
| Changeup | 377 | 46% | 26 | 8% |
| Slider | 36 | 4% | 161 | 48% |
| Not Charted | 29 | 4% | 3 | 1% |

## Great Move to First

Ross Ohlendorf — a right-handed pitcher — led the National League in 2009 with 8 base runners picked off. Since 2002, 25 pitchers have picked off seven or more base runners in a single season — but just three of them were right-handed.

# St. Louis Cardinals

| 2009 TEAM OVERVIEW | ML RANK | 18th | 13th | 12th | 21st | 15th | 22nd |
|---|---|---|---|---|---|---|---|
| | Team | 730 | 160 | .263 | 528 | .747 | 75 |
| **91-71** | | RUNS | HOME RUNS | BATTING AVG. | WALKS | OPS | STOLEN BASES |
| **1** st place NL Central | Opp. | 640 | 123 | .258 | 460 | .706 | 44 |
| | ML RANK | 2nd | 2nd | 10th | 1st | 3rd | 1st |

## Key Players

| Pos | Player | G | AB | R | H | 2B | 3B | HR | RBI | SB | CS | BB | SO | AVG | OBP | SLG | OPS | WS |
|---|---|---|---|---|---|---|---|---|---|---|---|---|---|---|---|---|---|---|
| C | Yadier Molina | 140 | 481 | 45 | 141 | 23 | 1 | 6 | 54 | 9 | 3 | 50 | 39 | .293 | .366 | .383 | .749 | 20 |
| 1B | Albert Pujols | 160 | 568 | 124 | 186 | 45 | 1 | 47 | 135 | 16 | 4 | 115 | 64 | .327 | .443 | .658 | 1.101 | 39 |
| 2B | Skip Schumaker | 153 | 532 | 85 | 161 | 34 | 1 | 4 | 35 | 2 | 2 | 52 | 69 | .303 | .364 | .393 | .757 | 18 |
| 3B | Mark DeRosa | 68 | 237 | 31 | 54 | 10 | 1 | 10 | 28 | 2 | 1 | 18 | 58 | .228 | .291 | .405 | .696 | 4 |
| SS | Brendan Ryan | 129 | 390 | 55 | 114 | 19 | 7 | 3 | 37 | 14 | 7 | 24 | 56 | .292 | .340 | .400 | .740 | 14 |
| LF | Chris Duncan | 87 | 260 | 25 | 59 | 15 | 2 | 5 | 32 | 0 | 1 | 41 | 67 | .227 | .329 | .358 | .687 | 6 |
| CF | Colby Rasmus | 147 | 474 | 72 | 119 | 22 | 2 | 16 | 52 | 3 | 1 | 36 | 95 | .251 | .307 | .407 | .714 | 13 |
| RF | Ryan Ludwick | 139 | 486 | 63 | 129 | 20 | 1 | 22 | 97 | 4 | 2 | 41 | 106 | .265 | .329 | .447 | .775 | 19 |

## Key Pitchers

| Pos | Player | G | GS | W | L | SV | IP | H | R | ER | SO | BB | BR/9 | ERA | WS |
|---|---|---|---|---|---|---|---|---|---|---|---|---|---|---|---|
| SP | Adam Wainwright | 34 | 34 | 19 | 8 | 0 | 233.0 | 216 | 75 | 68 | 212 | 66 | 11.01 | 2.63 | 21 |
| SP | Chris Carpenter | 28 | 28 | 17 | 4 | 0 | 192.2 | 156 | 49 | 48 | 144 | 38 | 9.39 | 2.24 | 21 |
| SP | Joel Pineiro | 32 | 32 | 15 | 12 | 0 | 214.0 | 218 | 94 | 83 | 105 | 27 | 10.64 | 3.49 | 13 |
| SP | Kyle Lohse | 23 | 22 | 6 | 10 | 0 | 117.2 | 125 | 69 | 62 | 77 | 36 | 12.54 | 4.74 | 3 |
| SP | Todd Wellemeyer | 28 | 21 | 7 | 10 | 0 | 122.1 | 160 | 88 | 80 | 78 | 57 | 16.19 | 5.89 | 0 |
| CL | Ryan Franklin | 62 | 0 | 4 | 3 | 38 | 61.0 | 49 | 13 | 13 | 44 | 24 | 10.92 | 1.92 | 14 |
| RP | Trever Miller | 70 | 0 | 4 | 1 | 0 | 43.2 | 31 | 11 | 10 | 46 | 11 | 9.07 | 2.06 | 6 |
| RP | Dennys Reyes | 75 | 0 | 0 | 2 | 1 | 41.0 | 35 | 17 | 15 | 33 | 21 | 12.95 | 3.29 | 3 |

## Defense on Your Side

Starting 95 games at shortstop for the Cardinals, Brendan Ryan was 25 plays above average as a defensive shortstop — that is, he was +25 in John Dewan's Plus/Minus System. In those 95 games, the Cardinals went 58-37 and allowed 3.43 runs per game. When someone else started at shortstop for the Cardinals they went 33-34 and allowed 4.68 runs per game.

## Coach and Effect

In spring training, 2009, Cardinal pitching coach Dave Duncan suggested that Joel Pineiro make his little-used sinker his go-to pitch. Pineiro led the major leagues with 317 groundouts, cut his walk rate by 42%, and enjoyed his best major league season since 2003.

## You Da Man

Albert Pujols wasn't able to top Ryan Howard or Prince Fielder in RBI, but he did drive in a higher percentage of his team's runs than either of them. The three of them finished comfortably ahead of everyone else.

**Percentage of Team's RBI**

| Player | Pct |
| --- | --- |
| 1. Albert Pujols | 18.5% |
| 2. Prince Fielder | 18.0% |
| 3. Ryan Howard | 17.2% |
| 4. Derrek Lee | 15.7% |
| 5. Adrian Gonzalez | 15.5% |

## It May Not Have Worked, But At Least They Had a Plan

While there may be no good way to pitch to Albert Pujols, there seems to be something of a consensus on the least bad way to do it: Keep the ball down, and don't challenge him any more than you have to. Last year pitchers threw him 563 pitches that were down and out of the strike zone, fourth-most in the majors. They also threw him only 45.5% strikes. Only 7 hitters saw a lower proportion.

## Power Without the Side Effects

Albert Pujols swung and missed only 144 times last year while leading the majors with 47 homers. Prince Fielder, who had the second-most homers (46), swung and missed almost twice as often as Pujols (276 times). The majors' next two leading home-run hitters, Ryan Howard (45) and Mark Reynolds (44), each swung and missed more than three times as often as Pujols did (455 for Howard, and a major league-leading 487 for Reynolds).

### Albert Pujols — 2009 Pitch Analysis

#### Overall

| | | |
|---|---|---|
| Pitches Seen | 2,526 | |
| Taken | 1,459 | 58% |
| Swung At | 1,067 | 42% |

#### Pitches Taken

| | | |
|---|---|---|
| Taken for a Strike | 398 | 27% |
| Called a ball | 1,061 | 73% |

#### Pitches Taken by Pitch Location

| | | |
|---|---|---|
| In Strike Zone | 398 | 27% |
| High | 120 | 8% |
| Low | 462 | 32% |
| Inside | 138 | 9% |
| Outside | 339 | 23% |

#### Swung At

| | | |
|---|---|---|
| Missed | 144 | 13% |
| Fouled Off | 411 | 39% |
| Put in Play | 512 | 48% |

#### Swung At by Pitch Location

| | | |
|---|---|---|
| In Strike Zone | 749 | 70% |
| High | 38 | 4% |
| Low | 101 | 9% |
| Inside | 54 | 5% |
| Outside | 122 | 11% |

## Reaching for the Stars

When given a pitch up and out of the strike zone, Brendan Ryan chased it 53.3% of the time, the highest percentage in the majors. He saw 90 such pitches and chased 48 of them; Nick Johnson saw more than twice as many (186) but swung at only 12.

## Adjusting on the Fly

The Cardinals' opening-day starters accounted for only 57% of their regular-season starting lineup, a remarkably low figure for a playoff team. All other teams that made the postseason were at 62% or higher. The Cardinals saw turnover at five of the eight positions: Skip Schumaker replaced Brendan Ryan as the second baseman; Brian Barden shared time at third with Joe Thurston until Mark DeRosa was acquired in midseason; Khalil Greene shared shortstop with several others before Brendan Ryan took over in the second half; left fielder Chris Duncan gave way to Matt Holliday; and Rick Ankiel lost the center field job to Colby Rasmus.

**Games Played by Opening Day Starter At Each Position**

| Pos | Player | Starts |
|-----|--------|--------|
| C | Yadier Molina | 136 |
| 1B | Albert Pujols | 158 |
| 2B | Brendan Ryan | 105 |
| 3B | Brian Barden | 24 |
| SS | Khalil Greene | 39 |
| LF | Chris Duncan | 71 |
| CF | Rick Ankiel | 90 |
| RF | Ryan Ludwick | 122 |
| | **Total** | **745** |

## Chalk One Up for the "Good Hitting Beats Good Pitching" Side

Matt Holliday batted .360 against pitchers with an ERA of 3.50 or better, second-best in the majors to Joe Mauer's .361. It was the third straight year Holliday had hit over .300 against good pitchers.

**Matt Holliday — 2009 Batting Performance By Quality of Opposing Pitcher**

|  | AB | H | HR | RBI | AVG | OPS |
|---|---|---|---|---|---|---|
| Pitcher with ERA <= 3.50 | 150 | 54 | 6 | 24 | .360 | .996 |
| Pitcher with ERA 3.51 to 4.25 | 181 | 51 | 8 | 30 | .282 | .844 |
| Pitcher with ERA 4.26 to 5.25 | 134 | 36 | 5 | 27 | .269 | .829 |
| Pitcher with ERA over 5.25 | 116 | 41 | 5 | 28 | .353 | .989 |

## Yadier's Defense

Yadier Molina was credited with 4 Defensive Runs Saved in 2009, tying him for sixth among major league catchers. Since becoming a regular in 2005, he twice has led major league catchers in defensive runs, and has placed in the top 10 in all five seasons. Over the five-year period, he has saved 42 runs, 45% more than the next-highest total (posted by his brother Jose).

**Most Defensive Runs Saved by Catchers — 2005-09**

| | |
|---|---|
| 1. Yadier Molina | 42 |
| 2. Jose Molina | 29 |
| 3. Ivan Rodriguez | 26 |
| 4. Gerald Laird | 21 |
| 5. David Ross | 19 |

## Walks Don't Always Lead to Trouble

Chris Carpenter walked 38 hitters in 2009 — which is a very low number to begin with — but allowed only 4 of those batters to come around and score. That's 10.5% — the second-lowest percentage among ERA qualifiers. J. A. Happ allowed only 5 out of 56.

# The Attribution Problem (in Baseball and in Life)

by Bill James

WE ATTRIBUTE THE VICTORY WON BY THE TEAM TO THE INDIVIDUAL pitcher — and then conclude, based essentially on that attribution, that the pitcher is the key to victory. It sounds silly, but people have been misled by this attribution problem for a hundred years.

In baseball the pitcher attribution problem is relatively simple to understand, if you can just let go for a moment of what you think you know and drift along with the flow of the logic. A similar fallacy in baseball is the confusion of run creation (from the standpoint of the team) with runs batted in (from the standpoint of the individual). From an offensive standpoint, which is half of the game, the goal of the team is to generate as many runs as possible. The handiest traditional instrument to measure the runs created by each individual player is his runs batted in, his RBI total.

*People have been misled by this attribution problem for a hundred years.*

The problem is that this often leads to confusion between RBI and actual offensive value — again, a confusion between the individual accomplishment and the good of the team. Most runs result from a sequence of actions by several hitters. The number of runs a team scores depends on how many long sequences they can muster — thus, on how many people they get on base. The RBI count is essentially an indicator of who stands where in the offensive sequence. I'm overstating the case — great RBI men are usually great hitters — but maybe you get my point?

When a new manager or general manager takes over a bad team, what he will very often say is "the thing we need most on this team is an RBI man." In reality, the vast majority of the time, an RBI man is the *last* thing that a bad team ought to be worrying about. What they almost always need is more people on base — thus, more people contributing to the sustained sequences of events that lead to three-run innings.

What a manager or general manager is really saying, when he says that "what we need here is an RBI man," is "we need somebody else here to take credit for the meager successes of this team." It's the wrong thing to worry about. If the team is more successful, *somebody* will get the credit for it, and you can worry later about who.

It's an attribution problem. Managers, media and fans are prone to attribute to the individual what is actually accomplished by the team — and thus, are prone to recommend changes in personnel that are really of no use at all to the team.

But is the attribution problem a unique problem to baseball? Not at all — in fact, the same sorts of attribution problems occur throughout American life. In America — and certainly in other countries, but I don't know anything about other countries — in America we are constantly trying to fix something that isn't really the problem. Children playing unsupervised in city parks, for example. Parents in America in the 1950s routinely allowed children as young as six to play around the neighborhood. Then there were news stories about child-snatching, more news stories about child-snatching, more grisly and horrific stories about children seized by predators and never again seen alive. Eventually we all quit allowing our children to play around the neighborhood until they were 23.

Am I saying that you are wrong to protect your children? Of course not. You, me, any of us would do and will do everything we can to protect our children.

What I am saying is, *addressing the problem from the standpoint of the individual doesn't really do anything at all to fix the problem from the standpoint of society as a whole.* You have just as many people who will victimize children after you do that as you did before. Adding an RBI man to a bad team doesn't really do anything at all to improve the team's ability to produce runs. If you add a low-average power hitter to a bad team, the low-average power hitter will lead the team in RBI — and

*Managers, media and fans are prone to attribute to the individual what is actually accomplished by the team.*

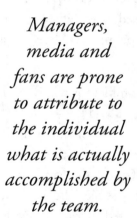

the team will score fewer runs, not more. For essentially the same reason, protecting your own child from child predators doesn't really do anything at all to reduce the problem of child predators. In fact, in some ways, it makes the problem worse.

How does it make the problem worse? Suppose that you see a small child, a six-year-old child, playing alone in the park. In the 1950s, this would not have been at all unusual; now, it would be extremely unusual. So what do you say to yourself, if you see a young child playing unsupervised?

You think to yourself, "My God, that child shouldn't be playing in the park without supervision" — even though you yourself may well have done the same thing when you were that age. I certainly did.

"Yes," you think to yourself, "I did that, but the world has changed." Bingo. That's how we've made the problem worse. We've created the idea that snatching a child out of the park if he is left unsupervised is a sort of normal and natural risk — rather than an extraordinary event. That doesn't make me or you any more likely to grab a child out of the park, because you and I aren't going to do that anyway. But to a potential child predator, the idea that this is a sort of normal and natural risk is a form of permission. In our world, an unsupervised child is a sort of advertisement for a child molester. It shouldn't be that way. Children playing should be a normal sight — *even* if they are unsupervised.

This syndrome of changing public behavior for no real public benefit has been repeated in many different areas. I remember once, when I was maybe eight years old, we were driving home from the nearby town, my nine-year-old sister and I in the car. We happened across two black men whose car had broken down, who were hitchhiking into town. My father was something of a racist, not a virulent racist, but...he wasn't Spencer Tracy. All the men of that generation that I knew were somewhat racist — yet he stopped to pick up the hitchhikers.

Why? Because, at that time, you just did. You saw

somebody in need of a ride, you gave them a ride. That's the way it was.

That was maybe 1958. Within a year, I remember reading news stories in the paper: Altoona Man Killed by Hitchhiker; Tennessee Woman Assaulted, Slain by Hitchhiking Soldiers. "Assault" was newspaper code, at that time, for rape. Ann Landers began counseling her readers: For heaven's sake, don't pick up hitchhikers. You never know what they might be up to. By the early 1960s, radio announcers were warning people not to pick up hitchhikers. By the late 1960s, there were public service announcements from the police, pleading with people not to pick up hitchhikers — although I found myself, from time to time, sticking up a thumb by the side of the road. I remember that in the early 1970s my brother-in-law Ned West would still stop and pick up hitchhikers, and my sister Rosalie, his wife, would get furious about this. They're both dead now, and a hitchhiker didn't kill either one of them. By the late 1970s, hitchhiking was nearly extinct.

Of course there are other factors in this. A lot of young people hitchhiked in the 1950s because that was the only way they could get around. I knew people in the 1950s who worked ten miles from their home and hitchhiked to work every day. Everybody has a car now, and the cars are vastly more reliable than they used to be; they used to break down by the side of the road regular as rain.

But my point is, *eliminating the practice of hitchhiking didn't really do anything at all to reduce the incidence of violent crime.* Society derived no benefit whatsoever from this change. There are, in the world, a certain number of violent people who commit random crimes until they are arrested and put away. Whether people pick up hitchhikers or whether they don't, that number is exactly the same, and the number of crimes they are going to commit before the short arm of the law catches up with them is essentially the same.

I don't pick up hitchhikers now either; what do you think, I'm crazy? We all acted rationally to protect ourselves — yet the chance that we would be killed

*In America we are constantly trying to fix something that isn't really the problem.*

by some random nut was the same afterward as it was before. In the same way that adding an RBI man to a bad lineup simply changes who gets credit for creating the runs, eliminating hitchhiking simply changes the details of the crimes which are committed. If you started picking up random strangers, somebody would probably rob you or worse within six months — but if we *all* started doing it together, we would all be just as safe as we are now.

Here's another example of the principle of misattribution to the individual. It used to be that, when people didn't feel well, they went to the hospital. A mother, after delivering a baby, might spend a week in the hospital, getting a good night's sleep every night, being taken care of by nurses, and letting her body recover. It might have cost $5 a night to stay in a hospital — literally — and there are still women around who remember how much they enjoyed that week, relaxing and letting other people worry about the kids.

When I was in the third grade I had my tonsils out. I spent three nights in the hospital. We were paupers, but...if you needed medical care, you went to the hospital.

Hospital costs began to rise. Hospitals began charging more for a night in the hospital. The "bed" wasn't really what you were paying for; it was just an accounting mechanism. You were actually paying for malpractice insurance, drug research, drug representatives, medical school and hi-tech equipment, but this was all paid for on a per-bed basis.

So the insurance companies, to reduce their costs, began pushing people to spend fewer nights in the hospital. A week spent recovering from childbirth became four days, became three days, two days... eventually the government had to step in and legislate at least one day, or the insurance companies would have insisted that you drop the kid and run. The three-day hospital stays to have your tonsils out dropped to about a half an hour.

As the number of the "beds" sold by the hospital

diminished, the price for each bed had to increase…$50 a night, a hundred, two hundred; eventually it cost hundreds or even thousands of dollars to rent a hospital bed for one lousy night. When this no longer served to defray the hospital's costs, they began charging fantastic fees for other things. An aspirin from a hospital in the 1950s was free, then it cost a quarter, 50 cents, a dollar, $20. God knows what an aspirin costs anymore; only God could afford one.

Of course, reducing the number of hospital beds the insurance company is paying for does nothing whatsoever to reduce the costs of medicine, because you're not really paying for the bed. That's just an accounting trick. Like RBI. The health care system was being fooled by its own accounting tricks.

If *one* insurance company stopped paying attention to the cost of a hospital bed, that insurance company would go bankrupt in a matter of weeks. But if *all* the insurance companies stopped paying attention to the cost of a hospital bed at the same time, it would make virtually no difference to any of them, since the overall costs of medicine, which is what the companies are *really* paying for, would be spread among the insurance companies the same afterward as before. In fact, the focus on the cost of a "bed" makes the problem worse, in this way: that if people could afford to go to the hospital when they don't feel well, they would. If a hospital bed had a reasonable cost, sick people would check themselves in. But now, you don't go to the hospital unless you're desperate — thus, the number of people sharing the cost of medicine is artificially reduced, and the cost is pushed artificially higher once again.

And, because the number of beds used is reduced, it no longer makes sense for the hospitals to maintain beds. What would happen if there was a serious pandemic in which people, for some reason, needed to be kept near their doctors? There are no longer enough hospital beds in which to treat people.

*An aspirin from a hospital in the 1950s was free, then it cost a quarter, 50 cents, a dollar, $20. God knows what an aspirin costs anymore; only God could afford one.*

The misattribution problem is not *causing* hospital costs to explode. Hospital costs are exploding for other reasons. But misattributing those costs to beds — or to aspirin, or whatever—is making the problem worse.

I got this question in the "Hey, Bill" section of Bill James Online. It was a coincidence, in that I had already written the above:

*As you have college age kids, I wondered if you have thoughts on the costs of higher education. I think we should contract some of the college departments that offer programs with little hope of leading to future employment, but my concern about that is the departments in demand today will not necessarily be the same as what will be in demand in 30 years. What do you think? And how much should we expect our students to fund their own education? Is a system that charges $50,000 in tuition annually but offers a lot of financial aid a good thing? In the public colleges, what should be the ratio of student/state funding?*

This question was from Michael Kirlin. As to whether I have any thoughts on the costs of higher education, the answer is: Will the government please stop trying to make higher education more affordable?

It's the same problem…and understand, I am speaking as someone who could never possibly have gone to college without the help of the government and am extremely grateful for that help. If there is a day in my life when I forget to be grateful for that, I should be ashamed of myself.

But it's the same problem; what is good policy on the individual level is insane government policy on the macro level. College is expensive. People need help to afford it. The government steps in to provide help.

What this does is increase the amount of money available to purchase higher education — which causes the cost of higher education to rise, which makes college more unaffordable to more people. The demand for higher education rises; the price increases — so the government needs to do more, and more, and more. We allocate ever more money to help more people go to college, and the cost of a college education goes higher, and higher, and higher. Every dollar that is spent to make college education more affordable makes it more unaffordable. The same with health care. Every dollar the government spends to make health care more affordable increases the cost of health care by one dollar — but we're trapped in a cycle of trying to do more, trying to do more, trying to do more.

Everything that government spends money to make more affordable, without exception, becomes dramatically more expensive. What one can do to make college more affordable is exactly the opposite of that suggested by Mr. Kirlin: work to increase the supply. If the government spends money to increase the supply of higher education — which, in fairness to the government, it does — that does make education more affordable. Working to increase the *supply* of education is like increasing the team on-base percentage. Working to make education more affordable to individuals is like trying to find more RBI men.

One more example, and I'll stop. Public Stadium financing. Let us say that Alston, Brighton, Cambridge and Danvers are all cities of 1.8 million each, and they

*Working to make education more affordable to individuals is like trying to find more RBI men.*

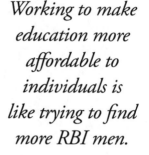

would all like to have an NFL team, which at the present Cambridge and Danvers do but Alston and Brighton do not. Alston thinks "To attract an NFL team, we need to build a $400 million stadium," and so they do. But whose NFL team do they attract? The voters of Cambridge are in effect told, "We have an offer of a $400 million stadium. Build us a $500 million stadium, or we're leaving." Then Brighton wants in on the action, so they build a $600 million stadium.

The only thing is, after billions of dollars are spent to build stadiums, there are no more teams than there were before. What is rational policy for each city is utterly irrational from the standpoint of *all* the cities — spending taxpayer money to enrich the NFL.

Kay Barnes was elected Mayor of Kansas City about ten years ago, on a program of "let's build a beautiful new arena and attract an NBA team to come back to Kansas City." She wasn't a bad mayor, really. We have the beautiful new arena now, the Sprint Center. The Kansas City Innovators, maybe you're heard of them? I think they're in the NBA finals by now.

# San Diego Padres

## Key Players

| Pos | Player | G | AB | R | H | 2B | 3B | HR | RBI | SB | CS | BB | SO | AVG | OBP | SLG | OPS | WS |
|---|---|---|---|---|---|---|---|---|---|---|---|---|---|---|---|---|---|---|
| C | Nick Hundley | 78 | 256 | 23 | 61 | 15 | 2 | 8 | 30 | 5 | 1 | 28 | 76 | .238 | .313 | .406 | .719 | 10 |
| 1B | Adrian Gonzalez | 160 | 552 | 90 | 153 | 27 | 2 | 40 | 99 | 1 | 1 | 119 | 109 | .277 | .407 | .551 | .958 | 34 |
| 2B | David Eckstein | 136 | 503 | 64 | 131 | 27 | 2 | 2 | 51 | 3 | 1 | 39 | 46 | .260 | .323 | .334 | .657 | 17 |
| 3B | Kevin Kouzmanoff | 141 | 529 | 50 | 135 | 31 | 1 | 18 | 88 | 1 | 0 | 27 | 106 | .255 | .302 | .420 | .722 | 16 |
| SS | Everth Cabrera | 103 | 377 | 59 | 96 | 18 | 8 | 2 | 31 | 25 | 8 | 46 | 88 | .255 | .342 | .361 | .703 | 14 |
| LF | Chase Headley | 156 | 543 | 62 | 142 | 31 | 2 | 12 | 64 | 10 | 2 | 62 | 133 | .262 | .342 | .392 | .734 | 16 |
| CF | Tony Gwynn | 119 | 393 | 59 | 106 | 11 | 6 | 2 | 21 | 11 | 7 | 48 | 65 | .270 | .350 | .344 | .693 | 13 |
| RF | Will Venable | 95 | 293 | 38 | 75 | 14 | 2 | 12 | 38 | 6 | 1 | 25 | 89 | .256 | .323 | .440 | .763 | 8 |

## Key Pitchers

| Pos | Player | G | GS | W | L | SV | IP | H | R | ER | SO | BB | BR/9 | ERA | WS |
|---|---|---|---|---|---|---|---|---|---|---|---|---|---|---|---|
| SP | Kevin Correia | 33 | 33 | 12 | 11 | 0 | 198.0 | 194 | 92 | 86 | 142 | 64 | 11.91 | 3.91 | 8 |
| SP | Chad Gaudin | 20 | 19 | 4 | 10 | 0 | 105.1 | 105 | 69 | 60 | 105 | 56 | 14.18 | 5.13 | 0 |
| SP | Chris Young | 14 | 14 | 4 | 6 | 0 | 76.0 | 70 | 47 | 44 | 50 | 40 | 13.26 | 5.21 | 1 |
| SP | Josh Geer | 19 | 17 | 1 | 7 | 0 | 102.2 | 116 | 73 | 68 | 54 | 23 | 12.54 | 5.96 | 0 |
| SP | Tim Stauffer | 14 | 14 | 4 | 7 | 0 | 73.0 | 71 | 31 | 29 | 53 | 34 | 13.56 | 3.58 | 3 |
| CL | Heath Bell | 68 | 0 | 6 | 4 | 42 | 69.2 | 54 | 21 | 21 | 79 | 24 | 10.08 | 2.71 | 12 |
| RP | Edward Mujica | 67 | 4 | 3 | 5 | 2 | 93.2 | 101 | 47 | 41 | 76 | 19 | 11.53 | 3.94 | 4 |
| RP | Luke Gregerson | 72 | 0 | 2 | 4 | 1 | 75.0 | 62 | 29 | 27 | 93 | 31 | 11.52 | 3.24 | 5 |

## One Man Show

Adrian Gonzalez totaled 34 Win Shares in 2009, which was 15.1% of the Padres' team total, the highest percentage of any player in baseball. The second best Win Shares total in San Diego belongs to David Eckstein (!), at 17 Win Shares. Gonzalez became the first player since 2005 to have twice as many Win Shares as the second-best player on his team.

## Is He a Hundley or Isn't He?

If you are wondering — and I was — Padres catcher Nick Hundley is not related to Randy and Todd Hundley. He could be, though. These are their career batting records through the end of their first major league seasons as regulars or near-regulars:

| Player | G | AB | R | H | 2B | 3B | HR | RBI | BB | SO | SB | AVG | OBP | SLG | OPS |
|---|---|---|---|---|---|---|---|---|---|---|---|---|---|---|---|
| Nick (2009) | 138 | 454 | 44 | 108 | 22 | 3 | 13 | 54 | 39 | 128 | 5 | .238 | .298 | .385 | .683 |
| Randy (1966) | 157 | 542 | 51 | 125 | 22 | 3 | 19 | 63 | 35 | 118 | 1 | .231 | .279 | .387 | .666 |
| Todd (1992) | 180 | 485 | 45 | 97 | 23 | 1 | 8 | 41 | 31 | 108 | 3 | .200 | .254 | .301 | .555 |

So far, Nick is actually the best hitter of the three.

## The Negative of Colorado

San Diego's home park is by far the most difficult place to hit in the major leagues. The Padres in 2009 scored 278 runs at home, 360 on the road. They allowed 321 at home, 448 on the road. Their three-year park run index is 76, meaning that the park reduces runs scored by 24%. No other major league park reduces runs scored by more than 9%.

Over the last two seasons, Adrian Gonzalez in San Diego has hit .246 with 26 homers, 85 RBI. On the road, he has hit .307 with 50 homers, 133 RBI.

## Maybe Better Sunglasses?

Chase Headley has a career batting average of .198 in day baseball.

|  | G | AB | R | H | 2B | 3B | HR | RBI | BB | SO | AVG | OBP | SLG |
|---|---|---|---|---|---|---|---|---|---|---|---|---|---|
| Day | 72 | 247 | 33 | 49 | 11 | 1 | 8 | 28 | 35 | 78 | .198 | .306 | .348 |
| Night | 183 | 645 | 64 | 186 | 40 | 3 | 13 | 74 | 59 | 163 | .288 | .353 | .420 |

## 97 In a Row

Despite no previous experience above single-A, Everth Cabrera made the team out of Spring Training and garnered 4 starts at shortstop in April before going in for wrist surgery. Bud Black wrote him into the lineup the first day he was eligible to come off the DL (June 19) and the young shortstop didn't look back. The 22-year-old started the final 97 consecutive games of the season at the position, more than any other player at any position except Prince Fielder (who started all 162 games at first base for Milwaukee).

## What's In a Name?

Not much, apparently, if the name is "Silva". Carlos Silva in 2005 pitched 188 innings, and walked 9 hitters. Walter Silva in 2009 pitched 25 innings for the Padres, and walked 15.

## Revolving Door

Fifty-six different players (including pitchers) made it into the San Diego lineup in 2009 — the highest total in baseball.

### Road Warrior

Kevin Kouzmanoff has a higher career OPS in road games than any of the following players:  Billy Butler, Michael Cuddyer, Johnny Damon, Jermaine Dye, Aubrey Huff,  Torii Hunter, Ian Kinsler, Mike Lowell, Lyle Overbay, Dustin Pedroia, Carlos Quentin, Ivan Rodriguez, Ichiro Suzuki, Miguel Tejada, Troy Tulowitzki, B. J. Upton, Justin Upton, Vernon Wells, Michael Young, Ryan Zimmerman, Ben Zobrist.

For roughly half of those players, Kouzmanoff beats them in road OPS by 50 points or more.

### Kouzman-notlead-off

Kevin Kouzmanoff led off 124 innings for the Padres in 2009, and in those innings the team scored only 28 runs, or 2.03 runs per nine innings.  This was the lowest average in the majors for any hitter leading off 100 or more innings.

### Station to Station

Will Venable had 11 opportunities to go from first to third on a base hit and never did. All other major leaguers with that many opportunities managed to make it at least once, including all three of the Flying Molina Brothers.

## Quality of Opposition Pitching

What major league team in 2009 faced the strongest quality of opposition pitching?

The Padres.

One could offer any number of theories as to what makes the quality of pitching faced by a team, over the course of the season, better or worse — random chance, for example, or the quality of the team. Good teams, perhaps, face more quality pitchers than bad teams?

No.

The quality of pitching faced by different teams is certainly not even, and it certainly does not even out over the course of the season. The dominant variable is: the number of good pitchers in your division. Over the last ten years, the best pitching faced by any major league team, over the course of a season, was by the 2005 New York Mets. Look at the division.

The Braves had John Smoltz and Tim Hudson, both having fine seasons. The Marlins had Dontrelle Willis (22-10, 2.63 ERA), A. J. Burnett (12-12, 3.44 ERA, 198 strikeouts) and Josh Beckett (15-8, 3.38). The Phillies had Jon Lieber (17-13), Brett Myers (13-8, 3.72 ERA, 208 strikeouts), and Cory Lidle (13-11). Washington — a .500 team that season — had Livan Hernandez (15-10, 3.98 ERA) and Esteban Loaiza (12-10, 3.77, strikeout-to-walk ratio of 173 to 55.) Everybody in that division had good starting pitching, but the Mets had less of it than anybody else, so they had to face more of it than anybody else.

The quality of pitching faced by the Padres last year wasn't quite at the same level as the 2005 Mets, but it was the toughest in the major leagues by a substantial margin. How do we know that?

We start by figuring a "Season Score" for every major league pitcher, which just puts Innings Pitched, ERA, Wins, Losses, Strikeouts, Walks and Saves all along a common scale so that we can add them together. Then we figure the average Season Score of the starting pitchers faced by each team.

The average Season Score of a pitcher starting against the Padres was 97.1 — the highest in the majors by more than five points:

| Rank | Team | Avg Opp | | Rank | Team | Avg Opp |
|------|------|---------|---|------|------|---------|
| 1. | Padres | 97.1 | | 16. | Angels | 81.0 |
| 2. | D'backs | 91.9 | | 17. | Orioles | 80.6 |
| 3. | Dodgers | 89.1 | | 18. | Mariners | 80.2 |
| 4. | Astros | 88.5 | | 19. | Blue Jays | 80.0 |
| 5. | Brewers | 88.5 | | 20. | Tigers | 78.6 |
| 6. | Mets | 86.5 | | 21. | Rangers | 78.2 |
| 7. | Rays | 85.5 | | 22. | Cardinals | 77.9 |
| 8. | Indians | 85.3 | | 23. | Braves | 77.7 |
| 9. | Pirates | 84.1 | | 24. | Marlins | 77.7 |
| 10. | Nationals | 83.9 | | 25. | Royals | 77.1 |
| 11. | Rockies | 82.7 | | 26. | White Sox | 76.7 |
| 12. | Reds | 82.7 | | 27. | Phillies | 74.2 |
| 13. | Athletics | 82.2 | | 28. | Red Sox | 72.5 |
| 14. | Giants | 82.0 | | 29. | Cubs | 72.2 |
| 15. | Twins | 81.3 | | 30. | Yankees | 71.6 |

The difference between the Padres and the Yankees in 2009 amounts to about 15 games started by a Cy Young-quality pitcher as opposed to a replacement-level pitcher. It's a huge difference.

The 2009 data for the Yankees and Red Sox is dramatically different than the 2008 data for the same teams. The biggest reason was the Blue Jays. The Blue Jays in 2008 had a front four of Roy Halladay (20-11), A. J. Burnett (18-10), Jesse Litsch (13-9) and Shaun Marcum (9-7 with an excellent 3.39 ERA). Last year, with Marcum and Litsch hurt, Burnett gone and even Halladay down a little, their starting pitching was nowhere near as good. With the Rays' starting pitching also down some from 2008, the only really strong starting staffs in the division were the Yankees and the Red Sox — who thus had a lot of games against starting pitchers of limited accomplishment.

In 2008 the Yankees and Red Sox ranked 5th and 7th among the 30 teams in the quality of pitching faced. In 2009 they ranked 28th and 30th.

## The Loyal Opposition

You will hear it said, several times this summer, that a team's #1 pitcher tends to be matched up, over the course of the season, against the other team's #1 pitcher.

Having studied this issue — I believe for the first time in a long career of studying this kind of crap — I can report that this is untrue. It is totally untrue; it is absolutely untrue, and it is zero percent true. This is not a mixed or tentative report. It simply is not true to any extent whatsoever that good pitchers tend, over the course of the season, to be matched up against other good pitchers.

We took ten years of Retrosheet data, and studied the pitching matchups. When I say "we", I mean myself and my son Isaac; Isaac pulled the data from Retrosheet and put it into spreadsheets, and then I studied the spreadsheets.

Let's start with the Season Scores for pitchers. In the last ten years there have been 11 starting pitchers with Season Scores over 300. Of those 11 pitchers, 8 won the Cy Young Award. All of the other Cy Young winners of the last ten years had Season Scores of 245 or higher. This chart summarizes the number of starting pitchers at each level (#), the number of Cy Young Award winners in that group (Cy), the number of starts made by those pitchers (all of them, not just the Cy Young winners), and the average Season Scores of the opposing starting pitchers in those games:

| Season Score | # | Cy | Starts | Avg Opp Season Score |
|---|---|---|---|---|
| 300 and up | 11 | 8 | 366 | 68.88 |
| 200 to 299.99 | 136 | 11 | 4,093 | 77.67 |
| 150 to 199.99 | 152 | 0 | 4,660 | 80.13 |
| 100 to 149.99 | 316 | 0 | 8,987 | 78.01 |
| 50 to 99.99 | 451 | 0 | 10,151 | 77.89 |
| Zero to 49.99 | 980 | 0 | 11,614 | 79.40 |
| Below Zero | 963 | 0 | 8,711 | 81.63 |

As you can see, the lowest average opponent season score (68.88) is actually for the *best* starting pitchers, the Cy Young Award winners, while the highest average opponent season score (81.63) is for the *worst* starting pitchers.

I would be reluctant to draw the conclusion that weaker starting pitchers actually face stronger opposition starters. Sometimes, when a pitcher reaches a certain level of performance, opposing teams start to focus on the other games of the series. I'm talking about "super Cy Young pitchers", like Randy Johnson at his peak, or Pedro Martinez. When the Dodgers had Koufax and the Giants had Marichal, Marichal rarely matched up against Koufax, because the Giants would figure they probably weren't going to beat Koufax anyway, but they could win the series by matching Marichal against Drysdale and Gaylord Perry against Osteen. You don't want to *admit* that you're probably not going to beat the Big Unit, but you *know*. It is probably rational and appropriate for the manager to focus on the games he has a better chance to win.

But the number of games in that portion of the study is pretty small (366 games), and we can't treat that as a reliable data point. Without that data point we don't have a clear pattern showing that weaker pitchers face better opponents, nor do we have a solid explanation for why that would be true. I don't think we can reach that conclusion.

We can clearly conclude, however, that the opposing pitchers faced by #1 pitchers are not *better* than the opposing pitchers faced by the Chris Reitsmas and Dewon Brazeltons and Scott Aldreds and Dennis Tankersleys of the world.

# San Francisco Giants

## Key Players

| Pos | Player | G | AB | R | H | 2B | 3B | HR | RBI | SB | CS | BB | SO | AVG | OBP | SLG | OPS | WS |
|---|---|---|---|---|---|---|---|---|---|---|---|---|---|---|---|---|---|---|
| C | Bengie Molina | 132 | 491 | 52 | 130 | 25 | 1 | 20 | 80 | 0 | 0 | 13 | 68 | .265 | .285 | .442 | .727 | 12 |
| 1B | Travis Ishikawa | 120 | 326 | 49 | 85 | 10 | 2 | 9 | 39 | 2 | 2 | 30 | 89 | .261 | .329 | .387 | .715 | 9 |
| 2B | Emmanuel Burriss | 61 | 202 | 18 | 48 | 6 | 0 | 0 | 13 | 11 | 4 | 14 | 34 | .238 | .292 | .267 | .560 | 2 |
| 3B | Pablo Sandoval | 153 | 572 | 79 | 189 | 44 | 5 | 25 | 90 | 5 | 5 | 52 | 83 | .330 | .387 | .556 | .943 | 27 |
| SS | Edgar Renteria | 124 | 460 | 50 | 115 | 19 | 1 | 5 | 48 | 7 | 2 | 39 | 69 | .250 | .307 | .328 | .635 | 10 |
| LF | Fred Lewis | 122 | 295 | 49 | 76 | 21 | 3 | 4 | 20 | 8 | 4 | 36 | 84 | .258 | .348 | .390 | .738 | 7 |
| CF | Aaron Rowand | 144 | 499 | 61 | 130 | 30 | 2 | 15 | 64 | 4 | 1 | 30 | 125 | .261 | .319 | .419 | .738 | 15 |
| RF | Randy Winn | 149 | 538 | 65 | 141 | 33 | 5 | 2 | 51 | 16 | 2 | 47 | 93 | .262 | .318 | .353 | .671 | 16 |

## Key Pitchers

| Pos | Player | G | GS | W | L | SV | IP | H | R | ER | SO | BB | BR/9 | ERA | WS |
|---|---|---|---|---|---|---|---|---|---|---|---|---|---|---|---|
| SP | Tim Lincecum | 32 | 32 | 15 | 7 | 0 | 225.1 | 168 | 69 | 62 | 261 | 68 | 9.67 | 2.48 | 22 |
| SP | Matt Cain | 33 | 33 | 14 | 8 | 0 | 217.2 | 184 | 73 | 70 | 171 | 73 | 10.75 | 2.89 | 20 |
| SP | Barry Zito | 33 | 33 | 10 | 13 | 0 | 192.0 | 179 | 89 | 86 | 154 | 81 | 12.56 | 4.03 | 10 |
| SP | Jonathan Sanchez | 32 | 29 | 8 | 12 | 0 | 163.1 | 135 | 82 | 77 | 177 | 88 | 12.62 | 4.24 | 7 |
| SP | Randy Johnson | 22 | 17 | 8 | 6 | 0 | 96.0 | 97 | 55 | 52 | 86 | 31 | 12.19 | 4.88 | 4 |
| CL | Brian Wilson | 68 | 0 | 5 | 6 | 38 | 72.1 | 60 | 27 | 22 | 83 | 27 | 10.95 | 2.74 | 15 |
| RP | Jeremy Affeldt | 74 | 0 | 2 | 2 | 0 | 62.1 | 42 | 14 | 12 | 55 | 31 | 10.97 | 1.73 | 10 |
| RP | Bob Howry | 63 | 0 | 2 | 6 | 0 | 63.2 | 50 | 26 | 24 | 46 | 23 | 10.60 | 3.39 | 5 |

## Giants Starters

The Giants led baseball in starts by their first five starters, with 144.

### Starts Made by First Five Starters — 2009 National League

| Team | Apr | May | June | July | Aug | Sept | Total |
|------|-----|-----|------|------|-----|------|-------|
| Arizona | 18 | 19 | 16 | 22 | 23 | 14 | 112 |
| Atlanta | 21 | 26 | 21 | 21 | 23 | 18 | 130 |
| Chicago | 21 | 24 | 20 | 17 | 18 | 21 | 121 |
| Cincinnati | 21 | 27 | 22 | 21 | 15 | 11 | 117 |
| Colorado | 19 | 23 | 23 | 20 | 20 | 22 | 127 |
| Florida | 21 | 21 | 22 | 19 | 19 | 21 | 123 |
| Houston | 19 | 24 | 23 | 26 | 19 | 15 | 126 |
| Los Angeles | 19 | 18 | 23 | 21 | 21 | 18 | 120 |
| Milwaukee | 22 | 28 | 24 | 21 | 20 | 27 | 142 |
| Washington | 21 | 24 | 15 | 12 | 5 | 6 | 83 |
| New York | 20 | 23 | 18 | 20 | 17 | 10 | 108 |
| Philadelphia | 20 | 25 | 16 | 15 | 13 | 16 | 105 |
| Pittsburgh | 21 | 29 | 23 | 15 | 16 | 16 | 120 |
| St Louis | 20 | 25 | 23 | 24 | 21 | 24 | 137 |
| San Diego | 19 | 17 | 13 | 8 | 6 | 6 | 69 |
| San Francisco | 20 | 29 | 26 | 22 | 23 | 24 | 144 |

## Barry's Best?

To say that Barry Zito had his best year with the Giants is a bit like saying that Steve Martin has made his best movie in several years, or saying, perhaps, that you don't know when you have seen Charles Krauthammer so upbeat. It's like saying you don't know how long it's been since Notre Dame has had such a good football team.

It is true, nonetheless, that Barry Zito had his best year with the Giants, finishing near .500 with an ERA not much over 4.00. Comparing 2008 to 2009, he increased his strikeouts by 34 and cut his walks by 21. You have to start somewhere.

When Barry Zito was on top of the world in Oakland, he threw a fastball-curve-changeup mix, with a big, wide curve being the key pitch. From 2006 to 2008, for some reason he de-emphasized the curveball and threw the changeup more often. This didn't seem to be working; it seemed like he was losing his fastball, and his curveball was no longer effective.

Last year he added a slider, which he had (essentially) never thrown before; he'd thrown it once in awhile. Maybe this helped. It didn't help a whole lot. As long as he is healthy and making his starts, he's got a chance to put things back together.

## Improved Baserunning

The Giants' baserunning improved dramatically from 2008 to 2009, going from a net loss of 53 bases versus an average team in 2008 to a net gain of 67 in 2009 — a pickup of about 120 bases, or about 30 runs. The improvement was across the board:

| Pos | Player | 2008 | | Pos | Player | 2009 |
|---|---|---|---|---|---|---|
| C | Molina | -20 | | C | Molina | -17 |
| 1B | Aurilia | -14 | | 1B | Ishikawa | +11 |
| 2B | Durham | -1 | | 2B | Burris | +10 |
| 3B | Castillo | -12 | | 3B | Sandoval | -2 |
| SS | Vizquel | -2 | | SS | Renteria | -12 |
| LF | Lewis | +13 | | LF | Lewis | +14 |
| CF | Rowand | -16 | | CF | Rowand | +8 |
| RF | Winn | +41 | | RF | Winn | +26 |
| Bench | Burris | +3 | | Bench | Uribe | +9 |
| Bench | Velez | -5 | | Bench | Velez | +13 |
| Bench | Bowker | -10 | | Bench | Schierholz | +8 |

Some of this improvement did result from replacing the aging Rich Aurilia and Ray Durham with the younger and faster Travis Ishikawa and Emmanuel Burriss, but those gains were really offset by Edgar Renteria and by Randy Winn not being on base as much. A lot of the gain was just almost everybody running the bases a little bit better.

## Tough Getting On

The 2009 Giants had a team on-base percentage of .309. This was the lowest on-base percentage in the majors since 2003. They drew 56 fewer walks than any other team in the National League.

## Bengie Bust

In 2008 Bengie Molina was one of the best clutch hitters in baseball, hitting .306 in clutch situations, and driving in 95 runs with just 16 homers.  In 2009, he couldn't buy a hit in a big-game situation:

| Year | AB | H | 2B | 3B | HR | RBI | BB | SO | GIDP | AVG | OBP | SLG |
|------|-----|-----|----|----|----|-----|----|----|------|------|------|------|
| 2002 | 59 | 17 | 3 | 0 | 3 | 18 | 1 | 6 | 4 | .288 | .302 | .492 |
| 2003 | 38 | 12 | 2 | 0 | 1 | 15 | 2 | 2 | 4 | .316 | .341 | .447 |
| 2004 | 45 | 12 | 1 | 0 | 5 | 18 | 3 | 2 | 2 | .267 | .313 | .622 |
| 2005 | 81 | 27 | 5 | 0 | 2 | 22 | 5 | 7 | 3 | .333 | .368 | .469 |
| 2006 | 37 | 13 | 1 | 0 | 1 | 7 | 3 | 3 | 2 | .351 | .400 | .459 |
| 2007 | 81 | 15 | 2 | 0 | 0 | 15 | 2 | 12 | 3 | .185 | .205 | .210 |
| 2008 | 62 | 19 | 2 | 0 | 4 | 23 | 4 | 8 | 3 | .306 | .319 | .532 |
| 2009 | 64 | 9 | 3 | 0 | 2 | 12 | 4 | 13 | 3 | .141 | .186 | .281 |
| Totals | 467 | 124 | 19 | 0 | 18 | 130 | 24 | 53 | 24 | .266 | .296 | .422 |

## Fly Ball King

For the second consecutive season Bengie Molina led the National League in sacrifice flies, 11 in each season. His ratio of ground balls to fly balls was .58 to 1, lowest in the National League.

Molina has 57 career sac flies in 1,244 games.  The only other player with that many sacrifice flies in that few games was Jeff King, who played even fewer games than Molina and had 71 sacrifice flies.

## K-Factor

The Giants led the National League in strikeouts in 2009 for only the 4th time in the last 100 years, and only the second time in the last 98 years.  Since 1912 the Dodgers have led the National League in team strikeouts 33 times; the Giants, twice.  The Mets and Astros, which didn't even exist until 1962, have led the league in strikeouts 19 times between them.

## Home Cookin'

Pablo Sandoval's .361 batting average at home was the best in the National League. He created 9.6 runs per 27 outs, also a league leading figure.

| Split | PA | AB | H | BA | OBP | SLG | OPS |
|-------|-----|-----|-----|------|------|------|-------|
| Home | 308 | 280 | 101 | .361 | .412 | .600 | 1.012 |
| Away | 325 | 292 | 88 | .301 | .363 | .514 | .877 |

## Kung Fu Panda Philosophy: When Entering Battle, Swing First!

Pablo Sandoval swung at the first pitch he saw 47.2 percent of the time and hit .357 when he put the first pitch in play. Jeff Francoeur (43.8%) was the only other hitter in the majors that swung at more than 40 percent of the first pitches he saw.

**Pablo Sandoval — 2009**

| | AB | H | HR | RBI | AVG | OBP | SLG | OPS |
|--------------|-----|----|----|-----|------|------|------|------|
| One and done | 115 | 41 | 7 | 28 | .357 | .368 | .621 | .988 |

## Nearly Perfect

Jonathan Sanchez fired a no-hitter against the visiting Padres on July 10. He struck out 11 and walked none, but Juan Uribe kicked a Chase Headley grounder in the 8th to ruin the perfect game. Sanchez' game score of 98 was the highest in the majors this season, and the third-best in the National League this decade.

### Don't Get Behind Him

When Tim Lincecum retired the first batter in 2009, he allowed just 0.99 runs per nine innings.  This was the lowest runs allowed rate (in that situation) since Jason Schmidt in 2004.

| Tim Lincecum 2009 | |
| --- | --- |
| Innings Pitched | 225.1 |
| Got First Man Out | 164 |
| Runs Scored in Those Innings | 18 |
| Runs/9 Innings | 0.99 |

### Who Made This Mess?

Jonathan Sanchez left 30 runners on base for his bullpen to deal with and Barry Zito left 27. These were the two highest figures in the National League.

### Hold On

Jeremy Affeldt led the National League with 33 holds, the most by any Giant since Mike Jackson in 1993 (34). And the most by any lefty ever in the National League (tied with J.C. Romero who also had 33 in 2002).

Affeldt also led the league in relief ERA, 1.73 (minimum 50 innings pitched).

# Percentage of Full Career

by Bill James

WHENEVER I LOOK AT WILLIE MAYS' RECORD, I AM ALWAYS astonished by how close he came to realizing 100% of his career potential. He was in the majors when he was 20; he was there when he was 42. He played something very close to the full schedule every year until he was 35 years old, and he had good years every year; he never took a year off and hit .255 with 18 homers, the way almost everybody else did. The only part of his career that he is missing is the 1952-1953 portion when he was in the Army. That took about 1.8 years out of his 20-year career, so that's about a 9% gap, but other than that, he was astonishingly close to having a perfect career.

*Is there some way to estimate what percentage of a player's "career potential" the player has been able to achieve?*

Mickey Mantle, you wouldn't say that; Mantle was as good or better than Mays at his best, but he had some injuries and was basically finished at 32. The players in the current generation who are (so far) having near-perfect careers are Albert Pujols and Carlos Beltran, and on the other end there is Milton Bradley and Carlos Pena; if it's not one damn thing with those guys, it's another. Ted Williams has major gaps in his career, when he was out of action with military obligations; Pete Rose is free of major gaps.

Norm Cash played for a long time, but he had a lot of years when he just really was not that good. Is there some way, I wondered, to estimate what percentage of a player's "career potential" the player has been able to achieve?

I decided to approach it this way. We establish the player's career potential by his three best consecutive years. In other words, since Willie Mays' three best consecutive seasons are 1963-64-65 (a total of 119 Win Shares), his "peak value", which establishes his potential, is 39.7. Since Mickey Mantle's three best consecutive seasons are 1955-56-57 (a total of 141 Win Shares), his "peak value" is 47.0. Since Keith Hernandez' three best consecutive seasons are 1984-1986, a total of 89 Win Shares, his peak value is 29.7. Since Don Mattingly's three best seasons are 1984-1986, a total of 95 Win Shares, his peak value is 31.7.

Not quite; when I got some data later on, one of the problems with it was that I had too-high percentages for some players — like Mattingly — who reached very high peaks early on in their careers, but then were prevented by injuries from moving on to another level in what should have been their prime seasons. To adjust for that, I figured two "peaks" for each player — his three best consecutive seasons, and his three best consecutive seasons ending no later than age 25. The second figure, his "young peak", I increased by 10%. If the "young peak", increased by 10%, was greater than the other peak, then I used the young peak. Mattingly's peak three-year period was increased from 95 to 104.5, because he was young when he had those years, and thus his peak value was increased to 34.83.

This peak value, to get the career potential value, was multiplied by a number of years representing a full career. A full career is longer for a superior player than for a weaker player, since the best players can stay around longer. After experimenting with different formulas, I assigned each player a potential number of years, which was:

- 11.2 years (every player has a potential of at least 11.2 years in his career),
- Plus his three-year peak, to the power 0.400.

Mattingly's three-year peak (adjusted) is 104.5. 104.5 to the power 0.400 is 6.42. 6.42 plus 11.2 is 17.62, so Mattingly has a potential of 17.62 seasons. 17.62 — his potential seasons — times 34.833 — his peak value — is 614 Win Shares. Don Mattingly has a potential value of 614 Win Shares.

Mattingly actually earned 263 Win Shares in his career. Thus, what Mattingly was actually able to do in his career was 43% of his career potential — 263, divided by 614.

I should be done explaining the method here, but I had to make one more stupid adjustment. I had very high values, at this point, for those few players — almost all of them pitchers — who were able to hang around to an advanced age. Tommy John, for example, now shows at 289 over 290. He shows as having essentially a 100% full career.

Tommy John, as we know, did not have a 100% full career; he took off a couple of seasons in mid-career to invent Tommy John surgery. But he shows as having a full career because:

1) His peak value is not terribly high,
2) He pitched until he was 46, and
3) He won 13 games when he was 44 years old, 9 when he was 45.

I needed another adjustment. To avoid guys like John (and Moyer) showing up as having full careers when we know they didn't, I discounted their Win Shares, after the age of 42, by two-thirds. This only effects a handful of players in major league history, since there are only a handful of players who have been effective in the majors past the age of 42 — and almost all of those players, as we will see later, still show up with a very high percentage of their potential value achieved.

Let's look at some players, chosen kind of at random, but establishing a pattern which you will see shortly.

 *Nineteenth-century baseball really is not major league baseball, regardless of what people might tell you.*

### Luis Aparicio

| | |
|---|---|
| Peak Seasons | 1964-1966 |
| Peak Value | 20.0 |
| Potential Seasons | 16.34 |
| Potential Career | 327 Win Shares |
| Actual Career | 293 Win Shares |
| Percentage of Potential Value achieved | 90% |

### Dwight Evans

| | |
|---|---|
| Peak Seasons | 1984-1986 |
| Peak Value | 24.7 |
| Potential Seasons | 16.79 |
| Potential Career | 414 Win Shares |
| Actual Career | 347 Win Shares |
| Percentage of Potential Value achieved | 84% |

### Buddy Bell

| | |
|---|---|
| Peak Seasons | 1982-1984 |
| Peak Value | 22.7 |
| Potential Seasons | 16.61 |
| Potential Career | 376 Win Shares |
| Actual Career | 301 Win Shares |
| Percentage of Potential Value achieved | 80% |

### Early Wynn

| | |
|---|---|
| Peak Seasons | 1954-1956 |
| Peak Value | 24.3 |
| Potential Seasons | 16.76 |
| Potential Career | 408 Win Shares |
| Actual Career | 309 Win Shares* |
| Percentage of Potential Value achieved | 75% |

* Adjusted to 305 Win Shares because of performance beyond age 42

### Bob Friend

| | |
|---|---|
| Peak Seasons | 1961-1963 |
| Peak Value | 18.3 |
| Potential Seasons | 16.17 |
| Potential Career | 296 Win Shares |
| Actual Career | 207 Win Shares |
| Percentage of Potential Value achieved | 70% |

### Willie McCovey

| | |
|---|---|
| Peak Seasons | 1968-1970 |
| Peak Value | 35.33 |
| Potential Seasons | 17.66 |
| Potential Career | 624 Win Shares |
| Actual Career | 408 Win Shares |
| Percentage of Potential Value achieved | 65% |

### Devon White

| | |
|---|---|
| Peak Seasons | 1991-1993 |
| Peak Value | 21.0 |
| Potential Seasons | 16.44 |
| Potential Career | 345 Win Shares |
| Actual Career | 207 Win Shares |
| Percentage of Potential Value achieved | 60% |

### Mike Morgan

| | |
|---|---|
| Peak Seasons | 1991-1993 |
| Peak Value | 15.7 |
| Potential Seasons | 15.86 |
| Potential Career | 249 Win Shares |
| Actual Career | 137 Win Shares |
| Percentage of Potential Value achieved | 55% |

### Larry Doby

| | |
|---|---|
| Peak Seasons | 1952-1954 |
| Peak Value | 31.0 |
| Potential Seasons | 17.33 |
| Potential Career | 537 Win Shares |
| Actual Career | 268 Win Shares |
| Percentage of Potential Value achieved | 50% |

### Elston Howard

| | |
|---|---|
| Peak Seasons | 1962-1964 |
| Peak Value | 26.7 |
| Potential Seasons | 16.97 |
| Potential Career | 453 Win Shares |
| Actual Career | 203 Win Shares |
| Percentage of Potential Value achieved | 45% |

### Dan Pasqua

| | |
|---|---|
| Peak Seasons | 1989-1991 |
| Peak Value | 12.7 |
| Potential Seasons | 15.48 |
| Potential Career | 196 Win Shares |
| Actual Career | 79 Win Shares |
| Percentage of Potential Value achieved | 40% |

### Damaso Garcia

| | |
|---|---|
| Peak Seasons | 1982-1984 |
| Peak Value | 16.7 |
| Potential Seasons | 15.98 |
| Potential Career | 266 Win Shares |
| Actual Career | 94 Win Shares |
| Percentage of Potential Value achieved | 35% |

### Oddibe McDowell

| | |
|---|---|
| Peak Seasons | 1986-1988 |
| Peak Value (Young Peak Adjustment Applied) | 16.9 |
| Potential Seasons | 16 |
| Potential Career | 270 Win Shares |
| Actual Career | 82 Win Shares |
| Percentage of Potential Value achieved | 30% |

### Ed Bouchee

| | |
|---|---|
| Peak Seasons | 1957-1959 |
| Peak Value | 17.7 |
| Potential Seasons | 16.09 |
| Potential Career | 284 Win Shares |
| Actual Career | 71 Win Shares |
| Percentage of Potential Value achieved | 25% |

### Herb Score

| | |
|---|---|
| Peak Seasons | 1955-1957 |
| Peak Value (Young Peak Adjustment Applied) | 17.6 |
| Potential Seasons | 16.09 |
| Potential Career | 283 Win Shares |
| Actual Career | 58 Win Shares |
| Percentage of Potential Value achieved | 20% |

### Lyman Bostock

| | |
|---|---|
| Peak Seasons | 1976-1978 |
| Peak Value | 21.7 |
| Potential Seasons | 16.51 |
| Potential Career | 358 Win Shares |
| Actual Career | 73 Win Shares |
| Percentage of Potential Value achieved | 20% |

Lyman Bostock's value achieved is about the lowest it can go, just in the way that we're measuring it. Players do, of course, show potential in less than three years, but we're measuring potential over a three-year period, which makes it difficult for our measurements to go much lower than 20%.

Let's go on to some lists now. The first thing we have to do, to make our lists work, is to get rid of the 19th-century pitchers. If we don't get rid of the 19th-century pitchers, most of our lists will be completely dominated by 19th-century pitchers, many of whom were spectacularly good for one or two years — often when they were 19 and 20 years old — but many of whom had very short careers. Nineteenth-century baseball really is not major league baseball, regardless of what people might tell you.

There are several basic questions we need to ask, with variations on that for Hall of Fame and non-Hall of Fame and pitcher and non-pitcher categories:

## 1) What players came closest to achieving 100% of their full career potential?

By my math, the number one player of all time, in terms of achieving his full career potential, was Jake Beckley, a turn-of-the-last-century first baseman who had 2,930 career hits and is in the Hall of Fame. Beckley, who hailed from the home town of Mark Twain and Joe Hardy, was never a great player; he was just a good player for a really long time:

| | Player | Peak Value | Career Value | Career Pot | Pct | | Player | Peak Value | Career Value | Career Pot | Pct |
|---|---|---|---|---|---|---|---|---|---|---|---|
| 1. | Jake Beckley | 20.5 | 318 | 337 | 94% | 13. | Luis Aparicio | 20.0 | 293 | 327 | 90% |
| 2. | Tommy John | 18.0 | 272 | 290 | 94% | 14. | Frank Robinson | 33.3 | 519 | 584 | 89% |
| 3. | Hank Aaron | 38.5 | 643 | 689 | 93% | 15. | Jimmy Dykes | 17.3 | 245 | 278 | 88% |
| 4. | Rickey Henderson | 32.6 | 532 | 570 | 93% | 16. | Dennis Martinez | 16.7 | 230 | 266 | 86% |
| 5. | Pete Rose | 32.7 | 530 | 570 | 93% | 17. | Rafael Palmeiro | 27.0 | 395 | 459 | 86% |
| 6. | Danny Darwin | 12.7 | 182 | 196 | 93% | 18. | Don McMahon | 10.0 | 130 | 151 | 86% |
| 7. | Bob McClure | 5.7 | 75 | 81 | 93% | 19. | Don Sutton | 22.3 | 318 | 370 | 86% |
| 8. | Al Kaline | 28.2 | 443 | 483 | 92% | 20. | Steve Carlton | 25.3 | 366 | 427 | 86% |
| 9. | Warren Spahn | 26.3 | 407 | 446 | 91% | 21. | Dave Winfield | 28.3 | 415 | 485 | 86% |
| 10. | Bad Bill Dahlen | 25.7 | 394 | 433 | 91% | 22. | Stan Musial | 39.3 | 604 | 706 | 86% |
| 11. | Chili Davis | 19.3 | 285 | 315 | 91% | 23. | Roger Clemens | 29.0 | 425 | 497 | 85% |
| 12. | Willie Mays | 39.7 | 642 | 713 | 90% | 24. | Benito Santiago | 14.3 | 190 | 225 | 84% |
| | | | | | | 25. | Joe Judge | 19.7 | 270 | 321 | 84% |

As you can see, most — but not all — of the players that we recognize as achieving a very high percentage of their potential career are outstanding players, and Hall of Fame players. Perhaps the most surprising name on the list is Chili Davis. When Chili Davis came to the majors in 1982, he was regarded as having a very high upside. He had knee troubles early in his career, and for much of his career he was regarded as a player who wasn't what he should have been, because of his early loss of speed.

Our system doesn't see it that way. The way our system sees it is, here is a player who hit just .233 with 11 homers in his second major league season, and who up to the age of 32 had never driven in 100 runs and had hit .300 just once. He stayed in the lineup and continued to progress as a hitter until he was in his mid-30s. He played 154 games when he was 22 years old; he played 146 games when he was 39. Although he was never a great player, he was healthy and productive throughout that long span. He had a full career.

*Most of the players that we recognize as achieving a very high percentage of their potential career are outstanding players, and Hall of Fame players.*

## 2) Among players of modest skills, who came closest to having a full career?

That list would be dominated by pitchers. My top 25 are Danny Darwin (93%), Bob McClure, Don McMahon (86%), Clarence Mitchell, Jim Dwyer, Mike Stanton, Ray Sadecki (80%), Woodie Fryman, Johnny Klippstein, Tom Gordon, John Burkett, Jeff Reardon, Mike Timlin, Kent Mercker (75%), Rick Honeycutt, Royce Clayton, Grant Jackson, Bob Forsch, Stan Javier, Todd Jones, Dennis Cook, Rick Aguilera, Don Slaught, Alan Ashby and Rube Benton (70%).

## 3) How about non-pitchers?

Clarence Mitchell was a half-and-half, pitching in 390 games but getting into another 259 as first baseman, outfielder or pinch hitter. Setting those aside, I have Jim Dwyer (81%), Royce Clayton (75%), Stan Javier, Don Slaught, Alan Ashby (70%), Heinie Peitz, Wilbert Robinson, Sandy Alomar Jr., Todd Pratt, Greg Myers, Rollie Hemsley, Charlie Moore, Dave Martinez, Otto Miller, Howard Shanks, Malachi Kittredge, Charlie Ganzel, Jimmy Austin (65%), Tom Brookens, Pat Kelly, Walt Weiss, Joe Quinn, Ed Kranepool, Joe Girardi and Blondie Purcell (64%). Blondie is another half-and-half, so I owe you one. Clyde McCullough.

## 4) Who had the lowest career percentages?

Jim Viox ranks last in my study, not because he probably deserves to, but because he perfectly fits the criteria of the study: He played regularly for three years, played very well, but then disappeared quickly from the major leagues. I didn't include anyone in my study who didn't earn at least 50 Career Win Shares; Viox had 61. He was the second baseman for the Pirates at the tag end of the Honus Wagner era, had an excellent .361 career on-base percentage in a very short career. I have Viox as achieving 18% of his career potential.

Behind him I have a pitcher named Fred Blanding, who pitched very well for the Cleveland Indians in 1912-1913, disappeared from the majors in 1914, presumably because of an arm injury.

Then we have what is at least a recognizable name, Sam Jethroe. Sam Jethroe was a Negro League star who was in his thirties by the time the color line broke, a good center fielder who scored 100 runs for the Braves in 1950 and 1951. Then we have Boo Ferriss — a 25-game winner with the 1946 Red Sox — and Milt Byrnes, a war-time third baseman who helped the Browns win the pennant in 1944, never got into a game before or after the war despite a nice .373 on-base percentage during the war. Byrnes is at 19%, then Dickie Kerr — kicked out of baseball by Landis for playing exhibition games against the Black Sox — then a couple of Federal League players, Duke Kenworthy and Dutch Zwilling. That's eight. Rounding out the bottom ten are Lou Fette, who won 20 games as a rookie for the Braves in 1937, and Gerald Young, who hit .321 in a half-season as a rookie for the Astros in 1987, stole 65 bases in 1988, then totally stopped hitting.

The next 15: Bob Lee (1960s reliever, dominant for a couple of years), Joe Connolly (outfielder who was part of the Miracle Braves in 1914), Alex Metzler (hit .319 for the White Sox in 1927), Steve Busby, Hod Eller, Tom Bradley, Herm McFarland, Rube Ellis, Ed Summers (one of the inventors of the knuckleball), Paul Dean, Josh Devore, Lyman Bostock, Buster Adams, Luke Easter, and Herb Score.

## 5) What is the historic norm?

The norm for all players, not including 19th-century pitchers, is 46%. Most players are able to achieve a little less than one-half of what they reasonably might, in a full career.

## 6) What is the norm for pitchers?

The historic norm for pitchers is 45%; for non-pitchers, 47%.

## 7) What is the norm for Hall of Famers?

The norm for Hall of Famers, still excluding 19th-century pitchers, is 64%. Hall of Fame players typically achieve about 64% of what they might have achieved without career interruptions of any kind. I listed eleven Hall of Famers earlier — Beckley, Aaron, Kaline, Spahn, Mays, Aparicio, Frank Robinson, Don Sutton, Steve Carlton, Winfield and Musial. Behind them are Babe Ruth (83%), Bid McPhee (82%), Gabby Hartnett, George Davis, Zack Wheat, Cap Anson (81%), Phil Niekro (80%), Sam Rice, Nap Lajoie (79%), Fred Clarke, Mel Ott, Carlton Fisk, Tris Speaker, and George Brett (78%).

## 8) And the lowest percentages for Hall of Famers?

Mostly — not entirely — a list of pitchers who had short but brilliant careers:

| Player | Pct | Player | Pct | Player | Pct | Player | Pct |
|---|---|---|---|---|---|---|---|
| 1. Dizzy Dean | 31% | 7. Freddy Lindstrom | 40% | 13. Joe Medwick | 43% | 19. Lefty Grove | 47% |
| 2. Sandy Koufax | 37% | 8. Hack Wilson | 41% | 14. Rube Waddell | 44% | 20. Rube Marquard | 47% |
| 3. Hal Newhouser | 38% | 9. Roy Campanella | 41% | 15. Home Run Baker | 45% | 21. Earle Combs | 48% |
| 4. Hughie Jennings | 38% | 10. Ed Walsh | 42% | 16. Tommy McCarthy | 46% | 22. Chuck Klein | 48% |
| 5. Addie Joss | 39% | 11. Jackie Robinson | 43% | 17. Monte Ward | 47% | 23. Stan Coveleski | 49% |
| 6. Ross Youngs | 39% | 12. Ralph Kiner | 43% | 18. Bob Feller | 47% | 24. Arky Vaughan | 49% |
| | | | | | | 25. Chick Hafey | 49% |

It seems remarkable that there are that many Hall of Famers who achieved less than one-half of what they might have achieved, but I think it stands up to skepticism. Look at Chick Hafey. He had 1,466 hits in his career. All we're really saying is that, given a longer run, given that his eyesight doesn't fail him in mid-career, given a chance to play earlier in his career, rather than starting out as a minor league pitcher, he might have had 3,000 career hits. I don't think that's unreasonable.

*It seems remarkable that there are that many Hall of Famers who achieved less than one-half of what they might have achieved, but I think it stands up to skepticism.*

## 9) Who does our system see as having the greatest upside potential of all time?

We should acknowledge here that we're departing into potentially controversial claims, with a speculative method that is clearly in need of more testing and refinement. In other words, I'll give you a list if you don't take it too seriously, OK? I don't want to be hearing about this ten years from now.

In the view of our system, the potentially greatest player of all time, if you mark off his high spots and project from there, is Mickey Mantle. These are what we would see as the 25 most promising careers of all time, and how they worked out. I'll mark with an asterisk those whose Peak Values were adjusted upward because of outstanding seasons as young players.

| Player | Peak Value | Career Value | Career Pot | Pct | | Player | Peak Value | Career Value | Career Pot | Pct |
|---|---|---|---|---|---|---|---|---|---|---|
| 1. Mickey Mantle* | 51.7 | 565 | 968 | 58% | | 13. Rogers Hornsby | 42.0 | 502 | 761 | 66% |
| 2. Ty Cobb* | 49.9 | 722 | 928 | 78% | | 14. Joe Jackson* | 41.1 | 294 | 742 | 40% |
| 3. Honus Wagner | 49.7 | 652 | 924 | 71% | | 15. Arky Vaughan* | 40.3 | 356 | 726 | 49% |
| 4. Babe Ruth* | 49.1 | 756 | 912 | 83% | | 16. Joe Morgan | 40.3 | 512 | 726 | 70% |
| 5. Walter Johnson* | 48.4 | 560 | 897 | 62% | | 17. Joe Medwick* | 40.0 | 312 | 719 | 43% |
| 6. Barry Bonds | 47.3 | 705 | 874 | 81% | | 18. Willie Mays | 39.7 | 642 | 713 | 90% |
| 7. Monte Ward* | 47.3 | 409 | 873 | 47% | | 19. Stan Musial | 39.3 | 604 | 706 | 86% |
| 8. Ted Williams | 44.0 | 555 | 803 | 69% | | 20. Hal Newhouser* | 38.9 | 264 | 696 | 39% |
| 9. Tris Speaker | 44.0 | 630 | 803 | 78% | | 21. Eddie Mathews* | 38.9 | 450 | 696 | 65% |
| 10. Eddie Collins* | 42.9 | 574 | 780 | 74% | | 22. Will Clark* | 38.9 | 331 | 696 | 48% |
| 11. Lou Gehrig* | 42.5 | 489 | 772 | 63% | | 23. Jimmie Foxx* | 38.5 | 435 | 689 | 63% |
| 12. Pete Alexander | 42.3 | 476 | 768 | 62% | | 24. Hank Aaron* | 38.5 | 643 | 689 | 93% |
| | | | | | | 25. Joe DiMaggio* | 37.8 | 387 | 673 | 57% |

Monte Ward is left off of a couple of other lists as a 19th-century pitcher; I decided to go ahead and include him here. So I still owe you one:

| Player | Peak Value | Career Value | Career Pot | Pct |
|---|---|---|---|---|
| 26. Mel Ott* | 37.4 | 528 | 666 | 79% |

All of the potentially greatest players of all time are in the Hall of Fame except Barry Bonds and Joe Jackson, who are not eligible, and Will Clark. Among players with very, very high peaks who ultimately didn't (or haven't yet) made the Hall of Fame: Tim Raines, Don Mattingly, Dale Murphy, Mark McGwire, Pedro Guerrero. Mostly 1980s players. All 1980s players.

# Seattle Mariners

## Key Players

| Pos | Player | G | AB | R | H | 2B | 3B | HR | RBI | SB | CS | BB | SO | AVG | OBP | SLG | OPS | WS |
|---|---|---|---|---|---|---|---|---|---|---|---|---|---|---|---|---|---|---|
| C | Rob Johnson | 80 | 258 | 21 | 55 | 19 | 2 | 2 | 27 | 1 | 1 | 26 | 60 | .213 | .289 | .326 | .615 | 9 |
| 1B | Russell Branyan | 116 | 431 | 64 | 108 | 21 | 1 | 31 | 76 | 2 | 0 | 58 | 149 | .251 | .347 | .520 | .867 | 14 |
| 2B | Jose Lopez | 153 | 613 | 69 | 167 | 42 | 0 | 25 | 96 | 3 | 3 | 24 | 69 | .272 | .303 | .463 | .766 | 12 |
| 3B | Adrian Beltre | 111 | 449 | 54 | 119 | 27 | 0 | 8 | 44 | 13 | 2 | 19 | 74 | .265 | .304 | .379 | .683 | 10 |
| SS | Yuniesky Betancourt | 63 | 224 | 15 | 56 | 10 | 1 | 2 | 22 | 3 | 1 | 10 | 18 | .250 | .278 | .330 | .609 | 4 |
| LF | Endy Chavez | 54 | 161 | 17 | 44 | 3 | 1 | 2 | 13 | 9 | 1 | 14 | 22 | .273 | .328 | .342 | .669 | 3 |
| CF | Franklin Gutierrez | 153 | 565 | 85 | 160 | 24 | 1 | 18 | 70 | 16 | 5 | 46 | 122 | .283 | .339 | .425 | .764 | 21 |
| RF | Ichiro Suzuki | 146 | 639 | 88 | 225 | 31 | 4 | 11 | 46 | 26 | 9 | 32 | 71 | .352 | .386 | .465 | .851 | 28 |
| DH | Ken Griffey Jr. | 117 | 387 | 44 | 83 | 19 | 0 | 19 | 57 | 0 | 0 | 63 | 80 | .214 | .324 | .411 | .735 | 7 |

## Key Pitchers

| Pos | Player | G | GS | W | L | SV | IP | H | R | ER | SO | BB | BR/9 | ERA | WS |
|---|---|---|---|---|---|---|---|---|---|---|---|---|---|---|---|
| SP | Felix Hernandez | 34 | 34 | 19 | 5 | 0 | 238.2 | 200 | 81 | 66 | 217 | 71 | 10.52 | 2.49 | 26 |
| SP | Jarrod Washburn | 20 | 20 | 8 | 6 | 0 | 133.0 | 109 | 42 | 39 | 79 | 33 | 9.81 | 2.64 | 14 |
| SP | Erik Bedard | 15 | 15 | 5 | 3 | 0 | 83.0 | 65 | 29 | 26 | 90 | 34 | 11.17 | 2.82 | 8 |
| SP | Ryan Rowland-Smith | 15 | 15 | 5 | 4 | 0 | 96.1 | 87 | 43 | 40 | 52 | 27 | 11.02 | 3.74 | 7 |
| SP | Jason Vargas | 23 | 14 | 3 | 6 | 0 | 91.2 | 98 | 53 | 50 | 54 | 24 | 12.27 | 4.91 | 3 |
| CL | David Aardsma | 73 | 0 | 3 | 6 | 38 | 71.1 | 49 | 23 | 20 | 80 | 34 | 10.47 | 2.52 | 16 |
| RP | Miguel Batista | 56 | 0 | 7 | 4 | 1 | 71.1 | 79 | 37 | 32 | 52 | 39 | 15.14 | 4.04 | 5 |
| RP | Mark Lowe | 75 | 0 | 2 | 7 | 3 | 80.0 | 71 | 39 | 29 | 69 | 29 | 11.25 | 3.26 | 8 |

## Is There a Pattern?

The 2009 Mariners became the 13th team since 1900 to have a winning season after losing 100 games the year before.

In year three of the sequence the first 12 teams averaged a .487 winning percentage.

| Year | Team | Wins | Losses | Win Pct |
|------|------|------|--------|---------|
| 2004 | Royals | 58 | 104 | .358 |
| 1990 | Orioles | 76 | 85 | .472 |
| 1987 | Giants | 90 | 72 | .556 |
| 1987 | Indians | 61 | 101 | .377 |
| 1981 | A's | 64 | 45 | .587 |
| 1975 | Rangers | 79 | 83 | .488 |
| 1968 | Cubs | 84 | 78 | .519 |
| 1964 | Cubs | 76 | 86 | .469 |
| 1963 | Phillies | 87 | 75 | .537 |
| 1948 | A's | 84 | 70 | .545 |
| 1919 | Pirates | 71 | 68 | .511 |
| 1906 | Phillies | 71 | 82 | .464 |
| | **Total** | **901** | **949** | **.487** |

## Rickey Would Be So Proud

Chone Figgins scored 23 runs in 2009 in the 54 games where he went without a hit. Nick Punto (21) was the only other major league player who scored more than 16 runs in his hitless games.

**Chone Figgins — 2009 Games with X Hits**

| | G | AB | R | H | 2B | 3B | HR | RBI | AVG |
|--------|----|-----|----|----|----|----|----|-----|------|
| 0 Hits | 54 | 180 | 23 | 0 | 0 | 0 | 0 | 4 | .000 |
| 1 Hits | 47 | 186 | 18 | 47 | 4 | 0 | 1 | 11 | .253 |
| 2 Hits | 37 | 153 | 44 | 74 | 15 | 6 | 3 | 24 | .484 |
| 3 Hits | 18 | 84 | 26 | 54 | 7 | 1 | 1 | 10 | .643 |
| 4 Hits | 2 | 12 | 3 | 8 | 4 | 0 | 0 | 5 | .667 |

## Who to Lead Off

It is not our place to tell the Mariners who should lead off between Chone Figgins and Ichiro, but Figgins in 2009 scored on a single by another hitter 54 times — 14 more than anyone else in baseball. Albert Pujols, who led the majors with 124 runs scored — 10 more than Figgins — scored on a single only 33 times. Dustin Pedroia, who scored more runs than Figgins, scored on a single only 31 times.

Figgins also scored 39 runs after reaching on a walk or hit-by-pitch, most in the majors. Adrian Gonzalez (119) and Adam Dunn (116) each had more walks than Figgins (101), but each scored less than half as many runs following a walk or a hit batsman.

### Chone Figgins — 2009 Runs Scored Analysis

| Reached on | | Runs Scored After | |
|---|---|---|---|
| Home Runs | 5 | | 5 |
| Triples | 7 | Scored after Triple | 4 |
| Doubles | 30 | Scored after Double | 14 |
| Singles | 141 | Scored after Single | 46 |
| Walk/HBP | 102 | Scored after Walk/HBP | 39 |
| Reached on Error | 8 | Scored after ROE | 3 |
| Reached on Forceout | 13 | Vultured Runs | 2 |
| Other | 3 | Other | 1 |
| | | Total Runs Scored | 114 |

| Brought in by | | Driven in by | |
|---|---|---|---|
| Single | 54 | Bobby Abreu | 35 |
| Double | 16 | Torii Hunter | 19 |
| Triple | 4 | Maicer Izturis | 15 |
| His own home run | 5 | Vladimir Guerrero | 14 |
| Other home run | 12 | Juan Rivera | 7 |
| Sac Fly | 9 | Kendry Morales | 5 |
| Walk, Error, or Other | 14 | Himself | 5 |
| | | No RBI | 5 |
| | | Erick Aybar | 4 |
| | | Gary Matthews Jr. | 2 |
| | | Mike Napoli | 2 |
| | | Howie Kendrick | 1 |

## Ichiro

- In 2009 Ichiro became the first player ever to lead the majors in base hits in four consecutive seasons.
- He has now led the majors in hits six times in his career, trailing only Ty Cobb and Pete Rose who each led the majors seven times.
- Ichiro had his ninth consecutive 200-hit season, the most in major league history. He was tied with Willie Keeler with eight consecutive seasons.
- Mr. Suzuki tied Ty Cobb for the most 200-hit seasons in American League history. Pete Rose's ten 200-hit seasons is the major league record.
- All nine seasons he has been in the American League he has led the league in singles — the most times any batter has led the league in that category. Nellie Fox led the American League eight times in singles in the 1950's.
- He became the first player to have five 220+ hit seasons in his career, breaking a tie with two of baseball's most genteel players, Roger Hornsby and Jesse Burkett. There have been 91 seasons in which a player had 220 or more hits.
- The three fastest players to 2,000 hits in major league history are Al Simmons (1,390 games), Ichiro Suzuki (1,402), George Sisler (1,414).
- Four players have had 2,000 hits in a single decade. Sam Rice and Rogers Hornsby in the 1920's, Pete Rose in the 1970's, and Ichiro in the 2000's.

## Mariner Batting — "Out of Order"

Mariner leadoff men in 2009 — mostly Ichiro — had an OPS of .837, which was second-best in the American League.

Mariner fifth-place hitters — a mix of Beltre, Branyan and Gutierrez — also had an .837 OPS, which was fourth-best in the American League.

At every other batting order position (2, 3, 4, 6, 7, 8, 9) the OPS of Mariner hitters was among the worst in the American league.

| Pos | OPS | League Rank |
|-----|-----|-------------|
| 1 | .837 | 2 |
| 2 | .673 | 13 |
| 3 | .735 | 12 |
| 4 | .731 | 12 |
| 5 | .837 | 4 |
| 6 | .710 | 12 |
| 7 | .578 | 14 |
| 8 | .689 | 11 |
| 9 | .617 | 12 |

## Branyan Goes Deep

Russell Branyan set a new career high in homers with 31. His home runs per plate appearance were right in line with what he had done over the past decade, but this was the first time he had gotten more than 300 plate appearances since 2002.

| Year | Team | Age | PA | HR | PA/HR |
|------|------|-----|-----|-----|-------|
| 2000 | CLE | 24 | 220 | 16 | 13.8 |
| 2001 | CLE | 25 | 361 | 20 | 18.1 |
| 2002 | TOT | 26 | 435 | 24 | 18.1 |
| 2003 | CIN | 27 | 205 | 9 | 22.8 |
| 2004 | MIL | 28 | 182 | 11 | 16.5 |
| 2005 | MIL | 29 | 242 | 12 | 20.2 |
| 2006 | TOT | 30 | 282 | 18 | 15.7 |
| 2007 | TOT | 31 | 194 | 10 | 19.4 |
| 2008 | MIL | 32 | 152 | 12 | 12.7 |
| 2009 | SEA | 33 | 505 | 31 | 16.3 |
| **Totals** | | | **2,778** | **163** | **17.0** |

## A Contrast in Styles

Russell Branyan swung at the first pitch he saw more frequently than any other player in the American League. He took a rip at 37.3% of the first pitches he saw.

Franklin Gutierrez took the other approach, swinging at just 7.7% of the first pitches he saw.

**Russell Branyan — 2009**

|  | AB | H | HR | RBI | AVG | OBP | SLG | OPS |
|------|-----|-----|-----|-----|-----|-----|-----|-----|
| One and done | 65 | 27 | 5 | 18 | .415 | .415 | .723 | 1.138 |

**Franklin Gutierrez — 2009**

|  | AB | H | HR | RBI | AVG | OBP | SLG | OPS |
|------|-----|-----|-----|-----|-----|-----|-----|-----|
| One and done | 23 | 8 | 1 | 8 | .348 | .348 | .542 | .889 |

| Highest First Swing % — American League | | Lowest First Swing % — American League | |
|------|------|------|------|
| 1. Russell Branyan | 37.3% | 1. Joe Mauer | 6.5% |
| 2. Carlos Pena | 36.7% | 2. Dustin Pedroia | 6.6% |
| 3. Magglio Ordonez | 36.3% | 3. Franklin Gutierrez | 7.7% |

Minimum 502 PA

The interesting thing is that Branyan is actually NOT a swing-at-everything guy. He actually takes a lot of pitches. He just likes to swing at the first one.

## A New Focus on Defense — Part I

Defensive Efficiency Rating (DER) is the percentage of balls that are put into play that are turned into outs. In 2008 the Mariners DER was .679, the second-worst in the American League. In 2009 with the addition of two strong defensive outfielders and a mid-season upgrade at shortstop, the team's DER zoomed to .710. That is the highest percentage of balls in play turned into outs that any American League team has posted since 2005.

## A New Focus on Defense — Part II

Defensive Runs Saved compiles all of the defensive ratings into a single number that estimates the number of actual runs saved or allowed by the fielder, compared to average.

Seattle's 110 runs saved in 2009 is the largest number in this category of any major league team since we began tracking it in 2003. The only other team to save more than 100 runs defensively in a season is the 2005 Phillies.

**Team Defensive Runs Saved**

| Year | Team | P | C | 1B | 2B | 3B | SS | LF | CF | RF | Total |
|------|------|----|----|-----|----|----|-----|----|----|----|-------|
| 2007 | Seattle | 11 | -9 | -16 | 1 | 4 | -7 | -9 | 6 | 0 | -19 |
| 2008 | Seattle | -1 | -4 | 0 | -2 | 25 | -13 | -6 | 0 | 17 | 16 |
| 2009 | Seattle | 12 | 12 | 1 | 6 | 27 | -6 | 8 | 36 | 14 | 110 |

## Spreading It Around

Only two pitchers for the Mariners pitched more than 100 innings in 2009, Felix Hernandez with 238.2 innings pitched, and Jarrod Washburn with 133. Those two threw 26% of the Mariners' innings while 18 other pitchers split up the other 74%. Despite that, the Mariners' 3.87 ERA led the American League, 27 points ahead of the second-place White Sox.

## Offense, Not So Good

The Mariners were last in the American League in runs scored, walks drawn, batting average, and on-base percentage. Their good season was entirely created by pitching and defense. OK, Felix Hernandez and defense.

## Quality Starts

Felix Hernandez' 29 quality starts in 2009 broke the Mariners' team record of 25 set by Floyd Bannister in 1982. Randy Johnson is the only pitcher in the 21st century to have more quality starts than King Felix did last year. The Big Unit had 30 quality starts in 2002 in Arizona.

## Counting on Felix

Seattle won 25 of Felix Hernandez' 34 starts, two more wins than any other team got from any one pitcher's starts in 2009. The last time a team had more wins in one pitcher's starts was in 2006 when the Twins won 27 of Johan Santana's 34 starts.

## Pitching When It Counts Most

Leverage Index is the amount of swing in the possible change in win probability, compared to the average swing in all situations. The average swing is indexed to 1.00. A Leverage Index of 2.0 would be twice as crucial as a typical situation; likewise, a Leverage Index of 0.5 would be half as crucial as a typical situation. It is a measure of whether the pitcher has pitched in game-crucial situations, when a hit or a run would lead to defeat.

David Aardsma was the third-highest leveraged pitcher in the American League.

### Highest Leveraged Relievers — American League

| Player | Games | Leverage Index |
|---|---|---|
| 1. Jonathan Papelbon, Bos | 66 | 2.17 |
| 2. Brian Fuentes, LAA | 65 | 2.13 |
| 3. David Aardsma, Sea | 73 | 2.11 |
| 4. Joakim Soria, KC | 47 | 2.05 |
| 5. Bobby Jenks, CWS | 52 | 1.90 |

Minimum 25 games in relief

## Pitching When It Counts Least

The pitchers who were consistently used in lowest leverage situations in 2009:

### Lowest Leveraged Relievers — MLB

| Player | Games | Leverage Index |
|---|---|---|
| 1. Luis Perdomo, SD | 35 | .28 |
| 2. Elmer Dessens, NYM | 28 | .31 |
| 3. Chris Smith, Mil | 35 | .35 |
| 4. Tyler Walker, Phi | 32 | .39 |
| 5. Carlos Fisher, Cin | 39 | .46 |

Minimum 25 games in relief

## Can I Come Back to Seattle?

Jarrod Washburn had the largest percentage of outs from fly balls of any starter in the majors in 2009, at 35%. What happened to him when he went to Detroit was, those fly balls started leaving play. With the Mariners he allowed 1 homer per 44 at-bats (11/488). As a Tiger his ratio was 1 in every 14 at-bats (12/170).

## As Paris Hilton Would Say, " That's Hot"

Mark Lowe had the fastest fastball of any reliever in the American League, with an average speed of 96.3 miles per hour.

### Fastest Average Fastball – Relievers

| Player | MPH |
|---|---|
| 1. Mark Lowe | 96.3 |
| 2. Kevin Jepsen | 96.2 |
| 3. Fernando Rodney | 95.8 |
| 4. Matt Thornton | 95.7 |
| 5. Kerry Wood | 95.5 |

Minimum 50 IP

## Blown Saves

The Mariners had the most blown saves in the American League with 28. Seattle starting pitchers left the game in position for a win 23 times, but the game was blown by the bullpen six more times than any other team in the league.

## Controlling the Running Game

The average American League team allowed 108 stolen bases and caught 26% of the runners who attempted to steal in 2009.

The Mariners allowed 67 steals, the lowest figure in the league, while throwing out 40% of all would-be base stealers, the best figure in the league.

Kenji Johjima threw out 22 of the 41 attempted base stealers he faced last season. His 54% caught stealing rate led the league. The Mariners other two catchers also stopped the running game effectively. Rob Johnson caught 31% (18 of 59) and Jamie Burke gunned down 44% (4 of 9).

## Good Catcher Defense as Well

Rob Johnson's rookie season was strong defensively. He led the majors in catcher's ERA at 3.22, and was ranked first among catchers in Runs Saved.

**Catcher 2009**

| Player | Runs Saved |
|---|---|
| 1. Rob Johnson | 8 |
| 2. Koyie Hill | 7 |
| 3. Miguel Montero | 6 |
| 4. Russell Martin | 5 |
| 5. Gerald Laird | 5 |

# Tampa Bay Rays

## Key Players

| Pos | Player | G | AB | R | H | 2B | 3B | HR | RBI | SB | CS | BB | SO | AVG | OBP | SLG | OPS | WS |
|---|---|---|---|---|---|---|---|---|---|---|---|---|---|---|---|---|---|---|
| C | Dioner Navarro | 115 | 376 | 38 | 82 | 15 | 0 | 8 | 32 | 5 | 2 | 18 | 51 | .218 | .261 | .322 | .583 | 5 |
| 1B | Carlos Pena | 135 | 471 | 91 | 107 | 25 | 2 | 39 | 100 | 3 | 3 | 87 | 163 | .227 | .356 | .537 | .893 | 17 |
| 2B | Ben Zobrist | 152 | 501 | 91 | 149 | 28 | 7 | 27 | 91 | 17 | 6 | 91 | 104 | .297 | .405 | .543 | .948 | 27 |
| 3B | Evan Longoria | 157 | 584 | 100 | 164 | 44 | 0 | 33 | 113 | 9 | 0 | 72 | 140 | .281 | .364 | .526 | .889 | 24 |
| SS | Jason Bartlett | 137 | 500 | 90 | 160 | 29 | 7 | 14 | 66 | 30 | 7 | 54 | 89 | .320 | .389 | .490 | .879 | 23 |
| LF | Carl Crawford | 156 | 606 | 96 | 185 | 28 | 8 | 15 | 68 | 60 | 16 | 51 | 99 | .305 | .364 | .452 | .816 | 19 |
| CF | B.J. Upton | 144 | 560 | 79 | 135 | 33 | 4 | 11 | 55 | 42 | 14 | 57 | 152 | .241 | .313 | .373 | .686 | 13 |
| RF | Gabe Gross | 115 | 282 | 31 | 64 | 16 | 1 | 6 | 36 | 6 | 3 | 42 | 79 | .227 | .326 | .355 | .681 | 8 |
| DH | Pat Burrell | 122 | 412 | 45 | 91 | 16 | 1 | 14 | 64 | 2 | 0 | 57 | 119 | .221 | .315 | .367 | .682 | 6 |

## Key Pitchers

| Pos | Player | G | GS | W | L | SV | IP | H | R | ER | SO | BB | BR/9 | ERA | WS |
|---|---|---|---|---|---|---|---|---|---|---|---|---|---|---|---|
| SP | Jeff Niemann | 31 | 30 | 13 | 6 | 0 | 180.2 | 185 | 84 | 79 | 125 | 59 | 12.60 | 3.94 | 12 |
| SP | James Shields | 33 | 33 | 11 | 12 | 0 | 219.2 | 239 | 113 | 101 | 167 | 52 | 11.96 | 4.14 | 11 |
| SP | Matt Garza | 32 | 32 | 8 | 12 | 0 | 203.0 | 177 | 93 | 89 | 189 | 79 | 11.84 | 3.95 | 12 |
| SP | David Price | 23 | 23 | 10 | 7 | 0 | 128.1 | 119 | 72 | 63 | 102 | 54 | 12.41 | 4.42 | 6 |
| SP | Scott Kazmir | 20 | 20 | 8 | 7 | 0 | 111.0 | 121 | 77 | 73 | 91 | 50 | 14.27 | 5.92 | 2 |
| CL | J.P. Howell | 69 | 0 | 7 | 5 | 17 | 66.2 | 47 | 22 | 21 | 79 | 33 | 11.21 | 2.84 | 11 |
| RP | Grant Balfour | 73 | 0 | 5 | 4 | 4 | 67.1 | 59 | 38 | 36 | 69 | 33 | 12.56 | 4.81 | 5 |
| RP | Dan Wheeler | 69 | 0 | 4 | 5 | 2 | 57.2 | 41 | 22 | 21 | 45 | 9 | 7.80 | 3.28 | 6 |

## Navarro's Platoon Splits

Dioner Navarro had a breakout season in 2008, a terrible year in 2009, but here's the weird part. Navarro's a switch hitter. Batting right-handed, he was actually much *better* in 2009:

### Dioner Navarro Batting Right-Handed

|      | AB  | R  | H  | 2B | 3B | HR | RBI | BB | SO | AVG  | OBP  | SLG  |
|------|-----|----|----|----|----|----|-----|----|----|------|------|------|
| 2008 | 109 | 12 | 28 | 8  | 0  | 3  | 13  | 9  | 12 | .257 | .314 | .413 |
| 2009 | 141 | 17 | 39 | 7  | 0  | 5  | 19  | 4  | 13 | .277 | .309 | .433 |

That just wasn't nearly enough to compensate for his 126-point decline in batting average from the left side:

### Dioner Navarro Batting Left-Handed

|      | AB  | R  | H  | 2B | 3B | HR | RBI | BB | SO | AVG  | OBP  | SLG  |
|------|-----|----|----|----|----|----|-----|----|----|------|------|------|
| 2008 | 318 | 31 | 98 | 19 | 0  | 4  | 41  | 25 | 37 | .308 | .361 | .406 |
| 2009 | 235 | 21 | 43 | 8  | 0  | 3  | 13  | 14 | 38 | .183 | .234 | .255 |

I would speculate that, in all the history of baseball, you'd have a hard time finding another example of a switch-hitting regular whose batting average dropped 77 points — but whose average actually went *up* from one side of the plate.

## Shift

Carlos Pena hit 88 ground balls in 2009 — 71 toward right field, 15 toward center, 2 toward left. He is the most extreme pull hitter in the major leagues.

### Carlos Pena

| Ground Balls          | NO | OUT | H | AVG  |
|-----------------------|----|-----|---|------|
| Ground Balls to Left  | 2  | 1   | 1 | .500 |
| Ground Balls to Center| 15 | 13  | 2 | .133 |
| Ground Balls to Right | 71 | 64  | 7 | .099 |

## That All-Important Leadoff Batter

James Shields and Adam Wainwright each allowed the leadoff batter to reach base 82 out of about 235 times in 2009, a fairly high total. However, while Wainwright allowed only 59 runs in innings where the leadoff batter reached, Shields allowed 92 — the most in the majors. After watching his opening day starter get into jam after jam, Rays manager Joe Maddon pulled him from the game 22 times in the middle of the inning, also more than any starter in baseball.

When Shields breezed through that first batter, however, he was headed for an easy inning. He was also second in the majors in "Quick Innings", those that last 10 pitches or less.

| James Shields — 2009 Inning Analysis | |
| --- | --- |
| Innings Pitched | 219.2 |
| Runs Allowed | 113 |
| Innings Started | 233 |
| Runs in Those Innings | 119 |
| Shutout Innings | 166 |
| One-Run Innings | 35 |
| Two-Run Innings | 18 |
| Three-Run Innings | 10 |
| Four-Run Innings | 2 |
| Five-Run Innings | 2 |
| Got First Man Out | 151 |
| Runs Scored in Those Innings | 27 |
| Runs/9 Innings | 1.61 |
| First Man Reached | 82 |
| Runs Scored in Those Innings | 92 |
| Runs/9 Innings | 10.10 |
| 1-2-3 Innings | 86 |
| 10-pitch Innings (or less) | 58 |
| Long Innings (20 or more pitches) | 38 |
| Failed to Finish Inning | 22 |

| Adam Wainwright — 2009 Inning Analysis | |
| --- | --- |
| Innings Pitched | 233.0 |
| Runs Allowed | 75 |
| Innings Started | 237 |
| Runs in Those Innings | 87 |
| Shutout Innings | 187 |
| One-Run Innings | 33 |
| Two-Run Innings | 9 |
| Three-Run Innings | 5 |
| Six-Run Innings | 2 |
| Nine-Run Innings | 1 |
| Got First Man Out | 155 |
| Runs Scored in Those Innings | 28 |
| Runs/9 Innings | 1.63 |
| First Man Reached | 82 |
| Runs Scored in Those Innings | 59 |
| Runs/9 Innings | 6.48 |
| 1-2-3 Innings | 88 |
| 10-pitch Innings (or less) | 54 |
| Long Innings (20 or more pitches) | 56 |
| Failed to Finish Inning | 6 |

## Tampa Bay Road Runners

The 2009 Rays were the first major league team since the 2001 Mariners to have three players with 30 or more stolen bases. Carl Crawford (60), B.J. Upton (42), and Jason Bartlett (30).

## Rare Feat

After a strong Rookie of the Year season, Evan Longoria established himself as an elite third baseman in 2009, capturing both the Gold Glove and Silver Slugger awards at age 23. Only two other players have won both a Gold Glove and a Silver Slugger in the same season at age 23 or younger: Ken Griffey, Jr. (1991) and Benito Santiago (1988).

## Getting Some Lift

The major league batting average on ground balls in 2009 was .236, but the slugging percentage was .237.
The batting average on fly balls was .235, but the slugging percentage was 200 points higher, .445.
The batting average on line drives was .722. These numbers are all pretty much the same every year.
Jason Bartlett's offensive breakout in 2009 occurred essentially because he got under the pitch. In 2008 he hit 49% ground balls. In 2009 he hit more fly balls and more line drives — thus, better results.

| | Ground Balls | Line Drives | Fly Balls |
|---|---|---|---|
| 2008 | 49.0% | 20.7% | 30.3% |
| 2009 | 35.0% | 26.0% | 39.1% |

## Excellent and Versatile Defense

Not even in the opening day lineup, Ben Zobrist played seven of nine defensive positions at some point during the 2009 season, more than any other major leaguer. On top of the position flexibility, he had an excellent defensive season, totaling an estimated 18 runs saved at second base and an estimated 12 runs saved in right field, his two semi-regular positions. The versatility was a tremendous benefit for the Rays. When Akinori Iwamura hit the disabled list in late May, Zobrist slid into the everyday lineup and by late July had worked his way into the cleanup spot. When Iwamura returned at the end of August, Zobrist made starts in right field to boost production from the disappointing platoon of the two Gabes (Kapler and Gross). In the offseason, the Rays traded Iwamura to open up a regular lineup spot for the surprising 29-year-old slugger.

## Run Support

The Rays scored 179 runs in the 30 games started by Jeff Niemann, but only 122 in Matt Garza's 32 starts. Niemann won 13 games and lost 6 while Garza finished at 8-12. If he wants a winning record in 2010, Matt Garza should grow a few inches and change his name to Jeff.

**Performance by Starting Pitcher**

| Games Started | GS | Run Support | Runs Allowed | Won | Lost |
|---|---|---|---|---|---|
| James Shields | 33 | 153 | 158 | 15 | 18 |
| Matt Garza | 32 | 122 | 137 | 15 | 17 |
| Jeff Niemann | 30 | 179 | 128 | 18 | 12 |
| David Price | 23 | 122 | 110 | 14 | 9 |
| Scott Kazmir | 20 | 119 | 99 | 12 | 8 |
| Andy Sonnanstine | 18 | 91 | 93 | 7 | 11 |
| Wade Davis | 6 | 17 | 29 | 3 | 3 |
| **Total** | **162** | **803** | **754** | **84** | **78** |

## The Hook

Rays closer J.P. Howell threw 402 curveballs last season, more than any other reliever in baseball.

# The 2009-2010 Young Talent Inventory

by Bill James

WHICH MAJOR LEAGUE TEAM HAS THE MOST YOUNG TALENT IN THEIR organization? Two years ago, in the 2008 *Bill James Handbook*, we introduced a method to study that issue. We repeated the study in the 2009 Handbook, and then this year, to give us more time to study the issue and improve the methodology, we moved the study from the *Handbook* to the *Gold Mine*.

We begin by assigning to every player in major league baseball an "Inventory Value", based on his age and major league performance. The method that was used here, while essentially similar to the original method, has been revised and extended. In the Bill James Online, I explained every step of the calculation. Here, in the interest of saving trees, I'm going to abbreviate.

*We're interested in the good young players.*

We figure two scores for every major league player, an "Established Value Score" and a "Youth Score", then we put these together into a "Youth/Value Score" or Inventory Value. We also gave Inventory Value Scores to the 50 players designated by MLB in January, 2010, as the 50 best prospects in the game.

By our method, the 20 "most valuable properties" in the majors at this moment are:

| Rank | Player | 2009 Age | Inventory Value | Rank | Player | 2009 Age | Inventory Value |
|---|---|---|---|---|---|---|---|
| 1. | Felix Hernandez, Sea | 23 | 267 | 11. | Matt Kemp, LAD | 24 | 238 |
| 2. | Prince Fielder, Mil | 25 | 267 | 12. | Dustin Pedroia, Bos | 25 | 238 |
| 3. | Hanley Ramirez, Fla | 25 | 265 | 13. | Zack Greinke, KC | 25 | 238 |
| 4. | Ryan Braun, Mil | 25 | 261 | 14. | Ryan Zimmerman, Was | 24 | 238 |
| 5. | Pablo Sandoval, SF | 22 | 255 | 15. | David Wright, NYM | 26 | 234 |
| 6. | Tim Lincecum, SF | 25 | 252 | 16. | Joe Mauer, Min | 26 | 232 |
| 7. | Evan Longoria, TB | 23 | 249 | 17. | Troy Tulowitzki, Col | 24 | 232 |
| 8. | Justin Upton, Ari | 21 | 248 | 18. | Adam Lind, Tor | 25 | 232 |
| 9. | Miguel Cabrera, Det | 26 | 241 | 19. | Jair Jurrjens, Atl | 23 | 227 |
| 10. | Nick Markakis, Bal | 25 | 239 | 20. | Mark Reynolds, Ari | 25 | 226 |

Probably you do not exactly agree with all of those listings, and you may be inclined to write to me and argue that the top twenty list should have included Adrian Gonzalez, or Jonathan Broxton, or Aaron Hill, or Adam Jones, or Curtis Granderson, or some other slacker. If you are determined to write me such a letter, then it is my sad duty to inform you at this time that you are a moron, and in the future you should refrain from engaging in public discourse, out of consideration for others.

No, I'm joking, of course. I have no doubt that your list of the top 20 young players in baseball right now would be every bit as good as mine; indeed, I have no doubt that it would be better than mine. But here's my point: *We don't really know.* There is no right answer. What we are talking about here is who is going to be a good ballplayer in the future. We don't know; I don't know, you don't know. We're guessing. We should make the best guess that we *can* make, but we could spend the next 90 days debating who should be where and refining our method, and we would still be wrong.

We would still be wrong, *and* we would never get to the question of which *teams* have the most young talent. This is not an article about whether Felix Hernandez is a more valuable young player than Tim Lincecum or vice versa. This is an article about whether Seattle has more young talent than San Francisco. In order to get to the doorway of *that* question, we have to close off debate about this one. So…I don't want to hear about it. If you have objections to my list, keep them to yourself; it's not helpful.

OK, next we eliminated from the list players whose Inventory Value was less than 25. Less than 25 is less than one-half the current value of Julio Lugo. Players with Inventory Value of 25 are routinely non-tendered, not offered contracts, and there are a billion of them, so…we're not interested in them; we're interested in the good young players. There were 737 major league players and prospects in 2009 with an inventory value of at least 25 points.

However, I didn't count all of those players in the inventory totals. I counted:

*The major league team with the most young talent at this moment is, as it was in our first survey two years ago, the Tampa Bay Rays.*

1) All players with an Inventory Value of 70 or more, and

2) At least 15 players on each team.

70 points is not a lot of inventory value; that's Jody Gerut, Manny Parra, Kyle McClellan or Torii Hunter. But only 8 of the 30 major league teams have more than 15 players of that value. For those 8 teams, I counted everybody with a value of 70 or greater. For the other 22 teams, I counted their top 15 players. Brayan Pena and Ross Gload score around 50. When you ask the question, "which teams have the most young talent", you're not talking about who has more Brayan Penas and Ross Gloads.

OK, let's get to the list. The major league team with the most young talent at this moment is, as it was in our first survey two years ago, the Tampa Bay Rays. This chart summarizes the totals of the 30 major league teams:

**1. Tampa Bay Rays (2,864 points).** 1,446 points worth of young major league position players (3rd in the majors), 894 points worth of young pitching (9th in the majors), and 523 points worth of prospects (first in the majors). They have 21 players with an Inventory Value of 70 or more, the most in the game. Top five young players: Evan Longoria, B.J. Upton, Carl Crawford, Ben Zobrist and Big Game James Shields.

**2. Colorado Rockies (2,529).** The Rockies rank 2nd in young position players, 7th in young pitching, 19th in prospects. The Rockies have 18 young players with an Inventory Value of 70 or more, the top five of whom are Troy Tulowitzki, Huston Street, Ubaldo Jimenez, Brad Hawpe and Seth Smith.

**3. Minnesota Twins (2,441).** The Twins, who have 18 players with an Inventory Value of 70 or higher, rank in the top half in both young pitching and young position players, although in the bottom half in prospects. Their top five properties are Joe Mauer, Jason Kubel, Justin Morneau, Denard Span and Scott Baker.

**4. Arizona Diamondbacks (2,385).** The Snakes' collection of young position players is actually the best in baseball, although they rank below average in the two other areas (young pitching and prospects.) Their top five young players are Justin Upton, Mark Reynolds, Dan Haren, Stephen Drew and Edwin Jackson.

**5. Boston Red Sox (2,310).** The Red Sox have 16 players with an Inventory Value of 70 or higher. They rank 4th in the majors in young pitching, and 9th in prospects. Their top five properties: Dustin Pedroia, Jon Lester, Jon Papelbon, Jacoby Ellsbury and Josh Beckett.

**6. San Francisco Giants (2,284).** The Giants rank 3rd in minor league prospects, 6th in pitching. The Giants have gained more since we first did this study two years ago than any other team. The top five: Pablo Sandoval, Tim Lincecum, Matt Cain, Brian Wilson and Buster Posey.

**7. New York Yankees (2,197).** The Yankees still don't have a lot in the way of young position players, but they are now third in the majors in young pitching, and about the midpoint in prospects. They have 17 players with an Inventory Value of 70 or higher. The Yankees' top five are Robinson Cano, CC Sabathia, Mark Teixeira, Curtis Granderson and Nick Swisher.

**8. Texas Rangers (2,121).** The Rangers, with 17 players listed, are 2nd in the majors in prospects, and 6th in young position players. Their top five: Ian Kinsler, Josh Hamilton, Neftali Feliz, Nelson Cruz, and Justin Smoak and Joke.

**9. Chicago White Sox (2,106).** The White Sox have been aggressive in the last year about increasing the young talent on their roster, claiming Alex Rios off of waivers and Jake Peavy and Mark Teahen in dollar-driven trades. They have no prospects listed, but are second in the majors in young pitching. Their top five: John Danks, Carlos Quentin, Jake Peavy, Gavin Floyd and Gordon Beckham.

**10. Florida Marlins (2,106).** The Marlins are 4th in the majors in prospect value, and a little above the midpoint in the other two areas. Their top five: Hanley Ramirez, Josh Johnson, Chris Coghlan, Mike Stanton and Ricky Nolasco.

**11. Los Angeles Dodgers (2,092).** Despite the presence on their roster of Kemp, Ethier, Martin and Loney, the Dodgers are actually fairly near the bottom of the list in young position players. They rank first in young pitching, however. Their top six: Kemp, Billingsley, Ethier, Broxton, Loney and Kershaw. (If the system worked perfectly, Kershaw would rank ahead of Loney.)

**12. Philadelphia Phillies (2,036).** Phillies are above the midpoint in young pitching, with Hamels, Happ and Madsen, near the midpoint in the other two areas. The top five: Cole Hamels, Ryan Howard, Shane Victorino, Chase Utley and J.A. Happ. (Howard and Utley are not really "young" players, but players of that quality retain value for a long time, and thus remain counted among the young stars.)

**13. Atlanta Braves (2,035).** The Braves are 5th in the majors in the possession of young position players, and 6th in prospects. The lack of young major league pitching, other than Jurrjens, is keeping them in the middle of the pack. Their top five are Jair J-J-J Jurrjens, Brian McCann, Nate McLouth, Yunel Escobar and Jason Heyward.

**14. Los Angeles Angels of Anaheim (2,033).** The Angels rank 5th in the majors in young pitching, behind the Dodgers, White Sox, Yankees and Red Sox. They rank low in the possession of young position players, and have no minor league prospects who registered in this accounting. Their top five: Kendry Morales, Jered Weaver, Scott Kazmir, Joe Saunders and Howie Kendrick. Napoli and Aybar are essentially even with Kendrick.

*This is an article about whether Seattle has more young talent than San Francisco.*

**15. Kansas City Royals (1,971).** The Royals' "front five" is actually far superior to the Angels', the Braves', or even the Phillies', but their talent base is very thin. They rank no higher than 10th and no lower than 16th in any of the three areas. Their top-five young talents: Greinke, Billy Butler, Joakim Soria, Alberto Callaspo and David DeJesus. They would be far ahead of where they are if Gordon and Teahen had developed as expected.

**16. New York Mets (1,939).** The Mets are 8th in young position players and middle-of-the-pack in young pitching, but have nothing in the way of prospects. Jose Reyes' failure to advance certainly hampers them, and makes David Wright—coming off a subpar season—their number one future talent, followed by K-Rod, Reyes, Francoeur, Bay and Santana.

**17. Chicago Cubs (1,898).** The Cubs have 17 properties valued at 70 or more points, making them the only team ranked lower than 9th with more than 15. As you can infer from this, there is a lack of true top-of-the-line talent. The disappointing season of Geovany Soto is a significant setback for them, in terms of their young talent profile. Their top five: Carlos Zambrano, Rich Harden (now with the Rangers), Soto, Carlos Marmol and Randy Wells. (Zambrano is now 29).

**18. Seattle Mariners (1,885).** The Mariners have gained ground in the last two years; they ranked 25th two years ago. The biggest gainers since we first did this study are the Giants, Braves, Cubs and Mariners; the biggest losses have been by the Brewers, Indians and Pirates. The Mariners are above the median in young pitching, led, of course, by Felix Hernandez. Their top five: Felix, Jose Lopez, Franklin Gutierrez, Cliff Lee and David Aardsma.

*It would be better if 25 to 30% of the value in the study was the minor leaguers.*

**19. Milwaukee Brewers (1,827).** The Brewers ranked 4th when we first studied this issue two years ago. They have two of the four most valuable young properties in baseball, in Braun and Fielder, but the developmental failures of Weeks, Hall, Hardy and Hart, and the lack of good young pitching, has made the crop in some ways disappointing. Their top five: Fielder, Braun, Hart, Gallardo, and McGehee. (I would rather have Braun than Fielder, but obviously any organization would love to have either one of them.)

**20. Baltimore Orioles (1,817).** The Orioles are making extremely good progress in their young position players, but their failure to develop hard-throwing young pitchers has been a disappointment. Their top five: Nick Markakis, Adam Jones, Matt Wieters, Brian Matusz and Nolan Reimold.

**21. Oakland A's (1,789).** Our system is set up to give modest values to young players who could be good, but who have not yet proven that in the major leagues. The A's lead the world in those kind of guys, and thus they *could* improve much more, in the next couple of years, than is suggested by our math. Their top-five young players: Andrew Bailey, Kurt Suzuki, Kevin Kouzmanoff, Ryan Sweeney and Brett Anderson.

**22. Toronto Blue Jays (1,756).** The Blue Jays have kind of been on a treadmill, with exciting new players being added to the mix (Hill and Lind), but no growth from Rios (now with the White Sox), and mass injuries to the young pitchers. Their top five: Adam Lind, Aaron Hill, Edwin Encarnacion, Brett Wallace, Kyle Drabek.

**23. Washington Nationals (1,743).** Nationals need to see forward strides from one of the young outfielders—Dukes, Milledge, or Nyjer Morgan. Morgan was fantastic in his few weeks in Washington, but...we've seen hot streaks before. Because Strasburg is considered a "prospect", rather than a "pitcher", the Nationals are dead last in my survey in young pitching, although they actually are top ten in the other two areas. Their top five: Ryan Zimmerman, Adam Dunn, Stephen Strasburg, Josh Willingham, John Lannan.

**24. St. Louis Cardinals (1,727).** We're getting now into the teams that are seriously short of young talent. The Cardinals have three outstanding players who are still in their prime years (Wainwright, Pujols and Holliday), but Pujols and Holliday turned 30 on consecutive days in mid-January, and Wainwright can see 30 on the horizon. The Cardinals are being sustained in the pennant race, to this point, but the facts that a) Albert Pujols is one of the greatest players of all time, b) Dave Duncan is a wizard with marginal pitchers, and c) the Cubs and Brewers have more or less fizzled. But they're going to need to come up with some young players. Their top five: Wainwright, Pujols, Holliday, Ryan Ludwick, Colby Rasmus.

**25. Pittsburgh Pirates (1,662).** Now entering the third decade of their rebuilding effort. The retrogression of Gorzelanny (now with the Cubs) and Matt Capps (now with the Nationals) is a serious problem. Their top five young players: Andrew McCutchen, Pedro Alvarez, Garrett Jones, Paul Maholm, Andy LaRoche.

**26. Cleveland Indians (1,661).** In my many years as a baseball fan, I've rarely seen things go bad for an organization, through no fault of their own, the way they have gone bad for the Indians. Two years ago the Indians appeared ready take on the world. Two years later, with Sabathia and Lee long gone, Victor Martinez gone, Fausto Carmona having imploded, and even Grady Sizemore not playing as well, they've been pushed down to near the back of the line. I've never really seen anything like it. Their top five: Grady Sizemore, Shin-Soo Choo, Asdrubal Cabrera, Jhonny Peralta and Carlos Santana.

**27. Cincinnati Reds (1,579).** Where have all the young outfielders gone? Top five: Joey Votto, Brandon Phillips, Edinson Volquez, Jay Bruce, Johnny Cueto.

**28. Detroit Tigers (1,559).** The Tigers have a young talent nucleus—three or four players—that is very good. Their problem is that what's outside of those three or four players is not much of anything. Their top five: Miguel Cabera, Justin Verlander, Rick Porcello, Jose Valverde, Zach Miner.

**29. San Diego Padres (1,478).** Kevin Kouzmanoff (now with the A's) was their #2 young player. They do have several young pitchers who have good arms, but haven't established themselves yet. Their top-five young players are Adrian Gonzalez, Adrian Gonzalez, Adrian Gonzalez, Adrian Gonzalez and Adrian Gonzalez. Other than Adrian: Chase Headley, Jon Garland, Scott Hairston and Heath Bell. And Bell is 32.

**30. Houston Astros (1,334).** The Astros have a couple of good young outfielders, Hunter Pence and Michael Bourn, but still rank last by far in young position players. Wandy Rodriguez is 31, Oswalt 32. Praying hard for Jason Castro to be Joe Mauer. Top five: Pence, Bourn, Wandy Rodriguez, Oswalt, Brandon Lyon.

*We're getting now into the teams that are seriously short of young talent.*

In this study, the age spectrum of the value analyzed is as follows:

| Age | Percent of Total Value |
|-----|------------------------|
| 18  | 0.3%                   |
| 19  | 2.0%                   |
| 20  | 1.4%                   |
| 21  | 2.3%                   |
| 22  | 5.1%                   |
| 23  | 6.2%                   |
| 24  | 6.8%                   |
| 25  | 16.1%                  |
| 26  | 14.3%                  |
| 27  | 11.2%                  |
| 28  | 9.7%                   |
| 29  | 6.0%                   |
| 30  | 8.6%                   |
| 31  | 5.1%                   |
| 32  | 3.3%                   |
| 33  | 1.6%                   |
| 34  | 0.0%                   |

With this method, players aged 35 or older have zero value by definition. Thirty-four-year-old players do have value, but no player aged 34 had *enough* value to be listed on his team's roster of the 15 most valuable properties.

The methodology I have used to study this issue at this time is better than the method that was used in previous years, but it still needs some work. The two biggest issues are these:

1) That more minor league players should be included in the study. In the past, we ignored minor leaguers. In this study we included them, but they account for only 8% of the value. It would be better if 25 to 30% of the value in the study was the minor leaguers.

2) That there is a problem with players making a minors-to-majors transition. Clay Buchholz, Cameron Maybin and Luke Gregerson, for example, fail to make their teams' lists of the most valuable young players. They are too far advanced to be regarded by MLB as "prospects", but what they have accomplished so far in the majors is not enough to establish significant major league performance value. This is not optimal; players like that *should* be included, and should make the lists.

# Texas Rangers

**2009 TEAM OVERVIEW**

## 87-75

**2**nd place
AL West

| | ML RANK | 10th | 2nd | 19th | 26th | 10th | 2nd |
|---|---|---|---|---|---|---|---|
| **Team** | | 784 | 224 | .260 | 472 | .764 | 149 |
| | | RUNS | HOME RUNS | BATTING AVG. | WALKS | OPS | STOLEN BASES |
| **Opp.** | | 740 | 171 | .260 | 531 | .747 | 99 |
| | ML RANK | 11th | 14th | 12th | 10th | 13th | 13th |

## Key Players

| Pos | Player | G | AB | R | H | 2B | 3B | HR | RBI | SB | CS | BB | SO | AVG | OBP | SLG | OPS | WS |
|---|---|---|---|---|---|---|---|---|---|---|---|---|---|---|---|---|---|---|
| C | Jarrod Saltalamacchia | 84 | 283 | 34 | 66 | 12 | 0 | 9 | 34 | 0 | 2 | 22 | 97 | .233 | .290 | .371 | .661 | 6 |
| 1B | Chris Davis | 113 | 391 | 48 | 93 | 15 | 1 | 21 | 59 | 0 | 0 | 24 | 150 | .238 | .284 | .442 | .726 | 7 |
| 2B | Ian Kinsler | 144 | 566 | 101 | 143 | 32 | 4 | 31 | 86 | 31 | 5 | 59 | 77 | .253 | .327 | .488 | .814 | 24 |
| 3B | Michael Young | 135 | 541 | 76 | 174 | 36 | 2 | 22 | 68 | 8 | 3 | 47 | 90 | .322 | .374 | .518 | .892 | 17 |
| SS | Elvis Andrus | 145 | 480 | 72 | 128 | 17 | 8 | 6 | 40 | 33 | 6 | 40 | 77 | .267 | .329 | .373 | .702 | 17 |
| LF | David Murphy | 128 | 432 | 61 | 116 | 24 | 1 | 17 | 57 | 9 | 4 | 49 | 106 | .269 | .338 | .447 | .785 | 11 |
| CF | Marlon Byrd | 146 | 547 | 66 | 155 | 43 | 2 | 20 | 89 | 8 | 4 | 32 | 98 | .283 | .329 | .479 | .808 | 20 |
| RF | Nelson Cruz | 128 | 462 | 75 | 120 | 21 | 1 | 33 | 76 | 20 | 4 | 49 | 118 | .260 | .332 | .524 | .856 | 16 |
| DH | Hank Blalock | 123 | 462 | 62 | 108 | 21 | 4 | 25 | 66 | 2 | 0 | 26 | 108 | .234 | .277 | .459 | .736 | 6 |

## Key Pitchers

| Pos | Player | G | GS | W | L | SV | IP | H | R | ER | SO | BB | BR/9 | ERA | WS |
|---|---|---|---|---|---|---|---|---|---|---|---|---|---|---|---|
| SP | Scott Feldman | 34 | 31 | 17 | 8 | 0 | 189.2 | 178 | 87 | 86 | 113 | 65 | 11.96 | 4.08 | 14 |
| SP | Kevin Millwood | 31 | 31 | 13 | 10 | 0 | 198.2 | 195 | 88 | 81 | 123 | 71 | 12.55 | 3.67 | 15 |
| SP | Tommy Hunter | 19 | 19 | 9 | 6 | 0 | 112.0 | 113 | 55 | 51 | 64 | 33 | 11.89 | 4.10 | 8 |
| SP | Vicente Padilla | 18 | 18 | 8 | 6 | 0 | 108.0 | 120 | 61 | 59 | 59 | 42 | 14.17 | 4.92 | 5 |
| SP | Derek Holland | 33 | 21 | 8 | 13 | 0 | 138.1 | 160 | 98 | 94 | 107 | 47 | 13.73 | 6.12 | 2 |
| CL | Frank Francisco | 51 | 0 | 2 | 3 | 25 | 49.1 | 40 | 21 | 21 | 57 | 15 | 10.22 | 3.83 | 9 |
| RP | Darren O'Day | 64 | 0 | 2 | 1 | 2 | 55.2 | 36 | 12 | 12 | 54 | 17 | 9.22 | 1.94 | 9 |
| RP | C.J. Wilson | 74 | 0 | 5 | 6 | 14 | 73.2 | 66 | 29 | 23 | 84 | 32 | 12.71 | 2.81 | 11 |

## Pitching and Defense

How did the Rangers get to the bright side of .500 for the first time in five years? Pitching and defense, and pitching and defense. Their offense actually was dragging them quite forcefully in the opposite direction. They scored 117 fewer runs than they had the year before, the third-largest decline in the majors. The club overcame this by allowing 227 fewer runs, the biggest improvement in baseball by more than 50%. They did that by keeping opposing hitters off the bases much more effectively. Rangers pitchers allowed only five fewer homers than the year before, but allowed 215 fewer hits and 94 fewer walks — a difference of nearly two baserunners per game.

## Shortstop — the Key to Defense

According to John Dewan's Defensive Runs Saved, the Rangers' defense improved by 69 runs in 2009, the third-biggest improvement among the 30 major league teams:

| Team | Runs |
|------|------|
| Mariners | 94 |
| Angels | 73 |
| Rangers | 69 |
| Reds | 64 |
| Tigers | 52 |

The bulk of the Rangers' improvement came in the middle infield, where they improved by 26 runs at second base and 23 at shortstop.  At shortstop, the Rangers replaced the veteran Michael Young with rookie Elvis Andrus.  Dewan's method evaluated Young as being five runs worse than the average shortstop in 2008, and Andrus as being 14 runs better than average in 2009 – the third-best mark among major league shortstops.

Each of the other four teams with the most-improved defensive units also changed shortstops in 2009 or mid-season 2009. In every case, the player or combination of players who manned the position in 2009 represented a clear defensive upgrade over the 2008 arrangement: The Mariners replaced the declining Yuniesky Betancourt with the still-stellar Jack Wilson halfway through 2009; the Angels went with a combination of Erick Aybar and Maicer Izturis in 2008 but pretty much handed over the position to Aybar, the better fielder of the two, in 2009; the Reds pressed Jeff Keppinger into service as a shortstop in 2008 but turned to Alex Gonzalez and then glove-whiz Paul Janish, in '09; and the Tigers went from a fading Edgar Renteria to Adam Everett.

| Team | Original | Replacement |
|------|----------|-------------|
| Mariners | Yuniesky Betancourt | Yuniesky Betancourt/Jack Wilson |
| Angels | Erick Aybar/Maicer Izturis | Erick Aybar |
| Rangers | Michael Young | Elvis Andrus |
| Reds | Jeff Keppinger | Paul Janish/Alex Gonzalez |
| Tigers | Edgar Renteria | Adam Everett/Ramon Santiago |

## No Runs

Frank Francisco did not give up a single run in any of the 25 appearances in which he recorded a save. He was the only pitcher with 20+ saves to do so in 2009.

## Hitting Like a Pitcher

Neftali Feliz pitched 31 innings for the Rangers in 2009. An average hitter facing Feliz performed at essentially the same level as an average pitcher will hit. Pitchers as hitters in 2009 hit an aggregate .136, with 6 runs scored, 13 hits and 39 strikeouts per 117 plate appearances. Neftali Feliz faced 117 hitters, who hit .124 with 6 runs scored, 13 hits and 39 strikeouts.

## Can I Get a Day Off, Please?

Rangers relievers had a 6.14 ERA when pitching on zero days' rest, worst in baseball by nearly a full run. The two main offenders were C.J. Wilson (an 8.00 ERA in 21 appearances) and Frank Francisco (a 9.00 ERA in 13 appearances). Each of them was highly effective when given at least one day off between appearances (a 1.17 ERA for Wilson, 2.41 for Francisco).

## Power Hitting 101

The major difference between Nelson Cruz in 2009 — when he hit 33 homers — and in 2007 — when he hit only 9 in 307 at-bats — is that Cruz has learned to pull the ball. In 2007, he hit the ball to the opposite field nearly as often as he pulled it: 72 balls pulled to left, and 71 hit to right. In 2009, he hit 78% more balls to the pull field than to the opposite field: 141 to left, and 79 to right.

## Going Down Swinging

On pitches in the strike zone, Josh Hamilton swung 82.5% of the time, the highest percentage in baseball. He took only 103 called strikes, which works out to about one for every 3.5 plate appearances.

## Scoops Davis

Chris Davis chased 51.7% of the low pitches thrown to him, the only player to chase more than one-half of the low pitches he saw. This helps explain why he missed connections on 37% of his swings, second-highest in baseball behind Mark Reynolds.

## First Pitch Fancy

When he hit the first pitch, Chris Davis in 2009 hit .500 (22 for 44) with 7 homers, giving him a 1.556 OPS in one-pitch at-bats. That was the highest in baseball, and he was almost as good when he hit the first pitch in 2008 (.424 with an OPS of 1.248).

Of course, the problem with trying to make a living off of the first pitch is that you wind up hitting 0-1 a lot, and, in Davis' case, 0-1 can give way quickly to 0-2. But it's great when it works.

### Batting Ninth, Leading Off

Surprisingly, the Rangers scored the most runs in innings led off by their weakest-hitting regular, Elvis Andrus. They averaged .79 runs per innings when Andrus led off the inning, but no more than .57 runs per inning when any other of the regulars did. A couple of odd developments combined to make this happen. First, Andrus happened to perform way over his head when leading off innings, batting .351 and reaching base at a .430 clip. And second, his habitual spot at the bottom of the batting order meant that he was followed by, arguably, the most productive part of the Rangers' lineup, the leadoff and #2 spots. Most teams' lineups are clearly strongest in the middle, but the Rangers were the exception in 2009, thanks to strong seasons from Ian Kinsler and Michael Young at the top of the order, and disappointing seasons from several players who often hit in the middle of the order, including Josh Hamilton, Andruw Jones and Hank Blalock. Kinsler, batting leadoff, nearly led the team in RBI.

**Elvis Andrus — 2009 Performance as Leadoff Man**

|  | Times | Team Runs | Runs/Inning |
|---|---|---|---|
| Innings Led Off | 107 | 84 | .79 |
| Reached Base Leading Off | 46 | 49 | 1.07 |
| Did Not Reach | 61 | 35 | .57 |
| Other Innings for Team | 1,326 | 700 | .53 |

### Stealing Third

The Rangers led the majors with 32 steals of third, and they were thrown out only three times trying. Elvis Andrus and Ian Kinsler each did it 11 times, and Nelson Cruz did it 7 times. Brian Roberts (14), Jacoby Ellsbury (13) and B.J. Upton (11) were the only other players with more than 10 steals of third.

### Only One Way to Go

In 2009 Hank Blalock hit 51 fly balls to left. Fifty of them were caught, giving him a .020 average on them. None left the park. He also hit 56 fly balls to right. Twenty-nine of them fell safely, including 19 that left the park, giving him a .518 average on those.

## Pitcher's Duels

What was the best pitcher's duel of 2009? The best of the last decade? What was the greatest pitcher's duel ever?

The concept of a pitcher's duel has three elements:

1) Quality starting pitchers,

2) Strong performances from those starting pitchers, and

3) A close, low-scoring game.

Obviously these three are entangled in every possible permutation. I represented these three elements in a simple formula, which I will post on the internet for those of you who care enough to look it up (billjamesonline. com).

These were the five best pitcher's duels of 2009:

**5. July 24, 2009, Texas at Kansas City, Scott Feldman against Zack Greinke.** Greinke pitched 3-hit ball through 7 innings, striking out 10 — but Scott Feldman pitched eight shutout innings. Greinke gave up a solo homer to Marlon Byrd in the 4th, and a reliever allowed another run in the 8th. Rangers won 2-0.

**4. May 9, 2009, Kansas City at the Angels, Zack Greinke against Joe Saunders.** Greinke pitched a complete game, giving up 4 hits and no walks, but the Angels scratched out a run in the 3rd on a double, a sac bunt and a sac fly. Joe Saunders pitched a five-hit shutout for a 1-0 Angels win.

**3. May 8, 2009, Tigers at the Indians.** Justin **Verlander against Cliff Lee.** Verlander dominated the Indians while Lee mystified the Tigers, and the game was 0-0 through 7 innings. Granderson manufactured a run in the 8th inning with a walk and a stolen base, giving the Tigers a 1-0 lead. Verlander pitched a 2-hit shutout and struck out 11. Tigers won, 1-0.

**2. August 25, 2009, Astros at St. Louis. Wandy Rodriguez against Adam Wainwright.** St. Louis scored in the first on a double by You-Know-Who. Rodriguez limited the Cardinals to three hits through seven innings; Wainwright limited the Astros to two singles and a double through eight innings. Cardinals won, 1-0.

**1. May 25, 2009, Cardinals at Milwaukee. Chris Carpenter against Yovani Gallardo.** Both Carpenter and Gallardo pitched eight innings of 2-hit, shutout baseball, and the game was scoreless through nine innings. The Brewers scratched out a run in the bottom of the tenth on an error, two ground balls and a single, and the Brewers won 1-0.

I feel that I should also mention the Red Sox/Yankees game of August 7, which was nothing-nothing through 14 innings, finally won by the Yankees 2-0 in the 15th, Josh Beckett starting against A. J. Burnett. Twelve relievers pitched in the game, and eleven of them pitched scoreless baseball. A great pitcher's duel, obviously; it just doesn't happen to score at the top of the list by the system I set up. Not that it couldn't. . .I wanted a system to identify the best pitcher's duel of the year, this is the system I set up, and this is the answer I got.

# Toronto Blue Jays

<table>
<tr><td rowspan="2">2009 TEAM OVERVIEW<br><br>75-87<br><br>4 th place<br>AL East</td><td>ML RANK</td><td>8th</td><td>4th</td><td>9th</td><td>16th</td><td>8th</td><td>23rd</td></tr>
<tr><td>Team</td><td>798</td><td>209</td><td>.266</td><td>548</td><td>.773</td><td>73</td></tr>
<tr><td></td><td></td><td>RUNS</td><td>HOME RUNS</td><td>BATTING AVG.</td><td>WALKS</td><td>OPS</td><td>STOLEN BASES</td></tr>
<tr><td></td><td>Opp.</td><td>771</td><td>181</td><td>.270</td><td>551</td><td>.772</td><td>89</td></tr>
<tr><td></td><td>ML RANK</td><td>22th</td><td>19th</td><td>23rd</td><td>13th</td><td>23rd</td><td>8th</td></tr>
</table>

## Key Players

| Pos | Player | G | AB | R | H | 2B | 3B | HR | RBI | SB | CS | BB | SO | AVG | OBP | SLG | OPS | WS |
|-----|--------|---|----|----|----|----|----|----|-----|----|----|----|----|-----|-----|-----|-----|----|
| C | Rod Barajas | 125 | 429 | 43 | 97 | 19 | 0 | 19 | 71 | 1 | 0 | 20 | 76 | .226 | .258 | .403 | .661 | 12 |
| 1B | Lyle Overbay | 132 | 423 | 57 | 112 | 35 | 1 | 16 | 64 | 0 | 0 | 74 | 95 | .265 | .372 | .466 | .838 | 12 |
| 2B | Aaron Hill | 158 | 682 | 103 | 195 | 37 | 0 | 36 | 108 | 6 | 2 | 42 | 98 | .286 | .330 | .499 | .829 | 25 |
| 3B | Scott Rolen | 88 | 338 | 52 | 108 | 29 | 0 | 8 | 43 | 4 | 2 | 26 | 42 | .320 | .370 | .476 | .846 | 12 |
| SS | Marco Scutaro | 144 | 574 | 100 | 162 | 35 | 1 | 12 | 60 | 14 | 5 | 90 | 75 | .282 | .379 | .409 | .789 | 21 |
| LF | Travis Snider | 77 | 241 | 34 | 58 | 14 | 1 | 9 | 29 | 1 | 1 | 29 | 78 | .241 | .328 | .419 | .748 | 4 |
| CF | Vernon Wells | 158 | 630 | 84 | 164 | 37 | 3 | 15 | 66 | 17 | 4 | 48 | 86 | .260 | .311 | .400 | .711 | 8 |
| RF | Alex Rios | 108 | 436 | 52 | 115 | 25 | 2 | 14 | 62 | 19 | 3 | 31 | 78 | .264 | .317 | .427 | .744 | 10 |
| DH | Adam Lind | 151 | 587 | 93 | 179 | 46 | 0 | 35 | 114 | 1 | 1 | 58 | 110 | .305 | .370 | .562 | .932 | 21 |

## Key Pitchers

| Pos | Player | G | GS | W | L | SV | IP | H | R | ER | SO | BB | BR/9 | ERA | WS |
|-----|--------|---|----|----|----|----|----|----|----|----|----|----|------|-----|----|
| SP | Roy Halladay | 32 | 32 | 17 | 10 | 0 | 239.0 | 234 | 82 | 74 | 208 | 35 | 10.32 | 2.79 | 21 |
| SP | Ricky Romero | 29 | 29 | 13 | 9 | 0 | 178.0 | 192 | 88 | 85 | 141 | 79 | 14.21 | 4.30 | 10 |
| SP | Brian Tallet | 37 | 25 | 7 | 9 | 0 | 160.2 | 169 | 99 | 95 | 120 | 72 | 13.84 | 5.32 | 4 |
| SP | Scott Richmond | 27 | 24 | 8 | 11 | 0 | 138.2 | 147 | 90 | 85 | 117 | 59 | 13.37 | 5.52 | 3 |
| SP | Brett Cecil | 18 | 17 | 7 | 4 | 0 | 93.1 | 116 | 59 | 55 | 69 | 38 | 15.33 | 5.30 | 3 |
| CL | Jason Frasor | 61 | 0 | 7 | 3 | 11 | 57.2 | 43 | 17 | 16 | 56 | 16 | 9.52 | 2.50 | 10 |
| RP | Brandon League | 67 | 0 | 3 | 6 | 0 | 74.2 | 72 | 40 | 38 | 76 | 21 | 12.05 | 4.58 | 3 |
| RP | Jesse Carlson | 73 | 0 | 1 | 6 | 0 | 67.2 | 67 | 37 | 35 | 51 | 21 | 12.10 | 4.66 | 3 |

### Blue Jays 2009

The Blue Jays dropped from 86 to 75 wins in 2009, and it's easy to diagnose what went wrong. They lost four-fifths of their starting rotation. In 2008 their starting rotation and bullpen each were outstanding, and as a result they allowed the fewest runs in baseball. In 2008, Roy Halladay headed a terrific rotation. By the second week of the 2009 season, he was all that was left of it. A.J. Burnett had fled via free agency, and Shaun Marcum, Dustin McGowan and Jesse Litsch were all wiped out by arm injuries.

The Blue Jays filled the void by 1) bringing in Brian Tallet from the bullpen, and 2) promoting unprepared rookie starters *en masse*. Tallet, who'd pitched well out of the pen in 2008, proved unable to maintain his effectiveness after the first time through the order. The rookies — particularly Ricky Romero and Marc Rzepczynski — were surprisingly decent at times, but ultimately could not compare to the pitchers they replaced. The Blue Jays sent a rookie starter to the hill in 87 of their games. Three teams used even more — which seems unusual — but those were all teams that were rebuilding and knew they were.

Toronto's offense, thanks to power explosions from Aaron Hill and Adam Lind, improved by 84 runs, but it didn't matter, since their run prevention declined by nearly twice as much. The Blue Jays allowed 161 more runs in 2009 than 2008 — essentially an increase of one per game.

### Best Against Best (and Against Worst)

Roy Halladay pitched 40 innings against teams with a winning percentage over .600 in 2009, 8 more than any other pitcher. He was 3-1 with a 2.70 in those innings.

He also pitched more innings against teams with a record between .500-.599 than any other pitcher, 146. He went 8-9 with a 3.02 ERA in those innings.

When he did face off against losing teams he was 6-0 in seven starts, with a 2.21 ERA in 53 innings pitched.

### The Famous Triple Double Home Run Cycle

The only major league hitter to hit 10 home runs to left, center and right was Ryan Howard, but Adam Lind came as close as you can come: 12 to left, 9 to center, 14 to right.

## Impact Felt

At the trade deadline, the Blue Jays and Reds swapped starting third basemen as part of a four-player trade, with the Blue Jays giving up Scott Rolen and acquiring Edwin Encarnacion. Over the previous three seasons, the two players' contributions with the glove had consistently appeared at opposite ends of the spectrum, according to the Defensive Runs Saved metric:

| Year | Edwin Encarnacion Runs Saved | Rank | Scott Rolen Runs Saved | Rank |
|---|---|---|---|---|
| 2006 | -11 | 33 | 14 | 5 |
| 2007 | -11 | 30 | 11 | 5 |
| 2008 | -16 | 35 | 10 | 3 |

During 2009, each player spent considerable time with both Toronto and Cincinnati, with both of them starting at least 38 games for both clubs (Rolen started 87 for Toronto and 38 for Cincinnati; Encarnacion started 42 for each). Both clubs allowed dramatically fewer runs per game in games started by Rolen than in games started by Encarnacion.

**Runs Allowed per Game**

| Team | Encarnacion Runs/Game | Rolen Runs/Game |
|---|---|---|
| Toronto | 5.17 | 4.39 |
| Cincinnati | 5.40 | 3.61 |

## Rod Barajas, Hitting Analysis

Most home runs are hit to the pull field, so to hit home runs you generally must be able to pull the ball in the air. The player who pulled the ball in the air in the highest percentage of his plate appearances last year was — don't bother trying to guess — Rod Barajas. He pulled 71 fly balls to left field out of 460 plate appearances for 15.4%. The top five:

| Player | Pct |
|---|---|
| 1. Rod Barajas, Tor | 15.4% |
| 2. Jose Lopez, Sea | 15.2% |
| 3. Ian Kinsler, Tex | 14.2% |
| 4. Jorge Cantu, Fla | 12.9% |
| 5. Carlos Pena, TB | 12.8% |

## I Like Trouble

Ricky Romero allowed the leadoff man in an inning to reach base 45.4% of the time, more often than any other qualifying major league starter.

**Ricky Romero — 2009 Inning Analysis**

| | |
|---|---|
| Innings Pitched | 178.0 |
| Runs Allowed | 88 |
| Innings Started | 185 |
| Runs in Those Innings | 88 |
| | |
| Shutout Innings | 134 |
| One-Run Innings | 26 |
| Two-Run Innings | 17 |
| Three-Run Innings | 4 |
| Four-Run Innings | 4 |
| | |
| Got First Man Out | 101 |
| Runs Scored in Those Innings | 21 |
| Runs/9 Innings | 1.87 |
| | |
| First Man Reached | 84 |
| Runs Scored in Those Innings | 67 |
| Runs/9 Innings | 7.18 |
| | |
| 1-2-3 Innings | 67 |
| 10-pitch Innings (or less) | 27 |
| Long Innings (20 or more pitches) | 43 |
| Failed to Finish Inning | 11 |

## Tallet and Romero

Brian Tallet and Ricky Romero had very different pitching records.  Romero was 13-9 with a 4.30 ERA; Tallet was 6-9 with a 5.32 ERA.  But the batting records of batters facing the two was strikingly similar, with a one-point difference in OPS:

| Player | AB | R | H | 2B | 3B | HR | RBI | BB | SO | AVG | OBP | SLG | OPS |
|--------|-----|----|-----|----|----|----|-----|----|-----|------|------|------|------|
| Brian Tallet | 631 | 99 | 169 | 43 | 4 | 20 | 94 | 72 | 120 | .268 | .345 | .444 | .789 |
| Ricky Romero | 676 | 88 | 192 | 39 | 1 | 18 | 80 | 79 | 141 | .284 | .366 | .425 | .790 |

The difference?  Double plays.  Romero got 30 double play balls; Tallet got 10.  That was 90% of the difference.  Romero also was more effective with runners in scoring position.

## Givin' Some Love to the Changeup

Brian Tallet threw his changeup 26% of the time, third-highest among qualifying starters, behind only noted changeup artists Johan Santana and Cole Hamels.

## Marc R., the One with the Last Name of Random Letters

Marc Rzepczynski pitched well in 11 starts as a rookie in 2009, but there's one thing he might want to work on: efficiency. He started 65 innings but completed only three "quick innings," the worst ratio of any starter who started 50 innings.

## He's Got a Rocket for an Arm!

Jose Bautista gunned down 7 baserunners from left field in 2009, despite starting only 35 games there. Only three left fielders had more baserunner kills, and all three of them were regulars: David DeJesus (11), Jason Bay (8) and Raul Ibanez (8).

## Catch Me If You Can

Randy Ruiz hit 10 fly balls to left, and got six home runs, two doubles and a single out of them. Only one was caught.

Have you guys seen Randy Ruiz, by the way? The man is HUGE. God, I hope he stays in the league. He's fun to watch.

## Vernon Wells on Offense

Over the past three years, Vernon Wells has hit .331 with 41 home runs on fly balls to left, and .073 with zero home runs on fly balls to right.

## Vernon Wells on Defense

Vernon Wells, who'd been a legitimate Gold Glover from 2004-'06, was a serious defensive liability in 2009. The area where he's regressed the most has been his ability to go back on the ball. It used to be one of his biggest strengths, but in 2009 his plus/minus on balls hit deep was -20, worst in the majors. This was the main reason his 2009 Defensive Runs Saved due to his range was -16, the worst among major league center fielders.

### Vernon Wells — Fielding Bible Plus/Minus

| Year | Inn | Outs Made | Basic | Shallow | Medium | Deep | Enhanced | Runs Saved | Rank |
|------|---------|-----------|-------|---------|--------|------|----------|------------|------|
| 2004 | 1,135.0 | 327 | +3 | -13 | +1 | +27 | +15 | 8 | 3 |
| 2005 | 1,358.0 | 351 | 0 | -10 | +6 | +8 | +4 | 2 | 16 |
| 2006 | 1,290.1 | 332 | +9 | -1 | +7 | +8 | +14 | 8 | 4 |
| 2007 | 1,279.0 | 321 | +5 | +1 | -4 | +10 | +7 | 4 | 10 |
| 2008 | 889.0 | 217 | -8 | -2 | -10 | -6 | -17 | -10 | 32 |
| 2009 | 1,356.2 | 352 | -21 | -9 | 0 | -20 | -29 | -16 | 35 |

## Bret Saberhagen Lives

What does Scott Rolen, 2009, have in common with Mike Campbell, 1988? Well, look at it. Scott Rolen made 344 batting outs in 2009. Mike Campbell in 1988 pitched 115.1 innings, which is 346 outs.

Mike Campbell struck out 63 batters in 1988. Scott Rolen struck out 62 times in 2009.

Mike Campbell walked 43 batters in 1988. Scott Rolen walked 45 times in 2009.

Mike Campbell allowed 81 runs in 1988. Scott Rolen created 82 runs in 2009.

See; they're really the same. Scott Rolen's record is Mike Campbell's record; it is merely looked at from a different perspective. Of course, you need to remember that what is good for a pitcher is bad for a hitter. When the batter fails, the pitcher succeeds. The worse a record looks, when looked at from the pitcher's standpoint, the better it is as a hitter's record. You can't find a pitcher who has a record that matches Albert Pujols, for example, because no pitcher is that bad. If a pitcher was that bad, he'd be sent back to the minors after a week or two.

The following are the pitchers who match the Toronto Blue Jay batting records for 2009.

### Rod Barajas.
Matches Scott Sanderson, 1985, Dave Schmidt, 1982, and Bret Saberhagen, 1999:

| Player | Year | G | IP | W | L | WPct | R | ER | SO | BB | ERA |
|---|---|---|---|---|---|---|---|---|---|---|---|
| Scott Sanderson | 1985 | 19 | 121.0 | 5 | 6 | .455 | 49 | 42 | 80 | 27 | 3.12 |
| Dave Schmidt | 1982 | 33 | 109.7 | 4 | 6 | .400 | 45 | 39 | 69 | 25 | 3.20 |
| Bret Saberhagen | 1999 | 22 | 119.0 | 10 | 6 | .625 | 43 | 39 | 81 | 11 | 2.95 |

### Lyle Overbay

| Player | Year | G | IP | W | L | WPct | R | ER | SO | BB | ERA |
|---|---|---|---|---|---|---|---|---|---|---|---|
| Oliver Perez | 2005 | 20 | 103.0 | 7 | 5 | .583 | 68 | 67 | 97 | 70 | 5.85 |
| Ron Moeller | 1961 | 33 | 113.0 | 4 | 8 | .333 | 80 | 73 | 87 | 83 | 5.81 |
| Terry Felton | 1982 | 48 | 117.3 | 0 | 13 | .000 | 71 | 65 | 92 | 76 | 4.99 |

### Aaron Hill

| Player | Year | G | IP | W | L | WPct | R | ER | SO | BB | ERA |
|---|---|---|---|---|---|---|---|---|---|---|---|
| Esteban Loaiza | 1998 | 35 | 171.0 | 9 | 11 | .450 | 107 | 98 | 108 | 52 | 5.16 |
| Armando Reynoso | 2000 | 31 | 170.7 | 11 | 12 | .478 | 102 | 100 | 89 | 52 | 5.27 |
| Brian Meadows | 1998 | 31 | 174.3 | 11 | 13 | .458 | 106 | 101 | 88 | 46 | 5.21 |
| Paul Maholm | 2007 | 29 | 177.7 | 10 | 15 | .400 | 110 | 99 | 105 | 49 | 5.02 |

### Scott Rolen

| Player | Year | G | IP | W | L | WPct | R | ER | SO | BB | ERA |
|---|---|---|---|---|---|---|---|---|---|---|---|
| Mike Campbell | 1988 | 20 | 114.7 | 6 | 10 | .375 | 81 | 75 | 63 | 43 | 5.89 |
| Brian Rose | 2000 | 27 | 116.7 | 7 | 10 | .412 | 78 | 75 | 64 | 51 | 5.79 |
| Wes Obermueller | 2004 | 25 | 118.0 | 6 | 8 | .429 | 80 | 76 | 59 | 42 | 5.80 |
| Kevin Correia | 2008 | 25 | 110.0 | 3 | 8 | .273 | 80 | 74 | 66 | 47 | 6.05 |

### Edwin Encarnacion

| Player | Year | G | IP | W | L | WPct | R | ER | SO | BB | ERA |
|---|---|---|---|---|---|---|---|---|---|---|---|
| Paul Lindblad | 1969 | 60 | 78.0 | 9 | 6 | .600 | 37 | 36 | 64 | 33 | 4.15 |
| Rocky Biddle | 2002 | 44 | 77.7 | 3 | 4 | .429 | 42 | 35 | 64 | 39 | 4.06 |
| Ben McDonald | 1995 | 14 | 80.0 | 3 | 6 | .333 | 40 | 37 | 62 | 38 | 4.16 |

### Marco Scutaro

| Player | Year | G | IP | W | L | WPct | R | ER | SO | BB | ERA |
|---|---|---|---|---|---|---|---|---|---|---|---|
| Steve Sparks | 1999 | 28 | 147.7 | 5 | 11 | .313 | 101 | 89 | 73 | 82 | 5.42 |
| Johnny Klippstein | 1954 | 36 | 148.0 | 4 | 11 | .267 | 104 | 87 | 69 | 96 | 5.29 |
| Don Carman | 1989 | 49 | 149.3 | 5 | 15 | .250 | 98 | 87 | 81 | 86 | 5.24 |

### Travis Snider

| Player | Year | G | IP | W | L | WPct | R | ER | SO | BB | ERA |
|---|---|---|---|---|---|---|---|---|---|---|---|
| Kerry Wood | 2005 | 21 | 66.0 | 3 | 4 | .429 | 32 | 31 | 77 | 26 | 4.23 |
| Will Ohman | 2006 | 78 | 65.3 | 1 | 1 | .500 | 30 | 30 | 74 | 34 | 4.13 |
| Scott Williamson | 2003 | 66 | 62.7 | 5 | 4 | .556 | 30 | 29 | 74 | 34 | 4.16 |
| Kyle Farnsworth | 2006 | 72 | 66.0 | 3 | 6 | .333 | 34 | 32 | 75 | 28 | 4.36 |

### Adam Lind

| Player | Year | G | IP | W | L | WPct | R | ER | SO | BB | ERA |
|---|---|---|---|---|---|---|---|---|---|---|---|
| Casey Fossum | 2004 | 27 | 142.0 | 4 | 15 | .211 | 111 | 105 | 117 | 63 | 6.65 |
| Jack Morris | 1993 | 27 | 152.7 | 7 | 12 | .368 | 116 | 105 | 103 | 65 | 6.19 |
| Dave Burba | 2001 | 32 | 150.7 | 10 | 10 | .500 | 112 | 104 | 118 | 54 | 6.21 |

### Vernon Wells

| Player | Year | G | IP | W | L | WPct | R | ER | SO | BB | ERA |
|---|---|---|---|---|---|---|---|---|---|---|---|
| Harry Brecheen | 1950 | 27 | 163.0 | 8 | 11 | .421 | 77 | 69 | 80 | 45 | 3.81 |
| Jim Bunning | 1968 | 27 | 160.0 | 4 | 14 | .222 | 75 | 69 | 95 | 48 | 3.88 |
| Brian Bannister | 2007 | 27 | 165.0 | 12 | 9 | .571 | 76 | 71 | 77 | 44 | 3.87 |

### Alex Rios

| Player | Year | G | IP | W | L | WPct | R | ER | SO | BB | ERA |
|---|---|---|---|---|---|---|---|---|---|---|---|
| Camilo Pascual | 1967 | 28 | 165.0 | 12 | 10 | .545 | 73 | 60 | 106 | 43 | 3.27 |
| John Montefusco | 1977 | 26 | 157.0 | 7 | 12 | .368 | 82 | 61 | 110 | 46 | 3.50 |
| Woodie Fryman | 1971 | 37 | 149.3 | 10 | 7 | .588 | 61 | 56 | 104 | 46 | 3.38 |
| Joe Nuxhall | 1965 | 32 | 149.0 | 11 | 4 | .733 | 57 | 57 | 117 | 31 | 3.44 |

### Jose Bautista

| Player | Year | G | IP | W | L | WPct | R | ER | SO | BB | ERA |
|---|---|---|---|---|---|---|---|---|---|---|---|
| Doug Bair | 1979 | 65 | 94.3 | 11 | 7 | .611 | 47 | 45 | 86 | 51 | 4.29 |
| Juan Cruz | 2006 | 31 | 94.7 | 5 | 6 | .455 | 45 | 44 | 88 | 47 | 4.18 |
| Eric Plunk | 1987 | 32 | 95.0 | 4 | 6 | .400 | 53 | 50 | 90 | 62 | 4.74 |

### Kevin Millar

| Player | Year | G | IP | W | L | WPct | R | ER | SO | BB | ERA |
|---|---|---|---|---|---|---|---|---|---|---|---|
| Joey McLaughlin | 1982 | 44 | 70.0 | 8 | 6 | .571 | 27 | 25 | 49 | 30 | 3.21 |
| David Weathers | 2008 | 72 | 69.3 | 4 | 6 | .400 | 27 | 25 | 46 | 30 | 3.25 |
| Dwayne Henry | 1991 | 52 | 67.7 | 3 | 2 | .600 | 25 | 24 | 51 | 39 | 3.19 |

# Cooperstown and the 'Roids

by Bill James

FOR THE LAST TEN YEARS OR SO PEOPLE HAVE BEEN ASKING ME to comment on the issue of steroids and the Hall of Fame. To this point I have resisted addressing these questions, arguing — as I do with the Hall of Fame status of active players — that there is nothing to be gained by trying to guess where objects still in motion will eventually land. With the passage of time the dust will settle, and we will see the issue more clearly.

After ten years, however, the dust does not seem to be settling very rapidly. There seem to be as many different and contradictory opinions on the issue now as there were five or eight years ago. We are all tired of arguing about it, but we still don't agree. In any case, I am finally ready to say what I have to say about it. It is my opinion that, in time, the use of steroids or other Performance Enhancing Drugs will mean virtually nothing in the debate about who gets into the Hall of Fame and who does not.

*I am finally ready to say what I have to say about it.*

The process of arriving at this conclusion began when I was studying aging patterns in the post-steroid era. One of the characteristics of the steroid era was that we had several dozen players who continued to improve beyond the normal aging time frame, so that many of them had their best seasons past the age of 32. This is historically not normal. In the post-steroid era we are returning to the historic norm in which players hit a wall sometime in their early thirties. But what does this mean?

It means that steroids keep you young. You may not like to hear it stated that way, because steroids are evil, wicked, mean and nasty and youth is a good thing, but…that's what it means. Steroids help the athlete resist the effects of aging.

Well, if steroids help keep you young, what's wrong with that?

What's wrong with that is that steroids may help keep players "young" at some risk to their health, and the use of steroids by athletes may lead non-athletes to risk their health as well. But the fact is that, with time, the use of drugs like steroids will not disappear from our culture. It will, in fact, grow, eventually becoming so common that it might almost be said to be ubiquitous. Everybody wants to stay young. As we move forward in time, more and more people are going to use more and more drugs in an effort to stay young. Many of these drugs are going to be steroids or the descendants of steroids.

If we look into the future, then, we can reliably foresee a time in which everybody is going to be using steroids or their pharmaceutical descendants.

We will learn to control the health risks of these drugs, or we will develop alternatives to them. Once that happens, people will start living to age 200 or 300 or 1,000, and doctors will begin routinely prescribing drugs to help you live to be 200 or 300 or 1,000. If you look into the future 40 or 50 years, I think it is quite likely that every citizen will routinely take anti-aging pills every day.

How, then, are those people of the future — who are taking steroids every day — going to look back on baseball players who used steroids? They're going to look back on them as pioneers. They're going to look back at it and say "So what?"

The argument for discriminating against PED users rests upon the assumption of the moral superiority of non-drug users. But in a culture in which everyone routinely uses steroids, that argument cannot possibly prevail. You can like it or you can dislike it, but your grandchildren are going to be steroid users. Therefore, they are very likely to be people who do not regard the use of steroids as a moral failing. They are more likely to regard the banning of steroids as a bizarre artifice of the past.

Let us suppose that I am entirely wrong about all of that; let us suppose that our grandchildren do not wind up regularly ingesting chemicals to extend their youth. I would still argue that, in the long run, the use of steroids will eventually become a non-issue in who gets into the Hall of Fame.

My second argument is this:

a) Eventually, some players who have been associated with steroids are going to get into the Hall of Fame. This is no longer at issue. One cannot keep Barry Bonds, Roger Clemens, A-Rod, Manny Ramirez, Mark McGwire, Sammy Sosa and all of the others out of the Hall of Fame forever. Some of them have to get in. If nothing else, somebody will eventually get in and then acknowledge that he used steroids.

b) Once some players who have been associated with steroids are in the Hall of Fame, the argument against the others will become un-sustainable.

When the time comes at which two or three or four players are in the Hall of Fame who have acknowledged some steroid use, the barrier to other steroid users rests upon some sort of balancing test. Did this player use too many steroids to be considered legitimate? Is his career a creation of the steroids? Would he have been a Hall of Fame player without the steroids?

I am not suggesting that it is inappropriate for any one sportswriter or any one Hall of Fame voter to balance these considerations as best he can. But one does not build a house upon a well-balanced rock.

*I am not suggesting that it is inappropriate for any one sportswriter or any one Hall of Fame voter to balance these considerations.*

The way that each sportswriter looks at these issues is most likely going to be different from the way the others look at them. There can only be a consensus on one of two positions:

a) that steroid users should not be in the Hall of Fame, or

b) that steroid use is not an issue in the debate.

Between the two extreme positions, it becomes a fluid discussion. Once we move away from the one extreme, in my view, we will begin to drift inevitably toward the other.

I would liken this to attitudes about sexuality and television. At one point there was a firm consensus that there was no place for sex on TV. Married couples, on TV, slept in twin beds. The first departures from this firm position were small and insignificant…PBS specials on prostitution, chewing gum and soft drink commercials that pushed the boundaries of "taste", and edited-for-TV movies that were not quite as edited as they would have been a few years ago. Once there was no longer a firm consensus at an extreme position, there was a fluid standard that moved inevitably toward more and more openness about sexuality.

I will note that this happened without the consent and without the approval of most of the American public. It was never true that most people wanted to see more sex on TV. Probably it was generally true that most Americans disliked what they regarded as the erosion of standards of decency. But it was always true that some people wanted to see more sex on TV, and that was all that mattered, because that created a market for shows that pushed the envelope, and thus eroded the barriers. It was like a battle line that disintegrated once the firing started. The importance of holding the battle line, in old-style military conflict, was that once the line was breached, there was no longer an organized point of resistance. Once the consensus against any sexual references on TV was gone, there was no longer any consensus about what the standards should be — thus, a constant moving of the standards.

I think the same thing will happen here: Once there is no longer a firm consensus against steroid users in the Hall of Fame, there will be a fluid situation which moves inevitably in the direction of more and more inclusiveness.

It is not necessary that people approve of this movement in principle. It is only necessary that there be advocates for those who are still on the outside looking in…for Sammy Sosa, let's say, and Manny Ramirez. And there is no question that there will be those advocates.

Third argument. History is forgiving. Statistics endure.

At the time that Dick Allen left the major leagues,

*History will rally on the side of the steroid users in the same way that it has rallied on the side of Dick Allen, Joe Jackson, Orlando Cepeda, Hack Wilson and many others.*

virtually no one thought of him as a Hall of Fame player. In his first year of eligibility for the Hall of Fame, he received the support of a little less than 4% of the voters. In his fifteen years of eligibility for BBWAA selection, he never reached 20% in the voting.

Dick Allen did not have imaginary sins or imaginary failings as a player. He had very real offenses. But as time passes, the details of these incidents (and eventually the incidents themselves) are forgotten, and it becomes easier for Allen's advocates to re-interpret them as situations in which Allen was the victim, rather than the aggressor or offender. The people who were there die off. A certain number of people want to play the role of Dick Allen's advocate. No one — including me — wants to play the role of persistently denigrating Dick Allen; in fact, I'm pretty sure you can go to hell for that. People who were friends of Dick Allen speak up; the dozens or hundreds of ex-teammates who despised Dick Allen keep silent, or speak of him as well as they can manage.

For very good reasons, we do not nurture hatred. We let things pass. This leads history to be forgiving. Perhaps it is right, perhaps it is wrong, but that is the way it is. Sometime between 2020 and 2030, Dick Allen will be elected to the Hall of Fame.

The same thing has happened, more slowly, with the Black Sox. In 1950 no one thought Joe Jackson should be in the Hall of Fame. Now it is a common opinion — perhaps a majority opinion — that he should. People question whether he "really" did the things that he clearly admitted doing. His virtues are celebrated; his sins are minimized.

Perhaps this is right; perhaps it is wrong. It is the way of history.

History will rally on the side of the steroid users in the same way that it has rallied on the side of Dick Allen, Joe Jackson, Orlando Cepeda, Hack Wilson and many others.

But with the steroid users, we are not talking about a single isolated "offender", but about a large group of them, representing the bulk of the dominant players of their generation. The forces that push for their acceptance will get organized much more quickly and will move with much greater force. This, in my view, will make the use of steroids a non-factor in Hall of Fame discussions within 30 to 40 years.

Fourth argument. Old players play a key role in the Hall of Fame debate. It seems unlikely to me that aging ballplayers will divide their ex-teammates neatly into classes of "steroid users" and "non-steroid users."

One of the key reasons that Dick Allen will eventually be in the Hall of Fame is that one of his ex-teammates — Goose Gossage — feels strongly that he should be, and is outspoken on this issue. Goose Gossage is now a Hall of Famer. His voice carries weight.

Eventually, younger players who were teammates of Mark McGwire, Sammy Sosa, A-Rod and Roger Clemens are going to be in the Hall of Fame. Andy Pettitte is probably going to be in the Hall of Fame. When he is in the Hall of Fame — if he gets there before Roger — he is going to speak up for Roger Clemens. Hell, somebody might even speak up for Barry Bonds.

Once this happens, it will erode the prejudice against steroid users in the Hall of Fame, to the extent that that prejudice might otherwise exist. You might choose to divide the world of baseball players into steroid users and non-steroid users, but this is not a division that makes intuitive sense when you know the people involved. Therefore, this is not the division that will ultimately endure, once the long historical sorting-out process that makes Goose Gossage relevant and Lindy McDaniel irrelevant has run its course.

I have a fifth argument here, but before I get to that, let me speak for a moment on the other side of the issue. Let us adopt, as the face of the non-steroid user, Will

*It seems to me that, at some point, this becomes an impossible argument to sustain — that all of these players were "cheating", in a climate in which most everybody was doing the same things, and in which there was either no rule against doing these things or zero enforcement of those rules.*

Clark. Will Clark and Rafael Palmeiro were college teammates, and apparently were not the best of friends. As players they were rivals. Texas had Palmeiro (1989-1993) and then had Clark (1994-1998), while Palmeiro went to Baltimore.

After the 1998 season the Orioles — then a strong franchise — signed Clark, while Palmeiro went back to the Rangers. Later on Palmeiro went back to the Orioles, so that both the Rangers and the Orioles had Palmeiro, then Clark, then Palmeiro. There was always a debate about which was the better player.

I've always been a great admirer of Will Clark, who I think was a great player and is a historically under-rated player in part because his numbers are dimmed by comparison to the steroid-inflated numbers that came just after him. Will Clark, in the pre-steroid era, was a much better player than Palmeiro, although Palmeiro was good. Palmeiro, as we entered the steroid era, gradually pulled ahead of Clark. I have no idea whether Will Clark ever used steroids or not, but let us use Will Clark as the face of the player who chose not to use steroids in order to stay in the game, the player who chose the natural route and suffered the consequences of that.

Is it fair to Will Clark to compare him to players who chose to cheat in order to move beyond that level? No, it is not. Absolutely, it is not. But the critical issue is: Is this cheating? If you choose to regard it as cheating, if you choose not to support the Hall of Fame candidacy of a steroid user because you regard it as cheating, I would not argue with you. I think that Will Clark has a perfect right to feel that he was cheated out of a fair chance to compete for honors in his time, and, if you choose to look at it from the standpoint of Will Clark, I don't think that you are wrong to do so.

But at the same time, I do not believe that history

will look at this issue from the standpoint of Will Clark. I don't see how it can. What it seems to me that the Will Clark defenders have not come to terms with is the breadth and depth of the PED problem, which began in the 1960s and expanded without resistance for almost 40 years, eventually involving generations of players. It seems to me that the Will Clark defenders are still looking at the issue as one of "some" players gaining an advantage by using Performance Enhancing Drugs. But it wasn't really an issue of some players gaining an advantage by the use of Performance Enhancing Drugs; it is an issue of many players using Performance Enhancing Drugs in competition with one another. Nobody knows how many. It would be my estimate that it was somewhere between 40 and 80%.

The discrimination against PED users in Hall of Fame voting rests upon the perception that this was cheating. But is it cheating if one violates a rule that nobody is enforcing, and which one may legitimately see as being widely ignored by those within the competition?

It seems to me that, at some point, this becomes an impossible argument to sustain — that all of these players were "cheating", in a climate in which most everybody was doing the same things, and in which there was either no rule against doing these things or zero enforcement of those rules. If one player is using a corked bat, like Babe Ruth, clearly, he's cheating. But if 80% of the players are using corked bats and no one is enforcing any rules against it, are they all cheating? One better: if 80% of the players are using corked bats and it is unclear whether there are or are not any rules against it, is that cheating?

And...was there really a rule against the use of Performance Enhancing Drugs? At best, it is a debatable point. The Commissioner issued edicts banning the use of Performance Enhancing Drugs. People who were raised on the image of an all-powerful commissioner whose every word was law are thus inclined to believe that there was a rule against it.

*At the end of the day, Mark McGwire is going to be in the Hall of Fame, and Roger Clemens, and Sammy Sosa, and Rafael Palmeiro, and probably even Barry Bonds.*

But "rules", in civilized society, have certain characteristics.

They are agreed to by a process in which all of the interested parties participate. They are included in the rule book. There is a process for enforcing them. Someone is assigned to enforce the rule, and that authority is given the powers necessary to enforce the rule. There are specified and reasonable punishments for violation of the rules.

The "rule" against Performance Enhancing Drugs, if there was such a rule before 2002, by-passed all of these gates. It was never agreed to by the players, who clearly and absolutely have a right to participate in the process of changing any and all rules to which they are subject. It was not included in any of the various rule books that define the conduct of the game from various perspectives.

There was no process for enforcing such a rule. The punishments were draconian in theory and non-existent in fact.

It seems to me that, with the passage of time, more people will come to understand that a commissioner's periodic spasms of self-righteousness do not constitute baseball law. It seems to me that the argument that it is cheating must ultimately collapse under the weight of carrying this great contradiction — that 80% of the players are cheating against the other 20% by violating some "rule" to which they never consented, which was never included in the rule books, and for which there was no enforcement procedure. History is simply not going to see it that way.

The end of the day here is about the year 2040, perhaps 2050. It will come upon us in a flash. And, at the end of the day, Mark McGwire is going to be in the Hall of Fame, and Roger Clemens, and Sammy Sosa, and Rafael Palmeiro, and probably even Barry Bonds. I am not especially advocating this; I simply think that is the way it is. I only hope that, when all of these players are enshrined, they will extend a hand up to a few players from the Will Clark division of the game.

# Washington Nationals

## Key Players

| Pos | Player | G | AB | R | H | 2B | 3B | HR | RBI | SB | CS | BB | SO | AVG | OBP | SLG | OPS | WS |
|---|---|---|---|---|---|---|---|---|---|---|---|---|---|---|---|---|---|---|
| C | Josh Bard | 90 | 274 | 20 | 63 | 18 | 0 | 6 | 31 | 0 | 1 | 24 | 50 | .230 | .293 | .361 | .655 | 4 |
| 1B | Nick Johnson | 98 | 353 | 47 | 104 | 16 | 2 | 6 | 44 | 2 | 2 | 63 | 66 | .295 | .408 | .402 | .810 | 12 |
| 2B | Anderson Hernandez | 77 | 231 | 25 | 58 | 9 | 2 | 1 | 23 | 5 | 3 | 20 | 41 | .251 | .310 | .320 | .630 | 3 |
| 3B | Ryan Zimmerman | 157 | 610 | 110 | 178 | 37 | 3 | 33 | 106 | 2 | 0 | 72 | 119 | .292 | .364 | .525 | .888 | 21 |
| SS | Cristian Guzman | 135 | 531 | 74 | 151 | 24 | 7 | 6 | 52 | 4 | 5 | 16 | 75 | .284 | .306 | .390 | .696 | 9 |
| LF | Josh Willingham | 133 | 427 | 70 | 111 | 29 | 0 | 24 | 61 | 4 | 3 | 61 | 104 | .260 | .367 | .496 | .863 | 11 |
| CF | Willie Harris | 137 | 323 | 47 | 76 | 18 | 6 | 7 | 27 | 11 | 4 | 57 | 62 | .235 | .364 | .393 | .757 | 9 |
| RF | Elijah Dukes | 107 | 364 | 38 | 91 | 20 | 4 | 8 | 58 | 3 | 10 | 46 | 74 | .250 | .337 | .393 | .729 | 7 |

## Key Pitchers

| Pos | Player | G | GS | W | L | SV | IP | H | R | ER | SO | BB | BR/9 | ERA | WS |
|---|---|---|---|---|---|---|---|---|---|---|---|---|---|---|---|
| SP | John Lannan | 33 | 33 | 9 | 13 | 0 | 206.1 | 210 | 100 | 89 | 89 | 68 | 12.39 | 3.88 | 9 |
| SP | Shairon Martis | 15 | 15 | 5 | 3 | 0 | 85.2 | 83 | 52 | 50 | 34 | 39 | 13.24 | 5.25 | 2 |
| SP | Craig Stammen | 19 | 19 | 4 | 7 | 0 | 105.2 | 112 | 67 | 60 | 48 | 24 | 11.84 | 5.11 | 3 |
| SP | Jordan Zimmermann | 16 | 16 | 3 | 5 | 0 | 91.1 | 95 | 51 | 47 | 92 | 29 | 12.61 | 4.63 | 3 |
| SP | Garrett Mock | 28 | 15 | 3 | 10 | 0 | 91.1 | 114 | 65 | 57 | 72 | 44 | 15.67 | 5.62 | 0 |
| CL | Mike MacDougal | 52 | 0 | 1 | 1 | 20 | 50.0 | 45 | 25 | 20 | 31 | 31 | 14.22 | 3.60 | 5 |
| RP | Ron Villone | 63 | 0 | 5 | 6 | 1 | 48.2 | 54 | 25 | 23 | 33 | 29 | 15.72 | 4.25 | 2 |
| RP | Jason Bergmann | 56 | 0 | 2 | 4 | 0 | 48.0 | 50 | 28 | 24 | 40 | 25 | 14.63 | 4.50 | 2 |

## Cleaning Up

In 2008, Nationals cleanup hitters drove in only 73 runs — the lowest total in baseball.   In 2009, Nationals cleanup hitters (primarily Adam Dunn) hit .269 with 42 homers, 119 RBI and 120 walks.   The OPS of the slot was .934 — the 4th highest of any batting order position in the National League, behind Cardinals third-place hitters (Pujols), Milwaukee cleanup hitters (Fielder), and Florida #3 hitters (Hanley).

## Using the Whole Field

Ryan Zimmerman set a new career high with 33 homers.  Prior to 2009 Zimmerman had pulled 71% of his dingers over the left-field wall. In 2009 70% of his home runs were hit to center and right.

Zimmerman tied for the second-most home runs to centerfield in the majors, and was tied for fourth in homers to right field by right-handed batters.

### Ryan Zimmerman

| Total Hit | 2009 | | 2005-2008 | |
|---|---|---|---|---|
| | HR | Pct | HR | Pct |
| To Left | 10 | 30.3% | 41 | 70.7% |
| To Center | 16 | 48.5% | 9 | 15.5% |
| To Right | 7 | 21.2% | 8 | 13.8% |

## Streaking

Ryan Zimmerman had a 30-game hitting streak from April 8 to May 13.  The last Washington player to have a longer hitting streak was Heinie Manush, who had a 33-game hitting streak in 1933.

## Starting Off Behind the Eight Ball

Nationals relievers inherited 336 runners this season, 68 more than any other team in the league. They allowed 109 runners to score, 19 more than the second-worst team. Their inherited runners scoring rate was 32%, two percent above the league average.

The 336 runners they inherited was the second-largest total of any National League team this decade.

### Most Inherited Runners — National League 2000-2009

| Year | Team | Inherited Runners | Scored | Pct |
|------|------|-------------------|--------|-----|
| 2004 | Giants | 381 | 94 | 25% |
| 2009 | Nationals | 336 | 109 | 32% |
| 2002 | Padres | 330 | 98 | 30% |
| 2005 | Giants | 325 | 87 | 27% |
| 2007 | Reds | 313 | 109 | 35% |
| 2006 | Rockies | 313 | 106 | 34% |
| 2007 | Nationals | 307 | 97 | 32% |
| 2008 | Giants | 304 | 80 | 26% |
| 2000 | Expos | 303 | 120 | 40% |
| 2008 | Mets | 301 | 86 | 29% |

## Allowing Hits and Walks Will Kill You

The Nationals gave up the most hits and the most walks in the league while striking out the fewest batters. That is the short version of why they allowed 56 more runs than any other National League team.

## Limited Quality

The Nationals had 63 quality starts, the fewest in the National League. For the second consecutive year they were the only team in the league without any starting pitcher posting a game score above 80.

## Bullpen Losses

The Nationals' relievers lost 39 games, 9 more than any other team in the majors. The last team to have 39 or more losses in relief was the 2004 Rockies.

## He Didn't Fit In

Mike MacDougal signed a minor league deal with the Nationals on May 3 after being released by the White Sox. He joined Washington's major league club on May 29 and earned his first save on June 17 in his ninth game with the Nats.

On a staff on which the bullpen lost 39 games, MacDougal saved 20 games with only one blown save as the closer for Washington, the best save conversion rate in the National League.

He was not offered a contract for the 2010 season.

| Player | Saves | Blown Saves | Pct |
|---|---|---|---|
| Mike MacDougal, Was | 20 | 1 | 95% |
| Huston Street, Col | 35 | 2 | 95% |
| Francisco Cordero, Cin | 39 | 4 | 91% |
| Trevor Hoffman, Mil | 37 | 4 | 90% |
| Ryan Franklin, StL | 38 | 5 | 88% |

## Clips of Clippard

2009 was Tyler Clippard's seventh season as a professional pitcher. He had pitched only three games in relief in the previous five seasons. The Nationals converted him to a full-time reliever in 2009, and he posted a 0.92 ERA in 24 games at Syracuse before he was promoted on June 24.

Clippard led all Washington relievers with 60.1 innings pitched and 67 strikeouts. He allowed a batting average of .172, the third-best of any National League reliever. The right-hander also led all National League pitchers with a .122 batting average allowed against left-handed batters, minimum 125 batters faced.

## Whiff Woes

John Lannan struck out 3.88 batters per nine innings pitched, the lowest rate of any major league pitcher who qualified for the ERA title.

He managed to stay in the rotation because he induced 28 batters to ground into double plays, he controlled the running game (10 SB/7 CS), he's left-handed, and he stayed healthy.

## Please Stay Put

Elijah Dukes was thrown out in 10 of his 13 stealing attempts. That resulted in a -17 Stolen Bases Gained figure. That ties Duke with Juan Uribe (2007), Juan Rivera (2005), and Luis Castillo (2003) for as the worst single-season Stolen Base Gains since 2002.

## Deep Sixed

1. The 2009 Nationals gave up six or more runs in a game 74 times.
2. The other 15 teams in the league did this an average of 50 times.
3. The normal winning percentage of teams allowing 6 or more runs was .155.

### Washington Nationals 2009

|  | Scored | Allowed |
|---|---|---|
| 10 runs+ | 9-1 | 1-16 |
| 9 runs | 3-1 | 1-12 |
| 8 runs | 7-3 | 1-8 |
| 7 runs | 4-3 | 1-13 |
| 6 runs | 6-8 | 5-16 |

## Too Many Miscues

The Nationals committed 143 errors, most in the league and 47 more than the league average. Only two National League teams committed more errors in the past decade, the 2002 Mets, who booted 144 balls, and the 2001 San Diego Padres with 145.

## Chilly

Bill James Online does a daily Hot and Cold Summary for all teams during the season. This gives you a quick read on how hot or cold a team is at the moment, and identifies their hottest and coldest points in the season. Every team starts the season at "room temperature" (72 degrees) and then tracks upward or downward with each game, depending on what the club does.

We track how many days a team dips below 50 degrees, and the Nationals were under 50 on 90 days. The Pirates' 58 days below 50 degrees was the next-most in the majors in 2009. In the eight years we have tracked this only two teams have had more days below 50 degrees than the Nats did in 2009.

| Washington Nationals 2009 | |
|---|---|
| Season Ending Temperature | 92° |
| High Point of the Season (Aug. 9) | 104° |
| Low Point of the Season (July 20) | 23° |
| Days Over 100° | 1 |
| Days Under 50° | 90 |
| Average Daily Temperature | 51.4° |

## Fewer Fans

After an attendance bump with a move to a new park in 2008, the Nationals' attendance fell to a new low since their move to the States.

| Year | Attendance | NL Rank |
|---|---|---|
| 2005 | 2,731,993 | 8th |
| 2006 | 2,153,056 | 11th |
| 2007 | 1,943,812 | 14th |
| 2008 | 2,320,400 | 13th |
| 2009 | 1,817,226 | 13th |

## First Base Defenseless

Adam Dunn played 540 innings of first base for the 2009 Nationals — 60 games worth — and was 24 plays below average as a fielder, according to John Dewan's Plus/Minus System.    The only other first baseman in the league who was -10 or worse was Washington's other first baseman, Nick Johnson, who played 806 innings there (for Washington), and was -13.

## That's a Wrap

Among all pitchers who made 100 or more starts in the decade which has just ended:
- Livan Hernandez made the most starts (332),
- Darren Oliver had the highest average run support per start (5.64 runs), but also gave up the most (6.01 per game),
- Jamie Moyer had the most winning starts (186),
- Livan Hernandez had the most losing starts (170),
- Johan Santana had the lowest average runs allowed (3.48, including the runs allowed by the bullpen),
- Matt Cain had the least run support (3.72 runs per start),
- Chien-Ming Wang, despite his miserable 2009, still had the highest (team) winning percentage in his starts (.663, 69-35), and
- Jason Johnson had the lowest team winning percentage (.348, 65-122).

Among pitchers with 200 or more starts:
- David Wells had the highest offensive support (5.51 runs per start),
- Kip Wells had the lowest offensive support (4.14 runs per start),
- Sidney Ponson gave up the most runs per start (5.15),
- Johan Santana still gave up the fewest,
- Johan Santana had the highest winning percentage (.657, 153-80), and
- Kip Wells had the lowest winning percentage (.405, 83-122).

There were 26 pitchers who made 250 or more starts during the decade.   All of those pitchers' teams had winning records (in their starts) except Livan Hernandez; Livan was 162-170.    The best record belonged to Tim Hudson, 184-105, a .637 percentage.

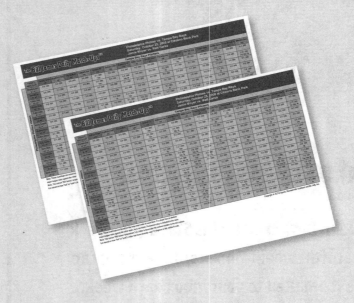